BILL MOYERS

A WORLD OF IDEAS

II

Also from Bill Moyers and Public Affairs Television

A WORLD OF IDEAS

JOSEPH CAMPBELL AND THE POWER OF MYTH

THE SECRET GOVERNMENT: THE CONSTITUTION IN CRISIS

REPORT FROM PHILADELPHIA: THE CONSTITUTIONAL CONVENTION OF 1787

BILL MOYERS

A WORLD OF IDEAS

II

Public Opinions from Private Citizens

ANDIE TUCHER, Editor

DOUBLEDAY

NEW YORK LONDON TORONTO SYDNEY AUCKLAND

PUBLISHED BY DOUBLEDAY
a division of Bantam Doubleday Dell Publishing Group, Inc.
666 Fifth Avenue, New York, New York 10103

DOUBLEDAY and the portrayal of an anchor
with a dolphin are trademarks of Doubleday,
a division of Bantam Doubleday Dell
Publishing Group, Inc.

"Finding the Father" from *This Body
Is Made of Camphor & Gopherwood*
by Robert Bly, copyright © 1977
by Robert Bly. Reprinted by
permission of HarperCollins, Inc.

DESIGN: STANLEY S. DRATE / FOLIO GRAPHICS COMPANY, INC.

Library of Congress Cataloging-in-Publication Data

Moyers, Bill D.
A world of ideas II : public opinions from private citizens
Bill Moyers : Andie Tucher, editor.—1st ed.
p.   cm.
1. United States—Civilization—1970–   2. United States—Politics
and government—1981–1989.   3. United States—Politics and
government—1989–   4. Civilization, Modern—1950–   5. Interviews—
United States.   I. Tucher, Andie.   II. Title.   III. Title: World
of ideas 2.   IV. Title: World of ideas two.
E169.12.M7   1990   90-38334
973.92—dc20   CIP

ISBN 0-385-41664-4
ISBN 0-385-41665-2 (pbk.)

Contents

This book is dedicated to the producers who have worked with me since Public Affairs Television was organized in 1986:

Madeline Amgott
Paul Budline
Tom Casciato
Leslie Clark
Richard M. Cohen
Judy Epstein
Wayne Ewing
Jan Falstad
David Grubin
Roy A. Hammond
Kathleen Hughes
Paul Kaufman
Kate Roth Knull
Alan M. Levin
Marc Levin
Christopher Lukas
Elena Mannes
Betsy McCarthy
Judy Doctoroff O'Neill
Gail Pellett
Richard Petrow
Matthew Pook
Greg Pratt
Catherine Tatge
Andie Tucher
Howard Weinberg
Arthur White

I am also fortunate in the executive producers who orchestrated the talent and ideas that have resulted in more than one hundred hours of television: Joan Konner, Judith Davidson Moyers, Alvin H. Perlmutter, and Jack Sameth. *A World of Ideas II* is dedicated to them, too.

These are the invisible hands and intelligence of what has been a delight of collaboration.

BILL MOYERS

Introduction

George Orwell believed that "all issues are political issues." So this is a political book. A political book, not a partisan one. The men and women you will meet in it are talking about America—the ideas that shape, sustain, and challenge us; ideas we constantly test against experience and refine through the trials and errors of democracy. They are talking about us as a community, the body politic, whose health is everyone's business.

Democracy as conversation is an old idea. At one point the very concept of "public" could be defined as "a group of strangers who gather to discuss the news." In early America the printing press generated a body of popular knowledge. Towns were small, and taverns, inns, coffeehouses, street corners, and the public greens—the commons—were places where people gathered to discuss what they were reading. Out of such exchanges "came much of the commonplace community development which preceded the Revolution and later proved to be essential to the governance of the city." These places of public communication "provided the underlying social fabric of the town and, when the Revolution began, made it possible to quickly gather militia companies, to form effective committees of correspondence and of inspection, and to organize and to manage mass town meetings.

"The public was no fiction," says James W. Carey, dean of the College of Communications of the University of Illinois, in a symposium published in *Center Magazine*. Nor was it a philosophical term. The public had no life, no social relationships, without news. The news was what activated conversation between strangers, and strangers were assumed to be capable of conversing about the news. In fact, says Carey, the whole point of the press was not so much to disseminate fact as to assemble people. The press furnished materials for argument—"information" in the narrow sense—"but the value of the press was predicated on the existence of the public, not the reverse." The media's role was humble but serious, and that role was to take the public seriously.

Not so today. The public has been left stranded by media that reduce important political ideas to a "sound bite" of 9.8 seconds, the average length of time presidential candidates were permitted to speak uninterrupted on network news in the campaign of 1988, and by political candidates, who speak to us but not with us. Vietnam and Watergate blew volcano-size holes in the legitimacy of our political discourse. More recently the lies that yet shroud the events of Iran-contra, the continuing deceit of "the budget process" by which both parties champion the free lunch, and the routine fraud of media politics have combined further to separate the language of government and politics from reality. The public conversation is mediated by politicians who have mastered the "sound bite" and by "experts" whose main appeal is not to reason and evidence but to status and tradition as the source of their authority. Their expertise, alas, is all too often the capacity for snappy one-liners in television talk shows that are the verbal and political equivalent of mud wrestling. The public has been transformed, writes J. R. Priestley, into "a vast crowd, a permanent audience, waiting to be amused. They look on more and more and join in less and less. . . ."

Priestley is not alone in his concern for the effects on us of this diminished conversation. George F. Will has written that "we need to talk about talk. We need a new respectful rhetoric. Respectful, that is, of the better angels of our nature. We are not just what we eat, we are to some extent what we and our leaders say we are." Writing in *The Atlantic Monthly*, David Denby laments that "Americans have ceased talking to one another. Instead, they entertain one another, and they do so in all sorts of places where entertainment is beside the point or corrupting. Under the tyranny of affability and simplicity, public discourse—in politics, religion, and education—has collapsed into smiling drivel." This leads to what Herbert Kohl calls "the impoverishment of personality." He warns that "if we do not provide time for the consideration of people and events in depth, we may end up training another generation of television adults who know what kind of toilet paper to buy, who know how to argue and humiliate others, but who are thoroughly incapable of discussing, much less dealing with, the major social and economic problems that are tearing America apart."

We see in Eastern Europe today the difference talk makes. The leaders of the emerging democracies there are not expert politicians but poets, painters, philosophers, and musicians. Celebrating the rise to leadership of playwright Václav Havel in Czechoslovakia and translator Arpad Goncz in Hungary, our own E. L. Doctorow told an American audience: "The credential for the post of President turned out to be the writer's faculty, which is the faculty of witness, of independent witness with no necessary loyalty to any institution—not the government, or the factory, or the church, or the party. Havel and Goncz both refused to lie. They were true patriots in that they refused to say that something that wasn't true was true. . . ." Havel has said that he and others like him are trying "to inject ideas of spirituality, mutual understanding, and mutual tolerance" into the affairs of state. Such ideas exposed the hollowness of Marxist shibboleths and forged the resistance to one-party domination. They kept alive the notion of a participatory public, of people accountable for their own destiny. Talk matters because ideas empower.

Our own public dialogue, by contrast, is a fiction spun from a narrow spectrum of voices and ideas. According to a recent study by the University of Minnesota School of Journalism, published in *Mother Jones*, network television turns again and again for commentary to the same sources: mostly white middle-aged males from official or quasi-official Washington whose critiques of the policy-making establishment are tempered by their membership in it. Once they and a handful of politicians have been heard, television considers the intellectual debate covered. Not here the voice of the poet or the philosopher, the historian or the artist—those men and women who speak to the soul and spirit of the American experience, or whose insights lift the debate beyond the Washington beltway to quicken the imagination of the public. A visitor to this planet from outer space, watching television for a week, could go home to report that America was a place where broccoli was the public enemy of choice and where people with the most media exposure had the least to say.

The public, I repeat, has been left stranded: the body unpolitic. A public emerges when citizens take part, not when they merely watch. Citizenship is more than voting; it means participating in the dialogue of democracy. Television, the modern commons, could make this possible. True, there are many more millions of us than there were in eighteenth-century America; the small towns have been swallowed up into mega-cities; life is fast and furious. But we could yet recover a sense of the public if only citizens could feel they were being addressed—and were themselves being heard—in a conversation of significance. Something transcendent to our mundane and parochial affairs happens when we are invited into the conversation of democracy. We know it was going on before we arrived and will continue after we are gone. But for now—in our time—we have not only caught the drift of the conversation, we have joined it. The exasperating but wondrous cacophony of American voices can produce a clear expression of ourselves as a people.

Critics respond that it is naive to expect too much of television. It is a limited medium and one to which people turn primarily for entertainment. I, too, understand the role the medium plays in our leisure time, and I do not expect its extraction from the rules of the economic game. However, you do not have to be a romantic to see television not only as an instrument of commerce but as a means of communication. You have only to experience it.

For example, during the Bicentennial of the Constitution in 1987, my associates and I produced a PBS series about the significance of the Constitution in contemporary life. Several members of the Supreme Court participated, and our documentaries also included legal scholars, historians, philosophers, and "ordinary" citizens who had taken their grievances all the way to the highest court in the land. Among the thousands of letters we received when the series ended was one from a housewife in a Western state:

> I have never written a letter like this before. I am a full-time wife and mother of four childen under seven years and I am entirely busy with the ordinary things of family life. However, I want to thank you very much for *In Search of the Constitution*. As a result of this series, I am awakened to a deep appreciation of many ideals vital to our democracy. I am much moved by the experience of listening at the feet of thoughtful citizens, justices, and philosophers of substance. All these are people with whom I will never converse on my own, and I am grateful to you for having brought these conversations within my sphere. I am aware that I lack eloquence to express the measure of my heart's gratitude. I can say, however, that these programs are a landmark among my life's experiences. Among all the things I must teach my children, a healthy interest in understanding the Constitution now ranks very prominently. Thank you.

Thousands of letters also poured in following another series based on Mortimer Adler's book *Six Great Ideas*. In devoting an hour to each of the ideas Adler had examined—liberty, justice, equality, truth, beauty, and goodness—we filmed a spirited debate between the opinionated philosopher and several educators, business executives, writers, lawyers, poets, and jurists. Of the letters provoked by the series, here is my favorite:

> Dear Dr. Adler: I am writing in behalf of a group of construction workers (mostly, believe it or not, plumbers!) who have finally found a teacher worth listening to. While we cannot all agree whether or not we would hire you as an apprentice, we can all agree that we would love to listen to you during our lunch breaks. I am sure that it is just due to our well-known ignorance as tradesmen that not a single one of us had ever heard of you until one Sunday afternoon we were watching public television and Bill Moyers came on with *Six Great Ideas*. We listened intensely and soon became addicted and have been ever since. **We never knew a world of ideas existed** [emphasis added]. The study of ideas has completely turned around our impression of education.

We only wish we had not wasted 25–35 years in the process. But we do have you to thank for the next 35–40 years that we have before us to study and implement the great ideas into our lives and into the lives of our communities. We have grown to love the ideas behind our country's composition, and since reading and discussing numerous of your books we have all become devout Constitutionalists. We thank you and we applaud you. We are certain that the praise of a few plumbers could hardly compare with the notoriety that you deserve from distinguished colleagues, but we salute you just the same. One last thought—we may be plumbers during the day, but at lunch time and at night and on the weekends, we are Philosophers at Large. God bless you!

A final example: In 1980 PBS commissioned a series about the political campaigns. My colleagues and I set out to cover the election with respect for the whole motion of the race and not just the impassioned moments of conflict and controversy. Among the outpouring of letters generated by the series was this one from a man in Colorado:

Your series accomplished the impossible. As a sixties college graduate, disillusioned Vietnam combat veteran, embittered anti-war author, and indifferent citizen, I never thought I'd see the day when I'd register to vote, much less enter a voting chamber. But yesterday I registered and November 4 I'll vote. [The series] spurred me to again participate in our democracy. Thanks. It's good to be back.

Reading such letters, I think back to those citizen discussions that took place when America was new and people gathered in taverns, inns, and coffeehouses to join the conversation of democracy. In their own way they were philosophers at large, the folk to whom this experiment in self-government was daringly entrusted. The men and women in this book are in the stream of that dialogue. They hold no office, and they are not among the usual suspects rounded up by mainstream television when it is time to debate the day's news. But how they do speak to the perils and promises of democracy! Listening, I am emboldened to believe that we might yet realize the importance attached by John Dewey (in *The Public and Its Problems* in 1927) to open and free communication in a democractic society:

The highest and most difficult kind of inquiry and a subtle, delicate, vivid and responsive art of communication must take possession of the physical machinery of transmission and circulation and breathe life into it. When the machine age has thus perfected its machinery, it will be means of life and not its despotic master. Democracy will come into its own, for democracy is a name for a life of free and enriching communion. It had its seer in Walt Whitman. It will have its consummation when free social inquiry is indissolubly wedded to the art of full and moving communication.

The consummation Dewey envisioned is a long way off, but enough voices occasionally break through to affirm its possibilities. Among those voices are the men and women in this book. I am indebted to them for taking a part in "A World of Ideas"—and to Jacqueline Onassis for encouraging this lasting record of their witness; Andie Tucher for patiently and intelligently editing the book even as she completed and received her doctorate in American Civilization from New York University; and Judy Doctoroff O'Neill and Judith Davidson Moyers for bringing such order to a journalist's chaos as to meet deadlines, fulfill commitments, and honor priorities. Like democracy, "A World of Ideas" is itself the result of exuberant collaboration.

BILL MOYERS

Editor's Note

Most of these conversations originally aired during the first part of the 1990 season of the weekly PBS series "A World of Ideas with Bill Moyers." The interview with John Henry Faulk derives from *The Man Who Beat the Blacklist*, a special broadcast in August of this year. The ninety-minute profile *A Gathering of Men with Robert Bly* aired in January.

Since these conversations have been edited for the page, not the air, this volume harmonizes with the television series but does not replay it note by note. I appreciate the willingness of the men and women who shared their ideas with us to allow their preservation in print.

Throughout this project I was lucky and grateful to have had the assistance of Caroline Claudepierre, the possessor of a keen eye, a fine judgment, a quick intelligence, and a buoyant good humor. Judy Doctoroff O'Neill was a wizard at smoothing paths, heading off disasters, removing obstacles, and soothing editors. I also want to thank Joe Tropiano for writing the biographical notes, Brynne Clarke Ferguson for her organizational help, and Karen Levy, Lynnette Caldwell, and Sarah Alpert for their gracious pinch-hitting. Shaye Areheart, Bruce Tracy, and Deborah Artman at Doubleday were efficient yet compassionate partners in our breakneck race with the deadline.

Most of all I want to thank Bill Moyers for his help and his inspiration. I feel proud, enriched, and grateful to be a citizen of this World.

ANDIE TUCHER

IMAGINING OURSELVES

"**I**f one advances confidently in the direction of his dreams," said Henry David Thoreau—who was speaking from experience—"and endeavors to live the life which he has imagined, he will meet with a success unexpected in common hours."

Now, a century and a half later, even Thoreau's own imagination might quail before our present absurdities. His Walden Pond was recently the site of a battle between conservationists and developers—a fight complete with benefit rock concerts, Hollywood celebrities, and protests from community members who *wanted* the development to proceed. The news abounds with such reports. Yet they cannot obliterate the persistence in this country of men and women who still cherish an unshakable confidence in the power of the imagination to design, inspire, and enrich our lives. Of such imagination is hope eternally born, and born again.

The immigrant experience especially reminds us again and again that America is still hospitable to the dreamer, the visionary, the inventor, the romantic. The moment Bharati Mukherjee was born into an upper-class family in the very traditional culture of India, her life seemed determined. In time her parents selected a bridegroom for her whose first name she never learned. But when Mukherjee deserted her familiar past and her ordained future to come to America, she found a land of "romanticism and hope" where she could invent a whole new history for herself. "America," she says, "is a total and wondrous invention."

Artists, of course, make a profession out of imagining life, but many also ponder their obligation to the truth. Maxine Hong Kingston believes that "a good strong imagination doesn't go off into some wild fantasy of nowhere." Still, a little fantasy can help set a direction for our dreams. "We need to imagine the humane being so we can put that archetype out there," Kingston says. "If we don't imagine it, how are we going to become it?"

Because art connects us to ennobling ideas, it challenges us to greater personal and social horizons. Peter Sellars, the theatrical director whose own imagination has poured forth ideas hailed as brilliant and criticized as banal, says that listening to a two-hundred-year-old Mozart opera is one of the toughest tests we can pose for ourselves today. It forces us to ask: "Are we good enough? Are we thinking big enough? Are we ambitious enough? Are we generous enough of spirit? What does our society look like next to the greatest things a human being ever uttered?"

Art is not the only incubator for our imagination. In his researches into the history of fame, Leo Braudy finds that the public people we observe in daily life—the television celebrities, movie heroes, and sports stars—are not simply empty figureheads; they are symbols who carry the meanings we imagine for them. "They are potentials for each person in the audience," says Braudy. "Perhaps none of the young people polled are going to become like Michael Jordan. But on the other hand, when they're on the basketball court, his image will be there with them. It's a potential. It's connected to all sorts of American myths."

Some of the world's most controversial scientific discoveries, the neurophilosopher Patricia Smith Churchland reminds us, have sprung from intellectual daring. "We mustn't let our own failures of imagination tell us what must be the case in the universe," says Churchland. "I'm thinking of philosophers right now who are wont to say, 'I can't imagine how it could be the case that consciousness could be explained in terms of the brain.' Well, so what? That's just a failure of imagination."

In a time so paradoxical and complex, in a country so full of hope and longing, the imagination is not to be wasted. If we can imagine anything, perhaps we can achieve anything we imagine. What we imagine then becomes our destiny.

Bharati Mukherjee

NOVELIST

Bharati Mukherjee's early novels spoke from India, the old world she left behind to marry a struggling American writer. But soon she set out to capture the New World experiences of Asian immigrants in two books of vivid, sensual short stories, *Darkness* and *The Middleman* (winner of the National Book Critics Circle Award in 1988). Her most recent novel, *Jasmine*, tells of a young Punjabi woman who, like the author, makes a heroic journey through America and claims the country as her own. Mukherjee currently teaches at the University of California at Berkeley.

MOYERS: You once said that your life has been a long process of searching for a home. Have you found it yet?

MUKHERJEE: Oh yes, absolutely. I feel very American. I've lived in many different countries, and I make many trips outside the United States for lectures or readings, but I'm always eager to come back here.

MOYERS: To what? What is it that makes you feel as if finally, after all of these wanderings, you belong somewhere?

MUKHERJEE: I knew the moment I landed as a student in 1961, at the Writer's Workshop at the University of Iowa, that this is where I belonged. It was an instant kind of love, a feeling of being at one.
You see for me, America is an idea. It is a stage for transformation. I felt when I came to Iowa City from Calcutta that suddenly I could be a new person. I didn't have to be the daughter of a very upper-class patriarch, a daughter who was guarded every moment of her life by bodyguards and so on.

MOYERS: So home is not a place. Home is an ideal, a state of mind, an attitude.

MUKHERJEE: Home is a state of mind. And that's a big change from what I was brought up to believe. In Bengali, the word for home is *desh*, which means "region." As a child, when I was asked, "Where is your home?" I would have to cite the name of the village, Faridpur, now in Bangladesh, where my father was born, even though I hadn't ever been there. So making the change from thinking of home as a place, to thinking of it as an idea, was a radical metamorphosis for me.

MOYERS: What does America mean to you as an idea?

MUKHERJEE: What America offers me is romanticism and hope. I came out of a continent of cynicism and irony and despair. A traditional society where you are what you are, according to the family that you were born into, the caste, the class, the gender. Suddenly, I found myself in a country where—theoretically, anyway—merit counts, where I could choose to discard that part of my history that I want, and invent a whole new history for myself.

MOYERS: That's what Americans have been doing for two hundred years, isn't it? Inventing, often romantically, an identity, a sense of themselves.

MUKHERJEE: Well, America as romanticism is what appeals to me. It's that capacity to dream and then try to pull it off, if you can. I think that the traditional societies in which people like me were born really do not allow the individual to dream. To dream big.

MOYERS: That's what America is to Jasmine, the character in your new novel. She has big dreams. She leaves Florida, comes to New York, leaves New York, goes to Iowa, then leaves for California, dreaming big dreams, "greedy with dreams," I think the phrase is, and "reckless with hope."

MUKHERJEE: What's also exciting for me about America is that my soul is always at risk here. The immigrant's soul is always at risk. There are no comforting stereotypes to fit into. I have to make up the rules as I go along. No one has really experienced what the nonwhite, non-European immigrants are going through in the States. We can't count on the wisdom and experience of the past of the old country; and we can't quite fit into the traditional Euro-centric experiences of Americans.

Many of my characters in fact are like Joseph Conrad's in their ambiguous morality, and their need for risky adventures. They have some call from the unconscious that forces them to undertake these journeys outside their circumscribed little, petty villages, and it gets them off and in trouble. It certainly gets Jasmine in trouble. But there's a morality and a purification involved in that. If Conrad had the "Heart of Darkness," I'm exploring the heart of light, if you like, through Jasmine.

MOYERS: And the light is—

MUKHERJEE: Where the Conradian character might say, "The horror, the horror," I am saying, "The wonder, the wonder." And light is tricky, too. Light can daze, light can blind. But it's coming in from the outside into the lighted interior, and one has to open one's eyes wide.

MOYERS: You have said a new American epic was washing up on our shores in the eighties.

MUKHERJEE: I meant new epic themes. We are going through lives that are larger than real in many ways, we new immigrants. And we're coming with such a hunger to find new meanings. We're coming with so much energy and curiosity in order to make new lives for ourselves, that to me, those are big stories to tell, very dense lives to chronicle. In a way, I am disappointed with the kind of fiction in magazines like *The New Yorker* or *The Atlantic*, which constantly records neat, miniaturized, suburban lives, and small crises, as opposed to the raw, raucous, messy lives that we nonwhites are leading during the same decade. It's as though some of the fiction editors don't want to acknowledge the rawness and messiness out there in America.

I think of it sometimes as fiction of fear. Of panic reaction to the changes that are going on in the country. Minimalist writing, with its codes, with its shorthand, with its very white suburban emphasis, is, I feel, an ostrich-with-head-in-the-sand kind of fiction.

MOYERS: So many of these editors have their roots in Central Europe, Poland, Italy, Germany—that part of the world that is itself white. Their parents and grandparents came here, and went through that raucous transformation that you and other Asians are now experiencing. How's this old-guard immigrant group reacting to the newcomer?

MUKHERJEE: In many ways, the Asian immigrant identifies with some significant aspects of the European immigration. We too believe in family-centeredness, and in education, and working very hard to improve oneself. But we're very different too because of race and religion.

Also, a lot of the South Asians, Pakistanis, and Indians have come in jets, rather than steerage. We've come with sophisticated degrees. We've come with the confidence to succeed in one generation, rather than wait for our children and our grandchildren to slowly cash in on America's promise. So in significant ways we have to deal with racism. If I have a message to deliver to America, it is a message of inclusiveness. That instead of thinking of the new Americans as new, or "we" versus "they," we should be thinking of all of us as a new kind of American.

MOYERS: Well, I hear that. But I don't see any evidence that the newcomers are integrating into the mainstream. I mean Pakistanis live here, and Indians live there, and Russians live there, and Thais live here, and Vietnamese live there, and El Salvadorans live there. They live to themselves. I don't see this integration taking place.

MUKHERJEE: I think psychologically, emotionally, it is occurring with the children who came when they were two years old, let's say, or who were born over here. They want to be American. But I sometimes think that liberal whites, out of their need to appease guilt of some sort, want the non-European to preserve her or his original culture. Multiculturalism, in a sense, is well intentioned; but it ends up marginalizing the person. And what I'm witnessing through my travels, and in the enormous amount of mail I get from immigrants, is that the parents quite often, out of either arrogance about their native culture or fear of American culture, will try to retreat back into an unreal, frozen image of the old world. Whereas the children want to be very American.

> *But I sometimes think that liberal whites, out of their need to appease guilt of some sort, want the non-European to preserve her or his original culture. Multiculturalism, in a sense, is well intentioned; but it ends up marginalizing the person.*

MOYERS: They want to become something new.

MUKHERJEE: A new being. Which is not to say that they want to be Anglo-Saxons, but yes, part of the new world. So I'm talking about psychological changes. Something has to be done at every level about marginalizing people into ghettos.

MOYERS: Have you experienced any racism here?

MUKHERJEE: Not in the United States, not personally, but I did in Canada. My husband, Clark Blaise, is also a writer, and his parents were Canadian. So when Clark and I were looking for our first jobs, after our degrees from the University of Iowa, we looked only in Montreal, and we went there in 1966. In the beginning, Montreal was a perfect city for a bi-racial, bi-cultural, multilingual couple like us. But by the early seventies, racism reared its ferocious head. And by 1980, I felt that not only was racism institutional there, but had gotten physically virulent.

MOYERS: Did you experience it physically?

MUKHERJEE: Yes, absolutely. I was spat on, and thrown to the back of the bus, and ejected from the lobby of a fancy hotel, and called a whore. These were not just my personal experiences, but they were every South Asian Canadian's experience during the seventies. I blame some of that on the mosaic theory of absorbing immigrants.

MOYERS: You mean the theory that culture is a variety of pieces placed side by side. They don't blend, or fuse into each other. It's just a mosaic.

MUKHERJEE: A mosaic, exactly, where the government and the national mythology encourage the newcomer to hang onto old-world cultures, old-world psyches. The intention was good. But if, in a multicultural system, unequal value is put on the various cultures, then I'm afraid that marginalization tends to work against the nonwhite immigrant. I wrote an essay called "An Invisible Woman" that was my good-bye to Canada. I said that the American system, in which everyone is encouraged to think of himself or herself as an American first, and then something else, works to the advantage of people like me, newcomers.

MOYERS: How did Canadians respond?

MUKHERJEE: This was the very first time that a writer of credibility was calling Canadians on racism, so initially there was shock and outrage among the mainstream Canadians. In the seventies the Canadians tended to believe that all racism occurred south of the border, in the United States, and that they were humane in their treatment of foreigners. But I got enormous amounts of mail on that essay, which showed that others too, German war-brides and so on, had also felt otherized, marginalized. On the last trip that I made to Toronto, which was just October of last year, I saw that letters to the editor and newspaper editorials are now agreeing with the ideas I had tried to bring into the consciousness of people in 1981.

MOYERS: Have you thought about why you would experience racism more in Canada than here?

MUKHERJEE: Yes. I think that we nonwhite new immigrants have profited in the United States from the long history of black-white racial conflict. The civil rights laws are already in place in the United States. I want for all of us to remember what it was like when there was no such equality, so that we don't relapse into racism again. In Canada, there hadn't been open conflict until the 1970s because, I think, the minorities hadn't challenged the mainstream. So there was a kind of smugness. And there was no constitution guaranteeing us rights. Canada depended in those days on good will, rather than law.

MOYERS: Your characters certainly experience some racism. Jasmine recognizes in America an infinite possibility for evil. Small wonder, since no sooner has she arrived than she's involved in a rape and in a murder. Even so, she manages never to feel like a victim.

MUKHERJEE: All American writers, even those who are offering messages of hope and possibility, must be very clear-eyed about the potential for evil. I hope that the stories in *The Middleman and Other Stories* or *Jasmine* present a full picture, a complicated picture of America. But I like to think that I, as well as my characters, constantly fight evil. We don't retreat from battle. And we don't like to be flattened altogether.

MOYERS: She fights back. Sometimes with an eye for an eye and a tooth for a tooth. I don't sense that *you've* done that, except through your stories.

MUKHERJEE: Have I murdered someone, have I blackmailed, did I come as an illegal alien? No, I didn't. But we, the new pioneers, who are still thinking of America as frontier country, do have a kind of ambiguous morality. We are improvising

> *Pioneering does not necessarily equate with virtue. I think that the original American pioneers had to have been in many ways hustlers, and capable of a great deal of violence, in order to wrest the country from the original inhabitants and to make a new life and a new country for themselves.*

morality as we go along. And so Jasmine, who does murder, who does blackmail, is nonetheless true to herself, and keeps her integrity in the course of her adventures.

I want to think that my work has a moral center, that there is a very deep sense of right and wrong located inside the novel. But it does not necessarily have to be conventional Judaeo-Christian morality. Not all my characters are virtuous. Pioneering does not necessarily equate with virtue. I think that the original American pioneers had to have been in many ways hustlers, and capable of a great deal of violence, in order to wrest the country from the original inhabitants and to make a new life and a new country for themselves. So I like to think my characters have that vigor of possessing the land.

MOYERS: What has it taken for a Third World woman to survive in this culture?

MUKHERJEE: A lot of discipline, a lot of strength, a lot of optimism.

MOYERS: Weren't you brought up in India, like most Indian women, to please?

MUKHERJEE: Yes. To be very adaptable. Not to look a man straight in the eye. To sit right. And to be elegant and decorative. But I guess I was into subversion.

MOYERS: How did that happen? Who planted the seeds of subversion?

MUKHERJEE: I went outside India for the first time when I was eight years old. I went with my family to a school in England and Switzerland for three years. Suddenly, being removed from a very predictable world in which every second of my life was programmed, into a world in which I had some independence and just seeing the world out there was very exciting. I knew right then and there that I wanted more than what my family, my father, my privileged life could afford in Calcutta. I wanted psychological freedom.

MOYERS: Why did you leave to come to this country in the first place in 1961? What were you looking for?

MUKHERJEE: I thought, when I came as a student to Iowa, that I was coming simply to get a Master of Fine Arts degree in creative writing at the Writer's Workshop in the heartland. But now, thinking back on it, I realize that I was looking for more out of life; that I never really intended to go back to that very circumscribed, safe life that my parents had promised. While I was a student living in a dorm in Iowa City, Iowa, my parents did find for me the perfect Bengali groom for an arranged marriage. I didn't know the first name of this man. He had seen my photograph, and he'd said, "Terrific, I'll take her." I was expected, certainly, to do what girls of my class normally did—be happy in an arranged marriage; be content, anyway, in an arranged marriage. But deep down, I must have rejected that safe, circumscribed life. So fate sometimes is full of happy accidents, and I fell in love with a fellow student, Clark Blaise. After a two-week whirlwind courtship, we got married during lunchtime. And therefore, I made my life in this country.

MOYERS: What did you mean when you said some people, like your character Jasmine, like yourself, although born oceans away, are born American at heart?

MUKHERJEE: It's that capacity for dreaming. The desire for change, for seizing the good life; meaning not a bigger house and bigger car, but freedom from fate, from a predetermined life. The desire to discard the traditional world, and sink or swim in a new world, without rules.

MOYERS: Jasmine wants to reposition the stars. Is that what you wanted to do?

MUKHERJEE: I didn't know it when I actually left India, but yes. I want to reposition the stars. I want to conquer. I want to love and possess this country. I don't want to be simply an expatriate who always has her bags packed and is looking for greener pastures elsewhere.

MOYERS: What's the difference between an expatriate and an immigrant?

MUKHERJEE: An expatriate is someone who is nourished by the old world, whose psychic life is still totally attached to the discarded world thousands of miles away. An immigrant is someone who in psychological, social, psychic ways, has made herself or himself over in the new world. Who's accepting the new world as her own.

MOYERS: How do you become an American? How do you let go of the past and invent the future when you're up against a culture of which you have only the dimmest, if not crudest, understanding?

MUKHERJEE: I think you invent an America for yourself. America is a total and wondrous invention. Letting go of the old culture, allowing the roots to wither is natural; change is natural. But the unnatural thing is to hang on, to retain the old world. What is the point of hanging on to a culture that's thousands of miles away, and that probably not you, not your children, not your grandchildren, will ever see? Why not adjust and accommodate to the world around you?

MOYERS: It's hard. When I travel to foreign cultures, I've been hostage to nostalgia, to home sickness.

MUKHERJEE: I think nostalgia is a reaction of fear. It's a very understandable reaction, but it's one of panic or fear. Or it also can be in the case of, say, non-European immigrants, cultural arrogance. They feel that everything American is somehow inferior culturally to what they've left behind. I think if you've made the decision to come to America, to be American, you must be prepared to really, emotionally, become American and put down roots. Make that emotional commitment.

MOYERS: Roots are more than geographical implants.

MUKHERJEE: Absolutely. In doing that, we very painfully, sometimes violently, murder our old selves. That's an unfortunate, perhaps, but inevitable process. I want to think that it's a freeing process. In spite of the pain, in spite of the violence, in spite of the bruising of the old self, to have that freedom to make mistakes, to choose a whole new history for oneself, is exciting.

MOYERS: Even though you have not yourself experienced racism in the United States, I'm sure that you know that many Asians have. I can give you chapter and verse from South Texas to Chicago.

MUKHERJEE: There's going to be an increase in interminority violence in the nineties, I'm afraid. There's been a kind of disinvestment in America in the eighties that may continue in the nineties. People have not invested in the country. Instead they've been asking, "What part of the pie is for me?" They're privatizing, instead of saying, what kind of an America do we want? What kind of an America can we build?

As a result, I think that we are seeing large numbers of disenchanted minority

groups who watch new immigrants from Asia come in, work hard, and in their perception, do rather well. They hold down jobs, move into good homes, buy big cars. There's a real resentment against the Asians. They're misperceived as the model minority.

I was standing by a newspaper kiosk which is staffed by an Indian-American, and a homeless Afro-American came up and said, "Why is it that all the foreigners are taking over our jobs, and doing so well, while we are nowhere?" There's that kind of climate of scapegoating. We must do whatever is necessary, as a nation, as a whole country, to try and prevent that scapegoating. The Asians must make a commitment to America. If they've chosen to be Americans, then I think that they must really invest in their neighborhoods, invest in projects that help the homeless, or help solve problems for other minorities.

MOYERS: What have you learned since you've been here about the American language? Your novels and short stories are so precise in their slang, in their understanding of American pop culture. You seem to have a gift for listening.

MUKHERJEE: I can't help it. I find myself mimicking every person that I listen to for more than fifteen minutes. It's also a hunger to know America. My love for the country translates itself into a kind of hunger to absorb it whole. I'm married to a fellow writer who's very American, who has dragged me to endless baseball games, and I have to thank him for giving me access to American trivia. I usually say that I'm a four-hundred-year-old lady, because I've lived through colonial and post-colonial history in India, and then have ingested wholesale two-hundred-odd years of American history.

MOYERS: One of the most fascinating chapters in our story is coming now in the nineties, as the face of America is being changed by people who bring new ideas and are changed by the ideas that are here. Our story is changing even as we sit here.

MUKHERJEE: Yes. I think that we are creating American culture, daily. It is not something static. But through our art, and through the dangerous, improvised lives that we have to lead, we are creating a new American culture.

MOYERS: Dangerous lives?

MUKHERJEE: Well, there are no comforts, no old mythologies to cling to. We have to invent new American mythologies.

MOYERS: So tell me, your basic Protestant white male with Anglo-Saxon roots, what to expect from this new epic that is washing up on our shores.

MUKHERJEE: Vigor and energy and passion, and the hunger to belong to whatever mythology or dream this country can still offer. Maybe for the white, Anglo-Saxon males, the country is become depressing or no longer a dream. But the rest of us are coming with an eagerness to refashion ourselves. Letting go of the old notions of what America was shouldn't be seen as a loss. I hope that as we all mongrelize we will build a better and more hopeful nation.

MOYERS: You write of Americans that we're overalert but underinformed, suspicious but ignorant, coddled like babies by our politicians, and rattled by the media drum beat. Have you figured out this country, what makes it tick?

MUKHERJEE: No. I hope I haven't figured it out. Part of the excitement is constantly retooling and refashioning, trying to discover. My subject is not nostalgia for a known world, or chronicling of a real world—it's a continual discovery. I don't think of myself as a realistic writer, even though I hope that all the details ring true, whether it's about Iowa farmers going crazy, or Iowa bankers with their midlife crises shacking up with eighteen-year-old undocumented Punjabi girls like Jasmine.

But really, I'm writing a fable for the times. I'm trying to create a mythology that we can live by as we negotiate our daily lives. A mythology, a fable that can help us retain our integrity.

MOYERS: Do you think America has a soul?

MUKHERJEE: Oh yes. That's why I'm here. I would have left if I didn't believe that America has a soul. Whenever I come back from trips outside, I heave a sigh of relief when I come into this country. I know it's unfashionable to believe so wholeheartedly, but I do.

MOYERS: What is it you believe in?

MUKHERJEE: The visionariness of the Founding Fathers. The American Constitution, whether it is practiced every day or not, absolutely entrances me. The protection of human rights, at least in theory. I'm seeing the world through very fresh eyes, whereas I felt jaded, even though I was a very young person when I lived in India. I felt I was a jaded child, looking through large jaded, bulging eyes at the world. Irony was my natural form of expression. Here, I'm not afraid to be impassioned. I'm not afraid to make mistakes. And I certainly have made many.

MOYERS: We think of the immigrants in literature and in movies as sometimes pathetic figures. Whimpering, frightened creatures. You're painting a different portrait of the immigrant in America today.

MUKHERJEE: Yes. I'm not a pathetic creature, and my heroines are not pathetic creatures, because they don't think of themselves as victims. On the contrary, they think of themselves as conquerors. We have come not to passively accommodate ourselves to someone else's dream of what we should be. We've come to America, in a way, to take over. To help build a new culture. So we're pioneers, with the same guts and energy and feistiness that the original American Pilgrims had.

Maxine Hong Kingston

WRITER

When Maxine Hong Kingston was growing up in Stockton, California, she listened to her parents' stories and memories of their native China. In her highly acclaimed memoirs, *The Woman Warrior* and *China Men*, she linked those tales of tradition to the story of her own American experience, blending childhood memory, meditation, and magic. They are the most widely taught books by a living American author on college campuses today. In her most recent work of fiction, the 1989 novel *Tripmaster Monkey*, she created Wittman Ah Sing, a young Chinese American whose imagination guides his search for meaning.

MOYERS: So much of what you write about—your own childhood, your ancestry—sounds so exotic to mainstream Americans. It's another world, and I wonder what they take away from that world.

KINGSTON: I should hope that at some point they would not think "exotic" anymore. They will see that I write about Americans, that I am writing about this country and what it means to be a human being. I think I teach people how to find meaning. I write about the most chaotic, tragic, hard-to-deal-with events, and these events are sometimes so violent and so horrible that they burst through bounds of form and preconceptions. I'm hoping that readers will find how to get the meaning out of those events. How do you find beauty and order when we've had this bloody horrible past?

MOYERS: How *do* you do it?

KINGSTON: Well, one way is to use the mind, the emotions, to know history and to see what happens. One way is to take a raw human event and put it through the process of art. I did that at the beginning of *The Woman Warrior*. I wrote about my aunt, who died a seemingly senseless death. Her entire village rose up against her and forced her to kill herself and her illegitimate child. She had threatened to break the community because she broke taboos.

I heard this story and it just tore me up inside. I didn't know what to do with it. So I worked with it and wrote it out and put it through a process of art and looked at it from all kinds of angles; I tried to find the beautiful accurate words for it. As I was writing it, I thought, "I'm not going to publish this. I'm telling family secrets, I'm not going to publish this."

Telling myself that gave me the freedom to write the story. When I got through writing it, maybe ten, twelve drafts, then I knew I had a resolution. I had a beautiful story. Most important of all, I gave this woman's life a meaning. Then I felt, "Okay, now I can publish it."

MOYERS: When you said "beautiful story," did you mean that in the artistic sense of form? There is a symmetry to that story. It has the appearance of a wonderfully composed piece of art, and the composition as well as the content make it beautiful.

KINGSTON: The form and the order of the words and the poetry of the words are beauty. There's also a moral goodness that comes out of that story. There's a redemption of that woman.

She was a person whom the villagers wanted to wipe out of the book of life. They wanted to take a person who was born into this world, who existed, and they just wanted to wipe her out in memory and in history. That's a horrible thing to do to a living creature. But by writing it, I brought her back to life. I gave her life and I gave her immortality.

MOYERS: She lives forever now, in your story.

KINGSTON: Yes, and that's part of the beauty.

MOYERS: When I think about your life, I think often of the invisible violence at work in the world. Your mother was trained to be a doctor, but when she came to this country, she had to work in the fields as a field hand. Your father was a scholar and a poet as a young man in China, but here he spent the rest of his life working in a gambling house and in a laundry. How have they coped with that? Do they see you fulfilling their own lifelong yearnings?

KINGSTON: My parents have immense lives and immense souls. I don't sense a bitterness; that doesn't seem to be in them. My father did have an artistic yearning, and I think that died because his poetry came out of the land of China. He came here and he couldn't hear the poetry anymore. However, after my books were published, my father said, "You're leading the life that I wanted," and I know that's an immense satisfaction to him.

> In China Men, *I put out a challenge to him, an old Chinese Kung Fu challenge. I said, "Father, I'm going to write your stories, and you'll just have to speak up if I've got you wrong."*

MOYERS: Does he comment on the books?

KINGSTON: Oh well, the poetry has come back to him. In *China Men*, I put out a challenge to him, an old Chinese Kung Fu challenge. I said, "Father, I'm going to write your stories, and you'll just have to speak up if I've got you wrong." So he did. The Chinese translation of *China Men* has wide margins on each page, and my father wrote commentary in his copy. He did it in *Woman Warrior*, too.

MOYERS: That's a tradition in ancient Chinese writings—that after the author finished, the scholars would come in and comment in the margins of ancient scripture. What did you think when you read his commentary?

KINGSTON: A lot of it is so reconciling. I wrote a lot of angry stuff about sexism, especially in *Woman Warrior*, but everywhere I made those angry feminist accusations, he would add something wonderful like "Women hold up half the sky."

I wanted his poetry to live somewhere, to be honored somewhere, so I gave his annotated copies to the Bancroft Library at Berkeley, where they had a reception and exhibition of all my work. I took my father there without telling him what he was going to see, and I took him right up to the display case and showed him. A wonderful smile came to his face. He looked around at all the people and he said in English, "My writing." So he didn't just live through me. The words came to him.

MOYERS: What a wonderful conversation between daughter and father in the margins of a book. Your mother was born in China, too. Did she ever respond to your writing? Did she ever tell you, "You've got it right" or "No, Maxine . . ."?

KINGSTON: Oh yes. "How did you describe China so accurately?" is what she asked me.

MOYERS: Because you had never been there.

KINGSTON: No, I'd never been there. I told her the reason that I could describe China accurately was that through her "talk story" she had told me China.

MOYERS: "Talk story." She was the troubadour, in a way, of the family. She told the stories that had been passed on or that she remembered. But in your books you didn't tell the stories her way. You reinvented many of the stories that you tell in *Woman Warrior* and *China Men* and *Tripmaster Monkey*—still they rang true. What does that say about the imagination and about art?

KINGSTON: For one thing, it says I have a very strong imagination. I believe that the strong imagination imagines the truth, sees a vision of the truth. A good strong imagination doesn't go off into some wild fantasy of nowhere. It goes to the truth. It also tells a lot about the "talk story" tradition. Thousands of years of people passed on history and genealogy by speaking them. When they took these stories across the ocean and gave them to me, I didn't have to invent what had gone before. I had to invent the next stage. I went on.

MOYERS: You picked up the story and continued it.

KINGSTON: Yes, yes, I continued it. Every human being who speaks the story does it in a new way. We can try to tell the same old story and it will come out different. And so what? It means that human beings carry on the next stage, the next evolution of the story. So what I've told are the new American stories.

MOYERS: Growing out of your mother's stories and the stories of your grandmother and your great-great-grandmother.

KINGSTON: Yes, they go back forever.

MOYERS: Do you think you're imposing a burden on the reader to expect us to move back and forth between fiction and fact? You said once that when you were a little girl you told your mother, "Stop telling me those stories. I don't know if they're lies; I don't know if they're true." Isn't there a danger that your reader won't know either if your story is true or not? How can we decide whether the story you're telling is fact or fiction?

KINGSTON: Of course I should put burdens on readers. I should give them challenges because readers—and all people—already have this burden. All human beings have this burden in life to constantly figure out what's true, what's authentic, what's meaningful, what's dross, what's a hallucination, what's a figment, what's madness. I think we all need to figure out what is true, what is valuable, constantly. As a writer, all I'm doing is posing the question in a way that people can see very clearly. I'm being very helpful. I'm saying, "This is one of your challenges as a human being," and you work it out in this book and then you work it out in life, too.

MOYERS: I liked something you said about growing up, that growing up means gaining the ability to carry ideas forth into the world. I like that idea of maturity. You're not talking just artistically there. You're talking about being able to carry out thoughts into the real world of action.

KINGSTON: That's what I'm working with in *Tripmaster Monkey*, actually, because it is a book about a reader. Wittman Ah Sing is a reader. His mind was shaped by his being an English major and reading those books that we all read in college. You know who he's like. He's like Emma Bovary and he's like Don Quixote. Both of those people were readers. Don Quixote read the chivalric romances. That was what made him go out on his quest. And Emma Bovary had her affair because she was reading those Harlequin romances and then she decided that was the way she was going to live.

Wittman Ah Sing is the same way. He's a liberal arts major and he's finished that amazing education and now what? Now there's no job that he's fit for. All employers want to know is if he can type. His idea is that he has to go out in the world and find a way. So throughout this book he tries to find a literary, artistic way. His solution is the theater, but I think in the next book he's got to sustain that. This is what growing up means too, to sustain carrying out your values into the real world.

MOYERS: Wittman Ah Sing is twenty-three in this book. Can you envision him at forty?

KINGSTON: Yes. In the sense that I can envision myself at forty. I mean I've been forty, so I know.

MOYERS: I have too, let's see—it was a long time ago. I hope he's more likable when he grows up. I have to tell you that I had to struggle to like him. He is so garrulous. He talks all the time, he just won't shut up.

KINGSTON: Many people have told me they don't like him. Maybe what's happening there is that he is responding to racism. This is why he's not likable. He means to be offensive. He says we ought to offend them. He does know how to be charming. Minority people in America all know how to be charming, because there are very charming stereotypes out there.

MOYERS: Like Charlie Chan in the movies I saw growing up.

KINGSTON: Yes. We loved him. He was charming.

MOYERS: And he was acceptable to the white majority.

KINGSTON: Yes. The Model Minority. There is also a nerdy kind of image, but they were both acceptable.

MOYERS: So by making him offensive, making him his own man, so to speak, irrespective of what the prevailing majority think about him, he's breaking that stereotype of the humble Chinese.

KINGSTON: Yes. What's sad is that when many people tell me that they don't like Wittman and his personality, what they're also telling me is that they don't like the personalities of a lot of actual Asian American men out there.

MOYERS: They can't be too uppity.

KINGSTON: Yes. It seems easier to write about a man, but it just occurs to me: what if I wrote about a woman who broke Chinese American stereotypes? Because there's another pleasant stereotype of the Chinese American woman, a sort of geisha girl, feminine and beautiful, and in that sense acceptable and not scary. But what if I were to break that stereotype? Then what would happen?

MOYERS: Well, some Chinese American critics of Chinese American and Asian American women writers say that they are reinforcing the stereotype by making the characters in their novels exotic, and that by appealing to the American interest in exotic characters they are making these women forever foreigners.

KINGSTON: And you know, all of this puts the writer into a terrible bind. How do I work with mystery if I'm denied the exotic? If exoticism becomes a stereotype and then we try not to be exotic in order to not fall into a stereotype, we deny ourselves certain wonderful true images. Exoticism cheapens real mystery. In life there is deep mystery, but what people in the West have done is to say no, mystery belongs to the Orient.

MOYERS: "The inscrutable Orient," yes.

KINGSTON: It's a schizophrenic way of thinking to put the burden of the exotic onto others and not face the exotic and mysterious that's in oneself. Many Asian American artists work in sort of an extreme realism because they don't want to appear exotic.

But then what happens is that we deny what's truly exotic and mysterious in ourselves. Besides, we do have things in our lives that are foreign. There are certain statues that we keep in the house, or there are incense and altars in a lot of houses. This is so common to us, but when you look from outside eyes it's exotic.

MOYERS: I don't want to be unfair to Wittman, because while I found him offensive at times, I also found him absolutely intriguing. The way he looks at the world, his fantasy of the world. He gets fired from his job in the department store because he stages a pornographic scene between a Barbie Doll and a battery-operated monkey. Then he imagines himself going to the loudspeaker system at the store during the crowded holiday season and announcing, "We have found an unconscious bleeding child, probably dead, in the toy department." And then he sees himself as a nuclear martyr. He has an atomic detonator in his body so that the President of the United States will have to kill him before he declares war.

KINGSTON: American surrealism.

MOYERS: It's all this that makes him an American. The moment he sees the world with that sardonic wit, then he becomes an American to me. And also when he's offensive, because I find a lot of Americans—when they truly are finally American—are offensive.

KINGSTON: Maybe what's happened is that I've written an archetype.

MOYERS: Discovered an archetype.

KINGSTON: Yes. The archetype behind the archetype of Wittman Ah Sing is the Monkey Spirit, the King of the Monkeys. What I've written is the new monkey, the modern one, that exists in America.

MOYERS: Well, that's why I have mixed feelings about your potentially growing him up in the sequel. I'm not sure that we would remember Huck Finn if Huck Finn were forty in a later Twain novel. Or Holden Caulfield from *Catcher in the Rye*. I mean, there are some characters in literature who live only because they are forever young. And Wittman Ah Sing has this modern, irreverent, sardonic—

KINGSTON: Bad. He wants to be bad.

MOYERS: Yes, in fact he speaks a line right out of black America when he says, "I want to be the first bad jazz blues man in America." Now there's a rhythm and a tempo in that sentence that's right out of Newark and a rap group. One of the questions I have about Wittman, if you grow him up, is whether his children will ever want to know anything about their distant Chinese past. Or will they only want to walk around with a Walkman of American music and be purely, totally Americans?

KINGSTON: I think about that for my own child. He's twenty-six. He doesn't speak Chinese and he doesn't read or write Chinese. He's a musician, but he's not a reader. How do we pass our culture on to this next generation? I think about how hard it would be to make a fictional character grow up. It's the same problem of how to make the next generation grow up.

MOYERS: What's that old Jewish prayer? "Lord, teach me when to let go"?

KINGSTON: Yes.

MOYERS: That's what a mother and a father and a writer have to do. Sooner or later, you have to let not only your real son, but Wittman Ah Sing go.

KINGSTON: I'll let him go after he grows up. I'm not ready to let him go yet.

MOYERS: Spoken like a real mother.

KINGSTON: I'm not going to let either of them go until I see that they are good men. And it's not yet.

MOYERS: What is a good man?

A good man is one who does not die tragically. Who does not die before he's fulfilled his service to the world.

KINGSTON: A good man is one who does not die tragically. Who does not die before he's fulfilled his service to the world. Maybe a good man is a Confucian man, one who comes into a chaotic scene, a chaotic home, or a chaotic country, and finds a way to bring order, community, peace, harmony. He is able to establish peace among people in a family. To set up harmonious relationships between people, between countries, within societies. At the core is a spirit of creation. The humane being evolves.

I think that all of life tends towards the good. We want to feel good. If there's a fire that's going to burn us, we instinctively pull away toward feeling better. The physical body pushes towards feeling better. Philosophy pushes towards the good. And I think that we want to find that which is good. We haven't gotten there. We still need to define it. There's something in us that knows what it means to be humane. It has to do with treating one another in ways that help us be better. It has to do with the way of finding the human community. And artistically, when we make a work that is aesthetically good, it's morally good.

MOYERS: I'll tell you, though, what you're up against. It comes out of your own tradition. The Three Books of Peace, and you know what happened to them. They were burned and the people who remembered them and tried to recite them had their tongues torn out.

KINGSTON: Yes, they were tortured and killed and sometimes were forced to burn their own books. But maybe we can retrieve those peace books by trying to figure out what was in them. I think of that as one of my tasks as a writer. I must write at least one of them. One of my mistakes I see now that I am older was in the *Woman Warrior* story. There are parts of the story that I left out on purpose, that maybe I shouldn't have left out.

I describe the woman warrior's battles against the Mongols. But I didn't say that when she returned, she brought her army with her, and she asked them to wait outside the house. Then she went inside and took off her armor, took a bath, and put on her feminine clothes. She did her hair and put flowers in it. Then she presented herself to her army as a beautiful woman. And she said, "I was the general who was leading you." They were flabbergasted that it was a woman.

When I wrote that story, I left that out because as a feminist, I wanted to get rid of all the feminine trappings of high-heeled shoes and makeup. I wanted to show women as being just as powerful as men. So I thought, "Forget this shaving under the arms and shaving legs and wearing makeup." But now I'm thinking, "No, don't leave it out, because the ancient storytellers had reasons for putting it in there." They wanted to let women have the credit for having those powers. Even more important, they wanted to say this woman went away to war and came back and was not brutalized. She came back and she could be whole. She could still be a woman, a family person and a community person. The reason she went to war was to take her father's place, and when she came back she took another kind of service: she was changed, and she will change the community by her presence in it. She will raise children and teach them new ways. She was not dehumanized or broken by the war. And so it's important to figure out how we can do that. How do you come back from a war and then turn back into a beautiful woman? And give that beauty to your family and community?

MOYERS: So you sometimes wish you could rewrite what you have written.

KINGSTON: Yes. We can change the past by figuring out new meanings of events that took place. I want to redo some of those events and say, "These are the meanings," such as the meaning of the *Woman Warrior*. The earlier meaning was we feminists have masculine powers, too. We can go into battle and lead armies. This new meaning I'm finding from that myth is that war does not have to brutalize us. In that sense I want to rewrite it, to bring in these new meanings that I've discovered in my life.

MOYERS: If we were only artists with our lives we could do in our own personal pasts what you're doing with your mythical figures. We're not allowed that privilege, living literally, are we?

KINGSTON: Oh yes we are. Of course, we're allowed it. We are all artists.

MOYERS: Can you look back at your life and either redo it or find a meaning in it that was hidden to you at the time?

KINGSTON: Yes. I can't actually redo it. People live with a lot of regrets about choices they think were wrong, or some part of life they think they've missed. There are a lot of regrets like that. You can't redo it in the sense of jumping into a fountain of youth. But we have a bank of memories. We work with memories and the feelings of other times. We find meanings and values there. That's how we change the past.

MOYERS: Do you think it's your job as the writer to imagine a healthy world?

KINGSTON: Yes. I have to imagine it because how are we going to build it if we don't imagine it? And writers and artists free themselves to imagine it. We need to imagine the humane being so we can put that archetype out there. So that we can become it. If we don't imagine it, how are we going to become it? This world is filled with role models of some very bad, violent, despairing people, and it may be there aren't enough actual living-in-the-flesh good people. We need to keep inventing them.

Peter Sellars

THEATER DIRECTOR

© Michael Oletta

Director Peter Sellars says it's fine with him if people hate his controversial theatrical work, and many have taken him up on the offer. But he's also been called brilliant, exciting, and innovative. He set a Mozart opera in New York's Trump Tower and Shakespeare in a swimming pool, and he even conceived an opera about Richard Nixon's trip to China. At age twenty-five, he was selected as a MacArthur Fellow and also took over as artistic director of the Boston Shakespeare Company. At twenty-seven, he was named head of the Kennedy Center. Fired two years later, he is now director of the Los Angeles Festival.

MOYERS: When did music first speak to you?

SELLARS: When I was about five years old my big ambition was to be a conductor. My father built me a little podium and after school I would come home and conduct the Toscanini recordings of the Beethoven symphonies. Then of course that faded, and when I was a teenager the Beatles took over my life and pop music became my world.

But gradually I returned to more of a classical music world through theater. What interested me was that music is the most specific language that exists. It can say things that no other language has words for. It can put its finger on moments of human feeling that go largely unacknowledged in a verbally dominated culture like our own, where for most people the only reality is a verbal reality. You know, if you can't write an essay about it, if it can't be quantified, then it can't be sold and therefore doesn't exist. Most people's lives are, again and again, reduced to what they can talk about. And that's a very narrow band of the world! The time you spend with music is time spent in that larger realm.

MOYERS: But why does music open the emotions? The question intrigues me because music is a mathematical operation, yet somehow touches a spring in us that has nothing to do with mathematics.

SELLARS: It's a unification of a Pythagorean sense of perfection which in its mathematical exactitude recalls what is divine. We realize that the world has been ordained, that it is ordered, that it does make sense, that it has been thought of, and behind every imperfect form that we see, there is a perfect form that has been badly imitated in our mortal world. We look at the imperfect mortal form, we peel off its surface, we ask what's underneath it, what's behind it, what would be inside this imperfect body. And inside this imperfect body is a perfect soul. Hiding.

MOYERS: This epiphany that you're describing does not occur to me very often at the opera, even though I have an untutored appreciation for the capacity and talent of the singers. That music does not move me.

SELLARS: Right. I would say most Americans are not as moved

by cultural experiences as they want to be because most of what they see isn't good enough. Most of the cultural establishment is dominated by a very cynical machine, which is satisfied to put out cut-rate goods at top prices, and nobody's around to blow the whistle. The person who pays for it is therefore the average American, who goes filled with the hope that this will be a nice night, and doesn't know enough to call anyone on what wasn't good enough. So he'll internalize it and say, "Well, maybe it's just me. I'm not having the full reaction that I thought I might have with this." In fact, opera was intended, by its most inspired creators, to be a very bright epiphany, to cut through the tangled web of politics and the large movements of nations. It connects those movements to the specific internal movements of an individual human heart, and then catapults the whole thing onto a kind of metaphysical and metaphorical plain.

MOYERS: Much of the early opera had a populist intent, too, didn't it?

> *The point about opera is that song is the one thing that connects all human bengs. Words, again and again, divide us. Song, again and again, brings us together.*

SELLARS: Absolutely! Opera had a mass audience when the Greeks invented it. Mozart and Verdi were sung in the streets. The point about opera is that song is the one thing that connects all human beings. Words, again and again, divide us. Song, again and again, brings us together. The voice goes so deep and connects to breathing, to what makes us alive.

In that regard, vocal music is an attempt to take the whole human being and project it into space. It is the ultimate gesture of getting out of yourself. You take the one part of you that is most private, most personal, most inward, and you hurl it out into space, you project it as far as you can. That gesture of opening this whole region of the body results in a tremendous spiritual release, and is felt by other people with tremendous impact.

MOYERS: That's true. But if classical music has the ability to open the soul, to transport us, why do you bring it into a wholly different world from the one in which it was written? I mean, you put *Don Giovanni* in Harlem, and the protagonist has a switchblade and eats Big Macs. You put *Così Fan Tutte* in a diner with some of the characters disguised as the Blues Brothers. You put King Lear in a Lincoln Continental onstage. Aren't you wreaking havoc with tradition?

SELLARS: In fact, what I'm doing is entering tradition, what I'm doing is finally respecting the tradition. Look at religious painting up through Rembrandt. When those Dutch artists presented the Crucifixion, they put contemporary Dutch burghers on the hillside. The point is not that this happened once two thousand years ago, and we'll tell you about it sometime. The point is it was true then, it is true now, it is ever present, it is constantly finding itself again in your life because it's true. And if it's true, it's enduring.

MOYERS: And in the Renaissance, the Madonna is very often a Florentine lass.

SELLARS: Which was not done smugly or tongue-in-cheek. It was done as the most serious way of honoring truth. I have to put these great masterpieces in an ordinary context because one has to say that there is something pure and divine that informs every moment of ordinary life. We're never separated from the great ideas, we're never separated from the great moments in history. The great moments in history live with us every day, and they are ours to summon up at any moment.

MOYERS: So if there is a truth in what the spirit is responding to, *Don Giovanni* will still be true in Harlem.

SELLARS: Well, I have to say, clearly, I also put our society up next to Mozart to test it, to ask how we measure up next to these great masterpieces. Are we good enough? Are we thinking big enough? Are we ambitious enough? Are we generous enough of spirit? What does our society look like next to the greatest things a human being ever uttered?

At the same time, what most people don't realize is how much Mozart has been co-opted by the commercial establishment. Mozart is now used to sell chocolates. In fact, when Mozart wrote *Don Giovanni*, it was not cute and it was not charming. If you put yourself back with the first audience that heard that piece in the 1780s, music of comparable violence to the opening notes of *Don Giovanni* had never been heard before in the history of the world. It was shattering music for that audience! We now think of Mozart as rest for the soul and something lovely. In fact, for his first audience, he was tough, he was shocking. People said the music was too intellectual, too forceful, too brutal, and couldn't it be a little nicer?

Part of my aggressively juxtaposing a modern context is to say "Excuse me, this stuff does have edges. This stuff isn't smooth, and wasn't intended to go down easy." Mozart himself was deeply committed on a wide range of social issues. He had all of the cast members in *Don Giovanni* come to the front of the stage at the end of the first act and sing thirteen times, at the top of their lungs in a C major mode, the march "Viva la libertà!" And this was two years before the French Revolution! He wouldn't have done it if he hadn't actually intended to push his public.

Don Giovanni is also a picture of personal exploitation. When the don brags he had three thousand women here, and two thousand there, it shows an understanding early on of pornography, an understanding of what happens when people become numbers, when women are objects. What is the nature of love? What is the nature of sexual attraction, and what are the political consequences of sexual exploitation?

Both *The Marriage of Figaro* and *Don Giovanni* inextricably tie the progress of world revolution to how one person treats another person. It's not a giant abstract political discourse. It's the fact that the political reality of our lives is about how husbands and wives interact, how children are treated. That's how you know what the political reality is.

MOYERS: In what sense?

SELLARS: Look at the Count's refusal to pay attention to his wife in *The Marriage of Figaro*. He's married to a perfectly beautiful woman, a wonderful one, whom we come to love because Mozart gives her the most beautiful music in the world. Meanwhile, her husband is philandering with anything that moves. Anyone would say, "Does this guy have eyes? What is he not getting? If he would just cultivate his own garden he wouldn't have to go and make all of these independent conquests! He wouldn't have to go to the servants and rape them!" Now, that wouldn't sound like any large nation in its treatment of Latin America, would it? I hope not! This question of just occupying ourselves with our own problems? Perhaps not.

MOYERS: That's a large leap.

SELLARS: And Mozart makes it. The point is that when you watch the Count, you realize that this is a society that must fall, and that will fall, because of how corrupt it is. Its foundations will no longer support it. And yet you see that the strange root of this corruption is a simple human failure to deal on the basis of one human being to another. To deal in a non-exploitative way, to begin to notice that one has been offered something that's beautiful and that all one has to do is notice it and treat it with some dignity, and allow it to blossom.

MOYERS: In *Così Fan Tutte* you had President Bush invading Panama six months before it actually happened. How did you foresee that?

SELLARS: It's given to the artist! My last show in Washington was *Ajax*, about the Greek general who went mad. It was military zeal and responsibility run amok. All of this happened while Iran-contra was going on, but six months before the public knew about it. It's wonderful—and I don't claim it for myself—but artists truly are extremely sensitive, not usually consciously, to the deep vibrations that are moving through a society. Again and again, if you look at the important performers and the important writers, their work is exactly anticipating very important political developments. That's why I feel that art is political, and art and politics are inextricably linked. You can't separate them, because artists are so sensitive to those vibrations.

MOYERS: But art is not speaking to power very forcefully in America today. Shakespeare and Molière wrote for the court theater. They infiltrated messages into the monarchy. We don't have a Shakespeare or a Molière today.

SELLARS: We don't. But even more interesting and powerful in America now is the creation of art within small communities, within officially marginalized or immigrant communities. This art is not decorative or commercially exploitable. It's a necessity, a social necessity, like the dance company founded by the Cambodian immigrants in Long Beach so they would know deeply and remember that they were Cambodian.

And because the artists are aware that they are meeting a compelling need, this art is not permitted to be self-indulgent, or self-reflexive; this art has to be essential. The audience is hungry, and they must be fed, and they're depending on it. The result is an art that's happening right now, not in any of the official cultural centers, not in any of the Lincoln Centers or the Kennedy Centers, but in small community centers, in neighborhoods, in garages. It's an art of and by people, and it's an art that puts forward alternative histories because the official history that is on the network news is not an adequate representation of the lives these people have led.

MOYERS: But the evening news reaches the masses. It is shaping the metaphor, deciding the images that seep into the general mentality.

SELLARS: That's less and less true. Already, you know, viewership is falling off for the major networks. We're moving into a phase which I would like to think of as a democratization of mass culture. The decisions about American culture will be made less and less on the seventeenth floor of buildings on Fifty-seventh Street in New York City. Right now we need Hollywood because it's the only place to get the capital to produce a film. But the means of production are gradually becoming cheaper and cheaper. Video equipment is now within reach of an artist, a neighborhood, a community.

MOYERS: Everyone a Steven Spielberg?

SELLARS: Absolutely. What's important is that people are taking their own histories into their own hands.

MOYERS: You think these are the real stories?

SELLARS: These are the real stories.

MOYERS: And regional theaters, amateur theaters, are doing a lot of this.

SELLARS: Right. While Hollywood continues to give us the same old sitcom format, while every TV show we see is a repeat of the same story, there are a whole bunch of Americans who have real stories to tell that are not the same old stories.

MOYERS: Where are they telling them?

SELLARS: They're telling them in small enclaves to themselves, because again, and again, and again, art is an important survival mechanism within the subculture. My point is now we have to rethink and reorient what we consider mainstream, so that we begin to include a whole range of things that have been kept outside on behalf of some imagined audience in Peoria living in a suburban mansion. The point is we've learned that the great American fifties image of suburban happiness hasn't helped the world. In fact, that image of suburban happiness has, as its subtext, alcoholism, the loneliness of women, the bizarre lives of wives who have bought into the consumer existence and then say, "What else is there?" Again and again, these big commercial images of American life are not panning out. Meanwhile, there are a whole bunch of people who can't buy into them, even if they wanted to. And the grit of their real lives generates more—what can I say?—human honor—

MOYERS: Spirituality?

SELLARS: Yes! Thank you! More genuine spiritual and moral force. The result is that the words which these people use to describe their lives have honor. They may seem to lack technique, but my God, they've got the content. That's why I think it's ironic—it's not ironic, it's in fact sad—that the art world is so obsessed right now with questions of style. Exactly because content is missing!

MOYERS: The art world right now is obsessed with art as commerce.

SELLARS: Correct. And that, of course, is the kiss of death. It's terrifying to behold. I grew up in the theater, and one of the terrible things to live with is the knowledge that Eugene O'Neill is the only American playwright who didn't get worse the longer he lived. The bitter, horrible truth of Arthur Miller is his great play is the first one. The terrifying fact of Tennessee Williams was the early work was great. The sad story of Sam Shepard is that the early plays were colossal, and then the decline.

MOYERS: And your conclusion from that sad litany?

SELLARS: America has always assumed that if something is commercially successful it will take care of itself. And there's always been this assumption that if you put economics and politics first, culture and the spiritual life will get along just fine. But it turns out not to be the case. It turns out that culture can't be an afterthought in the midst of a big commercial boom. It has to be specifically supported of and by and for itself, and it cannot be expected to do anything other than exist. It can't be expected to make a profit for anyone; it can't be expected to make a success story for anyone.

In fact, what's powerful about theater is it's the history of failure. Hamlet, Oedipus Rex, and King Lear are all people who didn't make it. That's why we look at their story. That's why we're obsessed with these people. They were failures, and we find that poignant. It leads us to search for another level of truth that we can depend on.

MOYERS: In the nineteenth century, great American actors would roam the countryside and the small towns. They'd get off at the railroad depot and they would perform Shakespeare for mill workers, in saloons, in mining camps. They were reaching an untutored but appreciative audience.

SELLARS: That's the point. First of all, Shakespeare was the great American playwright. He wrote all about America, all of his plays. The only place to see Shakespeare is America, the only way to do Shakespeare is for miners. Shakespeare really exists here and now. He wrote about a country that was a world power, in charge of commerce, whose grip was so big! His plays were cautionary tales of how to go from being a big adolescent to being an adult. America is the adolescent that Elizabethan England was. The question now is, "Will we live to adulthood?" Shakespeare's plays, the story of Prince Hal becoming a king, are about whether it's possible to survive your teen years. They're written and addressed to a nation to provoke the question "How do you want to grow up now?"

MOYERS: But Shakespeare has no audience today to speak of. He really doesn't.

SELLARS: Well, I would say the audience has been taught that Shakespeare is not theirs. Our audience has been taught that Shakespeare belongs to the British and to the Royal Shakespeare Company. What is maddening in America is most people have been separated from their culture. They have been told there's a special privileged class of artists who have a special insight. A normal person doesn't have this insight.

> *The special students are isolated in a class and told, "You're special, you go on. The rest of you, please become middle-class and boring."*

That is a monstrous lie, and it is hideous because it is taught to us early on. We are taught we're not artists. Every single day we're reminded. The special students are isolated in a class and told, "You're special, you go on. The rest of you, please become middle-class and boring."

That is a hideous betrayal, because every living soul is an artist; every living human being was invested with a view of the world that is his or her own. In fact, three quarters of my work is just to say, "Don't applaud politely because you were taught to applaud politely. If you hate it, say so. If you like it, say so."

MOYERS: We do. We've been very critical of your work.

SELLARS: The relief is that my work is controversial. It's such a relief, because at least it flushes people out of the bush. At least people can't say, "Oh, well, that was a nice evening." They have to say, "That was horrible" or "This annoyed me."

MOYERS: Some of it *is* boring.

SELLARS: I go out of my way to bore people because it's the one thing that is not allowed in America.

MOYERS: But I'm not going to pay you to bore me.

SELLARS: I hope you will. The most important art in the last fifty years in this country is boring art. What is important about John Cage or Jackson Pollock is it's boring. The whole idea is that you just *experience* something.

You have been genuinely mystified, have seen a whole series of things that you can't solve. Two years later you still think, "What was that?" The whole idea is that we must first allow people to be comfortable again with mystery, with the unknown, with the unspoken. Furthermore, I insist—I mean I just insist—that they be quiet for a moment, that repose be allowed. You know, in America everybody wants to interrupt you before you're done because they know what you're going to say. Insist for a second, "No, you don't know!"

What's so powerful about the late works of Eugene O'Neill—*Long Day's Journey into Night* and *The Iceman Cometh*—is this shocking thing: he makes his point in virtually the first three lines of the play, and then he repeats it four hundred times for the next five hours. And you say, "Thank you, we already heard that." And then he repeats it again, and you say, "Thank you, we already heard that." And he repeats it again, and you say, "Okay, we got the point. Go easy now." And he repeats it again, and you say, "This is enough!" Four hours later, after you've been saying, "We know this, we know this, we know this," he repeats it. And you say, "Oh, I get what he means."

MOYERS: If you've stayed with him and haven't fallen asleep. I don't have to pay twenty-five, thirty-five, forty-five dollars to buy a ticket to be put to sleep. I can do it on the couch in front of prime-time television.

SELLARS: But the reason to pay a little money is that when you do open your eyes, you see a vision. You see something you don't see on your sofa. You enter a world that's visionary and leads you to someplace where of course you've been, but you've forgotten how to live there. And you say, "Oh, I think I recognize that." Then suddenly some subterranean idea, something that's been running through your life all along but you never quite put your finger on it, says, "Hello. I'd like to meet you now." And you realize that of course, nothing is new in the world, that you did know this, but you had been taught that you had forgotten it.

MOYERS: Some of your critics just dismiss all of this as sophomoric horseplay.

SELLARS: The *New York Times*, for example.

MOYERS: "He's the Andy Warhol of opera production," they say, "screaming at us to look at sleazy banality with tolerant eyes and recognize it as a new profundity."

SELLARS: You know, I love it. I mean, you put something out there and people come up with all kinds of loony things. Mostly, though, what must be said? I'm not crazy, I'm not goofy, we're not doing this to do some weird oddball thing.

MOYERS: I'm struck that you don't let the criticism get to you. You've been fired from more jobs than George Bush has held. And you just keep going. You don't fear unemployment, do you?

SELLARS: No. In America, you have to hit and run. As soon as they figure out what you're doing, they take you out behind the barn and shoot you in the head. I mean, it's just known. So you have to move any way you can, and you have to use any strategy you can. I think what's so important is to first of all give audiences credit. Most people who tell you what audiences want or don't want are selling the audience terribly short. The reason the audience doesn't want anything else is they've never been given anything else, and they've been trained since birth that this is what they want.

When I was in high school, I had a theater for five summers in Denver, Colorado, where I did these shows for Denver housewives and their kids. I then took the same material to Harvard with me. Now, the Denver housewives had no problem. But the *Harvard Crimson* wrote articles saying, "This is so avant-garde, this is so alarming, this is so difficult to follow, how can this be allowed?" But the Denver housewives entered that work directly. They just were there! I never want to hear again that the mass public is not ready for serious art! Of course they're ready.

MOYERS: But where do you see it in a mass form?

SELLARS: What needs redoing is the distribution system. You just have to get it to the people. You have to get it so that it is available, it is there, it becomes part of the landscape, it becomes part of the surroundings. It should not be an extreme, unusual, bizarre occasion to have an art event. Rather it should be an ongoing engagement with your neighbors. That's what art is about.

It is about, why do we live together? Is there any reason to live near any other human being? If there is, there must be something that's shared. That thing is culture. And therefore the question is, "Should we cultivate it so that it could become cultured culture? Or should we just let it grow wild and kind of ignore it and not bother watering it and treat it like, you know, the dandelion between the cracks of cement in the sidewalk? And run it over and say, 'Gosh, it's hardy, it's still there, we can't get rid of it!'" Amazingly, no matter how we abuse it, there's still some weird little green sprig coming up through the cement. This becomes the question now in America. Could we now make a place for culture? Could we make a garden?

Leo Braudy

LITERARY HISTORIAN

If, as Andy Warhol contended, everyone gets to be famous for fifteen minutes, Leo Braudy can tell us why. The history of fame since ancient times and the phenomenon of celebrity in twentieth-century America have been the focus of his scholarship. He spent a decade researching his book *The Frenzy of Renown*, which traces how our collective attention has shifted from political leaders like Abraham Lincoln to television personalities like Vanna White. He teaches at the University of Southern California, where he is Leo S. Bing Professor of Literature.

MOYERS: I have here, hot off the presses, the new World Almanac, with its annual poll of young Americans' top heroes. The top hero this year was Michael Jordan, the basketball player, of the Chicago Bulls. There is also a recap of the heroes of the eighties: Burt Reynolds won twice, Alan Alda, Sylvester Stallone, Michael Jackson, Eddie Murphy won twice, Bill Cosby, and Tom Cruise. What does it say to you that young Americans' heroes every year come from either sports or entertainment?

BRAUDY: All of us have these categories of people that we pay attention to, and they have to be filled. They're inside of us. Some might say that we're manipulated, that we really wouldn't think about these people if we weren't told to by advertising people. But I think it's part of being in a mass society. We're constantly looking for symbolic people. They may symbolize goodness, badness, mediocrity, whatever it is. In part, it's a way to make sense of the world.

MOYERS: We make sense of things by choosing—

BRAUDY: By choosing somebody who embodies a constellation of traits. They may be heroic traits, they may be villainous traits. But these famous people embody them, and by personalizing these traits, we can make sense of what's going on around us.

It's not so hard to make sense between ourselves, in our family, at work. But then there's this vast world out there called the country, or the media, or the United States. How do we make sense of that? Well, we start by nominating people to represent certain kinds of things: political power, moral goodness, all sorts of elements.

MOYERS: But Michael Jordan has gained fame not only for his exploits on the basketball court. He's also famous for his endorsements of fast foods, breakfast cereals, sneakers, clothing, soft drinks, and so forth. It's not just for what he does as an athlete. He's become a pitchman.

BRAUDY: If you win fame for an actual achievement, somehow this fame is transferable to all sorts of other areas that would seem to have nothing whatsoever to do with it. For Jordan to say "You should eat this food," or use this detergent or whatever it is, "because I'm a great basketball player," that's an odd kind of logic. The hidden logic there is that fame is a spiritual quality.

That is, if you are famous, somehow you have a radiance, and somehow you have an authority that should persuade people to do virtually anything. And that authority is usable in commercials. Commercials are all about ideals and the way to become a better person. All commercials say, "You are lacking, you are empty. You need this product and then you will be wonderful." So the famous person who is the pitchman for these commercials says, "Be like me, be wonderful. If you do this, well, you may not necessarily become a great basketball player, but you will share in my aura."

> . . . if you are famous, somehow you have a radiance, and somehow you have an authority that should persuade people to do virtually anything. And that authority is usable in commercials.

MOYERS: This kind of fame has also given us something new in the dictionary of identity: the television personality. He or she is a "television personality." No one has any idea what a television personality *does*. It's just that he or she *is*. Vanna White, for example, is the essence of the television personality.

BRAUDY: Because these people are there on television, we start ascribing to them all sorts of characteristics. They're there as canvases on which we can project virtually anything. What does Vanna White do? She turns letters. But we watch her so often. We see her clothes; we see her so many times, we start ascribing characteristics to her. It hasn't quite gotten to the point where Vanna White is giving her views on what's happening in Eastern Europe, but that's only a small step.

MOYERS: One of your peers in the academy wrote recently that Vanna White is a harbinger of the return of traditional feminine behavior. "She's mute, obliging, and servile. She's also busty," he said, "which is important for family formation these days." This doesn't say much about the liberation of women from sexual stereotypes, when fame can be accorded to someone for being mute, obliging, servile, and busty. Or am I making too much of it?

BRAUDY: There are many different kinds of fame that satisfy different people. Vanna White is not in competition with Gloria Steinem, let's say, for anybody's attention. But Vanna White satisfies the audience that likes Vanna White.

MOYERS: Why do they like her? That's the question.

BRAUDY: They may like her for some of the reasons you cited. They may just like her because she's doing those things. They may have liked her to begin with because nobody else was paying attention to her, and they wanted to be the person who really liked her. We often pick up people on the sidelines in this way, people who aren't the center of attention, because we want to be thought of as fame mavens, experts in fame. We see so many different kinds of fame all the time, we want to have our say about who ought to be famous. As an audience, in general, we always have our say about who ought to be famous. When we stop paying attention to them, they're no longer famous.

MOYERS: But on the list of top heroes, there are no neurosurgeons who save lives; there are no statesmen who save countries; there are no teachers who save minds; and there are no religious leaders who save souls. These are all people who are known for their constant exposure, not for their genuine accomplishment. Are we giving up on the real people who make a difference in the world we live in?

BRAUDY: What these polls do show is which images carry meaning best for us. To the extent that somebody is famous for doing something, for being a great brain surgeon or a great philanthropist, that's very specific. They have done this, and therefore, they are famous for doing this.

But the people who win in this sort of poll have a vaguer image. They have not really done anything to merit that kind of attention. Michael Jordan is a basketball player. Sylvester Stallone is a movie actor. But they don't win in these polls because of their professions. They come out on top in these polls because the people who vote feel that they can load all this meaning onto them. What does Michael Jordan mean? I don't know. He means a certain kind of skill, a certain kind of aspiration, a certain kind of ambition. Every member of the audience probably has a somewhat different view of what Michael Jordan means.

I think this is true of the people who were grandly famous throughout the ages, on a much larger scale than this particular poll. The people who are grandly famous are people who are often famous for contradictory reasons. The more contradictions you can hold in yourself, the more contradictions your image has, the more famous you will be, because people will interpret you in different ways.

MOYERS: Give me an example.

BRAUDY: Jesus is a good example. Just think of the different ways that Jesus' message has been taken. Alexander the Great is another example. To one person, Alexander was the ruler of an empire. To another, Alexander was the great soldier. To still a third, Alexander was the soldier who was interested in the arts. In the Middle Ages, it wasn't Alexander's conquests that interested people so much as the fact that he had talked to the wise men of the East. The more different kinds of stories, and even contradictory stories, that can be told about someone, the more famous he will be, because he embodies ambivalences in the audience's own interest in him.

MOYERS: Was he Alexander the Great before his publicity agent got hold of him?

BRAUDY: He was Alexander III, in fact. It was not until several hundred years later that the Romans called him Alexander the Great. At the time, though, he had his own publicity people. When he went on his invasion of the East, he carried with him historians and sculptors and painters and even jewelers who made special rings to commemorate his triumphs. He had an instinct for doing the kind of thing that people would tell stories about. Whenever he came to a new region with his army, he would always ask about its myths. The locals would come in and say, "Well, you see that hill over there? That hill is so big and so difficult, that not even Hercules could climb that hill." Of course, Alexander would immediately zoom right to the top of that hill. He had a competitiveness with the famous of the past, which I think is an important element in that kind of grand fame. And he always won.

MOYERS: That's different from being a celebrity, isn't it? My late friend Joseph Campbell said that a celebrity serves only himself or herself, while a hero goes out and redeems society. Do you think we're losing the difference between a celebrity and a hero in this world?

BRAUDY: Oh, I think we have. We've certainly lost that distinction. We're not as interested in *doing* as we are in *being*. To me, a celebrity is someone who *is*, by his or her nature.

MOYERS: Is what?

BRAUDY: That's it. A celebrity only *is*. I think it's almost like an etiquette. In every age, there's a kind of central vocation that becomes the way in which fame, achievement, or whatever, is measured in other areas. It used to be the king. Everything was measured against the idea of monarchy. Or it could be the artist.

In our period, it's the performer. The performer doesn't *do* so much as *be*. We see the whole range of celebrities almost as a kind of etiquette book. How do you behave in public? What happens, let's say, when Bill Moyers comes and interviews you? How do you respond? It's intriguing to look at the news broadcasts over the last twenty or thirty years, and to see how reporters walk up to people on the street and ask them what they thought about whatever happened. People are so much more comfortable with that now, as if they've been rehearsing for it.

MOYERS: There is nowhere we can go today that the camera isn't accepted as a piece of furniture.

BRAUDY: I saw a film documentary the other day made by the Office of War Information during World War II. It was about the last bombing run of a plane—the *Memphis Queen*, I think it was. The camera had been along on their run, had filmed other planes shot down, and things like that. When the crew came back, the camera photographed them getting off the plane. And the voice-over on the sound track said, "The last thing they are interested in at this time is the camera." They had to explain it, because what we saw was people looking warily at the camera, not really wanting to talk about their experience. Of course, now, they would talk about it endlessly. It's normal to talk in front of the camera. In part, it's because we live in such a complicated society in which we are constantly forced into social situations. I remember reading recently that when Americans were asked what they're most afraid of, speaking in public beat death by a large margin. So we want to know how to be seen by others. We want to come off well.

> *. . . when Americans were asked what they're most afraid of, speaking in public beat death by a large margin.*

MOYERS: Why is Elvis Presley a bigger star dead than he was alive?

BRAUDY: Good career move, as they say.

MOYERS: His merchandise is bringing in 50 million dollars this year. Someone asked the manager of Graceland, which is Elvis's former home in Tennessee, how he explained the phenomenon. The manager said, "Somebody had to do the job. Somebody had to be the central figure in a cultural and social revolution." Elvis did it well—dead and alive. But what is this cultural and social revolution of which a deceased Elvis Presley is the Paul Revere?

BRAUDY: Elvis is fulfilling a certain function for his admirers. Elvis, I think, is the saint of failure. He embodies a particularly American kind of story. He had a fantastic success, but somehow, underneath it all, there was personal failure, problems, and, of course, finally, death—the greatest failure of all. Some have argued there's a particularly Southern aspect to this; that the South has a cult of failure that goes back to the Civil War. Failure, they say, is more noble than success.

I remember taking a walk in Baltimore once, and I noticed through a first-floor window a room full of images of Elvis. An older woman who was sitting on the steps said, "Do you like that? Would you like to see more?" She invited us in. Her entire front room was filled with pictures and statues of Elvis. Clearly, this was a kind of Adonis, if you want to go back to Greek mythology for precedents. A beautiful young man who had died too young. She had set up a shrine for him.

The most famous people—like Elvis—are the intersection of varieties of desire, varieties of attention, and they fulfill many different kinds of functions for the audience. For one fan, it's a cult of failure. For another, it's the great singer who could have been greater. For another, it's this lost beautiful boy.

MOYERS: But there is a sense of tragedy to it.

BRAUDY: I think Americans in general, and perhaps Southerners even in particular, have always had a soft spot for the underdog, for the noble failure. We are enamored of success—that's one side of it. But also, perhaps, because in our own lives we know the complexity of success and failure, we hanker after the noble failure, too. It's a resolution. You can fail and still be famous. You don't have to just succeed.

MOYERS: So it's fame for its own sake, not fame for its achievement.

BRAUDY: For all our adulation of the incredibly successful, there's still a feeling of bad faith about it. There's still a feeling that perhaps it's better not to strive so much. Perhaps it's better not to be in the spotlight. We have another set of heroes, who are heroes of reticence, who are heroes of failure.

MOYERS: But Elvis seemed to lust for fame, to revel in it.

BRAUDY: But he also seemed to be burdened by it, too.

MOYERS: Well, there is a burden of fame.

BRAUDY: I think that's true. I have a friend who is a painter. After he had been working for many years and had some degree of recognition, all of a sudden he was

being celebrated from one end of the country to the other. We went to his big show, and I said to him, "Well, you must be feeling terrible." And he said, "How did you know? Everybody else thinks I should be happy about it. But I feel awful. If I'm getting so much attention, my work must not be any good."

MOYERS: Not any good? Why did he think that?

BRAUDY: There's an idea that the more you are successful—and I think this is especially true in the arts—the more you attract an audience, in fact, the blander or the more boring or the less interesting your work really is. That is, the truly great artists are people who are appreciated after they're dead. The immediate audience, the audience that's around you all the time, the audience that celebrates you, is a purely commercial audience, and you don't want to appeal to that audience. You want to appeal to the audience that will be around once you're dead, when your true value will be revealed.

MOYERS: It's interesting to me that half of the top heroes of the 1980s on the World Almanac list were black. We've certainly democratized access to fame in the media.

BRAUDY: Oh, yes. That's a very striking thing. And it's happened in the last four or five years. I think you can see it in commercials in general. It used to be, of course, that blacks were seen only in commercials for products that were particularly targeted to blacks. But that's not true anymore. Just recently, when a tobacco company tried to introduce a cigarette aimed at blacks, it totally blew apart. That kind of obvious audience targeting is not acceptable anymore.

MOYERS: So fame has some positive results, too, when it enables a people long denied access to the mainstream imagery of America to become universally appealing.

BRAUDY: I think that's true. I don't like the way that many writers and media deplore fame because somehow it shows the corruption and degradation of Western civilization. I think that fame is connected with democracy in a very important way. It is the way we view people, and it is, in part, the way we view ourselves. The more people—different kinds of people—who are brought into this pantheon of the famous, the more democratic fame is.

MOYERS: That's a novel thought to me, because I've long thought of fame as that celebrity which comes from great accomplishment, that rises above the pack, that stands out beyond the masses, striking a path into the future. You're saying that we've leveled fame, even as fame is lifted up.

BRAUDY: Well, I wouldn't say leveled. The kind of fame that you're talking about, I think, is much more typical of a monarchical world, or a world that has a pyramid structure. The fame at the top is unique. But fame has changed since the democratic revolutions in America and in France in the eighteenth century. Now the unique person is also the representative person.

MOYERS: The man of the people.

BRAUDY: The spokesman for the people, who realizes a potential in everyone. That's really the essence of democratic fame. Not all of them, but a lot of the people we've been talking about, are famous because they are potentials for each person in the audience. Perhaps none of the young people polled are going to become like Michael Jordan. But on the other hand, when they're on the basketball court, his image will be there with them. It's a potential. It's connected to all sorts of American myths, certainly. You know, Abraham Lincoln writing his lessons on his shovel next to the fireplace, rising from the log cabin to the White House.

MOYERS: And on the way—becoming one of America's first corporate lawyers.

BRAUDY: That's right. Well, that is usually left out of the story. Lincoln was very much a member of the establishment of his own day and connected to political and social power. But what's left in the story, the myth, is that sense of potential. It happened to Lincoln, it could happen to me.

MOYERS: On the plane coming out here, an interesting thing happened. I was sitting next to an eighteen-year-old from Louisiana, who was on his way to San Diego to be inducted into the Marine Corps. It was his first airplane flight, and we were chatting. The stewardess, who did not recognize me, came up and said, "Did you fellows know that Lily Tomlin is up in the first-class cabin?" The young man said, "Who's Lily Tomlin?" His eyes were utterly blank. I said, "She's on television."

And he said, "She's on television! Is that right! She's up in first class!" He didn't know who Lily Tomlin was, but the fact that she was on television excited his imagination, and bonded him in some way with that stewardess who was excited about Lily Tomlin being up there. Then when we got off the airplane, I pointed out Lily Tomlin to him. She looked nondescript; she had on sunglasses and was obviously trying to avoid people. He said in a disappointed tone, "Oh, she's famous?"

BRAUDY: Yes, America is a country in which people have very little in common. There is no state religion. We live in different places with different laws. We all consider ourselves Americans, however. And one thing that connects us is that we all watch the same television programs. Or we all watch Television, with a capital *T*. The idea that somebody is on Television then becomes like a kind of instant coin of recognition around the country. These people bring us together as a country. They make us pay attention to the same things. They become a coin of conversation and controversy between us. So they perform a very important service for the United States.

MOYERS: You seem to be suggesting that people like Johnny Carson, Arsenio Hall, Roseanne Barr, Peter Jennings, are playing almost a spiritual role.

BRAUDY: Oh, I think they are minor deities of a sort. They're like fairy godparents who come down and tap you and turn the normal everyday you into something special. I think that myth is there underneath it.

MOYERS: But the saints of old pointed us towards God, beyond ourselves to another reality. I'm not sure that's happening with the minor deities, as you call them. They seem to do so little. What is Johnny Carson doing every night for us?

BRAUDY: He is directing our attention. He is directing our focus. He is saying, "I'm paying attention to these people. Therefore, they are people that you should pay attention to." And this is a great change, I think, in the career of the talk-show host in general. It used to be that the host was just there to bring these famous people on. Now it's the host who makes them famous *because* he brings them on.

We want to be told what's important. We get so much information; so many people are trying to get our attention. How do we know if this new singer, or this new actor or actress, or this new politician, is worth paying attention to? We look to the intermediaries. We look to the columnists, the journalists, the talk-show hosts, the producers, to tell us these things. Depending on our temperament, we might say, "Ah, they're all wrong." We might say, in fact, that this actress, this journalist, this politician that nobody else is paying attention to is really a lot more interesting than the other ones. But then we're still buying into the whole system. We're saying that in fact the fame machine makes mistakes, but we're going to rectify them. Either way, we're looking to have our choices and our will ratified.

MOYERS: You don't seem very cynical about this.

BRAUDY: Well, I think the cynical position is the most normal position. But the problem is that it somehow assumes that at some time there was an Eden in which this wasn't true. The cynic wishes that we were back then, when we weren't so corrupt, when there wasn't television or newspapers or whatever particular thing bothers the cynic most. I'm much more interested in how we deal with what's happening right now.

MOYERS: With this explosion of fame?

BRAUDY: How we understand it as part of what's going on in our culture, and in a sense, how it's unavoidable. I don't necessarily think it's going to keep increasing and continually expanding its bounds. But on the other hand, we're not going to get smaller as a society; we're not going to get less complex as a society. The modes of communication are going to become more and more elaborate. There's going to be more and more information. So I think the challenge is to try to understand it all. To figure out exactly what's valuable and what isn't valuable from all this information.

MOYERS: Are we going to become more critical of fame? Are we going to use our analytical powers to take apart the images of fame the way we take apart the sentences of an article or a book or an essay?

BRAUDY: I hope so. I think that's happening. We've created an audience that knows a lot about fame, and is interested in all the varieties of fame, the true fame and the false fame. The audience is testing the relationship between what it thinks about a person's private life and what it thinks about that person's public position and public image. Gary Hart was a victim of that kind of testing.

Now my more optimistic view is that in the future we'll know a little more about that because of the things that have happened now. We always go forward. We always get more sophisticated. I think the cynical view implies that we get less subtle, less sophisticated. But that's clearly not true.

MOYERS: What do you think about the writer who said, "The media know exactly what they're doing, focusing our attention on Arsenio Hall's hairstyle. If we didn't keep our brains brimming with rubbish, we might think about things."

BRAUDY: This is the updated version of religion as the opiate of the people. Now it's supposed to be the media that are the opiate of the people. That is, we get so filled with trivial details that we're not going to think about the important things. I don't think it's happening. In fact, we are more interested in the important things than we used to be. We are more attuned to scandals. We are more willing to follow out, say, the problems of the Department of the Interior, the problems of HUD, than we were twenty years ago. Twenty or thirty years ago, the inner operations of Washington were much more of a mystery to the general public than they are now, and I think that's all to the good.

MOYERS: I agree with that. But when the disclosures were made in the fifties about how presidential assistant Sherman Adams accepted a gift of a vicuña coat, for example, there was much more moral outrage, much more indignation in the country than there is now. I wonder if the diminished outrage isn't the price we paid for the explosion of fame. We're so interested in everything that everything is equalized at the trivial level.

BRAUDY: I think the outrage has been diffused in that sense. We're not so upset because we're more used to it. On the other hand, I want to give the media credit for their constant preoccupation with the operations of government. They're not just saying, "Oh, there's a scandal, let's pay attention now." They constantly pay attention. That seems to be a very important part of democracy. If you accept the common argument that we're only electing images to public office, you have to add the fact that we're also paying a lot more attention to the people who truly run the government, the people who run the day-to-day government.

So it works at both ends of the spectrum. At the same time that there's more empty famousness, there's also a lot more hard attention. Maybe we have to take the bitter with the sweet. One of my favorite analyses of America came actually from somebody who was on the wrong side in the Revolution, a fellow named Fisher Ames who supported England. He made a comparison between monarchy and democracy. Monarchy, he said, is like a great ship that rides the waves. But if one cannon hits it, it sinks right to the bottom. Democracy, he said, is like a raft. It's always half under water, but it never sinks. So, both of these things happen. It's the same with fame and image. A lot of negative things happen, a lot of superficial and trivial things. But on the other hand, we've learned a lot about fame, we've learned a lot about the famous, and we keep paying attention. I think that's part of a true democracy.

Patricia Smith Churchland

NEUROPHILOSOPHER

Patricia Smith Churchland, professor of philosophy at the University of California at San Diego, is probing a new frontier of brain research. She is convinced that exploration into physical functions of our "wonder tissue" can help us better understand what our thoughts mean and how we can control them. In her new book, *Neurophilosophy*, she describes how recent discoveries about the brain call into question such basic philosophical concepts as free will and rational thinking.

MOYERS: What's a philosopher doing studying the science of the brain? It seems to me that's more naturally the domain of the trained scientist.

CHURCHLAND: In a way that's true. But suppose, as it seems, that how we perceive and think and reason are all in fact brought about by the brain. If we really want to understand who we are, what kinds of things we are and what it is to think and to see, then we need to understand those processes in the brain.

I became very dissatisfied with much philosophy, and indeed with much psychology, when I was a graduate student, because it seemed to me that it really did ignore the brain. It didn't just say, "Well, I'm too busy to pay attention to the brain." It said, "The brain doesn't matter. How the brain does these things isn't actually very interesting because we want to understand the nature of cognition, the nature of language or vision, at a different level, and it's at the level that's analagous to a program in a computer." Just as you wouldn't care too much about the inner workings of the chips of a computer, but would want to care about the program. So philosophers said, "Why bother caring very much about the nature of the brain?" And I guess I was just stubborn enough to think that that was wrong.

MOYERS: Have you ever held a brain?

CHURCHLAND: Yes I have, several of them. When I initially decided that I wanted to understand more neuroscience, part of the motivation was this. I couldn't tell, from looking at a two-dimensional picture, where things were, because you could see a structure on one page, but on the next page it would look different. So I found someone at the University of Manitoba in the anatomy department and I said, "Look, I'm really having trouble knowing where things are in the brain," and he said, "The only way to do it is to take anatomy." So I went to the medical school and took all of the regular neuroscience, neuroanatomy courses. One of them was lab. And one day they wheeled in a big trolley and on the trolley were Tupperware pots, each of which contained a human brain. What we needed to do then, of course, was to dissect the brain so we could understand how the gross parts at least were put together.

MOYERS: We can hold a brain, see a brain, dissect a brain, put the tissue of a brain under the microscope. We can study the brain, but nobody has ever seen the mind. Right?

CHURCHLAND: No.

MOYERS: So how did you hope to study what you couldn't see?

CHURCHLAND: The way to think of it, I suppose, is that the mind would be the collection of capacities, the collection of psychological capacities that the brain has: to see, and to smell, for example. And then you would want to try to find out what in the brain are the mechanisms that subserve those capacities. So there wouldn't be anything which is somehow "vision itself" that you would see when you open up the brain. It's just that when a circuit of cells interacts in a certain way, they have the capacity to compute visual motion, let us suppose, or they have the capacity to compute color.

MOYERS: So when you held that brain, did you think, I'm looking at a mind?

CHURCHLAND: Well, I did, in a funny sort of way. When I first took the brain out of the pot, I was tremendously moved. I mean, this was a human brain that I held in my hands. It was somebody's, and somebody who had been alive and been a person and been somebody's mother. But of course what I always wanted was to know, but how does it work? How are the things put together? What is the mechanism, such that it works?

MOYERS: But no matter what we know about how the networks of neurons work, how the cells work, isn't it still just speculation about how language occurs and how thought occurs?

CHURCHLAND: Yes, we're a long way off, really. We don't understand at all what thinking is, or planning, or reasoning, but we are beginning to understand a little bit about vision. We are beginning to understand quite a bit about memory. We know that there are at least two very different memory systems. The one that we use when we consciously remember something requires a very special piece of tissue in the brain called the hippocampus, and we know quite a bit now about the cells that are in the hippocampus and how they are wired up together.

Now, the missing piece is we don't quite yet know how that functions to achieve memory. There was a patient, referred to as HM, who had intractable epilepsy, so that he was constantly having epileptic seizure. In order to treat the epileptic seizures, one of the things that they finally resorted to, after trying everything else, was surgery. The surgery involved taking out the hippocampus, a little structure in the inner part of the brain.

Now after they did that, he seemed to recover quite well and the epilepsy seemed much more tractable, but they discovered, to their horror, that he could no longer get anything into long-term memory. So that if you came to visit him and asked him what he had for breakfast that morning, he would not have a clue. If you then left the room and came back, one minute later, he would say, "Hello, who are you?" He wouldn't have a clue that he'd met you before, or who you were. And that could happen again and again and again, as long as you cared to come in and out of the room. And he has been like that since the surgery, some twenty years ago. There are one or two other patients who, not through surgery, but through disease, have also lost the hippocampus on both sides.

Now what they do have, more or less intact, is a retrograde memory, a good memory of past events before the surgery. So HM can converse about his life as a child or his life as a teenager. But he has no idea what has happened to him since the surgery. So that's how we know that the hippocampus is a crucial piece of tissue for memory.

Of course, as soon as neurophysiologists understood that, then they said, "But what exactly does the hippocampus do? What's it connected to? What are the cells in the hippocampus like?" And so they found out a lot about the circuitry and organization, and then they began to find out about the nature of the interconnection of cells within the hippocampus, and in particular, that certain cells are modified as a result of input. And that, of course, is very exciting, because if you get modification as a result of input, that is just an inch away from saying it's learning.

MOYERS: Sometimes I lie awake at night and my thoughts are like monkeys in trees, or shooting stars, or fireworks someone else set off. I have no control over them. I haven't summoned them, I don't want them there—but they come back. I have no control over what's going on up there. Does your study of the mind tell us what's happening?

I think we have an illusion of how much control we have over our thoughts and perhaps even our decisions and choices and so forth.

CHURCHLAND: I think we have an illusion of how much control we have over our thoughts and perhaps even our decisions and choices and so forth. But I suppose the fast answer to your question is we really don't know exactly where these things come from. We have a bit of an idea about dreaming now, but we really don't know about where those sorts of thoughts come from.

MOYERS: The traditional view that I grew up with is that the brain is sort of an engine of logic, and if the brain doesn't work logically, there must be something wrong with it. Are you challenging that notion?

CHURCHLAND: At least at the level of circuits, it doesn't look like the brain is a logic machine. It doesn't appear that the brain is a computer of the kind that we're used to having on our desktops. It looks like it's a very different kind of beast altogether, and that when we go through a sequence of reasoning, it may be underpinned by sort of a mulch of activity on the part of neurons. I suspect that activity won't look anything like logic. It may also turn out to be the case that some of what we think of as reasoning involves only a very little bit of logic. It's sort of mulch, mulch, mulch, mulch—whatever that turns out to be.

MOYERS: What I'm getting at is that our notion of personal responsibility centers on an individual making rational decisions. That seems to me to be the assumption of our society. And what you're suggesting, it seems to me, is the possibility that we may not be making rational decisions. We may be responding to activities and behaviors of these neurocells that we don't control. This is a threat, in a sense, to the idea of a rational society.

CHURCHLAND: Well, one way to think about it is that what we discover to underpin rationality may be very different from what we thought. We might have thought that in order to be rational, you had to go through a series of steps of conventional logic. It might turn out that, as a theory about what it is to make a rational decision, that's just not very good.

Now if it turns out that we can explain the difference between somebody's making a rational choice and their not, in terms of neurons, that isn't going to suddenly change how people make choices. You're still going to be a rational person, even though it's your neurons that are doing it, because they've always been doing it, and you've always been rational.

So I think we will achieve a deeper understanding of what it is to make a rational choice, but it may also help us to understand those circumstances where, as we now say, people do not make a rational choice: where a woman stays with a husband who batters her, for example. If we understood more about the way the brain worked, we might be able to understand a little better what happens in such circumstances.

MOYERS: Would this help to explain common sense—the tool that we use every day just to get through the world, without even thinking about it?

CHURCHLAND: Ideally, of course, we have to be able to explain all of these things.

MOYERS: Well, we get along without explaining them. You know, I reach out and touch your hand—or I throw a ball . . . or questions come without my knowingly composing sentences.

CHURCHLAND: Sure. But I mean that there is nothing mystical about common sense; it is the outcome of causal interactions in a physical system. But you might ask why would one want to know? And there are a number of reasons. Let's take the simplest reason first. And the simplest one would be biomedical. There are many kinds of diseases, some we call psychiatric, and some we call neurological, that humans have where we really desperately need to help people. So we need to be able to understand the brain in order to do that.

And then there is what one might call the scientific issue of just wanting to know. Just wanting to understand. It shouldn't be thought, of course, that that's merely a kind of romantic ideal without practical implications, because notoriously in the history of science, when people have tried to understand something just because they wanted to understand it, they stumbled upon something that had incredible practical results—results that they would never have got if they had gone for the practical results first.

If you had said to Marie Curie, "Now, my dear, what you must do is find me the means for being able to look inside the body so I can tell whether somebody's bones are broken," it would have been hopeless. And it was, she grubbed away on pitchblende and stumbled upon something—radiation—that had incredible implications. Thus we have X-ray machines.

And I think the same is true with regard to understanding the brain. One possible implication, of course, is technological. If we understand what kind of computer it is that fits in our heads, then, of course, we will be able to make computing machines that make the current best computers look like sledgehammers.

MOYERS: I think I understand the biomedical appeal, the scientific appeal, the technological appeal. But the philosophical appeal . . . What would this help us to understand philosophically? Would it, for example, help us to understand love?

CHURCHLAND: Sure. I think it would. Look, one way to think of it would be that the traditional questions that philosophers have wanted to answer from Plato on have had to do with the nature of knowledge and the nature of consciousness. And I'm assuming that, if we do understand the brain, we will understand the nature of knowledge: learning, memory, and so on, and that we will understand the nature of consciousness, of how it's possible that you can take just a brain— Just a brain!

MOYERS: Just a brain!

CHURCHLAND: And yet it has awareness, and yet it can introspect, and yet it can talk. You look at a cell under a microscope and you ask, "How could that thing have anything to do with my feeling pain or my seeing a color?"

MOYERS: Or falling in love.

CHURCHLAND: Yes. Two things need to be said about that. First of all, it isn't an individual neuron that does it. It isn't an individual neuron that feels pain. It's a whole interactive set of neurons that do. And similarly with falling in love. I mean it isn't that there's one little neuron out there in the parietal cortex that says, "Oh-h-h-h-h! This is the real thing!" Obviously it can't be like that. So that's part of what has to be realized.

The other part of the answer is this: with regard to understanding the neurobiological basis for psychological functions, like falling in love and seeing, we're where Aristotle was with respect to understanding the nature of motion. And we've a long, long way to go. Just as for Aristotle it would be impossible to imagine a space that wasn't Euclidean, a space that had a shape and that was deformed by large gravitational masses, so we might say, "God, it's impossible to imagine how the redness of an apple, the seeing of the redness of an apple, could be caused by or could be identical with the behavior of a set of neurons."

> *. . . we mustn't let our own failures of imagination tell us what must be the case in the universe.*

But the important thing—we mustn't let our own failures of imagination tell us what must be the case in the universe. Just because we can't imagine a non-Euclidean geometry doesn't mean that there isn't one. It turns out there is one. It turns out space is non-Euclidean. It's deformed. It doesn't have Euclidean straight lines. It means that parallel lines will eventually converge, for example. Now Aristotle would have thought that that was ridiculous. Kant would have thought that that was ridiculous. And yet it is so, and given the physics of the situation, we understand why it is so.

It might have been impossible to imagine that having a high temperature turns out to be a function of the activity of a whole lot of little molecules that make up the stuff. And yet, it is so! So we shouldn't be too impressed by what we can't imagine. In part, of course, I'm thinking of philosophers right now who are wont to say, "I can't imagine how it could be the case that consciousness could be explained in terms of the brain." Well, so what? That's just a failure of imagination. I mean, either it is or it isn't so explainable. But your inability to imagine it doesn't signify.

MOYERS: What is radical about saying that the mind is the brain?

CHURCHLAND: Well, although many people have thought, for a long time, that that's got to be the case, what is new now is that we're beginning to be able to see how particular aspects of the mind are related to particular structures in the brain. How, for example, being able to recognize a face is a function that's carried out by a fairly small region of the brain on both sides. Or that color vision seems to be handled mainly by a very small part of visual cortex. So we're getting more specific now. We used to just say, "The mind is the brain," and argued for that in a very general way. Now it's clear that we can say a whole lot more.

MOYERS: But we don't know everything we'll be saying.

CHURCHLAND: There's an awful lot that we don't know, and we are really now at the first step. But it's a very important first step. And it's more exciting than, perhaps, research in chemistry, because, after all, this is *us*. We're not talking now

about some distant aspect of the universe; we're talking about how we work, how we are, what makes us the kinds of things that we are, and understanding ourselves from an objective that is a neurobiological point of view, rather than just from a subjective point of view.

One of the things, I must say, that has impressed me rather a lot is this: a number of months ago, I, among a few other neuroscientists, was asked to give a tutorial on the brain to the Dalai Lama. We were told that he was simply very interested, that he wanted to know about the kinds of things that we were working on, and he wanted to understand in order to think about things more wisely. So we had a meeting with him in Newport Beach.

Now, the profoundly interesting thing about the Dalai Lama was this: he had no dogma. He was willing to change his mind about anything depending on the nature of the evidence. He seemed to take as the most important aspect of the religion of Buddhism those questions of how to live a life. And there he talked about compassion, about honesty, and so forth. But he didn't advert to any dogmas about the nature of the universe: about whether the earth is in the center of the solar system, or about whether species were created, or whether there was a mind independent of the body, and so on. He said, "If those are the facts, those are the facts."

MOYERS: What did you think when you came away from this session with him?

CHURCHLAND: What I thought was important was that on the issues of science, issues of the nature of the universe, he wanted information from the people who knew, or the people who had the most information available. And he was not going to insist that the universe be one way because the Buddhists had thought it was so for two thousand years. He is deeply concerned with how people live their lives and with political issues of compassion, and it seemed to me this kind of separation of matters of fact on the one hand and matters of morals on the other hand was really quite important to him.

MOYERS: It would not relieve us from the necessity of constructing ethical ways of dealing with one another.

CHURCHLAND: Absolutely not! I mean, I think that's all very much open, and I don't think that discovering facts about the way the brain works is going to tell us what sort of moral system is most appropriate. It might tell us some things that bear upon that question; it might give us facts about that that would be relevant.

MOYERS: Such as?

CHURCHLAND: About the kinds of flexibility people do and don't have in molding their character or in making difficult decisions, and, as it were, weakness of will.

MOYERS: The limits of free will.

CHURCHLAND: Yes. I think it might be very helpful with regard to those kinds of matters. But we would still have to reason together and make a decision about what to do with that knowledge. The knowledge is one thing, and then the decisions about how best to use that knowledge—well, that's a very different thing.

MOYERS: It's absolutely astounding to me that this organ can attempt to understand itself!

CHURCHLAND: Perhaps what we've done is underestimate the capacity of the brain when we look at it and say, "Well, you know, that's just three pounds of meat." It's three extraordinarily glorious, marvelous, almost miraculous pounds of meat.

IMAGING OTHERS

The brain is indeed the glorious, marvelous, almost miraculous three pounds of meat described by Patricia Smith Churchland. But one loose connection can grind it to a halt. For all its power, for all its beauty, sometimes imagination fails us, and never more so than when we try to grasp the lives, the thoughts, and the stories of others.

Jeannette Haien's novelistic vision was shaped by her life as a concert pianist and her commitment to honor the form chosen by the composer. "Within the strictures of so-called form is all the freedom in the world," she says. "In service is really freedom." The novelist, too, is bound by the form of reality, and the writer's role is to be "responsible to the truth."

Thus, she has Father Declan, the protagonist in her novel *The All of It*, say that to work one's imagination on someone else is evil. For Haien, the evil is "to look at other people and have the audacity to make a statement about them, born of your imagination, as *fact*, and then to work on it, to elaborate on it, to refine it, to twist it. This is done sometimes against a person, sometimes against race. I think in part, that's one of the elements of racial conflict. . . . Prejudice is one of the most vital acts of the imagination."

The American literature of the nineteenth century was driven by this vital but warped imagination. While slavery was tearing the nation apart, "the chances of getting a truly complex human black person in an American book in the nineteenth century were minimal," says the novelist Toni Morrison. When black characters appear at all in the fiction, they are symbols of darkness and fear. "The characters are discredited and ridiculed and purged," Morrison says. "But the idea of those characters, the construction of them as an outside representation of anarchy, collapse, illicit sexuality—all of these negative things that white Americans feared are projected onto this presence."

We do this to our enemies, too. It is a theme that long has obsessed Sam Keen. In his workshops on personal mythology, he encourages people to explore and claim their own stories, to discover what he calls the sacredness of their own lives. Public mythology, on the other hand, is often a profane story. The underlying vision that binds and governs a culture as a whole can easily translate into a license to demonize the lives of others. "A culture always has a mythology about evil," says Keen, "because one of the great mythic questions has always been: What is the source of evil? And if myth tells us who creates evil, it also can tell us who are not people, and whom we can kill without guilt."

When this limited imagination translates itself into language, language limits us. Evelyn Fox Keller, trained as a scientist, now focuses her attention on the language scientists have chosen to describe their work. Those choices have shaped the development of science. "It is a fantasy," she says, "that any human product can be free of human values. Science is a human product. It's a wonderful, glorious human product." Yet Keller also discovered that the human values usually associated with science encompassed only half of humankind: they were almost exclusively male, employed to "raise a masculine philosophy." This, says Keller, skewed scientific study for the past three hundred years.

Fortunately, many Americans are coming to realize that in this polyglot nation we can no longer afford such impoverishment. And for some, language actually unlocks the imagination. Richard Rodriguez, born to Mexican parents, underwent the "trauma" of being thrust into a school where everyone else spoke English. But the ordeal was his second birth, and he now refuses to consider himself Mexican, Mexican American, or Hispanic. He's American. His language is English: "You gave it to me, you held it out to me, and I took it and I bit it and I licked it and I swallowed it and now it's mine. . . . I've taken the thing that is closest to America's heart, and I've made it mine."

Sometimes, to imagine others is to discover one's self.

Jeannette Haien

MUSICIAN

Jeannette Haien has spent more than thirty-five years of her life performing as a concert pianist and teaching her students the liberating beauty of classical boundaries. Recently she composed some linguistic music of her own in her first novel, *The All of It*. The story of a parish priest in Ireland who hears a remarkable confession, the book was greeted by critics as a gem of style and grace. Whether at the keyboard or at the typewriter, she is concerned with artistic forms that both circumscribe and enhance our lives.

MOYERS: Where did you get the idea for your novel? The story of a man who, on his deathbed, confesses to his priest that the woman he is leaving behind as his widow is not his wife after all, but his sister. Where did that idea come from?

HAIEN: It came, oddly enough, out of several different circumstances. First there was a priest passing through the district in Ireland where my husband and I have a place. He was clearly from a poor parish, and he stood looking at the foreigners angling expensively on the river. I knew he was a frustrated angler. But then to my astonishment, at three that afternoon, I saw him being toasted. People were lifting their glasses saying, "Congratulations, how marvelous." He had gone to the head ghillie, who, being a good Catholic, said, "Ah, Father, I have an extra beat today. I'll not charge you for it, and I'll loan you a rod." He came in with this enormous salmon. He was thrilled. He was celestially humble, but mortally thrilled.

MOYERS: As happy as God with a sinner converted.

HAIEN: That's right. I started a short story based on that incident. But then, the next day, I went into our nearest village, and there was a funeral in progress. When I asked who was being buried, I was told, "Ah, well, there's a story." I was not made privy to the story. But the funeral was different from any other funeral I'd ever witnessed in Ireland. People understood that there was something extraordinary about it. So I thought, what would cause this? They were good people. Everyone said they were both darling people, the widow and the man. So I went thinking about what would make this so extraordinary, and I came up with this idea of the brother and sister who had run away from an abusive drunken father.

MOYERS: Did you read this story into the funeral, or did you do some reporting and find out what happened?

HAIEN: No, no. I read into that funeral.

MOYERS: You made this up.

HAIEN: Yes. I found out later that the funeral actually involved a gypsy who had married a woman whose husband was thought to have been killed in World War II. Then the first husband came back. He was not, in fact, dead. Suddenly there was the woman with two husbands. The local priest went to her, and asked her, "Which do you prefer?" And she said, "The gypsy." And he said, "So it shall be." Isn't that a marvelous story? And that's true.

MOYERS: So the two scenes from routine life—a priest fishing in a river in Ireland and a funeral—trigger your imagination, and you're off and running with a wondrous, complex, moral tale. Now this story takes place in the priest's mind as he is fishing. Do you fish?

HAIEN: I don't fish at all, but my husband fishes. The physical activity of fishing fascinates me. I used to sit on the riverbank with Frank, my husband's ghillie, the helper, who "serves on the rod" in the English phrase. The ghillie knows the river conditions and every creature on it. You see the water being rippled in a certain way, and there will be a little otter looking up and looking about, and above a heron flying over. The solemnity of the landscape is such, the quiet so great, that you can actually hear the very solemn wingbeats of the heron. And Frank would tell me the most extraordinary stories of his childhood, all the time keeping his eye on my husband. Once in a while he'd call up and say, "Sir, I'd suggest now you change to a 'Jock Scott,' or a 'Hairy Mary.' "

MOYERS: When you sat down to write, you remembered all of this, in much the same way you remember the notes of a Mozart concerto when you sit down at that piano.

> *I'm very fascinated by the notion of memory. I always have been. I have a very deep emotional memory. I can work myself back to a point of anger that overwhelmed me thirty years ago.*

HAIEN: I'm very fascinated by the notion of memory. I always have been. I have a very deep emotional memory. I can work myself back to a point of anger that overwhelmed me thirty years ago. I can remember the episode that vividly. I also have a terrific sense of memory of experience. You'll see no photographs in my house except of one or two people. I find that causing memory to *be*, in a sense, makes it more profound. It gives depth.

MOYERS: What do you mean, causing it to *be*?

HAIEN: By almost causing an experience to happen again through the process of reanimating the memory of it. The memory of something is a kind of image one calls up out of the past, or oneself, on one's own terms. It's not like a photograph, which is after all an object. But what I call a *working* memory exists in the flow of time and in relation to one's ability to call it back to life and fully into being.

MOYERS: Writing is a creative act. And playing the piano is a re-creative act. When you sit down before a blank sheet of paper, you have to invent what occurs there. But when you sit down at the piano bench, you're remembering a story already told by Mozart, in this case. Now what you're saying is they both have something in common; when you sit down and write *The All of It*, you're remembering the ghillie on the bank of the Irish river, the priest in the stream, angling, just as you're remembering Mozart, and the Twenty-first Concerto.

HAIEN: The most effective work a musician does, in music, is away from the instrument. I mean, we practice because we have to keep up our equipment, our technique. But music, the ideal performance, of course, always happens in the head.

That's where we live the performance. I always begin learning a new score away from the instrument. I don't like to take it to the instrument too soon. I read it as I do a novel. Musicians can do this. There are musicians, for instance, who've learned a new score on an airplane between New York and London. A musical score, to a musician, is narrative. You can take it to bed at night, and read it, and return to it as you would reread a Conrad novel, and find some new marvelous thing in it that you'd never noticed before.

MOYERS: I've never thought of a score of music as a narrative with a plot.

HAIEN: Yes. That's how I learned to write. Take the Mozart concerto you spoke of. It immediately opens with a theme, a subject. It has a key, a minor key or a major key. It is lively in tempo, vivace, or it is slow, adagio, so right away, you feel some mood. A novel too immediately sets forth a thematic subject and a mood, a description of a landscape or a village, or a place, or a character sitting alone thinking. Then the action begins. Or it begins with the action and then there's a contrasting second theme.

MOYERS: One of your former piano pupils said to me, "I always enjoyed taking lessons from Jeannette, because although I don't have any talent for the piano, she always explained the structure of the music to me." That's what you're talking about when you talk about the narrative form of music.

HAIEN: That's right. Structure is the word. Structure is the relationship of one idea to another, for instance, it's like the relationship in architecture of a window to a door. One of my problems with minimalist writing is that there is a concentration only on one thing, a door, say, and all that surrounds the door is left out. So it lacks the support of the whole view. Structure. Structure is about the relationship of this to that. So, yes, for me, the structure of a work is the essence of it. Its discipline, if you will, which makes great freedom possible. A wonderfully structured musical score is wonderfully proportioned. Under the laws of structure, you have the freedom to work in the freest way imaginable.

MOYERS: So you feel free at that piano, even though Mozart has written the story you must follow.

HAIEN: Let's just talk again about the opening of a musical work. You know its key; you know its tempo—whether it's going to be fast or slow; the composer has given you a dynamic marking. Let's say that dynamic is a "forte" or a "piano"—loud or soft. These elements are the first given. Yet there is no such thing as a fixed piano, or a fixed forte, except as the performer causes it to happen. When I walk out onto the stage and sit at the instrument, I have to enter the realm of the attitude of softness or of loudness. So it isn't a matter of dynamic so much as a kind of freedom for the performer's perception of a dynamic marking as it relates to the whole.

MOYERS: And your emotional involvement.

HAIEN: Well, no. You can't overwhelm Mozart with your emotions. What happens is that Mozart inspirits you. When you hear a performance where the performer gets in the way of the music, that's very bad. It's bad for music. It's bad for Mozart. It's a form of assassination.

MOYERS: There is something magical or mysterious or psychological that takes place for you and Mozart to play together. The hands are Jeannette Haien's. But the music is the music of Mozart. And you're saying, Mozart must be born again in you.

HAIEN: What he has written is that which I honor. Look, you can tack on for effect. You can do something phony. A composer can drive you, and drive you, and drive you, to a climax. And then you can turn all cute, and that's very effective to stir them up; to give them something different, if you're a bad artist. Musicians don't do that.

MOYERS: So Mozart's Twenty-first Concerto in C has helped to tell you something about writing a story.

HAIEN: Oh yes. The relationships between a first theme and a second theme are like the relationships between subplots. In a great work they inevitably complement each other.

MOYERS: When I begin to hear Mozart, I feel as if I were ready for it; as if there is a relationship back to something that I hadn't even been thinking of at the moment I hear the first chord.

HAIEN: That's the form again. You expect to hear the subject stated, and then the second subject, and then the development, and the recapitulation of those ideas; and then the ending. When you're studying composition, even if you aren't very gifted at composition you can write a sonata. But for a genius, within the strictures of so-called form is all the freedom in the world. The bad people are the self-expressers, who don't honor boundaries. Who don't know that in service is really freedom.

Now, I have sat as a judge on international competitions. Everyone who comes before you can do everything in the world at the instrument. The fastest octaves, the fastest etudes. My God, they gobble up and give out everything. Then there will come along someone with a terribly, terribly involved musical mind. And suddenly, you will have goose pimples. Whereas before, you just sat there, big-eyed, listening to the instrument, suddenly you forget whether you're listening to a violin or a piano or a cello; it's the music that is projected.

MOYERS: And that is?

HAIEN: It's talent.

MOYERS: Yes, that's presumed. But there has to be some kind of soul there, don't you think?

HAIEN: If by soul you mean emotional connection, yes. That's an ingredient of talent. Without it, there isn't talent.

MOYERS: Soul is an ingredient of talent.

HAIEN: For me. Yes, I'm sure. I was a kind of prodigy. So as a very young person, I wept over certain melodies, without knowing in the least bit why I was weeping. And I was happy, too. Now, of course, I know why. But as a child I only experienced the longing to play that melody. And I remember the longing to write a poem. I remember this in whatever the seat of the soul is. I remember it anatomically.

MOYERS: In the same way the fingers, so to speak, remember the music.

HAIEN: Oh, the fingers don't remember. The fingers will betray you. The brain remembers. I remember I was playing in Burma once, and they killed a cobra, just offstage. I was aware peripherally that the whole audience was sort of picking up its feet. I was in the middle of Schumann's Symphonic Etudes, just before the finale, and you know, you go on. But my concentration was broken, and right away, the fingers betrayed me.

MOYERS: Are you still teaching music?

HAIEN: I'm not training people anymore in the sense of undertaking them and seeing them through a long, long apprenticeship and then turning them loose in the world. As I said about a year ago to a colleague, I no longer nurse. I only doctor.

MOYERS: What do you look for in a potential pupil?

HAIEN: Stamina. And interior tension. Desire. They must really want it. That's a form of tension. It's like first love. That terrific tension between two people terribly, newly, innocently in love. The young talented mind, in its first stages, is innocent. And the responsible teacher never, never intrudes upon that innocence.

MOYERS: Your job is not to requite that love, is it? It's to nurture it there, and lead it on into a deep and long ongoing relationship.

HAIEN: I never say, "Do this because I say so." Never. Never. Then you turn out students like cookie cutters. You must realize that every potential artist is very individual. You don't corrupt by imposing your point of view. I only say, "I think this, what do you think? Why do you think that? How can we justify it?"

MOYERS: You have to work not to become possessive.

HAIEN: The student must form a relationship to the score, not a relationship to the personality of the teacher. The teacher-pupil relationship is the most delicate of all, more than any other relationship in life. More than between lovers, husbands and wives, families.

MOYERS: Tell me about performing. What happens to an audience when it really is with you?

HAIEN: There is a tension that develops. It's a wonderful tension. It's like the vibrato on a violin string. What you are conscious of is that when you are playing pianissimo, you are being attended to, pianissimo, by the audience. That is to say, something has happened where they realize that they must be quiet in order to receive a great and quiet moment. When a performer can cause a winter audience in New York City to be quiet, when a performer can cause people not to remember that they must cough, then the performer feels that. That's a wonderful thing. That's a happy performance.

MOYERS: So they participate in the art of the music with you.

HAIEN: Yes. And a performer also knows which audiences are there for the music, and which are there for the event. They are different audiences. You walk out to some audiences and you know that the people who comprise it have dropped their lives, had an early dinner at the end of a day, and have come to hear Mozart, Beethoven, Schubert, out of desire. If that desire is absent, it is very hard for a performer to win the ear of such a person.

MOYERS: How do you teach desire to a potential audience?

HAIEN: You have to do away with the notion that a record or a tape is a substitute for a live performance. The tape isn't a performance. First of all, it's an agony for every musician to make a recording. I remember when I was making recordings, I'd go back two years later and realize I don't play that work like that anymore. It's a frozen concept. And you're an evolving musician. So to go back and hear that performance that you passed on two years ago as a "final" thing is a positive agony.

It's wrong to let a young potential concert-goer think that sitting at home, listening to a tape recording, is the same as experiencing the unfolding of a work in a concert hall. In a concert hall, you can't hold the cassette. The work begins, and it's contained in a spatial way. You go away without it in your hand. You can't catalogue it in your library of tapes. You can't take it in the car and listen to it as you drive. You have only the experience of remembering it.

MOYERS: You spent so much of your career performing and teaching music, how did it come about that you started writing fiction?

HAIEN: I don't know what an audience hears, musically. I've played all over the world, and when someone comes backstage after a performance and says, "You know, Miss Haien, that one work you played reminded me of waterfalls," I have no idea what work they're talking about. So I wanted to say some things in words, not just in sound. I wanted to speak in a tongue that had a broader audience and that might remotely convey some things about my perceptions of life that I wanted to share. As a musician, one is a little sealed off from that kind of depth of colloquy that the spoken language can undertake.

MOYERS: Don't you feel a relationship when you sit down at that piano in that concert hall? Aren't you aware that out there in the darkness, several hundred, if not thousands, of people have paid money, come out of their homes, made their way to that place to listen to you? Don't you feel some relationship with them?

HAIEN: Yes, but it is very marginal. If you're really terribly conscious of those three thousand, or three hundred, or thirty people, your mind isn't on the right thing.

MOYERS: What do you do to narrow the gap between you and them when you're sitting at that silent keyboard?

HAIEN: You must let the music do it.

MOYERS: How about when you're writing? How do you narrow the gap between you and that invisible reader?

HAIEN: I never think about the reader. It never occurs to me to think of a reader.

MOYERS: For whom are you writing? For whom was *The All of It* written?

HAIEN: For myself. I had to write it. I wished to write it. I thought I had something to say. Also, I love words. I mean, the exercise of words, the making of a sentence. I work very slowly. I've had a celestial day if I have five sentences I can turn to the next morning. But I'm not a genius. I know some writers who verge on that and who write perhaps as many as sixteen or eighteen sentences a day. The pianist Artur Schnabel had a wonderful phrase that "No one is obliged to be a genius." I do wish I were a genius only because I'd like to be able to work faster. To say more, faster. To me, there's a kind of sound about language that echoes an idea, and a mood, or an image of a person who's saying the words, or even of the room in which it's being said. I think dialogue reflects the room you're in.

MOYERS: In what way?

HAIEN: Well, if you come into a dour, dark, damp, deprived circumstance, somehow your words reflect the place. Or the place, words.

MOYERS: Well, you've captured not only the climate of Ireland in this book, but also something deeply sorrowful in the moral conflict of that country. You've caught this moral tension between the rules prescribed by the Church and the frailty of the human heart on which those rules are dashed.

HAIEN: Right. The priest realizes, finally, that there are some circumstances in life that are not of God's making, almost. That things happen outside anyone's right to question except as a fatal flaw to the given of life.

MOYERS: That's a change. At one point early in the novel, the priest says, "Nothing is beyond God's boundary."

HAIEN: Everything is within God, yes. But at the end, he knows that some things happen that must surprise even God. That God is surprised on occasion.

MOYERS: I wonder if God imagined how difficult it is to be human, as people in your story are, and want to live by the rules of the Church. But the realities of their lives and their circumstances, the abusing alcoholic father, the necessity of keeping their secret from the neighbors, become—well, I started to say, it becomes a burden. Yet this is a very happy, joyful, brother and sister.

HAIEN: That's right. Enda refused to confess her situation, because she thought one confessed only those sins that one is responsible for, not the ones that circumstance plays upon one.

MOYERS: There is something that Father Declan says that has baffled me since I read *The All of It.* You have him mulling from the pulpit that to work one's imagination on someone else is evil.

HAIEN: It's evil to look at other people and have the audacity to make a statement about them, born of your imagination, as *fact,* and then to work on it, to elaborate on it, to refine it, to twist it. This is done sometimes against a person, sometimes against race. I think in part, that's one of the elements of racial conflict. We imagine other people's lives, imagine what they do. And it's contrary to what we do. Then we elaborate on it. We hear the worst of the news involving them, and by exaggeration the imagination forms itself into prejudice.

MOYERS: An act of imagination. I hadn't quite thought of prejudice as an act of the imagination.

HAIEN: Oh, I think prejudice is one of the most vital acts of the imagination.

MOYERS: Almost hallucinatory at times. I think of some of Hitler's more melodramatic speeches. There's imagination going to work there that is evil.

HAIEN: Yes. Or the Ku Klux Klan.

MOYERS: What do you think is the role of the artist, the artistic imagination, in dealing with that crude imagination that changes the nature of another human being? Is the artist's role to re-create an ideal human being?

HAIEN: No. The artist's role is to be responsible to truth. I can't stand the short story or the novel that just cuts off with the deed, and people walk away from it as if there is no consequence. Certain actions, certain deeds that we commit, have an inexorable, an inevitable consequence—perhaps down the line quite a way—but there. The seed is there in the initial act.

MOYERS: So the artist has to imagine the consequence? He can't just say they lived happily ever after?

HAIEN: That's right.

MOYERS: Is form, is symmetry, the truth to which you say the artist is ultimately accountable?

HAIEN: Form is a form of truth. Form frames consciousness. It gives a frame to our real consciousness of everything. And there is a truth larger than the capriciousness of individual conduct. Some people call it God or religion. But I think it is apparent in the way the universe functions on its own.

MOYERS: When you say that the artist has the responsibility to the truth, it's not to the truth of an idea. It's not to truth as some given, because every artist's truth is different.

HAIEN: But every artist knows that his work fails if the inevitable is false to the sequence of the action. It comes to a point, a denouement, the act is done, and there is a consequence. If you fiddle with that consequence, if it is out of focus with the old theories of consequences since the beginning of time, if you try and give it a cute or clever ending, it may be very titillating to an audience for now, but it won't last as truth.

MOYERS: You make me think of some movies of late that have been wonderfully inspired, but they lack plausibility at key moments. And so, you walk out of there saying no matter how imaginative the idea, the implausibility of certain things defied reality. Even that which is imagined must be true to reality.

HAIEN: There is, even now, among a certain genre of writers a falsification of reality. Flaubert really wished to create reality and did. But there is such a strain now to be horrible beyond words, to pervert and distort the world. But the world of and by itself won't necessarily yield.

MOYERS: I don't know. The world is fairly distorted.

> *But a story is the only thing the human mind can truly understand. And the best stories understand the inevitability of relationships, both in terms of consequence, and in terms of anticipation.*

HAIEN: But the form of the world itself is not. It is resistant. It will fight back. One knows that moment in a novel when it breaks down, where it doesn't come together and coalesce into an inevitable whole.

I spoke last week to a publisher who said to me that what the reading world is hungering for is stories. We've gone through a terrible desert-like period of minimalist writings, stories that don't have a beginning, and a middle, and an end—where you are put in a situation, in the present tense. These stories have no background, no nuance, no supports, and then they drop off.

But a *story* itself is the only thing the human mind can truly understand. And the best stories understand the inevitability of relationships, both in terms of consequence, and in terms of anticipation.

MOYERS: What has come before, what is coming after. Art does understand that, I think. But modern society has very little tolerance for connection.

HAIEN: And that's tragic. That makes all of our friendships, our loves, our familial life, schismatic. I often think of the literature of America, of a Willa Cather. You think of *O Pioneers!* and the astonishing, marvelous moments out on a prairie with a contained family, living together, terribly intimately, terribly involved in the relationship of time, and soil, but terribly alone. Then, on the horizon there's a speck moving towards them, and it's another family in a covered wagon. That coming together of those two families is something they would talk about for years, long after the second family has come and gone.

MOYERS: The speck seems to move so slowly, but deliberately. As if it were part of some eternal score that was taking its time getting to the epiphany.

HAIEN: For me one of the most extraordinary things is expectation. I was perhaps very fortunate. My life has been nothing but a dawning exercise every day of expectation. I have been so continuously surprised, that I am childlike to the point of glee sometimes.

MOYERS: Where did that come from?

HAIEN: I credit my parents. One begins, or doesn't, with that. One of my first memories is of my father calling excitedly to say, "Look." He was looking up at the sky. I couldn't see what I was to look at. Then he said, "Listen," and I heard this peculiar sort of sound, very distant. He kept saying, "Look higher, look higher," and I did. Then I saw my first skein of geese and heard their call. He took my hand and said to me, "Those are the whales of the sky." I have never forgotten it. And I never look up at a sky without the expectation of some extraordinary thing coming—airplane, owls at night. I'm a great looker up to the sky.

Toni Morrison

NOVELIST

Toni Morrison has transported millions of readers into the experience of being black in America. *The Bluest Eye, Sula, Song of Solomon*, and *Tar Baby* are peopled by characters whose vibrant but often tragic stories force us to confront the realities of race. In her painful and beautiful *Beloved*—winner of the Pulitzer Prize in 1988—she held up for contemporary America a mirror of forces that roil our society. Morrison is currently teaching in the humanities at Princeton.

MOYERS: You said recently that it's a great relief to you that terms like "white" and "race" are now discussable in literature. How so?

MORRISON: Because a language has been developed and has still some sovereignty in which we mean "white," and we mean "black," or we mean ethnic, but we say something else. There's an enormous amount of confusion. It's difficult to understand the literature of the country if you can't say "white" and you can't say "black" and you can't say "race." Now, at last, we can look clearly, for example, at Herman Melville, at Edgar Allan Poe, at Willa Cather, at real issues that were affecting founding American writers.

MOYERS: The public rhetoric of our time has been filled with "race" and "white" and "black." It seems a surprise to hear you say, "Well, now at least we can discuss those in literature." You're saying that they weren't a part of our tradition of story-telling?

MORRISON: Not in the critiques. Not in the discourse. Not in the reviews. Not in the scholarship around these works. It was not a subject to be discussed; race was not considered worthy of discussion. Not only that, there was an assumption that the master narrative could not encompass all of these things. The silence was absolutely important. The silence of the black person.

MOYERS: The silence. His voice is never heard.

MORRISON: Never heard. Blacks don't speak for themselves in the texts. And since they were not permitted to say their own things, history and the academy can't really permit them to take center stage in the discourse of the text in art, in literature.

But in public discourse, when we talk about neighborhoods, or policy, or schools, or welfare, or practically anything, the real subject is race or class. We may call it "disadvantaged," or "undeveloped," or "remedial," or all these euphemisms for poor people and/or black people, and/or any nonwhite person in this country. That is the subject of practically all of the political discourse there is. But it has been kept out of the art world.

This country is seething with the presence of black people. But it was always necessary to deny that presence when we discussed our literature. I read all those books in undergraduate school, as everybody did. We never talked about what was really going on. We talked about Huck Finn and Jim, and we thought about how wonderful the innocence of this radical child was as a paradigm for the American coming of age.

MOYERS: The white American . . .

MORRISON: The white American coming of age, because the story is about the construction of a white male. But Huck grows up and becomes a moral person because of his association with Jim, a black slave who is called a boy, never a man. To Mark Twain's credit, he provides the extraordinary scene where you realize that Jim has a wife and a child. He's trying to get home to them. Huck's trying to get out to the wild territory, while Jim is trying to get home. Jim tells Huck a terrible story about a time when he told his daughter to shut the door, and she didn't do it. He told her again, and she didn't do it. And he got annoyed and he hit her, and then later realized that while she had been sick recently, she had lost her hearing. And suddenly there's this man who has a context.

MOYERS: A family and emotions.

MORRISON: It's an overwhelming thing for Huck to say, these black people think about children the same way "we" do. It's a revelation to him. The question is, why is it a revelation?

MOYERS: The artist is supposed to carry our moral imagination. Yet in the 1840s and '50s, on the eve of the Civil War, in the period of traumatic conflict over abolition and slavery, the American novelists were not dealing with those issues. Hawthorne was writing European gothics with ruins and ghosts and the supernatural. James Fenimore Cooper was writing adventure stories set in primeval forests. The best-selling novels on the eve of the Civil War, in fact, were soppy stories written by women about courageous orphans. Your people never show up in the novels of that time. How do you explain that?

MORRISON: Well, they do. They do show up. They're everywhere. They're in Hawthorne's preoccupation with blackness. They're in all the dark symbols. They're in the haunting one senses in his fiction. What's he haunted by? What is the guilt? What is the real sin that is really worrying Hawthorne all his life? They're there. They're in Fenimore Cooper. They're in Melville. They're everywhere in Poe. I don't care where they find their story; writers are informed by the major currents of the world.

MOYERS: But blacks don't emerge in these stories as people with context, with family, with emotions.

MORRISON: No. The characters are discredited and ridiculed and purged. But the idea of those characters, the construction of them as an outside representation of anarchy, collapse, illicit sexuality—all of these negative things that white Americans feared are projected onto this presence, so that you find these extraordinary gaps and evasions and destabilizations. The chances of getting a truly complex human black person in an American book in the nineteenth century were minimal. Melville came probably very close with classic complexities, but not real flesh and blood people.

MOYERS: He used them as symbols.

MORRISON: Each one of the white men in *Moby-Dick* has a black brother. They're paired together. Fedallah is the shadow of Ahab. Queequeg is the shadow of

Ishmael. They all have them, and they work together in tandem all through the book. What I'm saying is that while there is no realistic representation, the subtextual information is powerful. It's all self-reflective. It's all about the fabrication of a white male American.

MOYERS: What is it in our makeup that just does not want to confront the reality of race? We didn't want to deal with it in the era of our founding. We just tried to act as if it wasn't there. It took a bloody and last-minute Civil War to cope with slavery itself, and then immediately after that war was over, the waters closed around and it was as if the war hadn't been. Even today, our political system seems such a complex evasion of race that we don't have to face it.

Learning how to be an adult is very hard. So much has to be disassembled. The past has to be revised.

MORRISON: Learning how to be an adult is very hard. So much has to be disassembled. The past has to be revised. The way one thinks about things has to change. Now, many people are not only willing to do it, they're eager to do it. They are tired of this sort of Kafka nightmare world that we're living in. But many other people cannot bear the thought of having to revise their own concept of themselves, their own neuroses, their own sense of the past. There's something else, though, that I am becoming convinced of. In some quarters, racism really feels good.

MOYERS: Everybody needs somebody to look down on.

MORRISON: I was looking at a television show recently in which somebody was roaming around South Africa talking about the imminent release of Nelson Mandela. Some of the white people were very upset by this and wanted apartheid to become even purer. They felt so strongly about it that they are willing to go off and establish their own little counties. They were so determined not to have any black people there that they decided on an extraordinary thing: to do their own work. They would allow no black laborers. They would plow their own land, empty their own slop jars, and so on. Now some of these people were twenty, twenty-five years old.

This sort of attitude is not a conversation; this is not dialogue. This is nothing. This is madness. This is scraping around in the bottom of the barrel of cliché in order to support the habit. The habit of disdain. So their racism is wasteful. It doesn't help. It's not economical, it's not profitable. You don't get anything for it. It has no reason for being. It has no scientific proof, no basis, nothing. Ever. Everybody knows that now. So why is it around?

MOYERS: Is it conceivable that you could write a novel in which blacks are not center stage?

MORRISON: Absolutely.

MOYERS: Do you think the public would let you? Since you've achieved such fame by writing about black people, does the public now expect you to write only about black people?

MORRISON: I will, but I won't identify them as such. That's the difference. There are two moments in *Beloved* when I tried to do that. I set up a situation in which two people are talking—two black people—and some other people enter the scene. They're never identified as either black or white, but the reader knows instantly, and not because I use the traditional language of stereotype. One moment comes when Paul D and Sethe are walking down the street, and he touches her shoulder to lead her off the sidewalk onto the ground because three women are walking this way. That's all. But you know who they are.

There's another moment when he's in despair, talking to a friend, and a man rides up on a horse and says, "Where is Judy?" He calls the woman by her first name. You can tell by the reactions of the black man who the rider is, but I don't have to say it.

What I really want to do, and expect to do, is not identify my characters by race. But I won't be writing about white people. I'll be writing about black people. It will be part of my job to make sure my readers aren't confused. But can you think what it would mean for me and my relationship to language and to texts to be able to write without having to always specify to the reader the race of the characters?

MOYERS: What does it do for us to talk about this now?

MORRISON: I think it's liberating. You can see what it is that has destabilized you. You know what has gone down beneath the cracks. I think racism feels crazy. I think people who really and truly are staunch, steady racists—the ones for whom it feels good, it's right and they know it, which is why they invent documentation from biblical sources and all sorts of odd places—I think at the same time there's a part of them that knows it's truly psychotic. Racism doesn't work intellectually. I think it was Robert Penn Warren who wrote about an incident when some black students were jailed for taking part in a sit-in demonstration. The sheriff who jailed them was furious about these demonstrations, and furious that they wanted to sit at whites-only lunch counters. Then he said, "But you know, I was raised by a black woman." With tears running down his face he said, "I loved her." His rage was at the students he had to lock up. But there was another rage: that he had to stop loving that woman. He really did love her. And the craziness was of having to say to her, "You don't belong to me; I can't love you anymore. It's over." Racism makes you deny the real world of your emotions.

MOYERS: There is such a gulf between the "inner city" today and the rest of the country in both imagination and reality, in politics and literature. If you were writing for the rest of the country about the "inner city" today, what metaphor would you use?

MORRISON: Love. We have to embrace ourselves. Self-regard. James Baldwin once said, "You've already been bought and paid for. Your ancestors already gave it up for you. It's already done. You don't have to do that anymore. Now you can love yourself. It's already possible."

I have a feeling of admiration and respect and love for these black people in the "inner city" who are intervening. Some of them are going in and saying, "You four girls—you come to my house every Thursday and we're going to eat, or I'm going to take you out." These are professional women who become companions to these children. I love those men I heard about in Chicago—black professional men—who went every lunch hour to the playgrounds in Chicago's south side to talk to children. Not to be authoritarian, but just to get to know them, without the bureaucracy, without the agencies. They simply became their own agency. Or some woman told me a couple of weeks ago that black men were going into shelters and spending time holding crack babies. Just holding them. Now I'm sure it does something for the baby, but think what it does for that man to actually give up some time and hold a baby. There are organizations, of course, there are still agencies, but there are also these individuals who do care for children—the caretakers, the lovers. That has to be the most glorious thing that is going on.

MOYERS: The love you're talking about is the love inspired by moral imagination that takes us beyond blood.

MORRISON: Absolutely.

MOYERS: A critic once said, "Toni Morrison writes about places where even love found its way with an ice pick." You say love is the metaphor. When I go back through your novels, love is there in so many different ways and forms. The women in your novels particularly do extraordinary things for love. There's a grandmother who has her leg amputated so that her insurance policy will buy a house and take care of her children as they grow up. There's Sethe, who is willing to kill her children before the slave catchers can come and seize them. What kind of love is that?

> *It is more interesting, more complicated, more intellectually demanding and more morally demanding to love somebody. To take care of somebody. To make one other person feel good.*

MORRISON: Some of it's very fierce. Powerful. Distorted. The duress they work under is so overwhelming. But I think they believed, as I do, that when people say, "I didn't ask to be born," they are wrong. I think we *did*. That's why we're here. We have to do something nurturing that we respect before we go. We must. It is more interesting, more complicated, more intellectually demanding and more morally demanding to love somebody. To take care of somebody. To make one other person feel good.

Now the dangers of that are the dangers of setting one's self up as a martyr, or as the one without whom nothing could be done. But like the acquisitions of knowledge, that's what the mind does. I mean, it may not get the knowledge you want it to have, but it's busy all the time.

MOYERS: In your novel *Beloved*, Paul D says to Sethe, "Your love is too thick." Is that what you're talking about?

MORRISON: It can be excessive.

MOYERS: How do we know when our love is too thick?

MORRISON: We don't. We really don't. That's a big problem. We don't know when to stop. When is it too much and when is it not enough? That is the problem of the human mind and the soul. But we have to try. Not trying is so poor for the self. It's so poor for the mind. It's so uninteresting to live without love. Life has no risk. Love just seems to make life not just livable, but a gallant, gallant event.

MOYERS: But I have a sense in so many of the love stories in your novels that love is destined to be doomed by the world.

MORRISON: In the stories, I place the characters on a cliff. I push them as far as I can to see what they are made of. I say to them, "You really think you're in love? Well, let me see what it's like under these circumstances. You think this is important; what about this?" I place them in that tragic mode so I can get at what those emotions really are. What is interesting to me is that under the circumstances in which the people in my books live there is this press toward love. They triumph in that sense. Which is not to say they don't get sick and die—everyone does. I mean, the decay is already out there somewhere because we're mortal. We really are mortal. That's what it means. The point is what is the process while you are here?

MOYERS: What about Ella in *Beloved* who says, "If anybody was to ask me I'd say, 'Don't love nothing' "?

MORRISON: I've heard that said many times. "Don't love nothing. Save it." You see, that was one of the devastating things in the experience of black people in this country, the effort to prevent full expression of their love. And the sentiment that Ella has is conservative. If you want to hang on to your sanity or hang on to yourself, don't love anything; it'll hurt. The next time they break its back, you'll have a little love left over. You kind of husband it. You hold it back. And of course that's true not just of African-Americans, it's true of all sorts of people. It's so risky. People don't want to get hurt; they don't want to be left; they don't want to be abandoned. It's as though love is always some present you're giving somebody else. It's really a present you're giving yourself.

MOYERS: On the other hand, there's Pilate, your character who reminds me of my aunt Mildred. In *Song of Solomon* she says, "I wish I'd a knowed more people. I would of loved them all. If I'd a knowed more, I would a loved more." There are people like that, too.

MORRISON: That's a totally generous free woman. She's fearless. She's not afraid of anything. She has very few material things. She has a little self-supportive skill that she performs. She doesn't run anybody's life. She's available for almost infinite love. If you need her—she'll deliver. And she has complete clarity about who she is.

MOYERS: Did you know people like that?

MORRISON: Yes, in my family there are women who presented themselves to me that way. They are just absolutely clear and absolutely reliable. They have this sort of intimate relationship with God and death and all sorts of things that strike fear into the modern heart. They have a language for it. They have a blessedness maybe. But they seem not to be fearful.

It's to those women that I really feel an enormous responsibility. Whenever I answer questions such as the ones you put to me about how terrible it all is and how it's all going down the drain, I think about my great-grandmother and her daughter and her daughter and all those women. Incredible things happened to those people. They never knew from one day to the next about anything, but they believed in their dignity. They believed they were people of value, and they had to pass that on. And they did it. So when I confront these little twentieth-century problems—

MOYERS: Well, you also created a twentieth-century woman in *Sula.* She's out there, independent, uncontained, and uncontainable, you said. You called her the New World black woman. Why?

MORRISON: Well, she's experimental. She's sort of an outlaw: she's not going to take it anymore. She's available to her own imagination. Other people's stories, other people's definitions are not hers. The thing about Sula is that she makes you do your own defining for yourself.

I think one of the interesting things about feminine intelligence is that it can look at the world as though we can do two things or three things at once—the personality is more fluid, more receptive. The boundaries are not quite so defined. I think that's part of what modernism is. And I think that we're probably in a very good position to do that as black women. I mean we're managing households and other people's children and two jobs and listening to everybody and at the same time creating, singing, holding, bearing, transferring the culture for generations. We've been walking on water for four hundred years.

MOYERS: Have these women you created taught you anything?

MORRISON: Oh yes. All the books are questions for me. I write them because I don't know something. In *Tar Baby*, for instance, there was something in there I really did not understand: what is the problem between a pair of lovers who really love one another but are culturally different? What is the battle about? Culture? Class? When Son and Jadine can't speak to one another, they're both a little right, but nobody will give—nobody will say, "Okay, I'll give you this little bit." What have they learned? How can you manage to love another person under these circumstances if your culture, your class, your education are that different? All the while I wrote that book I was eager for them to make it. You know, end up and get married and go to the seashore.

MOYERS: And yet?

MORRISON: They didn't. They each had to learn something else, I think, before that could happen. With *Beloved*, I began to think about motherhood. It's not the all-encompassing role for women now, it can be a secondary role, or you don't have to choose it. But on the other hand, there was something so valuable about what happened when one became a mother. For me it was the most liberating thing that ever happened to me.

MOYERS: Liberating? Isn't every mother a hostage to love?

MORRISON: Liberating because the demands that children make are not the demands of a normal "other." The children's demands on me were things that nobody else ever asked me to do. To be a good manager. To have a sense of humor. To deliver something that somebody could use. And they were not interested in all the things that other people were interested in, like what I was wearing or if I were sensual. All of that went by. You've seen the eyes of your children. They don't want to hear it. They want to know what are you going to do now—today? Somehow all of the baggage that I had accumulated as a person about what was valuable just fell away. I could not only be me—whatever that was—but somebody actually needed me to be that.

It's different from being a daughter. It's different from being a sister. If you listen to your children and look at them, they make demands that you can live up to. They don't need all that overwhelming love either. I mean, that's just you being vain about it. If you listen to them, somehow you are able to free yourself from baggage and vanity and all sorts of things, and deliver a better self, one that you like. The person that was in me that I liked best was the one my children seemed to want. Not the one that frowned when they walked in the room and said, "Pull your socks up." Also, you could begin to see the world through their eyes again—which are your eyes. I found that extraordinary.

MOYERS: You raised them by yourself, didn't you?

MORRISON: Yes.

MOYERS: Would you have liked to have had the help of a companion?

MORRISON: Yes. It would have been nice to have somebody else to think things through with you. The more the merrier. I needed a lot of help.

MOYERS: As I listen to you talk about the liberation of motherhood and love, I find all the more incredible Sethe's willingness to kill her daughter, Beloved, rather than let the slave trader kidnap her.

MORRISON: That was Margaret Garner's story. She was a slave woman who escaped from Kentucky and arrived in Cincinnati to live with her mother-in-law. Right after she got there the man who owned her found her. She ran out into the shed

and tried to kill all her children. Just like that. She was about to bang the head of one up against the wall when they stopped her.

She became a *cause célèbre* for the abolitionists because they were attempting to get her tried for murder. That would have been a big coup because it would have assumed she had some responsibility over those children. But the abolitionists were unsuccessful. She was tried for the "real" crime, which was stolen property, and convicted and returned to that same man.

I didn't want to know a great deal about her story because there would be no space for me to invent, but what struck me was that when they interviewed her she was not a mad-dog killer. She was very calm. All she said was, "They will not live like that. They will not live like that." Her mother-in-law, who was a preacher, said, "I watched her do it. And I neither encouraged her nor discouraged her." So for them, it was a dilemma. Shall I permit my children, who are my best thing, to live like I have lived, when I know that's terrible? So she decided to kill them and kill herself. That was noble. She was saying, "I'm a human being. These are my children. This script I am writing."

MOYERS: Did you ever put yourself in her position and ask, "Could I have done that to my two sons?"

MORRISON: I ask it a lot. As a matter of fact, the reason the character Beloved enters the novel is because I couldn't answer it. I didn't know whether I would do it or not. You hear stories of that in slavery and Holocaust situations, where women have got to figure it out—fast, really fast. But the only person I felt had the right to ask her that question was Beloved, the child she killed. She could ask Sethe, "What'd you do that for? Is this better? What do you know?" For me it was an impossible decision. Someone gave me the line for it at one time which I have found useful. "It was the right thing to do, but she had no right to do it."

MOYERS: And you've never answered it in your own case. "Could I do it?"

MORRISON: I've asked. I don't know. I really don't know. There are some things that I could imagine as the fate of my children, particularly when they were young, that I'd have to think very carefully about. Would I be willing to let certain things happen? There are terrible things in the world. Suppose you knew for sure, as some people have learned later, that your children have been sold to child pornographers?

MOYERS: What do you think is the primary role of the novel? Is it to illuminate social reality, or is it to stretch our imagination?

MORRISON: The latter. It really is about stretching. But in that way you have to bear witness to what *is*. The fear of collapse, of meaninglessness, of disorder, of anarchy—there's a certain protection that art can provide in the guise, not even of truth, but just a kind of linguistic shape of a life or a group of lives. Through that encounter, when you brush up against that, if it's any good, or it touches you in some way, it does really rub off. It enhances. It makes one or two things possible in one's own life, personally. You see something. Somebody takes a cataract away from your eye, or somehow your ear gets unplugged. You feel larger, connected. Something of substance you have encountered connects with another experience.

Novelists can do that. Art can do it in a number of ways. But it certainly should stretch. I don't want to read a book that simply reinforces all my prejudices and ignorances and things I half-know. I want one that says, "Oh, I'd forgotten—but that is exactly the way it looks," or "Oh, that's what that feeling is."

MOYERS: That's what you've done for so many others. The paradox to me is that I grew up in a small Southern town in the 1930s and '40s and '50s—twenty-two thousand people, half black, half white. It wasn't until I read your novels and the novels of people writing, as you do, about the past that I really knew what the folks on the other side of the tracks were thinking and feeling and experiencing.

MORRISON: That's important if a book can do that.

MOYERS: If only a book could do it now, for people who are in our circle of the present. Why do we have to wait so long for reconciliation?

MORRISON: You were ready for the information. You were available to the book. Some people are not available to the book, to that information. I'm sure there are books that I am just not ready to hear. It's not that the novel batters you down and gets rid of barricades or opens doors. The person inside you has to be accessible. There has to be a little crack in there already, some curiosity. Some willingness, you know, to know about it. Some moment when you really don't have the blinders on. We know people who just zip their eyes shut, who are totally enclosed in the neurotic and frequently psychotic prison of racism. But if ever any chink can be made from the inside or outside, then they become accessible to certain kinds of information.

MOYERS: Are you aware when you're writing that you're going to invade my imagination? That you're going to subvert my perception? Were you intentionally trying to do that?

MORRISON: Totally. I want the reader to feel, first of all, that he trusts me. I'm never going to do anything so bad that he can't handle it. But at the same time, I want him to see things he has never seen before. I want him to work with me in the book. I can rely on some things that I know you know. For instance, I know you don't believe in ghosts, none of us do, but—

MOYERS: I wouldn't go too far in that assumption.

MORRISON: Well, we were all children. We all knew that we did not sleep with our hands hanging outside the bed. To this day if you wake up and your hand is hanging out there you move it back in. So I can rely on readers to know those things. But I do want to penetrate the readerly subconsciousness so that the response is, on the one hand, an intellectual one to what I have problematized in the text, but at the same time very somatic, visceral, a physical response so that you really think you see it or you can smell it or you can hear it, without my overdoing it. Because it has to be yours.

I don't describe Pilate a lot in *Song of Solomon*. She's tall and she wears this ear thing and she says less than people think. But I felt that I saw her so clearly, I wanted to communicate the clarity, not of my vision, but of a vision so that she belongs to whoever's envisioning her in the text. And people can say, "Oh, I know her. I know who that is. She is . . ." and they fill in the blank because they have invented her.

Sam Keen

PHILOSOPHER

© Michael Oletta

Like our mutual friend the late Joseph Campbell, Sam Keen has focused his prodigious energies on how the world's mythologies affect our daily lives. His book *The Faces of the Enemy*, which he made into a film for PBS, probes the images we create of our enemies—personal or global—and the serious implications for daily behavior. A prolific writer and popular lecturer, Keen has described himself as "a lover of questions, a freelance thinker, a man rich in friendship and, in a former life, a professor."

MOYERS: Last night I watched again your film *The Faces of the Enemy*, and I was struck by how the decline of the Soviet Union as our enemy has left so many people with a sense of loss. Filmmakers and spy novelists in particular are having trouble finding a common standard villain these days. Where's the face of the enemy now?

KEEN: Well, the politicians don't have much trouble finding a face. They filled the vacuum quite rapidly with the splendid little invasion of Panama, where we used the Stealth bomber against people who have very primitive armed forces. Or look at how the Pentagon uses the language of war and warfare in the interdiction of drugs. That's one place the image of the enemy has gone. But it's also moved into a much more hopeful place, the whole environmental movement, where pollution and warfare itself are now seen as the enemies. That's a much more mature and hopeful direction.

MOYERS: What's the role of mythology in all of this?

KEEN: I use myth to mean the systematic, unconscious way of structuring reality that governs a culture as a whole, or a people, or a tribe. It can govern a corporation, a family, or a person. It's the underlying story. So, for instance, the underlying story that we all have in common in the Western world is the myth of progress, the belief that we are going to get better and better in every way, and our children are going to have a better world, and we are going to engineer our way into a kind of human utopia. We don't stand up and salute that, but in fact, that's what governs our lives. As the song "America the Beautiful" says, we are an alabaster city "undimmed by human tears."

MOYERS: Or as Ronald Reagan said in his final speech "a city upon the hill."

KEEN: Right. In that sense, you see, we all have a common myth. But then you realize that other nations also have their binding myths, and ethnic groups have their myths. Or you go into a corporation, and IBM is very different from Apple Computer about the stories they tell that give structure to that organization. And I think the way we structure and see enemies and evil is all mythology. The evil is not a myth, but the glass through which we see it is a mythology. A culture always has a mythology about evil, because one of the great mythic questions has always been: What is the source of evil? And if myth tells us who creates evil, it also can tell us who are not people, and whom we can kill without guilt. We can say there's one source of evil, and it's over there; and if we go clean that up, we can feel righteous ourselves in the process.

MOYERS: There *are* real enemies out there, though. Nazi Germany was a genuine threat to civilization. Communism, as manifested in its oppression of people, was a genuine enemy. The question is how to discriminate between the perceived enemy and the real enemy.

KEEN: That's always been the problem. Obviously some nations or people pose real threats and we have to do something about them. But when you see Nicaragua being portrayed as an embodiment of that same kind of evil, then you have to begin to realize, wait a minute, something mythic is going on here.

MOYERS: The myth of the enemy run amok.

KEEN: The myth run amok. In the Vietnam War the myth became so overwhelming that two mythic metaphors governed all our decisions: the domino myth and the myth of containment—the idea that wherever this thing called communism pops up, we have to respond. And nobody seemed to pause to say, "Well, what is the strategic importance or the political importance of Vietnam for us? Should we be fighting communism there, or are there other places where we should have responded to that very real challenge?"

MOYERS: You write that we must learn to change the face of the enemy. Will that really change our behavior?

KEEN: The images themselves do have a life of their own, and although it doesn't solve the problem of enmity, it solves that kind of surplus enmity that happens when we create images that are unrealistic. Changing our images allows us to begin to deal with our rivals in a much more reasonable way. The whole question of how we deal with Gorbachev is on a much more reasonable basis now than it was five years ago.

MOYERS: Your book *The Faces of the Enemy* came out just shortly before Gorbachev came to power, didn't it?

KEEN: Yes, and in 1984 I actually lectured before the USA Canada Institute in Moscow on images of the enemy. At that time, the lecture was not well accepted, but eventually it went up through the Soviet leadership hierarchy, and Gorbachev may have taken his phrase "image of the enemy" from that.

MOYERS: Gorbachev used that term?

KEEN: Yes, he said, "I'm going to take the image of the enemy away from you." He very consciously set out to do that. As a matter of fact, we had a conference in Moscow that was supported by the Soviet Government on the image of the enemy. It's the first time I know of that any major country ever said it was going to look at perception, it was going to admit that at least part of the problem of warfare and enmity is in the perception and not in real geopolitical differences that we have between us.

MOYERS: Well, given the state of its economy, it became hard to believe the Soviet Union was as powerful as the rhetoric on the right made it out to be. A country that weak couldn't have been that much of a real threat. But the perception was different.

KEEN: That's right. But it's strange, it's almost like there's a given quantity of enmity, like a balloon filled with water. When you squeeze it in one place, it goes to another. If you get rid of a major enemy like the Soviet Union—or the image of that enemy—you squeeze the balloon and part will go over to Qaddafi and part will go to the drug war and part will go to the environment and part will go to child abuse. See, we now have all these new enemies. Missing children are getting a lot of attention, and then you find out that a lot of these supposedly "missing" children were actually kidnaped by one of the parents who had been denied custody or visitation.

MOYERS: You're not laying all of this at the feet of Gorbachev, are you? You're not saying Gorbachev is causing child abuse in America.

KEEN: Well, Gorbachev is not causing it, but remember the journalist Lincoln Steffens once wrote a chapter in his autobiography called "I Make a Crime Wave." Just the reporting of something that was never noticed much before makes people think an epidemic has struck. Child abuse has gone on all along, but it's only recently become almost a national hysteria. Only recently have we discovered that we are dangerous to our children.

MOYERS: Do you think we can really defuse aggression just by changing the images? Many people think there is a certain aggression bred within us that comes with the turf.

> *I don't at all equate aggression and hostility. Aggression is very fine. Aggression merely means the focused use of energy. . . . Hostility is something else. Hostility is aggression mixed with some degree of hatred, paranoia, and fear.*

KEEN: I don't at all equate aggression and hostility. Aggression is very fine. Aggression merely means the focused use of energy. Right now you and I are being very aggressive in trying to define ideas and sharpen them. We're using the knife of decision and clarity to do that. Writing a book or making television requires a lot of aggression.

Hostility is something else. Hostility is aggression mixed with some degree of hatred, paranoia, and fear. So those are two separate questions. We could be quite aggressive and never be hostile.

MOYERS: And images can turn aggression into hostility.

KEEN: Yes. Probably the clearest example was what happened during the Second World War, when the United States and Japan had so hyped each other up with these demonic images that we couldn't call the war off when it was really strategically over. During the last year of the war, hundreds of thousands of people were killed, merely because we had demonized each other and we couldn't find a way to stop the demonization.

MOYERS: It's so much easier to arouse people to martial causes. Why is it so hard to inspire a sense of shared national purpose in the interest of peaceable pursuits?

KEEN: The problem is that the concept of peace lacks drama. I once took a screenwriting workshop in which the teacher started off by saying that in screenplays things only develop by conflict. This was in the middle of the peace movement. And I said, "Wait a minute, here we are talking about peace, and the fact is that we love drama and we love conflict." So one of my answers to that is that we have to have a concept of peace that includes conflict. Instead of looking at peace as a state without conflict, look at it as a state in which conflict is loving conflict.

The best example is of course dialogue. Karl Jaspers, the great philosopher, said every real dialogue is loving combat. Or a marriage is loving combat. There's lots of aggression, there's lots of my saying, Look, I stand here and you stand there. But we have a bond of love.

Now, I think that what's happened in *perestroika* and *glasnost* is exactly that. We are seeing a conflict leave the mode of hostility and become a more creative kind of conflict. There's a love affair now going on between the United States and the Soviet Union that wasn't there before. It's much more helpful than the way we see Qaddafi, for instance. There's no possibility of reconciliation with Libya because we don't consider it a creative conflict.

MOYERS: Which comes first? The changing of the metaphor, or the changing of the behavior?

KEEN: Oh, I think the answer's either. It can happen either way. Gorbachev set out specifically to change the image and the behavior, but it was a long time before we responded and said maybe this is trustworthy, maybe something is happening that isn't cosmetic. The early cartoons all said, look, it's just cosmetic, it's another Commie trick, they're disarming to fool us, you know. Look out, they'll commit suicide to get us off balance! And then gradually we realized, no, it wasn't just an image change.

MOYERS: If you were filming your documentary *Faces of the Enemy* now, in the era of Gorbachev and Bush, how would you change it?

KEEN: I would look at the Panama invasion, a totally inappropriate response to the situation. As Secretary of State John Hay said of the Spanish-American War, it was a splendid little war for symbolic and ideological purposes. I believe George Bush needed to beat up on somebody to change his image as a wimp.

MOYERS: The *New York Times* said he had proven his presidential manhood by sending men to combat.

KEEN: Yes. And it was all to get hold of one person, General Noriega, whom we had had all kinds of dealings with in the CIA, so we were complicitous in his power. Then the way that we handled that whole thing was totally inappropriate. So I think you have to see, when something like that happens, that it's symbolic, it's primarily an interior psychological drama.

Somebody once said in a critique of *Faces of the Enemy* that you shouldn't psychologize political events. Well, I say that's half a truth. The other half is that you shouldn't politicize psychological events. Our need for an enemy is a need to feel superior. It's a need also to have something dirty in the world that we can clean up, because in that act of cleaning up we can say God is with us, God is on our side, and we're really protecting the world from evil.

MOYERS: But there *are* dirty things in the world. There *is* evil.

KEEN: There is evil in the world, and there are places that we have to fight. But it's interesting that for a paradigm of the fight, we have to go back to the Second World War, where we had such a clear evil, and where the response to that was quite appropriately one of violence. As a matter of fact, we should have responded that way much earlier. But I don't think that we can use those same metaphors in a nuclear world. In the old world, we could go and clean the evil up and come back, and people could survive. Nuclear weapons changed all that.

MOYERS: Just believing a mythology doesn't make it true, though, does it? We're not necessarily more just because we think we're more just, or more democratic

because we think we're a democracy, or more kind because we think of ourselves as kind. Mythology can misinform, can it not?

KEEN: I would say that mythology inevitably misinforms. It's just a question of how much it misinforms. But the point is we don't have a true picture of the world the way it actually is without our perceptions to compare mythology to. All we have is our perceptions, which are always filtered through our values and through the stories that we told and the stories that we have been told.

MOYERS: Do you think we have a common mythology today in this country? Or are we so many different kinds of people from so many sources, that we no longer have a shared mythology?

KEEN: I think we do. I think if you had asked me this question twenty years ago I would have said no. In the 1950s Martin Heidegger said that all the old gods were gone, and Paul Tillich talked about the vacuum of waiting. All we could do, he said, is wait in this vacuum, because you can't just create myth. Myth isn't something you just create. I think what's happened in the last few years is the beginning of the emergence of a genuinely new myth. Our society is in a very creative kind of chaos at the moment where there are three mythic systems that are in conflict. One is the myth of progress we've been living on since the beginning of the Industrial Revolution. It's a secular myth that survives largely by not asking ultimate questions. When in the nineteenth century Nietzsche said God is dead, he didn't mean that people stopped believing in Him. Ninety-four percent of all people, as *Reader's Digest* tells you, still believe in God. But what Nietzsche was talking about was that the majority of people stopped structuring their lives as if there were a God, as if there were a sacred order, and they started structuring it in terms of what was technologically and economically possible.

MOYERS: And you think we're disillusioned about that now?

KEEN: I think that all over the world there's been a reaction to that, the conservative religious reaction, which is the second contending myth. In Iran, for instance, where the Shah tried to bring in all the secular ways, he didn't notice that there was a large community of Shiite Muslims who were saying, "We don't want the secular world! No! We are going to go back to an Islamic commonwealth. We want a society that is ruled by an authority, by a rule of God." We see that also in right-wing American fundamentalism.

MOYERS: Patrick Buchanan keeps sounding the alarms about the decline of Christian America.

KEEN: That's part of the myth. Now, the third myth is the spiritual revolution. It's not churchy, but it comes up out of I guess three sources, first out of quantum physics and the new biology, which says we are all in this together. The world is a connected network, it's not separate, it's not atomic. The second place it comes from in a more popular way is the ecological myth, the Gaia hypothesis. Look, everything is connected. And finally it comes up in feminism. These three combine to form the emerging myth of the twenty-first century: that there's no place to export our garbage, there's no place to export even our images of enmity. We are organically connected.

MOYERS: But you're talking about private myth at the moment, the stories people are telling themselves. Who's writing our public myths today, the myths about America?

KEEN: I think that *is* the new emerging public myth. In Europe you have the growing power of the Green Party. But I think it's the same thing here. What Earth Day showed in a sense is a kind of symbolic tribute to the emergence of this new mythology.

MOYERS: But there are polls that show that working-class and middle-class people do not buy into the environmental movement. Now, that may be because it's lily white, that may be because its leaders are primarily from the socially secure classes, but large numbers of American people have not yet bought into this myth.

KEEN: That's right. Joseph Campbell always says every new myth emerges from a heroic journey and from an elite who sees things differently. So I think that's true. It is certainly not a majority myth.

MOYERS: I guess what I'm saying is I don't yet see the arrival of a single dominant myth in American culture that would take the place of the one that has animated our thinking for so long, the individual who forges ahead into the wilderness creating a new society, the rugged individual of Hollywood, or the free market individual of entrepreneurialism. I don't see a new American rising to play out the myth that you're describing.

KEEN: Well, I do. I don't see anywhere near a majority yet, but I see it as a growing minority. Yesterday, my nine-year-old daughter and her friend were talking, and one of them said, "What is your dream?" And the other said, "Well, my dream is to marry . . ." somebody, some rock star, "and to have the world clean."

MOYERS: You've spent a lot of your time, in the last few years, leading seminars trying to help people discover what you call their personal mythology. What do you mean by that?

KEEN: If you look at a mythology of any tribe, you'll see that all mythologies give answers to certain primal and perennial human questions. Where did I come from, and where am I going? Who are my people, and what is my place? What is the meaning of suffering, what is the meaning of death, and what is sex about? How close should I be to people? For what am I guilty, and what should I avoid, what's taboo? In one sense, the modern myth was the myth that we didn't have myth because we had this scientific secular consciousness. I was raised in that, so were you. In seminary we talked about demythologizing, you know, we're going to get rid of all that primitive myth stuff.

Well, I began to examine my own experience at a very crucial and disturbed period in my life—when my own tenacious clinging to the Christian worldview and the Christian myth began to crumble, when I couldn't believe it anymore—and I had to ask myself the question, well, what do you believe? How do you find any rock upon which to put your feet? For a long time I was at a loss, and suddenly it occurred to me that instead of looking at the answers that myth gave, I could look at the questions. I began to interrogate my own life using those questions. Who are my heroes? Who are my villains? What is my source? Where did I come from? Who are my people? I discovered that I could find within my own autobiography, as it were, a complete but undeveloped mythology. And as I began to look at those stories and recover those stories for myself, I had a mythology that gave me a story by which I lived.

MOYERS: The poet Rūmī said we shouldn't take things that other people have told us, or other people's stories; we must find out our own story.

KEEN: We become alienated when we take somebody else's story as the story of our lives. Our deep sense of the sacredness of our own life begins to be eclipsed. And the only way to find that, when we go into these periods of chaos where we lose our identity, is to go back into our own memory system.

Personal history is exactly the same as world history. Santayana said those who don't know history are condemned to repeat it.

MOYERS: If you were going to write your mythic autobiography what would your title be? That would tell me something about your mythic journey.

KEEN: I think it would be something like *The Travels of a Mystic Cowboy*, or something of that kind. Integrating my sense of travel, of my life as an adventure and as a pilgrimage, that is in some sense spiritual; my sense of land and of the love of the outdoors, and of the love of which horses are a symbol for me.

MOYERS: Do you see yourself as a hero? John Wayne? Shane? The Durango Kid?

KEEN: No! My greatest hero in teenage years was Will James. I don't mean the philosopher Will James, I mean the cowboy who wrote *Lone Cowboy*. I read those stories as a sixteen-year-old, and I wanted to be a rancher. But I knew that *Lone Cowboy* wasn't going to be the title of my journey. He was very disconnected from people.

So I guess that's probably the title, although I change my title every few years. I think when you write an autobiography it should change every ten years or so. Your memories change, your values change, your sense of importance changes.

MOYERS: If you were writing the conclusion of your mythic journey, what would be the last scene?

KEEN: There's a biblical phrase, "And he died old and full of years." I'd like to live to be an old man. That's largely because I still have so much to learn. As my wife will tell you, I haven't learned a terrible amount of patience yet. I can slow down on occasion, but . . . My great hero was Howard Thurmond, and what he taught me was the value of silence. He never spoke until he thought, and he usually didn't speak until he had connected his mind with his spirit. So his word had to come from the thought, and the thought from a deep kind of listening to his whole experience. That requires more silence than I have most of the time.

MOYERS: You are a writer and an intellectual. Does this have any kind of practical application? Advising other people to take their mythic journey, write their own stories? Does it have any practical application for people who are not writers and intellectuals?

KEEN: Oh, enormous I think. In 1969 I wrote a book called *Apology for Wonder*. It was a good book, it was recognized well, and I got probably ten letters about it. About two years later I wrote the book *To a Dancing God*. At the ripe old age of thirty-three I was doing autobiography. Then I began to get letters. For twenty years now this book has been in print, and I still get letters, and they almost all start the same. They say something like, "Dear Sam, I never write authors, but I feel I know you because you've told so much of your story." And then they always go on in the second paragraph, "And here's my story." And I found out, quite inadvertently, that by saying, "I'm not telling this because I'm this great hero, I'm telling this because it's the only place I've got to start; I'm lost, so I'd better start on home ground"—I found that I had given permission for other people to take their stories seriously, too. They said, wait a minute, the dignity of my life is telling my own story, and seeing the world through my own eyes.

MOYERS: What happens when they see the world themselves?

KEEN: They're separating out their own experience of what is real and valuable from what they have been told is real and valuable. They are sorting out their sense of what their own gifts are versus what they've been told their gifts were.

MOYERS: In your new book you quote Herb Gardner's *A Thousand Clowns* where he says, "You have got to own your days and name them, each one of them, every one of them, or else the years go right by and none of them belong to you." In a sense, your story doesn't belong to you until you claim it.

KEEN: Until you claim it and name it. One of the simplest exercises I do in trying to teach people to tell their own story is to have them write an outline of their autobiography. It makes people have to think, well, what was important? When did I change? When was I on an up cycle? What were the peak experiences in my life? What were valley experiences? What enemies have I had? What battles have I fought? Who were my allies? Very often old people go through this process naturally, but I think we should begin the process much earlier.

MOYERS: What if you write your story and no one reads it?

KEEN: If you write your story only for yourself, there'll be important parts left out, because audience shapes our story, too. If I tell my story to you, it's going to be very different than if I tell it to myself in private. Story-telling is a communal act. It requires community and it creates community. It's not isolated, it is not something an individual does.

MOYERS: That I can understand, but you stressed the point that it's not just sharing stories, it's sharing our myth with each other. Why is myth so important to the story?

KEEN: Remember, I said myth is an unconscious systematic way in which your experience is informed. Jung once said, "I came to the middle point of my life, and I realized I didn't know what myth I was living." When I ask myself—somewhere usually near the midpoint of life—"Wait, what myth have I been living?" I begin in a certain sense to destroy that myth, because I'm trying to make it conscious. I say that the task of a life is to exchange the unconscious myth with a conscious autobiography. For the first twenty years of my life I was shaped unconsciously by the Christian myth and by the myth of being a Keen and by the myth of being a white Anglo-Saxon Protestant Southerner, all quite heavy information systems. But at twenty-five, I didn't know I'd been shaped that way. Then, at thirty-five, when I began to reflect on that, I said, wait a minute, something was shaping me. And when I did that, I began to get a distance between myself and that shaping myth, and I began then to write my own story. I realized there were some things I didn't like! I didn't like the macho part of the male myth, I didn't like that antiseptic, uptight part of the Protestant myth. I threw it out. See, I began then to weave my own story, using the myth, but still now trying to make it more conscious.

MOYERS: Underlying all of this is the power of story in our lives. The story is crucial to our understanding of who we are even if it's a story we don't wholly understand. That's where we find meaning. Joe Campbell said that life is in the experience, but I also think that life is in the meaning we give that experience. He and I differed on that.

KEEN: Well, I don't even think that we have an experience until we have a story about it. Experience is a moment in a story. Put another way, we are by definition narrative creating beings. That's what it means to be conscious. We are the only being that is in a very real sense condemned to tell a story. Jean-Paul Sartre, the French existentialist, said we're condemned to be free, because we're conscious. And therefore we are that animal that has to tell a story about our lives.

Evelyn Fox Keller

HISTORIAN OF SCIENCE

When in the 1950s Evelyn Fox Keller sallied forth to become a scientist, she discovered it was a man's world. Training as a theoretical physicist and working in both mathematical biology and the history of science, she wondered why most scientists were men and why the language of science reflected masculine metaphors and values. Keller has grappled with the meaning and consequences of these stereotypes ever since, especially in her pioneering works *Reflections on Gender and Science* and *A Feeling for the Organism*, a biography of the geneticist Barbara McClintock. She teaches in the Department of Rhetoric at the University of California at Berkeley.

MOYERS: What are you doing teaching in the Department of Rhetoric? What does rhetoric have to do with science?

KELLER: I have had a somewhat checkered career, and I have written in many different areas. So I pose a problem to the academy. Where can we put Evelyn Fox Keller? They can no longer put me in the physics department. They don't want to put me in a biology department anymore. I'm not formally a historian. And although I think of myself as working in the history and philosophy of science, there are very few history and philosophy of science programs in the country.

So when Berkeley offered me a job in rhetoric and women's studies with an affiliation in history of science, I thought, well, at the very least it's an imaginative solution. But it also made a certain kind of sense, because I realized over the last decade that what I was talking and thinking about kept coming back to the question of language and science. That's what I try to understand—how language works in science. Language is the mediator of human values and human expectations in our descriptions of nature. If we want to understand the ways in which science is reflecting back to us particular expectations, particular values, we have to look at the language of science and see how that works. How the traffic between ordinary and technical language works as a carrier, if you will, of ideology into science.

MOYERS: One of your chief contributions to this has been to clarify the significant role gender plays in the language scientists use to describe their work.

KELLER: It has played a very, very powerful role.

MOYERS: By gender you do not mean sex, our biological differences.

KELLER: No, I mean ideas of masculinity and ideas of femininity. We see it at the very beginning of modern science with the scientific revolution of the seventeenth century. The Royal Society of London, one of the first modern scientific societies, was founded in order to "raise a masculine philosophy." What did they mean by a masculine philosophy? Well, Francis Bacon said, "Let us establish a chaste and lawful marriage between Mind and Nature."

The purpose of this marriage was to bind nature and bring nature and all her children to your service. Bind her and make her your slave.

MOYERS: And the purpose of science was to give the mind—the husband—mastery over nature—the bride?

KELLER: That's right. The central metaphor for the scientific revolution was a marriage between the mind and nature that was modeled on a particular kind of marriage, a patriarchal marriage, the purpose of which was the domination of nature.

MOYERS: And the Royal Society of London was founded in 1662 but didn't admit a woman until 1945!

KELLER: Women were excluded from many domains, not just science. But scientists had a particular commitment to the notion that there was something special about what they were doing. It was a special kind of thinking. A special kind of philosophy. A special kind of activity. In the most general sense, science meant "thinking like a man." It was committed to an idea of objectivity that was from the beginning equated with masculinity in a very curious way.

> *I wanted to understand what it meant to say "thinking objectively" is "thinking like a man." What could it mean? Where does such an idea come from?*

In fact, it was that equation that motivated my entire inquiry. I wanted to understand what it meant to say "thinking objectively" is "thinking like a man." What could it mean? Where does such an idea come from? And more important, what consequences has it had for science? These early scientists used such language for a reason. People would respond in ways that the language intended. The scientists were trying to articulate a form of knowledge and the rules by which you could demarcate correct from incorrect modes of knowing. They were also demarcating who should be engaged in this pursuit and who should not. But it wasn't just the demarcation of men from women. In fact, it was very little about the demarcation of men from women. It was much more the demarcation of *values*. They invoked the language of gender in order to justify the exclusion of a certain domain of human activity, particularly the exclusion of feeling and emotion, from the pursuit of science.

Here is how Joseph Glanvill described it: "That Job himself cannot be *wise* and in *Love*; may be understood in a larger sense, than Antiquity meant it: Where the *Will* or *Passion* hath the casting voyce, the case of *Truth* is *desperate* . . . The *Woman* in us, still prosecutes a deceit, like that begun in the *Garden*; and our *Understandings* are wedded to an *Eve*, as fatal as the *Mother* of our *miseries*." He concludes: "Truth has no chance when the *Affections* wear the breeches and the *Female* rules."

MOYERS: He was saying that we have to exclude feeling, empathy, intuition from the search into how the world works.

KELLER: That's right. But he's doing it by attaching these to the female and excluding both. We're excluding "Affections"—feeling and emotion—because they're female, and we're excluding females because they carry these attributes with them. But once you've documented the pervasive gender imagery in the language of scientific development, once you have shown how prevalent these images of masculinity and femininity and domination were, the question remains—so what? That's really the question. Some people might say, yes, but that was just in the seventeenth century; we've left that long since behind. Well, we haven't left it behind. It is still with us. Listen to this passage from C. P. Snow's *The Masters*, written in 1951. He's describing a young scientist, Luke, who has just had a breakthrough.

"It's wonderful," he bursts out, "when you've got a problem that is really coming out. It's like making love. Suddenly your unconscious takes control and nothing can stop you. You know that you're making old Mother Nature sit up and beg, and you say to her I've got you, you old bitch. You've got her just where you want her."

MOYERS: So a mythology was created that objectivity, reason, and the mind are male attributes and subjectivity, feeling, and nature are female attributes. But what did that mean to the history of science? Did it change the content of science?

KELLER: That, of course, is the hardest question of all. Clearly, it mattered to the history of science in that the effect was the exclusion of women. Of course there have always been some women in science. I don't want to contribute to the erasure of the very brave and heroic and talented few women who managed to survive in that history.

But obviously a science that advertises itself in that language is not going to be hospitable to women. So one immediate consequence was that the domain of science was restricted to men, and to a particular world of men, and the development of science was deprived of a pool of talent. But it also meant the exclusion of certain kinds of talent in the men who did become scientists. Did that change the quality of it, did that affect the content of science?

That's the question, but it's a very, very difficult question. We have learned—the

hard way, I think—that it isn't true that science gives us a mirror or reflection of nature. We've learned that that picture of science doesn't work. What actually happens is that the descriptions of nature, the theories of nature, are very complexly influenced by all kinds of social, cultural, and psychological presuppositions.

MOYERS: That kind of presupposition has had a significant impact on a lot of people. Here is a passage from Jacques Monod, a biologist, whom you quote in one of your papers: "If he accepts this message in its full significance, man may awaken from his millenary dream and discover his total solitude, his fundamental isolation, and realize that like a gypsy he lives on the boundary of an alien world. A world that is death to his music and as indifferent to his hopes as it is to his suffering or his crimes."

KELLER: I think that's a wonderfully revealing passage. Monod is arguing for a mechanical universe, for a universe that is devoid of human emotions and human feelings. But he has projected onto that universe emotions that can only be human. It is only a human who can feel alien, abandoned, isolated. Atoms and molecules aren't deaf. They're neither deaf nor hearing; it is people who are deaf or hearing. So it's an interesting illustration of the way in which, despite our greatest efforts to objectify the universe, to remove ourselves from our pictures of nature, we're nevertheless importing our own language, our own expectations, our own categories. No matter how hard we try to eliminate those hopes and anxieties, they are still there.

MOYERS: The physicist Steven Weinberg talks about the universe as being overwhelmingly hostile. Do you feel the universe is hostile?

KELLER: How can the universe be hostile? Weinberg also says, "The laws of nature are cold and indifferent. We didn't want it to come out that way; it just came out that way." I think in a sense we did want it to come out that way. The language of hostility, of coldness, of indifference is a human language. It's written into the very notion of laws of nature.

MOYERS: In what sense?

KELLER: A law of nature is a very curious construct. Whose law is the law of nature? Where does the idea of a law of nature come from? And what is the function of a law of nature? The concept of a law of nature originally comes from the realm of God. They were God's laws to which the material universe must be obedient. So the very idea of a law of nature structures a notion of hierarchy, proscription, law-giving, and obedience to those laws.

Now in a contemporary sense, we don't believe in God's laws. But still, the laws exist in our imagination, somehow above the phenomena, and the phenomena must conform to the laws of nature. This is very important when you think about how physicists actually work, and how we develop our science. Francis Bacon gave us all kinds of memorable expressions about how we have to vex nature. That only under the act of vexation will nature reveal her truths. Well, we do vex nature. We vex nature quite a bit. It is no easy task to make nature conform to the laws of nature. Let me tell you as a scientist, it is very hard work to get nature to conform to the laws of nature. The natural phenomena have to be structured and constrained and twisted and vexed to an astonishing degree before they will obey the laws of nature.

MOYERS: So when Steven Weinberg says that the laws of nature are as impersonal and free of human values as the rules of arithmetic, you're not objecting to the formula as much as you are to the very language, the very use of the word "law" to describe the operations of nature.

It is a fantasy that any human product can be free of human values. Science is a human product. It's a wonderful, glorious human product.

KELLER: I'm objecting to both. I'm objecting to the language of laws and also objecting to the notion that they are as free of human values as the rules of arithmetic. It's not true. It is a fantasy that any human product can be free of human values. Science is a human product. It's a wonderful, glorious human product.

MOYERS: But what about nature? Nature is not a human product. The natural world is not a human product.

KELLER: Yes, but science doesn't give us nature. Science gives us a description of nature. Science gives us scientific theories of nature.

MOYERS: In the description of nature, we assign to that description our own subjective experience.

KELLER: There is no way of avoiding that. There is no magic lens that will enable us to see nature uncolored by the values, hopes, fears, anxieties, desires, goals that we bring to it.

MOYERS: Are you arguing that if there were more women in science, we'd be studying acid rain instead of Star Wars?

KELLER: I wish that were true. I wish all we had to do was to bring more women into science. But it's much more complicated because these social and ideological patterns get imprinted onto the very structure of science. What I worry about most is the ways in which science is used in the world. If this history of sexism, of patriarchy, of racism, of imperialism, of all the values that I find offensive, has had a hand to play in the actual science that has been developed, then I think that is far more important than the question of women in science.

The question of women in science is important. I don't want to say it's not important. But given the tremendous role that science plays in the world we live in, the idea that we might redirect science, that there could be changes in the way in which science is done and the direction in which it moves—that seems to me of even greater importance.

MOYERS: Do you think that has cost us something in our creative vision, in the creativity of science? Do we miss certain things about the world because science is gendered masculine?

KELLER: Well, that's my principal argument. My strongest case for that argument is the story of Barbara McClintock, who won a Nobel Prize in 1983 for her work in genetics. I titled my biography of McClintock *A Feeling for the Organism*. It wasn't for my agenda that I chose that title; the words are hers. It's her deepest belief that you cannot do good research without a feeling for the organism. I argued that it was her feeling for the organism that led her to recognize that genetic elements move within the chromosome.

MOYERS: What do you mean by "a feeling for the organism"?

KELLER: I mean the ability to identify with the subject you are studying. To feel kinship instead of a sense of a battle, a struggle, a state of opposition.

MOYERS: You really feel that's primarily a female mode of approaching science?

KELLER: No, I believe that it's been *called* a female mode of approaching science. I believe it is a human virtue, a human talent. We are talking about the capacity for empathy. I don't think that women have a corner on the market of empathy; I think all of us are capable of empathy. I do think that it's not a talent that is very well-developed in many men because of the ways in which they're raised. But it is precisely because it has been identified as a feminine virtue, as a feminine talent, that it has been excluded from science.

MOYERS: You make me think of something you wrote earlier. You said, "We have developed scientific methods and techniques to change the world without asking what we would change the world to. We've never acknowledged we were making choices that could change the world." My question is: what kind of world would you like to change us to?

KELLER: I'd like to change the world to make it better for humankind—for all people. I have only the most idealistic visions that we all can share. I want a world that will preserve and augment life. I want a world that will promote peace. I want what most people want, really, for the world. I'd like to see a science that serves the ideals of social justice. There's nothing novel in that. But we're not asking what our science is doing—what the knowledge that we're seeking is for. There's no way in which we are going to map all of nature. We are never going to have a complete science. So the question becomes what questions are we asking, what kinds of knowledge, what parts of nature are we seeking to engage, and for what purpose? What guides these choices? It's a selection process in the first place. What aspects of nature are we going to try to model, to develop theories of, and toward what end?

MOYERS: Assuming that we could move to a science that is gender free, how different would that science be? What would we see differently?

KELLER: I do believe that there is a history of complicity in science with the forces of aggression that has in part to do with the historic genderization of science. On an institutional level, complicity between physics and the military is well known. This is a social, structural complicity; remember, the military is another domain subject to very sharp gender demarcations. I hope a degenderization of science would break that complicity, would open science to a more erotic engagement with nature, to a more productive deployment of the uses of science toward the goals of life rather than death.

MOYERS: Is it possible that we could replace the strongly masculine image of the scientist with one that is gender neutral?

KELLER: Yes. But I don't know if that's enough. When I wrote my book in 1985, I was more optimistic than I am today.

MOYERS: What do you mean?

KELLER: In the early days I thought if we could just change the stranglehold of this gender ideology on science, it would have a tremendous effect. Not only would it open up the doors of science to women, it would allow men and women alike to think more freely. To make use of the full gamut of their human talents.

Now we have cleaned up the language of science. The gender ideology is not nearly as prominent or explicit as it was ten years ago, and we have far more women in science. But that's not enough. We can degenderize the language of science and not make very much of a dent in the structures that are in place. Science in the late twentieth century is a product of three hundred years of evolution. It's naive to think that we could just change that structure just by changing the metaphors. The metaphors are built in. They're already embodied in the institutional structures of science. Science is what it is. To change science, therefore, requires a much more complex, long engagement. It's a much more difficult endeavor than I had thought.

MOYERS: I remember the story of the great Danish seismologist who talked about her education at the first coeducational school in Denmark where boys and girls were treated equally. They played football alike and they learned needlework alike. Their intellects were not seen as being different. She said, "It wasn't until I left the coeducational school and went out into the world that I realized society was organized differently." So if you're going to change, replace the masculine gender with a gender-free science, you've got to start way back down there.

KELLER: It's not enough, though, to teach the boys needlework, although I think it's great to teach the boys needlework and the girls carpentry. I'm all for that. I think one has to carry that forward. It's very interesting to think about how it is happening that there are now more women in science. What kinds of arrangements are making that possible? What I had had in mind when I thought we could move more toward a gender-free science was an integration of the laboratory and the nursery. I had in mind a sharing of the responsibilities of men and women by men and women. What we are finding instead—it's a very familiar solution—is that child rearing, the principal task that has traditionally been the task of women, is being parceled off onto other women. The women who become scientists are now becoming scientists because they're liberated from the sphere of domesticity.

MOYERS: But every woman can't be a scientist just as every man can't be a scientist.

KELLER: Right. We need people to take care of children. But if you want to degender science then you have to engage men in the spheres that were traditionally those of women. Otherwise, you're not going to redistribute the gendered values in the culture.

MOYERS: And the world remains very much the way the world is. Recently, I read an article which moves us from science to politics, but I think the analogy is appropriate here. "Is Margaret Thatcher a woman?" the headline asks. And then the subheadline answers, "No woman is, if she has to make it in a man's world." The writer says that not only has Margaret Thatcher been the first Prime Minister since the war not to put a woman in the Cabinet, but she's actually appointed fewer women than any other Prime Minister. Her own children have been sacrificed the same way the families of men are sacrificed when they're consumed by politics. The point is that Margaret Thatcher's arrival as Prime Minister of England has succeeded by political standards because she acted, this author says, as if she were a man. She is a surrogate man; an imitation man, says this writer. What's your reaction to that?

KELLER: Probably the only thing I would defend in Margaret Thatcher is her right to choose her relation to the stereotypic roles that have traditionally been assigned to women. She is a woman as much as any other woman; she's just not a stereotypic woman. She has that right. The major thrust of the feminist movement in the twentieth century has been to struggle for the rights of individuals to choose their courses unfettered by traditional stereotypes. Margaret Thatcher has done that. That she has not appointed women to the Cabinet, that her politics are not good for women in England—that's another problem. That I will not defend. But I don't think one can both saddle her with the responsibilities of traditional womanhood and ask her to be a Prime Minister in the world. I think that those are incommensurable categories.

MOYERS: Do you think she's acting like a man?

KELLER: She's acting like a traditional, stereotypic man, yes. She has the right to act like a stereotypic man, just as I want to defend the right of men to act like stereotypic women. I want to break down these boundaries.

MOYERS: Who first interested you in science?

KELLER: The long and short of it is that I read a series of books by George Gamow for a composition class because I had to find something I could write a decent paper on. That was what turned me. Many people were encouraging me very strongly to go into science, but it was George Gamow's books that turned me around. I fell in love with physics.

MOYERS: You fell in love? That's a romantic notion.

KELLER: Yes. It was an appropriate notion. I fell in love with the life of the mind. It was a very compelling vision for me. But my career in physics was thwarted by my being a woman, in very conspicuous ways.

MOYERS: Do you know why?

KELLER: I was a graduate student in physics at Harvard in 1959, and that was extremely painful—in effect, it was impossible. I was one of three women in a class of a hundred. I could not get my professors to speak to me. I was scrutinized, laughed at, and humiliated. I came with a reputation of being very smart and so I was an object of enormous curiosity. It was terrible. And very lonely. I couldn't take it. I did actually get my degree in theoretical physics, but only after leaving the actual premises to do my dissertation on molecular biology. Finally, it was teaching my first women's studies course in 1974 that provided the occasion for me to talk about my experiences as a graduate student at Harvard. It had been so painful, and my efforts to talk about it at the time were met with such condemnation and dismissal, that I didn't try again until I was teaching in the State University of New York at Purchase. It became clear to me that it was important for women of my generation who had lived through this kind of experience to say what had gone on. To get it out in the open could serve a political function. I was prevailed upon by my students and colleagues to write that story, which I ultimately published in a book called *Working It Out.*

MOYERS: Your search invites many more ways of seeing the world. Is that popular in the scientific establishment?

I am advocating a pluralistic vision. . . . It stands to reason that different perspectives would be very productive, and would suggest other possibilities and other options. They would give us choices.

KELLER: I am advocating a pluralistic vision. I am trying to argue for more tolerance in the scientific community, and that's not popular because it's not seen as efficient. But I think it's just a simple, elementary, logical observation that the phenomena of the natural world are infinitely more complex, are infinitely larger in density and in number than any series of propositions we can articulate. The phenomenology of nature is infinitely more vast than anything that can be encompassed by our theoretical apparatus. Our theoretical representations are of a much lower dimensionality than the phenomena in nature. So there's no way in which any theory can fully encompass that rich array of phenomena. It stands to reason that different perspectives would be very productive, and would suggest other possibilities and other options. They would give us choices.

MOYERS: A more creative way of seeing the world. Or exploring the world.

KELLER: Or of seeing what we are exploring. Yes. Or considering the directions in which our explorations are taking us.

MOYERS: In your early work as a scientist you said you believed in the accessibility of an underlying and unifying truth and that you fully accepted science and scientists as arbiters of the truth. Do you still believe that there is an underlying and unifying truth?

KELLER: No. I like to think of that as the Truth. I believe in truths, but I don't believe in the Truth. Furthermore, I think that vision of an underlying Truth, with a capital *T*, that scientists are privy to, has been a very counterproductive vision. It has served scientists very well, but what it has done, above all, is enclose the world of science and immunize it from criticism. It has created a kind of insularity which protects the scientific world from the critical examination that I think is very necessary. Most of all, it insulates the scientific community from any examination of the recognition that we are making choices—any examination of the directions in which scientific inquiry is taking us. I think that it's absolutely essential that we engage in such examination.

MOYERS: What is your starting point now for your inquiry into the nature of this world?

KELLER: What I'm engaged in is the very difficult problem of trying to find a way of thinking and talking about science that does justice both to the cultural forces that give rise to it and the forces of nature with which science is engaging. To try and find a way of talking about science that both recognizes the force of language and also recognizes that theories do work.

Some theories *do* work. What does it mean to say a theory works? How are we going to account for the extraordinary success of scientific predictions—these extraordinary confirmations to thirteen decimal places between experiment and theory—without invoking this very counterproductive and sometimes even dangerous metaphor of science as a mirror of nature? How are we to redescribe it in terms of the negotiation between the language of theory and the experimental phenomena with which we engage? That's the task at hand.

MOYERS: So you still have a romance with science even though you've fallen out of love with physics.

KELLER: I wouldn't even say I've fallen out of love with physics. It's one of the most wonderful human endeavors that has ever been. I think it's marvelous. I want to see it better. It's a deeply satisfying inquiry into reality. I don't know if it's deeper than other kinds of inquiry, but it does seem to me capable of generating more stable accounts of phenomena. More reliable accounts that more of us could agree on if we were given the right place to stand.

Richard Rodriguez
W R I T E R

© 1990 Kate Kunz

Richard Rodriguez, the child of Mexican immigrants, calls himself "a comic victim of two cultures." He started school speaking nothing but Spanish, and now argues for education in nothing but English. In his memoir *Hunger of Memory*, he explores the paradox of the melting pot: that taking America for his own meant losing Mexico and his family.

MOYERS: You call your new book *Mexico's Children*. But it's not about Mexico.

RODRIGUEZ: Well, it's a book about California. And to live in California, as indeed to live in the Southwest, is to live in a land that was first Mexico and then America. It's a land populated by holy ghosts. Now America has always imagined itself coming upon an empty land, or at least a virgin land, but in fact there were other people here.

So in a way I'm a kind of betrayer of Mexico, I who have come here to the United States and who have in some way put Mexico away. In some way I've always been haunted by the fact that this *was* Mexico. That the land under my feet belonged to that place I thought my parents had escaped.

MOYERS: Do you live in that world? Do you keep one foot in that old world of Mexico?

RODRIGUEZ: The Mexican-American identity has always been a struggle between desire and memory. The culture of memory is Mexico, the culture of the past. The insistence that you are related to ancestors. The insistence that you belong to a community, as opposed to the American assurance that you can stand on your own, that you are new, that you, Richard Rodriguez, are your own man. That America gives you the freedom to become anything you want.

MOYERS: The America I think of is the America that says, put your roots behind you. Don't hold on to them. What gives one identity is not one's memory of one's grandparents, but one's opportunity to create for one's grandchildren a new world. And yet there is this paradox that people want to hold onto roots, even as they forge into the future.

RODRIGUEZ: The Mexican in the United States is unique for coming such a short distance. For literally falling within the echoing shadow of the mother. Most Mexican-Americans, and there are something like 12 million of us now, live within two or three hours of the mother country. It's an extraordinarily different experience of immigration than most other Americans have. There is not this sense of cutting. We also come from a nation that tells us in some way that we are always Mexican. We will never lose it. This is the home country.

MOYERS: But is that really so? Can one be Mexican *and* American, or mustn't you be one or the other? Isn't the hyphen a kind of illusion?

RODRIGUEZ: I think it's an illusion. But of course I have a lot of critics who tell me that I'm wrong. I think that in some way I've become more American than Mexican. I drifted away from a certain culture toward another culture. The culture of America has moved me toward a certain optimism, toward a certain comic assurance, toward a certain energy, toward a certain Protestantism, toward a certain assurance that I am not my father. And in that sense I have become more American than Mexican.

Frankly, I don't know what it means to be bicultural. The tensions within my own soul between Mexico and the United States, between what I call comedy and tragedy, between the tragic demands of Mexico and the comic assurances of America, are such that I always felt that I would betray one by admitting to the other.

MOYERS: What do you mean? What's tragic about Mexico?

RODRIGUEZ: Mexico is a tragic country for lots of reasons. There is a sadness in Mexico that I think is deeper than its history, although its history is certainly tragic. The country was invaded again and again and again. Raped. Its leaders betrayed the people. One generation of poverty is following on another. The deepest tragedy of Mexico is Indian and Spanish both, this strange mixture of pessimism in the culture. There is the extraordinary sadness of Spain. I mean go to a Mexican church one day if you want to see sorrow on the walls.

One day my father told me, a teenager, as we were polishing the blue DeSoto, that life is not easy. He said, "You think it will all happen to you." And I kept on telling him that nothing he knew in Mexico was going to happen to me. That Mexico had betrayed everything about him.

MOYERS: How did that happen?

RODRIGUEZ: He left Mexico during the last part of the revolution, when Catholic Mexico was undergoing an anti-Catholic persecution. His well-to-do uncle was hiding priests in cupboards and in closets as if it were Tudor England. My father remembers Mexicans fighting outside the door with knives in the dark, remembers this kind of mad display of violence in Mexico, remembers a priest swinging from a rope in a tree in Mexico. He never wanted to go back to that country. I say to him, "Do you not miss it? Do you not want to go back?" He says, "What is there to miss?"

MOYERS: So he's American.

RODRIGUEZ: He's American, but he is Mexican in the sense that he's a carrier of Mexico's tragic sense. He looks around America and he is not convinced of it. My father put his kids through college and achieved a two-story house and a big blue DeSoto and a stereo television combination. He has seen his daughters go off to junior proms and his sons go off in tuxedos. But if he heard you say, as many people have, "You've achieved so much in this country," my father would laugh at the illusion that he's achieved anything at all.

MOYERS: So he still has his Mexican soul.

RODRIGUEZ: Oh yes. After the earthquake in San Francisco recently, I saw an extraordinary interview on television. A woman was standing in the middle of what used to be her house in the Marina district of San Francisco and she said, "What I know now is that this house was nothing against the wind, that it was just wood. And that it would fall." I live in a rarefied San Francisco street of gentile houses where people remodel and remodel and remodel and live in this kind of pristine environment, and suddenly that voice came to me. That it is all—it's just wood in the wind. And it won't be there in time. That's a Mexican knowledge. It didn't come to me as an American knowledge.

MOYERS: But your father was wrong. America didn't destroy you.

RODRIGUEZ: It hasn't so far.

MOYERS: But what about America as a land of comic assurances?

RODRIGUEZ: I've remained a Roman Catholic, but I've always flirted with Protestantism. I remember as a young boy bicycling by the Fremont Presbyterian Church in Sacramento and hearing the Protestants sing. And I'd never heard singing like that. It was nothing like the sad Mexican songs, I'll tell you. These were people who knew where they were in the world. These were people who were standing upright. These were people who were facing God one to one. These were people who believed in Easter. I will tell you, that was not the reason we prayed to the sorrowful Virgin in my house. I mean we prayed in sorrow. We prayed out of the assurance that in fact man is helpless. We prayed in the knowledge that in fact on our own, we would drown. And suddenly these voices come pouring out of this California church, and I was entranced.

MOYERS: But what's comic about that assurance that you get out of the Protestant and American marriage?

RODRIGUEZ: You can be born again in this country. You can become a new man. You can even change your name. You can dye your hair. You can go to Muscle Beach and get a new body. You can become a billboard on Sunset Boulevard twenty feet tall with a beauty mark five feet tall. That's extraordinary. America is an enormously funny place. America is fifteen years old and America rides a skateboard and that guy who just went by us was Tom Paine. I mean America has that quality to it. It's a profoundly immature country, or it has been.

People always accuse me of having lost my culture, as though it was a little suitcase that I left in some train station back there. And I suppose I have, in the sense that I'm not my father. But that's inevitable I think. I belong to a different time. I belong to your culture.

MOYERS: What do you mean "my culture"?

RODRIGUEZ: That is to say, I'm an American. You know, I'm not a Mexican. I think of myself now as having been converted to America, and in that sense, I'm not a missionary from Mexico. The pity of America I think is always that we don't understand just how enormously seductive we are to the world. We always imagine ourselves as virgin, as somehow easily, easily upset by the foreigner. The American's inner phobia has always been that we are in this pristine place and these people are going to change us.

Well, in fact, America has been doing a lot of changing of the world these days. It is a culture. It is an idea. It is an advertisement. It's a lipstick. It's a Coke bottle. People always say, "Why did you choose to become American?" Well, James Farley, the British essayist who died recently, wrote an essay about coming to America from Britain. Just a few months after he'd come here he was walking down the street, and he saw a little kid of about four. The kid looked up to him and said, "Hi." And Farley fell in love with this culture, in which a child of four can say a remarkable American word, "hi," to an adult.

When I was a boy, in Sacramento, I remember a man saying hi to me. And that word came to me with such force, such informality against all the formal structure of Mexico, the *tu* and *usted*, the distinction between public and private, between formal and informal society. There was this Jeffersonian high that just came pouring at me. There was no way to resist it.

MOYERS: You said you chose to be an American. Did you really choose? Was there an option?

RODRIGUEZ: No, no, I didn't choose. It doesn't come to you as a choice. It comes to you, America comes to you.

MOYERS: You have grown up in America.

RODRIGUEZ: Absolutely. You learn it, you know, you learn it, just walking through the crowds. That energy, that ambition, that drive, that slouching American walk at intersections, the pace of traffic, the assertion of neon. These are not things you need to learn about in school. I mean you get the point of this country very early.

MOYERS: Do you feel lonely as an American? I ask that question because Ernest Cortes, whom you know, talked to me recently about how Americans are so atomized and alienated. It is not We the People, it is I versus the People. That's what's going to bring America down.

RODRIGUEZ: That also is what created America.

MOYERS: That's it, that's the paradox.

> *... what America gives the world is an "I," I the individual. The possibility that your father's ghost will not pursue you. That you can escape the civil wars of your ancestral village, that you can escape your ancestors, that you can escape all that ties you to the past.*

RODRIGUEZ: It's the brilliance of America. I think that there's a great sorrow in this country. I think it is decadent, on the other hand, for Americans not to realize the enormous privilege of that and the fragile gift of it. I mean what America gives the world is an "I," I the individual. The possibility that your father's ghost will not pursue you. That you can escape the civil wars of your ancestral village, that you can escape your ancestors, that you can escape all that ties you to the past. That you can begin anew. I was talking to a Mexican kid the other day in San Francisco. He's gay. He ran away from his home in Los Angeles and came to San Francisco, and the first thing somebody told him was that he should go to the Mission District, which is the Mexican part of town. He said, "That's the reason I'm here. I don't want to be in the Mission District. I don't want to be there. I want to be free. I want to be I." We mustn't forget the freedom and the extraordinary joy that comes with that.

MOYERS: This unbridled "I" that you talk about—the rampant individualism—doesn't it inflict great pain and suffering on Hispanics, Mexicans, other immigrants who are coming here used to a culture shared, not a culture separate?

RODRIGUEZ: Yes, they are pulverized by the extraordinary energy, the destructive qualities of the "I." But they are also romanced by that "I." Of course the history of the nineteenth century is the history of America's "I" gone bad. Yet the history of the nineteenth century is also the history of the great European migrations, where everybody also wanted to come.

MOYERS: What's the role of language in this?

RODRIGUEZ: The first thing I need to tell you is that, by all means, do not consider me a Mexican-American writer—because I don't know what that means. You should recognize that I'm a renegade, which is to say, I'm also a writer.

MOYERS: You're the ultimate "I" . . .

RODRIGUEZ: That's right. I'm not Mexican-American. I don't know what that means. I oppose very much the idea that there is a typical Mexican-American or Hispanic-American experience. I insist on the singularity of life experience.

What I insist also, however, as a writer is that you render the "I" fully. The more I indicate your story, and separate you from everyone else around you, the more this magic happens in literature. We begin somehow to share in that life. It's the most mysterious and paradoxical aspect of writing. The more you write about Richard Rodriguez—not his brother, who was more graceful, and who looked like Mario Lanza; not his sisters who looked Polynesian, and who floated in their own adolescent worlds—but Richard Rodriguez, the high-strung kid who read through the long Sacramento summers; Richard Rodriguez when he was twelve years old, in Sacramento, that afternoon. The more you specify him, the more you get these letters from people who will say, you know I'm five generations German-American; I know nothing of Mexican-Americans; but I'm you.

MOYERS: How can anybody establish a firm identity today?

RODRIGUEZ: People always ask me, "What do you think of yourself as?" And I say, "Well, I think of myself as an American." Then they ask, "What does that mean exactly?" "Well, I think of myself as Chinese," I say to them. Or, "I think of myself as Irish." I was educated by Irish immigrant nuns for my first eight years of schooling. A few years ago I was studying in England, and one weekend on a kind of lark, I decided to go to Ireland. I remember getting off the Aer Lingus plane in Dublin, and finding myself immediately—I mean, immediately—at home. I thought to myself, "This is odd that I should feel at home here in this culture." Then it occurred to me about two years later, that my closest friends have always been Irish Catholics.

What I'm trying to tell you is that kind of washing one soul against the other is not something we even decide upon. I've always thought that whites and blacks in the South are kin in a way that the rest of us in America cannot understand. You're all carrying on with each other in this kind of Masonic private language and you don't realize that the rest of us have no idea what you're talking about.

I don't mean to deny the cruelty, or the repression, or the vulgarity of the relationship. But I do insist that in some sense people create each other. People seated together on a bus are already exchanging some energy. And I say I'm Chinese in the sense that I live in San Francisco, the first mainline American city which is now Asian, and I am breathing it, I am tasting it. It is changing my life. Don't ask me what it means; I cannot tell you. But I know I'm becoming Chinese. I know that somehow my character is being changed. Do I want it? I don't even think that's the question. Is it happening? Yes.

MOYERS: There are some people whose pores are just open. They don't consciously push a lever . . . they just open to the world. And that may be what's happening for you.

RODRIGUEZ: It's America. People say to me all the time, "You're so anglicized."

Well, I'm not anglicized at all. I'm Americanized. I speak American English, I don't speak British English. Listen to this language that you and I are speaking. I have a California accent, with perhaps traces of Spanish; you have a Texas accent, with perhaps traces of Spanish.

There is no one in America who does not speak Black English; there is no one in America who does not speak Yiddish. There is no one in America who does not sigh with the sigh of Mexican grandmothers. It is an assimilationist language. It is an immigrant language, and in that sense, it's a world language— which is one of the reasons why it's such a vital language.

But we're creating somewhere between us this American tongue. It was something that was shoved down the throats of a lot of immigrant kids and it came up sounding very different. It has its own energies. There is no one in America who does not speak Black English; there is no one in America who does not sigh with the sigh of Mexican grandmothers. It is an assimilationist language. It is an immigrant language, and in that sense, it's a world language—which is one of the reasons why it's such a vital language.

MOYERS: Is that one of the reasons why you have opposed bilingual education? You've been roundly criticized for opposing bilingual teaching of Spanish in our schools.

RODRIGUEZ: I've opposed the ideological implications of bilingual education. Whenever people talk to me about using family language in the classroom, that's when I shudder. I don't think the classrooms are for family language. I think that by and large, what would have happened to me as a boy coming to a bilingual class, for example, is that I would have had to relearn Spanish. By and large, the Spanish of my home was family Spanish. The distinction between intimate private family language and public language is very severe for me. I don't like it when teachers start denying that distinction.

I acknowledge that teachers and parents should work together to get the child over that long border between the two worlds. But I think that border has to be maintained. I think those are separate worlds. When I hear educators talking about using family language in the classroom, what I want to say immediately is that there's no way that's possible. That there's no way family language exists in the classroom.

MOYERS: Because it's not a family, for one thing.

RODRIGUEZ: It's not a family. For children who have used that language as an intimate tongue, the illusion is that in fact a family is what's being given. And yes, you may get the student to feel less alienated by hearing Spanish. But the basic lesson of education will be postponed, perhaps denied, perhaps postponed forever. That is that education is a separation from family. It is a movement into another world.

When the Irish nun wrote my name on the board, "Richard Rodriguez," it was curious to me, because I'd never heard my name pronounced that way, I'd never seen it spelled. Then when she said to me, "Say it out to me," that was curious, too, because no one had ever asked me to say it in a public place. She said, "Speak it to all the boys and girls." Well, I simply wasn't able to do it. I didn't feel that I needed to speak to *you.* Do you understand what I mean? I was a minority, in the basic sense of that word. I didn't belong to your world. I didn't want you. I wanted to live with my grandmother, I wanted to live within Spanish, and here was this enormous Irish woman with this cross dangling from her breasts, saying that I had an obligation to speak to the boys and girls. I simply couldn't do it.

You know, when people talk to me today about why I don't want to acknowledge that I'm a minority, I think to myself of that boy. That boy was a minority. What he needed was not a linguistic breakthrough. It was a social breakthrough that he needed. He needed to believe that he had a relationship to that public space, that he belonged to public society, the majority.

MOYERS: And that has happened for you.

RODRIGUEZ: I remember a few years ago I was at this ludicrous literary conference in London, where mad Irish poets were going on and on about English as the oppressor's language. I thought to myself, "I don't feel that at all. English doesn't feel to me like the oppressor's language. It's my language. You gave it to me, you held it out to me, and I took it and I bit it and I licked it and I swallowed it and now it's mine. You can't have it back; you can't tell me, 'No, no, no, it was Spanish that was yours.' English is mine. I'm Caliban, I've taken your books, they're mine. I know what's in them now. You can't unwrite that. Your language is in fact mine. I've taken the thing that is closest to America's heart, and I've made it mine."

MOYERS: But the argument for the teaching of Spanish in a bilingual program is that it is a bridge, it's a facilitating bridge between the familiar world into the strange new world of America. Doesn't that have some appeal to you?

RODRIGUEZ: Not particularly. I've always liked the metaphor of the melting pot, not only because of the alchemy suggested by that, but also its violence in some way. I mean there was a radical remaking of Richard Rodriguez. Now, it came, in my case, with a certain trauma which I do not recommend to anybody else, but also I think with a certain clarity of vision about what the classroom was. I knew what it was about quite early. And I think I've never disregarded its value.

MOYERS: It was about remaking you?

RODRIGUEZ: It was about the public making of Richard Rodriguez, that's right. This voice speaks now not to boys and girls, but to ladies and gentlemen. I have this freedom, this enormous freedom to break out of what I call the minority culture. Now a lot of Hispanics hear that as a betrayal of my ethnic identity. I'm not even talking ethnicity, I'm talking something much more elemental. This is for me a much more private, in some sense a much more theological dimension. I don't think of ethnicity as tacos and serapes and weekend trips to Mexican resort towns. I think of ethnicity as having to do with my very soul and the nature of my relationship to my god. I've always thought of my Catholicism as somehow my Mexican side, and my difficulty with Mexico has also been my difficulty with the Catholic church.

MOYERS: But you see, so many people are making the point that it isn't a melting pot anymore, that if anything it's a mosaic. If it ever was a melting pot, it was a boiling cauldron in which a lot of people got hurt as well as transformed. The metaphor now is, it's a mosaic, many colors, many pieces, but one society.

RODRIGUEZ: It isn't that. America means that I don't know where I stop and you begin. I cannot predict in meeting you how I'm going to be changed. I can't decide it. It's risky to be an American, it's risky to live in San Francisco in the 1990s because I may become Chinese, I don't know. The idea that I'm a piece of glass in a mosaic, that that's an appropriate metaphor, denies the basic fluid experience of our lives. It doesn't feel that way to me. The soul is not this ice cube, it's not this piece of glass. The soul is, rather, water, the soul is something more movable. I think it's something that can be lost. In some sense I lost my soul in America, if you want to say it that radical way.

MOYERS: Explain that. You lost your soul?

RODRIGUEZ: I lost my Mexican soul in America. I was enchanted by Lucille Ball and by Walt Disney and by Technicolor and by the enchantments of this culture. And by the Protestant singing at the Presbyterian church. And I didn't want Mexico. In some way I'm terrified of Mexico.

MOYERS: Do you think the soul of Mexico still has something to teach America?

RODRIGUEZ: Oh, indeed. I think as America ages, for example, and as we get slower and our eyesight gives way, we are going to learn of necessity the lessons of Mexico. That life is not all youth. That life is not all new beginnings. We're going to miss the consolation of continuity. We are going to feel alone in this city.

In some way, the environmental movement's insistence on considering the global "we" is really the desperate cry of America at the other end of maturity, telling the premodern nations, "Don't come this way." Literally, don't do what we did to the plains. Don't do what we did to the forests. Don't do what we did to our birds and to our lakes. Save the forest. Save the sky. I think that we may have the irony of ironies. America's destiny was once to play a kind of piper to the children of the world. We may become the old men of the world, the old prophets warning people away from eternity.

MOYERS: That is the Indian in you speaking. That is the Mexican in you speaking.

RODRIGUEZ: Oh yes. But you see, that isn't exactly what the Hispanics want me to say. They want me to be better. They want me to be Jesse Jackson. They want me to talk about how we want to get jobs in the city and how we want to get better housing and how we want to be proud of Spanish and we have a contribution to make in this society. We want to be one of the stones in the mosaic.

MOYERS: You do want those things.

RODRIGUEZ: Yes, but that's not primarily how I see myself. I see myself as a much more subversive, a much dreamier sort of person. I was a very sad child. I was a very melancholy child. I was a child much like a fat girl with bad acne. I mean I read a great deal. And that's who I am. I've lived by myself a long time. I like long summers. I used to read with little old men who had green visors in the library in

Sacramento, and they would read faded newspapers from Detroit and from Philadelphia. And I would read these extraordinary novels. I wanted to know about Texas. I wanted to know about where you were. I wanted to be Texan.

One day I remember I read William Saroyan and I found out that I was Armenian! I'd never known that I was Armenian. And then I read James Baldwin, who had written this book of essays called *Nobody Knows My Name*. It was the first time I read Baldwin. I found out that I was black. No one had told me that I was black. I did not read Mark Twain until I was in high school, because I thought he wrote kids' books. And I wanted to read adult books when I was a kid because I was so precocious. But one American summer this Mexican kid read Huck Finn and I almost gave up. I was trailing Huck and I couldn't follow the dialect, and then Jim came in, and I couldn't follow that. And I was losing my footing on the levee and suddenly, somewhere in the middle of that book, I caught sight of the river. And that river is America and it is mine.

One of the things I deeply resent about the ethnic movement in America in the last few years is that it has denied me the possibility of being Irish, of being Chinese. I want to be more myself. I've always wanted that.

MOYERS: But you're talking about the imagination and ethnicity is a matter of fact. It is a matter of birth, inheritance, place.

RODRIGUEZ: Writers are always rebels against imagination. I'm always wondering what the woman feels as she's giving birth to the child. I'm always wondering what that moment is like on the other side of death. I've always wanted to know what the insides of great hotels were like. So the first time I had any money I went off to New York and stayed at the Carlyle Hotel. There was Bobby Short singing black music to this upper-class white audience. And I thought, "This is heaven. I have trespassed the boundary. I've gone to a foreign country."

MOYERS: You always wanted to be where you weren't, and wanted what you didn't have. That's very American.

RODRIGUEZ: Very American, and I think rebellious the way writers are rebellious. We're not nice people. But what I really fear is that Americans are afraid of themselves and are afraid of each other, and that we are really going to retrench in the next few years. We are going to use ethnicity not for the celebration of the mosaic, which it never was, but rather the old xenophobic assertion that we are separate, each discrete editors in this country. We are not discrete editors. I am your brother. I married you. You are my cousin. I have a niece who looks just like you. I have a brother-in-law with your surname. I'm your next-door neighbor. I am you. And in that sense I think that America is going to have to finally come to terms with the fact that it's not longer quite as Protestant as it used to be, with a sense of individuality. But also I think it has to realize that there are lots of people who have come precisely for that individuality and for that Protestant inheritance. And we are Chinese and Mexicans.

I was on the list at the American embassy speaker's bureau when I was studying in England. They would get requests from people who wanted a Yank to come out and speak, so I'd always go out to one of these Rotary societies in one of these small towns in England. We would sit around the pub beforehand and they would always be waiting for the Yank to arrive. I was there. But they always imagined that somehow the Yank was some astronaut, you know, he was crew cut, he was blond, and so forth and so on. I am a Yank. I am the American. And it's going to take some time to get used to that idea that Americans look like me.

FACING
EACH OTHER

The philosopher Arthur Schopenhauer tells how on one very cold day, several porcupines huddled close together for warmth. Because their spines made proximity uncomfortable, they spread out again and grew cold. After shuffling in and out for some time, they eventually found a distance at which they could warm each other without getting pricked. This distance they thenceforth called decency and good manners.

Moral: It's hard for porcupines and humans alike to live with one another; decency and good manners may seem the very least we owe each other. Yet those humble virtues are also the very foundation of many of our systems of values and ethics, our theologies and philosophies of life. They address a fundamental question: How can we treat with dignity the people with whom we share this earth?

Love, says M. F. K. Fisher, is one of the basic human needs. Throughout her long life she has enjoyed—and explored in elegant prose—a myriad of the ties that bind man and woman, traveler and native, parent and child, guest and host, husband and wife, sister and brother, the sick and the hale, the young and the old. Along the way, she says, she learned to love not unquestioningly but completely. "The best thing I can think of," she says, "is to live with somebody and go through thick and thin together and then come out the end and have good years of love and whatever is left."

Sometimes it is spiritual love that informs our relationships with and our responsibilities for others, even among people who profess no religion. Cornel West—professor, preacher, and philosopher—finds powerful and universal messages in the traditions of the black church. He often leaves the ivory tower to tell high school students in our inner cities: "The value of service to others, the value of caring for others, the value of attempting to keep one's eye on the forms of social misery, inadequate housing, health care, child care, unemployment, and underemployment—religion has no monopoly on these kinds of values. Religion may help motivate persons to act on these values in light of the stories within their traditions, but neither Christians nor Jews nor Muslims nor Hindus have a monopoly on this."

Nor on wisdom. In this increasingly global culture, many of us are enhancing our own spiritual experience with insights from other traditions. When Tu Wei-ming came to the United States from China, he told himself he would be willing to change his conception of the Confucian way of life if he learned anything "more viable, more persuasive, more in keeping with my experience as a modern human being in a different environment." Yet after much questioning and doubt Tu found that life in the United States enabled him better to appreciate his own tradition. All religions "ask the ultimate question. They are not satisfied with our living as ordinary human beings. They want us to be more, and in fact, we want to be more."

Ethics also is about being more—to other people. When Joanne Ciulla tells people that she teaches business ethics, they often respond: "Isn't that a contradiction in terms?" Yet Ciulla believes that ethics in business is no different from ethics in daily life. "I don't sit around telling my students that you should be honest and fair and just. That would be a fairly silly course. The point is, how are you honest in a variety of business contexts? What does honesty mean in the sales department? Does honesty mean you tell them every single thing about that product?" The main point of business ethics, says Ciulla, is "trying to help people to understand how moral behavior can function in the complex business environment in which we now operate."

Ruth Macklin, too, grapples with the practical application of ethical principles to everyday life—and death. As a bioethicist at a large New York hospital, she helps doctors, medical students, patients, and families to make intelligent decisions when the intellect is often battling the heart and soul. Ethical agreement is not always possible. On the tormenting issue of abortion, for instance, Macklin believes we are incapable of consensus. The danger is therefore real that decisions that should be based on moral principle will be made politically—for expedient rather than ethical reasons. "The difference between ethics and politics is that if there's an ethical right answer," says Macklin, "that right answer doesn't change from 1973 to 1990. If abortion was not legal before 1973 and was legally available after 1973, it surely does not mean abortion was ethically wrong before 1973 and became ethically right after 1973."

Given the demands of daily life, of getting through our days intact, simple decency can be a herculean life. I am constantly amazed to discover how many people I meet every day—including the people with whom I work—are the sons and daughters of Hercules, living up to the legend.

M. F. K. Fisher

ESSAYIST

Mary Frances Kennedy Fisher long has said that two things came naturally to her: cooking and writing. Now eighty-two, she has written more than twenty books and countless articles for *The New Yorker*. Her subjects are our three basic needs—food, security, and love—and how they intermingle. *Serve It Forth*, *The Gastronomical Me*, and *With Bold Knife and Fork*—to name but a few—are enduring works that display Fisher's distinctive views on taste and cuisine. Her forays into fiction—my favorite is the acclaimed book of short stories about aging, *Sister Age*—further attest to her literary powers and zest for living. She lives in Sonoma, California, where she is working on a book about the town of Dijon in France.

MOYERS: Sister Age has come to live with you. Is she what you thought she'd be?

FISHER: Well, she's still a good friend. Still a sister, I think. There are some things about aging that I don't like, but I think I'd rather be old than young. I can get away with more. Say more what I want to say and less of what I think people want to hear.

MOYERS: Here in the afterword of *Sister Age*, you write, "I notice that as I get rid of the protective covering of the middle years, I am more openly amused and incautious and less careful socially, and that all this makes for increasingly pleasant contacts with the world." We do indeed have that "protective covering of the middle years." Why do you suppose that is?

FISHER: I think we hide from a lot of things in the middle years that we're not conscious of hiding from at all until we get older and find that we've been hiding. You have to call on your own when you get older. In the middle years, you take on the protective coloration of your environment. But when you get old, you choose your own environment more and you choose your own friends more.

MOYERS: Did you choose this environment of central California? Did you come here because this is where you thought you wanted to grow old?

FISHER: No, I didn't want to grow old anyplace. I never thought of growing old. I don't think I've grown old. I've gotten older, but I've not grown very much. I haven't developed very much.

MOYERS: You seem to have thought about aging very early. You wrote even before you were thirty that there are two things we must do. We must grow old, and we must eat.

FISHER: I do believe that. I've always liked older people. I've always been interested in them. I think one of the main troubles about modern life is that the older people do not live with the younger people anymore. When I was a child, we had a big house, and my grandmother lived with us.

MOYERS: And that was important to you?

FISHER: She was a very Christian woman. I was not very Christian, ever. And she was a very severe woman. She was a rabid

Irish Protestant. I guess they're really all rabid. She never talked to Catholics, she always spoke with horror of Rome. She had terrible prejudices.

MOYERS: And yet it was still a good thing to live in the same house with her?

FISHER: Yes, it was very good for us because we had better manners when Grandmother was around. She demanded them and she got them. We had one set of manners for Grandmother, one set when she was gone. We always ate nicely at the table. Grandmother believed children should be seen and not heard, you know, except she heard me all the time reading. She taught me to read. I liked her very much but I wondered why I didn't love her.

MOYERS: Have you figured out the answer to that?

FISHER: She wasn't a very lovable person. But she was my protection. I liked her like a tree or something, she was just part of my life like a tree or a bush or something.

I admired her very much, and Mother admired her too, even though she didn't like Mother at all. Mother was an afterthought. In those days of Irish Protestantism and the Victorian Age, women had childbearing years, then they had to give up all that nonsense and they embraced the Church. Grandmother embraced the Church and then, bang, she had Mother many months later. So she resented her very much. Mother had a miserable childhood, I think. She loved her father, but her brothers were older than she. They teased her; so we never teased at home.

MOYERS: Was your home a happy place?

FISHER: Oh, very happy. I was very happy. Of course I was miserable about being the patsy for years. I was the oldest child, but I never got any privileges because my next youngest sister was the invalid of the family. She knew how to get all the attention and I didn't get any. So I would cook. I was always the cook on the cook's day off. And then I realized that I was being a patsy to get the admiration—I loved it. I wanted to get something away from my sister. So I would cook meals. I learned how to cook when I was very young.

MOYERS: Look what came of it. A lifelong art.

FISHER: Well, people ask me why I wrote about food. I think I wrote about everything all my life. I've always been a writer, but I eventually found I could earn some money by it. I supported the family for years. The only way I made money was from my magazine articles, not my books. I think I was twenty-three when I published the first thing for money.

But I never think of myself as a writer. I'm a journalist, a fifth-generation newspaper person. Father was a newspaper editor, a small-town newspaper editor, but he never thought of himself as a writer either. He wrote two thousand words a day for sixty years of his life, but he never used a byline. So when I used a byline, I hid it from my father for years. I was embarrassed by it.

MOYERS: Was it hard to make a living writing in those days? If I remember correctly, one year you made only thirty-seven dollars writing.

FISHER: Yes, I did. I had an agent then who didn't want me to be a best-seller. I could have been, but I would never have amounted to much.

MOYERS: Why?

FISHER: Well, I would probably have made a lot of money and then I would have gone back to newspaper work. But as it is, I've been a free-lancer most of my life. I was under contract once to five magazines, for once-a-month stuff. It was when my children were little. At that point I had divorced their father, and I was paying his alimony for two other wives. And I needed money badly. So I went under contract to five magazines at once. I wouldn't ever do that again.

MOYERS: But you never stopped writing after that.

FISHER: No, I write naturally. Just have to write.

MOYERS: An early compulsion?

FISHER: I think so, but I don't think I'm a real writer because I've not grown any. I think, well, now my books sell. The first books I published sell just as well now as they did then. Better, maybe.

MOYERS: Don't tell me this isn't growing. You're talking about moments of wisdom. "Once, I was lying with my head back, listening to a long program of radio music from New York, with Toscanini drawing fine blood from his gang. I was hardly conscious of the sound—with my mind, anyway—and when it ended, my two ears, which I had never thought of as cup-like, were so full of silent tears that as I sat up they drenched and darkened my whole front with little gouts of brine. I felt amazed, beyond my embarrassment in a group of near-friends, for the music I had heard was not the kind I thought I liked, and the salty water had rolled down from my half-closed eyes like October rain, with no sting to it but perhaps promising a good winter."

FISHER: Well, that's good. It's okay. But I don't think that's really writing. I just did it, you know.

MOYERS: No, I don't understand.

FISHER: Well, I said it; I didn't write it. I said it to myself. Then I just put it on paper. I've never rewritten it.

MOYERS: Even the metaphor of tears just came to you? You didn't have to sit at the desk and make it work for you?

FISHER: No.

MOYERS: And this: "Such things are, I repeat to myself, fortunately rare, for they are too mysterious to accept with equanimity. I prefer not to dig too much into their comings, but it is sure that they cannot be evoked or foretold. If anger has a part in time, it is latent, indirect—not an incentive. The helpless weeping and sobbing and retching that sweeps over somebody who inadvertently hears Churchill's voice rallying Englishmen to protect their shores, or Roosevelt telling people not to be afraid of fear, or a civil rights chieftain saying politely that there is such a thing as democracy—those violent, physical reactions are proof of one's being alive and aware. But the slow, large tears that spill from the eye, flowing like unblown rain according to the laws of gravity and desolation—these are the real tears, I think. They are the ones that have been simmered, boiled, sieved, filtered past all anger and into the realm of acceptive serenity."

FISHER: That's true, but I never heard it before. What is that from?

MOYERS: It's from "Moments of Wisdom," your opening chapter in *Sister Age.* You don't recognize it?

FISHER: I don't. I never read anything I write after I think it. I write in sentences and paragraphs and even chapters. So maybe I'm crazy, a phenomenon or something.

MOYERS: That's what they said of Mozart. He wrote down what he heard, and he often didn't know what he was writing down, or what he had heard. You've never gone back to your own sixteen, seventeen books?

FISHER: No, never. I wouldn't want to; I'd be embarrassed. Once I did get one of my grandsons to read me a chapter from my book *A Cordiall Water*. I think it's the best thing I've written. It's just old recipes and old receipts I found. How to cure warts and stuff like that. I wrote it when I had not read or spoken English for a long time so it's quite pure. But when my grandson read it all I can remember is that within two sentences there was a mistake, one misuse of a word. If I said it now I would not have said it that way. It was perfectly correct, you know, but I didn't like it.

MOYERS: You once wrote that women have an inner language that is peculiarly their own. Do you still think that's true?

FISHER: Yes, I do. Often they don't express it, though. They understand it, but they don't express it. Yes, I do think there's an entente between women. There's an entente between men, too, that women never understand. *You* could be with a man and you'd understand something about him that I could never get.

> *I like men very much. I think I would rather be with women, though, than men. I think men are less interesting than women in general. They're more limited. They don't feel the same pain. They don't have the same endurance.*

MOYERS: I agree with that, and yet I think many of my best friends are women.

FISHER: I like men very much. I think I would rather be with women, though, than men. I think men are less interesting than women in general. They're more limited. They don't feel the same pain. They don't have the same endurance. They don't know the same things women know. I don't think pleasure is real to most men. Do you?

MOYERS: I'm afraid we live too much in worlds that have been constructed for us and organizations that we didn't create. I grew up thinking that I had to succeed out there in a world I didn't make.

FISHER: You had to take care of people.

MOYERS: Well, men don't necessarily take care of people. They provide for them. I think the women take care of people. I don't somehow think of men as "civilizing"— to use your term.

FISHER: I don't think they are. Unfortunately, women will always kowtow to men.

MOYERS: Why?

FISHER: I don't know. I hate it. I hate the subservience of women to men. One reason women are in such a mess now is because of men in politics, for instance, but women are terrible politicians. Most women become strident, you know. They raise their voices. I don't like that.

Now, my mother and father were different. I realize now that we believed in equal rights and fair play and money for both people. Mother just happened to choose to raise us rather than work. Twice she got ready to get a job, I remember. Once Father was going into the First World War, and Mother practiced being editor of his paper. I don't know what it would have done to us, but then Father was turned down for the army. He was horrified, because he always wanted to wear a uniform.

MOYERS: Well, that's a difference, you know. Men do feel the empowerment of the uniform, and I don't know many little girls who do.

FISHER: Oh, he would have hated it, you know, he just would have loathed it, but he wanted to wear a uniform. Back during the Spanish-American War he ran away for Theodore Roosevelt. He became a Rough Rider. His father went down and nabbed him off the decks of the ship to Cuba. He lied about his age; he was not yet eighteen, you see. So he never did make it. And his son didn't make it either. His son said he never would wear a uniform. Never. He never did. His only son killed himself. Which was terrible for Father, and Mother, too. He was their last child, you see.

MOYERS: Your brother?

FISHER: Yes, my brother, David. He killed himself the night before he was to go into the Army for World War II. He was just passionate about not wearing a uniform for any country, any man. It absolutely ruined my father and mother. So I'm very bitter about it in a way. I don't really blame David because I've always believed in suicide. You know, my second husband Timmy killed himself, and I don't think he was unjustified. But it was unjustified in David's case because you never know what waves will spread out.

MOYERS: The unintended victims of a suicide—the survivors—carry the pain.

FISHER: It's terrible. It did awful things to my father and mother because we thought they'd have a wonderful old age together. They had been married almost fifty

years and they were mellowing beautifully, and they were more and more compatible, more congenial all the time. They'd gone through lots of thin and thick. Mostly thin, pretty thin times, I'm sure. And so we thought they'd have a wonderful old age together, but it drew them apart instead of together.

MOYERS: You said your second husband killed himself justifiably.

FISHER: He had Buerger's disease. He and the King of England were the only people we knew of who had it at the time. There were thirty-seven identified cases in the whole world. It was quite a rare thing, like a cancer of the blood.

MOYERS: Did he take his life because he was so ill?

FISHER: Oh yes. He was doomed. He had a wonderful heart, a very strong heart, that kept beating. His mother had it, and he had it. So this heart would have gone on beating until he was a basket case, which he would have been.

MOYERS: And he was in pain?

FISHER: Terrible pain.

MOYERS: Did you know he was going to take his life?

FISHER: Oh yes, sure.

MOYERS: Did you agree to it?

FISHER: Yes, I did. It was still a shock, though. I kept him from killing himself once, and then I said never again, I never would do that to anybody again. I held him back from jumping off a bridge. He couldn't help himself, though, he was insane with pain. So I think there was justification there. But most suicides are basically selfish.

MOYERS: How did you appease your grief?

FISHER: I never did, I guess. I just went with it. I didn't show it to anybody much, though. Timmy and I lived on an isolated place out in the desert. Everybody said, "Now, you must go to work, you mustn't stay here alone." And I thought, Why not? I have everything I need here, including my dog. One night about ten o'clock I said to Butch, my dog, "Now, Butch, you please turn off the radio." And I got a job the next day. I realized I'd just gone over the edge. Talked to my dog as though he could turn off the radio.

MOYERS: Just from reading your stories I've the sense that Timmy, your second husband, was your only true love.

FISHER: Well, not my only. I've loved many people. Really loved them, too. But he was the real one for me. I fell in love with him the first time I saw him, I think, or the second. I knew then it was hopeless, but it hadn't occurred to me yet to get a divorce or anything.

MOYERS: You've lived single for forty years now. Is that by choice?

FISHER: Well, I haven't been single, I've had several good affairs. But I like to be alone. I don't believe in marriage much. I think it's silly.

MOYERS: Now, you've got to explain that. Too many of us are married to be silly.

FISHER: The best thing I can think of is to live with somebody and go through thick and thin together and then come out the end and have good years of love and whatever is left.

MOYERS: So is marriage just a device? Just a form?

FISHER: Largely, now, I think. It doesn't keep enough people together. It's too easy to get a divorce. But I don't know, I'm a poor one to talk about it, I think. I've had three marriages, three good ones, too. I loved the men dearly. Always loved them dearly.

MOYERS: But you left your first husband.

FISHER: Yes, I did, because I fell in love with the second one. You see, I knew I couldn't lie; I had to get a divorce. But I never could do it until I found that Timmy loved me, too. Then I thought, "Well, pooh." I wasn't really in love with Al the way I was with Timmy.

My third husband and I should have never married, but I got from him two wonderful children. He didn't want any kids at all. He was horrified at the idea of one child. But he settled for one. And then two—my God, that was shocking. He'd been a single child, you see. His idea of children was the little boy who came in the room and said, *"Bonjour, Maman. Bonjour, Papa."* You'd kiss him on the forehead, and he left and never saw his parents again. He was raised by governesses and nurses and by nannies and by tutors.

MOYERS: You raised your two daughters by yourself. Would you have liked to have had some help?

FISHER: It was easier to raise them alone than to raise them and a man, too, you know?

MOYERS: You wrote once about the seasons of life. What was the finest season of your life?

FISHER: Well, I think when I was with Timmy. I was with him for seven years, though we weren't married for that whole time.

MOYERS: What made it so good?

> *I don't love unquestioningly, but I do love completely. And I think I learned a lot of that from Timmy Parrish. He taught me how to love because he knew we wouldn't be married very long.*

FISHER: Well, he was just right. I don't love unquestioningly, but I do love completely. And I think I learned a lot of that from Timmy Parrish. He taught me how to love because he knew we wouldn't be married very long.

MOYERS: When you were married were you aware that he was ill?

FISHER: No. But we learned soon after. And the last few years of his life we knew.

MOYERS: You've had so much independence in your life. Has it been hard to give up that independence with the coming of age?

FISHER: Oh well, there's some things I don't like about it. I think giving up driving a car was the worst because I started driving when I was ten years old. By eleven I was taking the whole family to the beach. But driving was different in those days, thank God.

MOYERS: What else have you had to stop doing?

FISHER: Well lately, I don't write anymore. I can't write with my hands. I dictate.

MOYERS: Somebody once asked de Gaulle if he feared anything. And he said, "I fear only one thing. The shipwreck of old age."

FISHER: Well, he was not shipwrecked. I don't think it's a shipwreck at all.

MOYERS: But when I think about having to give up driving, when I think about wheelchairs and failing hearts and arthritic joints and all of that, I think of the southern French wine that you used to write about; it peaked very slowly and then decayed very quickly. And sometimes I wish life were like that. That we peaked slowly and then we were gone instead of waiting around.

FISHER: So do I. I don't think it's worth living, but I do live. So I'm alive. So I make the best of it. I would have died twenty years ago if somebody had shown me this recent picture of me with, you know, pouches and bags, and stuff. I don't like those things. They're not very pretty, but I'm me.

MOYERS: You wrote once about an older woman who was "past vanity." Do any of us ever get "past vanity"?

FISHER: Oh yes. Although I don't think I ever was vain, so I didn't need to go past it. I've never really thought of myself as beautiful at all. I never thought one way or another about it until later. I had the kids when I was quite old, you see. And when Anne was almost seventeen, we went to Aix-en-Provence, and there was a young Englishman who was in love with her. One day I was sitting there and he said, "Your mother must have had lovely gams once." And I thought, Lovely gams once, what does that mean? It meant that when I was younger I must have had good legs. Now my legs were pretty much all right then, but they were gone for him forever, because I was too old to have them. I was thinking about that the other day. They're the same old legs. I never thought about it, never thought I had pretty legs, but I guess I did once.

MOYERS: You wrote once that our basic needs are food, security, and love. Would you add anything to that now that you're in your eighties?

FISHER: Well, in order to exist, you have to be warm and fed and protected by other people, which means love; and you're also protective to other people, you feed other people first usually and keep them alive. And security is the place where you can hide your head, go to bed with somebody you love. Well, there you are.

MOYERS: You write of one of your characters, "She does not need anything that is not already in her." I like that.

FISHER: Yes, I don't think any of us needs more than that. I have just enough, I think. I'm very fortunate, because I've always known more than many people do. Some people were born dumb. I wasn't born dumb.

MOYERS: What you seem to have done is to store up almost everything you ever experienced.

FISHER: Well, maybe that's stupid.

MOYERS: No, it's paid handsome dividends in terms of the richness of your writing, your memory. I mean, there is joy in your books, even when there is sadness. The tears of wisdom commingling with the joy. In a wonderful scene in *Sister Age*, you're a little girl in the house outside of Whittier, and a Bible salesman comes to the door.

FISHER: Yes, I remember that. That's the first time I cried for anybody but myself, I think. I was eleven or twelve then. The salesman knocked on the door, and he wanted to see Grandmother, who had died just a few days earlier. He stopped at the gate in the tangle, and plucked a rose, and at that moment tears fell—just fell out of my face. I didn't mean to cry at all.

MOYERS: What you called "the tears of new wisdom."

FISHER: I think I suddenly knew why he was old and tired and dusty, and I was so stupid, and Grandmother's gone, and I understood about a lot of things.

MOYERS: Did you ever try to give your daughters a certain treasure? Did you say to them, this is the right treasure to store?

FISHER: No, I don't think so. I just trusted them to find their own treasures. I'd say, well, I think this is good, or I think that's good, but I didn't say, "You should think that," ever. I don't think anyone should ever say that to anybody.

MOYERS: Did you finally do everything you wanted to do in life?

FISHER: I don't know. I think so. I think I never did enough, though.

MOYERS: You've traveled, you've loved, you've eaten, you've—

FISHER: Never enough, though.

MOYERS: A friend of mine said there's one question I want you to ask Ms. Fisher. What use are good wine and ripe tomatoes in the face of pain and evil in the world?

FISHER: Well, that's a silly question, I think. One has to live, you know. You can't just die from grief or anything. You don't die. You might as well eat well, have a good glass of wine, a good tomato. Better that than no wine and a bad tomato, or no crust of bread. Since we must live, we might as well live well. Don't you think?

Cornel West

CULTURAL CRITIC

To practice his unique brand of scholarship, Cornel West moves in many worlds. As an academic, he teaches religion and directs the Afro-American studies program at Princeton University. As an author, he has delved into subjects from liberation theology to postmodern architecture, from rap music to black politicians. As lay preacher, he can be found speaking to community groups and high school students and in the pulpits of various faiths.

MOYERS: You've been seen in some very unusual places for an intellectual: the storefronts and streets of Harlem, the shanty-towns of South Africa, one of the worst high schools in one of the worst districts in Brooklyn. Why? Those are so far from Princeton, so far from the ivory tower.

WEST: I understand the vocation of the intellectual as trying to turn easy answers into critical questions and putting those critical questions to people with power. The quest for truth, the quest for the good, the quest for the beautiful, all require us to let suffering speak, let victims be visible, and let social misery be put on the agenda of those with power. So to me, pursuing the life of the mind is inextricably linked with the struggle of those who have been dehumanized on the margins of society.

MOYERS: One black intellectual said you make him uncomfortable with your ease out there on the street.

WEST: Certainly I have tried, on the one hand, to uphold the discipline of the life of the mind, but on the other hand, to keep track of other people's humanity, their predicaments and plights. I want to empathize and sympathize with them the best that I possibly can.

MOYERS: Many Americans believe that a substantial portion of the black community in the inner cities is simply saying yes now to death, violence, and hate. What do you find when you go there?

WEST: I do find a lot of meaninglessness and hopelessness, but at the same time I find people who are struggling, trying to survive and thrive under excruciating conditions. So the question becomes: how does one attempt to transform this meaninglessness and hopelessness into a more effective kind of struggle and resistance? It's a very difficult task, but there are many highly courageous people, working people, ordinary people, who are trying to hold on to meaning and value in a society that revolves more and more around the market mentality, the market ethos that permeates almost every sphere of this society.

MOYERS: What does that ethos do to a community?

WEST: It makes it very difficult to hold on to nonmarket

values, such as commitment in relationships, solidarity, community, care, sacrifice, risk, and struggle. Market values encourage a preoccupation with the now, with the immediate.

MOYERS: The future is now.

WEST: That's exactly right. What that means then is people feel they no longer have to work or sacrifice. Why? Because the big money can be achieved right now. In the black community market activity is at its most pernicious and vicious right now in the drug industry. Young people want to make the easy buck now. In many ways they are mirroring what they see in society at large, what they see on Wall Street. It makes it very difficult for them to take, not only commitment and caring and sacrificing, but ultimately human life itself seriously. Profits become much more important than human life. What we see is a very coldhearted mean-spiritedness throughout these communities. I think again it reflects so much of our own culture and civilization. It's quite frightening.

MOYERS: You've been making a lot of speeches to young people in the high schools like those in Brooklyn, where the situation is fairly miserable. What do you say to those young people?

WEST: I tell them we live in a society that suffers from historical amnesia, and we find it very difficult to preserve the memory of those who have resisted and struggled over time for the ideals of freedom and democracy and equality. Then I provide some historical background of people who displayed this kind of courage in its highest form—people like Martin Luther King, Michael Harrington, Ida B. Wells Barnett, and other freedom fighters. Then I move up to the present and talk about how many of their parents and brothers and sisters in some way extend that kind of tradition. And I ask the kids: "Are you going to be part of this tradition? What's going to happen to this tradition? How can we keep it alive? How can we keep it vital and vibrant?"

MOYERS: You're suggesting that each one of them can matter, and yet they're living in communities where the institutions have broken down, where the family is fragmented; there's a kind of chaos all around them. Don't they need institutions that will nurture them? Institutions they can hold on to for the message of self-worth and self-determination to take hold?

WEST: Oh, very much so. In fact, when I talk about the historical leaders, I talk about the institutions that produced them—the families, the schools, the colleges, the churches, the synagogues, and the temples. It's true that many American families, neighborhoods, and associations are undergoing a kind of disintegration and decomposition, but it's not thorough. There are still some American families and some black families that are holding together. There are still some neighborhoods, black, white, brown, and Asian, that are holding together.

MOYERS: What do you tell them about how to signify?

WEST: They have to hope. They have to hold on to some notion that the future can be different if they sacrifice, if they fight, if they struggle. This is an old message. I learned this message in the black church years ago. I'm very much a product of a loving black family and a caring black church. And more than anything else, the church taught me the lesson of the cross. The only way to hope, to faith, to love, is through the blood. The cross is a symbol of the impossible possibility, to use Karl Barth's language, the impossible possibility of holding on to faith, hope, and love in the kind of world in which we live, the kind of world in which blood is in fact always flowing.

MOYERS: Once upon a time the church did provide that kind of lesson, it did provide that kind of community. But a poll I saw just recently said that in the black community, the church is less and less a part of the life of young people. Do you find that so?

WEST: The influence of the black church is declining as are churches around the country. But I do think that the message of the church remains relevant, even among those who are not Christians. The value of service to others, the value of caring for others, the value of attempting to keep one's eye on the forms of social misery, inadequate housing, health care, child care, unemployment, and underemployment—religion has no monopoly on these kinds of values. Religion may help motivate persons to act on these values in light of the stories within their traditions, but neither Christians nor Jews nor Muslims nor Hindus have a monopoly on this.

MOYERS: I've always been curious why so many blacks, when they were brought to this country, adopted Christianity, which was the religion that often defended the slavery that imprisoned them. How do you explain that?

WEST: I think large numbers of black people turned to Christianity for three basic reasons. The first had to do with issues of meaning and value. Black people arriving here 371 years ago had to come to terms with the absurd in the human condition in America, the place of enslavement.

MOYERS: So that image of the Exodus, of the slaves freeing themselves, was especially appealing to black slaves in America.

WEST: Yes. The God of history who sides with the oppressed and the exploited, a God who accents and affirms one's own humanity in a society that is attacking and assaulting black intelligence and black beauty and black moral character, namely white supremist ideology—this message spoke very deeply at the level of meaning and value. But Christianity is also important institutionally because black people appropriated primarily the left wing of the Reformation. The Baptists and the Methodists are much more democratically structured than the Catholics. The preachers are immediately accountable to the congregation, and the pew has access to leadership. Black humanity at the level of both leadership and followership could be accented.

Then I think there was also a political reason. Black people could engage in a form of critique of slavery, of Jim Crowism, of second-class citizenship, while holding on to the humanity of those whom they opposed. This is the great lesson of Martin Luther King, Jr., who is a product of this tradition.

MOYERS: We have opponents, but not enemies.

WEST: That's exactly right. Actually, the enemy is oppression and exploitation. It's legitimate to abhor and hate oppression and exploitation, but we cannot lose sight of the humanity of those who are perpetuating it. This is a very difficult and complex doctrine because it seems to promote a kind of a masochistic love of oppressor.

MOYERS: The negative side of religion was that it could breed apathy and compliance. Also, the black church could even became a haven for charismatic con men, as modern-day television is to some evangelists.

WEST: Sure. I think Karl Marx's critique of religion as an impotent form of protest against suffering has an element of truth. Religion has tended to legitimize and to undergird forms of oppression precisely because it provided a critique that remained spiritual and had very little understanding of the social and economic and political conditions that were sustaining the oppression. At its best, religion can provide us with the vision and the values, but it doesn't provide the analytical tools. One doesn't

> *At its best, religion can provide us with the vision and the values, but it doesn't provide the analytical tools. One doesn't look to the Bible to understand the complexity of the modern industrial and postindustrial society.*

look to the Bible to understand the complexity of the modern industrial and postindustrial society. It can give us certain insights into the human condition, certain visions of what we should hope for, but we also need the tools. They are found outside of religious texts and outside of religious sensibilities. We move to the social sciences for some handle on the maldistribution of resources and wealth and income and prestige and influence in our society. So all forms of prophetic religion must be linked in some sense with a set of analytical tools.

MOYERS: But there is still in that old scripture a very powerful moral message. You end one of your books, *Prophesy Deliverance*, with a quote of Jesus from Luke 4:18. "The spirit of the Lord is upon me because he has anointed me to preach good news to the poor. He has sent me to proclaim release to the captives and recovering of sight to the blind, to set at liberty those who are oppressed." Do you think that message still means anything in urban areas where you visit often?

WEST: Yes, I do. I think it means that there is still someone who cares for those who are socially invisible and politically marginalized. The spirit of the Lord is still empowering those who have been cast aside to struggle, enabling those who've been cast aside to not lose hope.

MOYERS: You have been on a long intellectual odyssey yourself. Are you still an active Christian?

WEST: Very much so. Jesus' words, along with many others, have helped sustain me as I encountered for myself the absurdity of being both an American and a person of African descent. W. E. B. Du Bois talked about this years ago in his American classic *Souls of Black Folk*. "All that people of a darker hue have ever wanted to be," he said, "is human beings who could be both American and also acknowledge their African heritage." This double consciousness, of living in many ways *in* America but not still fully *of* it, is a tension, I think, that all of us forever grapple with. Those words allow me to hold on to my sense of possibility.

MOYERS: You have talked about combative spirituality. What do you mean by that?

WEST: I mean a form of spirituality—of community and communion—that preserves meaning by fighting against the bombardments of claims that we are inferior or deficient. Combative spirituality sustains persons in their humanity but also transcends solely the political. It embraces a political struggle, but it also deals with issues of death or dread, of despair or disappointment. These are the ultimate facts of existence and they're filtered through our social and political existence. Ultimately all of us as individuals must confront these, and a combative spirituality accents a political struggle but goes beyond it by looking death and dread and despair and disappointment and disease in the face and saying that there is in fact a hope beyond these.

MOYERS: But isn't that hope deferred again? Isn't that justice deferred? Isn't that saying, "You have to put up with the miserable conditions in Brooklyn today, in Harlem, because one day there'll be a reward"?

WEST: No, because it calls into question all illusions that there'll be Utopia around the corner. When you talk about hope, you have to be a long-distance runner. This is again so very difficult in our culture, because the quick fix, the overnight solution, militates against being a long-distance runner in the moral sense, the sense of fighting because it's right, because it's moral, because it's just. That kind of hope linked to combative spirituality is what I have in mind.

MOYERS: So combative spirituality is that sense of subversive joy, as you once called it?

WEST: Subversive joy is the ability to transform tears into laughter, a laughter that allows one to acknowledge just how difficult the journey is, but to also acknowledge one's own sense of humanity and folly and humor in the midst of this very serious struggle. It's a joy that allows one both a space, a distance from the absurd, but also empowers one to engage back in the struggle when the time is necessary.

MOYERS: Some of that has come, has it not, from black music, from gospel and jazz and blues?

WEST: Yes.

MOYERS: What about rap? Does rap have any of that spiritual energy in it?

WEST: Oh, very much so. I mean, black rap music is the most important popular musical development in the last ten years. It is a profound extension of the improvisational character of what I call the Afro-American spiritual blues impulse, which is an attempt to hold at bay the demons and devils. What rap has done is to allow a kind of marriage between the rhetorical and the musical by means of some of the most amazing linguistic virtuosities we have seen in the language, the lyrics, the quickness, the speaking.

MOYERS: You have said that rap music is part and parcel of the subversive energies of the youthful black underclass. What do you mean by subversive energies?

WEST: They respond to their sense of being rejected by the society at large, of being invisible in the society at large, with a subversive critique of that society. It has to do with both the description and depiction of the conditions under which they're forced to live, as well as a description and depiction of the humanity preserved by those living in such excruciating conditions. It then goes beyond to a larger critique of the power structure as a whole. It is international in terms of its link to struggles in South Africa, so that in that sense it's part of a prophetic tradition. But I should say that what is lacking in rap music is vision and analysis. It's fun, it's entertaining, it helps sustain the rituals of party-going on the weekends, but it still lacks a vision. This is where again the church plays an important role, you see, because otherwise, it's quite easy to channel these energies into very narrow, chauvinistic, xenophobic forms that lack vision, that have no moral content or ethical substance.

MOYERS: Black have made an enormous contribution in this country through preaching, through music, through sports, yet we still see the black underclass sinking in a quagmire. Almost every analyst I know says nothing is helping, not black rap music, not the black church, not social programs, not capitalist economics. Nothing is helping this black underclass. And yet you still trumpet hope.

WEST: Yes I do. I mean, the condition of the black underclass is tragic, but they are still human beings who are getting about. Many are still making sense of the world. Many are actually still escaping. I don't want to lose sight of them. Many are outside of churches trying to hold on to their moral character. I don't want to view the black underclass as a monolithic homogeneous entity. These are actual human beings, children of God. Some are losing, many are losing, some are winning in terms of holding on to their sense of self and holding on to their sense of vitality and vibrancy.

That in no way excuses the structural and institutional forces that are at work: the unemployment, the failed educational system, the consumer culture that bombards them. The black underclass still has to contend with all of these in addition to the larger racist legacy. But it's not only about race. As we know, there are other factors as well. So that certainly a description of their conditions must include this, but I hold up hope. I'm talking about my cousins and friends and relatives who are seemingly locked into this condition, yet change can indeed come about.

MOYERS: Where is the moral outrage in society today? Do you see it?

WEST: Not enough. There's been a kind of anesthetizing, I think, in the 1980s toward forms of social misery. But there's the National Coalition for the Homeless. There's the NAACP. There's the Democratic Socialists of America, of which I'm an honorary chair. There's a whole host of groups that have been trying to sustain some moral outrage, filtered through a systemic analysis of our situation and regulated by a vision. It hasn't taken the way it has in past decades, but I think the 1990s will be different.

MOYERS: The conundrum is that if you are morally outraged today, you're relegated to the margins of society. It's almost considered out of the norm to be concerned about social misery. To be mature today means you're supposed to say we can't ameliorate certain circumstances in life.

WEST: But I think the important point there is that we have to understand why this is so. Why has cynicism become so pervasive over the past ten years for those who wanted to focus on social misery? And I see that cynicism more and more on the wane. I think Eastern Europe is providing us with a different lesson, you see. Up until the last few months, people did not believe that ordinary human beings organized could fundamentally change society. We had scholars around the world saying that the very notion of revolution was outdated and antiquated. We could not even imagine the transfer of power that we have witnessed in Eastern Europe in the past month and a half. So all of those assumptions and presuppositions are now being called into question, which means that the focus of ordinary people organizing, mobilizing, having impact on powers that be, once again moves to the center of the agenda.

Tu Wei·ming

HISTORIAN AND CONFUCIAN
THINKER

Tu Wei-ming was born in mainland
China, studied in Taiwan, and
pursued an academic career in
America at Princeton University
and the University of California at
Berkeley. Now professor of Chinese
history and philosophy at Harvard
University, he teaches and writes
about Confucianism, the ancient
Chinese system of ethics, and its
relationship to the modern world. In
Tu's view, the ways in which this
humanistic philosophy of the East
meshes with Western technology
and democratic values tell us much
about the future of China and
industrial East Asia, and about our
survival on an endangered planet.
He returns to China regularly to
lecture on Confucian thought.

MOYERS: Here we are approaching the twenty-first century
and the world's major religions are at least fifteen centuries old.
Do you think, in this new era, the old faiths have anything to say
to us?

TU: Oh yes. We should look at these great historical spiritual
traditions not as static structures, but as rivers of ideas, of rituals,
of spirituality, flowing over the historical landscape for more than
a millennium. They have been in communication with one another and influencing each other through a very long history.
China, for instance, has been deeply affected by Buddhism from
India. There was communication between Greek ideas and Christianity, not to mention Judaism, Christianity, and Islam. And of
course, there was continuous interaction between Hinduism and
Buddhism.

Now, they do diverge at times in the spiritual landscape, but
they all share some deep concerns for the human condition. So
religion, in this sense, may very well be understood not as something static but as a quest for ultimate self-transformation. Karl
Jaspers, the German philosopher, has characterized the first millennium, when most of the great historical religions first emerged,
as the Axial Age. It was then that the different human civilizations
turned toward their different spiritual orientations. That's one of
the reasons why we have different cultural traditions, informed by
different forms of ritual practices, and different forms of spirituality.

MOYERS: It was a time of convergence, when ideas came
together to combust into new forms and phenomena.

TU: Yes. And some people are arguing that we are now properly
entering into the second Axial Age. All these religious traditions
not only coexist in our global village, they coexist in such a way
that a Christian project, for example, would have to be understood
and perceived in a comparative religious context. And I think that
in the twentieth century, for the first time, all these major traditions are coming together to shape the human condition.

MOYERS: But so many of these religions are exclusionary.
They were built upon the idea that nonbelievers were to be kept

outside, if not persecuted. Can religions with that kind of tradition really find core values in common?

TU: It is true that quite a number of religious traditions with a powerful sense of the center tend to be exclusive—concerned only about a particular path and the exclusion of other equally valid paths in other religious perspectives. And whether or not there are powerful resources for developing a common ground within the orthodox traditions of these religious orientations, I think, really depends upon further research, further study, and further practice. It's a moral imperative for the twentieth century, and of course, the twenty-first century, that they find a common ground for communication. It is a moral imperative that they share a common concern for the human condition. Because for the first time in human history, we are questioning whether human beings are a viable species.

MOYERS: Do you really believe that we humans may not be a viable species?

TU: I think that for the first time, not only the possibility of self-destruction is real—so is the possibility of the destruction of the ecosystem. That is frightening. We know it may not happen. We hope it will never happen. But the very fact that it could happen, and that we're at the brink of allowing it to become a realizable possibility, is frightening.

MOYERS: What some people see as diversity, others see as chaos. Do you think we're living in an age of chaos?

TU: From the Taoist point of view, chaos can be very creative. But we certainly live in a pluralistic universe. And pluralism can be a form of relativism, in the sense that anything goes because I cannot judge others according to my own criteria. On the other hand, it can be an invitation to open-mindedness, in the sense that I should know what is the best for me but I also know that what is best for me may not be best for my neighbor. Self-awareness may therefore give the idea of pluralism a texture, a nuanced understanding of the human condition, that, of course, a traditional spiritual universe, where exclusivism is a matter of fact, is never able to really fully appreciate.

MOYERS: I hear this kind of insight from many thinkers of different faiths. I've talked to people of various persuasions and traditions. But the question becomes, is this concern limited just to intellectuals? And if it is, how do we get it into the body of society?

TU: Actually, what we see now in the academic study of religion is a fascinating situation. For a number of years, people in the academic community were not interested in religious matters. They considered them private. In America, we traditionally believed in the separation of church and state. So when the study of religion was accepted as a real major at Berkeley, there was a lot of controversy. At Harvard, it took a number of years to develop a program of religious studies in the arts and sciences.

Now in the last few years, the public demand and intellectual awareness outside of the ivory tower really provided an occasion for people to take religious matters seriously. When I first approached the study of Confucianism, I came to it as a historian. Then I studied it as a philosopher, analyzing the ideas and concepts. More recently, I really studied it as a religionist, not just as a form of life, but as a particular kind of faith—faith in the perfectibility of human self-transformation, and the perfectibility of human nature through self-effort. That change helped me to realize that Confucianism, as a subject, is no longer the province of people in the academic community. It is a concern of intellectuals who are not necessarily historians of China, or philosophers of Asia; but just humanly concerned about some of the perennial problems.

MOYERS: Would it be fair to say that you are a practicing Confucian?

TU: I'm trying to learn to be a Confucian. Or trying to learn to be a human being informed by my Confucian roots. And in this sense, I'm a practicing Confucian. But Confucianism is not a membership religion—you do not become a Confucian simply by adopting a certain kind of ritual. It is a process of learning to be human, as defined by the Confucianists.

MOYERS: My understanding is that it's really more an ethical way of life than a religion or a philosophy. Is that fair?

TU: That's right. But the ethical way of life has far-reaching religious implications. And it's also rooted in very profound philosophical ideas, especially moral philosophy and ethics. So it is not a form of life that can be easily characterized as a form of secular humanism, precisely because it's profoundly religious, and it has philosophical ideas and concerns that are not easily reducible to the ethical realm. Many people are not aware that they are Confucians, but they live by some of the basic Confucian ideas and they transmit some of these values to their children.

MOYERS: It's in the cultural DNA in a sense?

TU: It's in the cultural DNA. That's a marvelous way of putting it. And learning to be human is an ultimate concern.

MOYERS: And the notion of God—where does that come into focus?

TU: The functional equivalent of God in Confucian humanism is Heaven. In fact, we can say that the Confucian process of learning to be human involves not only being filial to one's parents, and faithful to one's friends, and loyal to one's society, it also involves one's ability to go beyond anthropocentrism. The highest ideal of Confucian self-realization is the unity of Heaven and the human.

MOYERS: So what I would call the will of God, in my Christian faith, you would call the mandate of Heaven.

TU: The mandate of Heaven. And the difference is that the mandate of Heaven is understood to be the ultimate reason for my human nature. In other words, my nature is confirmed and informed by the mandate of Heaven. Therefore, through my understanding of my own heart and mind, I will be able to understand my nature. If I understand my human nature, I will also be able to understand the nature of Heaven. So man or woman, in this sense, is considered the cocreator of the heavenly process. The transcending perspective of the Confucian tradition is also immanent in this world, in our nature. The mandate of Heaven reveals itself through the human heart and mind.

MOYERS: In my tradition, it is the Word made flesh.

TU: That's right. I think the whole notion of incarnation is that the will of Heaven realizes itself in the concrete human condition. It is not simply for the love of humanity, but also for its own revelation, that Heaven becomes concretized in the human project. That's the reason why the term "anthropocosmic" is the correct humanistic vision. We help Heaven to realize itself. There's a very powerful statement in the *Analects:* "It is not the Tao, or the heavenly way, that makes the human great; it is the human that makes the Tao, or Heaven, great!" Now first, especially when I was among Christian friends, I thought, "It's blasphemous! It's anthropocentrist, it's egotistic." I tried to hide it.

MOYERS: It's secular humanism!

TU: Secular humanism. But the more I read it, the more I was convinced that it's a statement about faith and responsibility and human self-understanding. It's saying, "Heaven doesn't need us; Heaven has its own structure and its own development; Heaven is always natural." To be sure, that's our naturalistic reading of it, and yet, by being human authentically, both individually and communally, we create new values, we create culture, we transform society. And so what Heaven originally doesn't need becomes greatly expanded as the unfolding of a new kind of vision which is anthropocosmically defined, rather than simply humanistically defined. Being human in this case therefore assumes a responsibility which is not just social, it's cosmological. What human beings do will have powerful consequences for the ecosystem or for the cosmos as a whole. Learning to be human is not simply anthropological. It also has profound cosmological implications.

MOYERS: You're talking about sacred humanism.

TU: A colleague of mine, Professor Herbert Fingarette, has written a marvelous book on Confucius. The title is *The Secular as Sacred*. I think it's a very beautiful description of the Confucian project. How to transform the secular world into a sacred domain for everyone. My own sense is that we can even characterize the Confucian idea of self-realization as transforming our biological reality—that which we are born with—into an aesthetic expression of the self. An artist usually tries to create something beautiful outside, by working with an object—a painting. But now the artist is trying to transform himself, or herself, into an aesthetic expression of the self. That is the realization of the will of God. And that is the process of trying to transform the secular world into a sacred domain.

MOYERS: One of my great professors at seminary, T. B. Maston, used to say that no matter how disfigured the lame and the halt might be, that person can still be the most beautiful revelation of God.

TU: Precisely. And humanity is aesthetically appealing not because it's given, but because it has been transformed. Any development of the person from *A* to *A plus 1* is aesthetically appealing, a transformation of the human spirit. Viktor Frankl has remarked that in the concentration camp everything is dehumanized, but if one person could still exhibit human-heartedness or kindness, that was an exemplification of the human spirit.

MOYERS: Frankl also said that he was not responsible for his circumstances, but he was responsible for how he responded to those circumstances. He came to this insight in the concentration camp. Is that Confucian as well?

TU: Totally Confucian. And I think it goes one step further. It is not just the response that counts, but also the willingness and the determination to transform those circumstances. In other words, I'm determined to transform the conditioning forces originally constraining me to be a limited human being—my ethnicity, my gender, my socialization, and so forth—into a concrete manifestation of myself as the center of relationships. On the surface, it's a very simple notion, but it's really more profound. It's difficult, and also it's enduring. I cannot choose my parents, I cannot choose my nation, I cannot choose my time in the world. Therefore, I'm responsible for my ability to respond to these conditioning forces.

But a further step is, by responding creatively to these conditioning forces, I can transform them into instruments of self-realization. Precisely because of the limitations of my gender, my ethnicity, and so forth, I become a fully embodied human being in the sense of human flourishing. In other words, I try to take the limitations of who I am as the nutrients, the nourishing forces, for me to become what I ought to become. The Confucians believe that this is a common human situation: I am not what I ought to be. And yet, what I ought to be is structured in the whole universe of what I am.

MOYERS: Or what I should become. But what should I become? What does it mean when we're truly human?

TU: It means that I am established in meaningful harmonious relationships with an ever-enduring and expanding network of relationships—the larger community. I'm not simply an isolated individual now—I am a responsible parent, a worker, a bureaucrat, a teacher. At the same time, I have a deepening self-awareness. I become more and more aware of the dimensions of myself, not simply as a body, but also as a heart and mind, as a soul, as a spirit. But to become more aware of myself in those dimensions is not to depart from my body. In fact, there's no exclusive dichotomy between the body and the mind. The body is a vehicle through which I become an aesthetic expression of the self.

MOYERS: So mature human beings are self-sufficient but—

TU: They are not islands, but always a stream, allowing other streams, other waters to come in. They have their own direction, but they are also able to open themselves up to other possibilities; they may eventually flow into the ocean.

MOYERS: There's a sense of reciprocity there. Life is taking and giving.

TU: That's right. But it's not altruism in an ordinary sense.

MOYERS: It's not doing good for goodness' sake.

TU: Right. It is, in fact, a necessary condition for my self-development, for my self-transformation. I am sympathetic to others because my own sensitivity has to be heightened and empowered for me to be truly human. So a fundamental quality of being human is sympathy. And sympathy has to be cultivated. It's not something just given.

MOYERS: The Confucius golden rule says, "Do not do to others what you would not want others to do to you." And the Christian is, "Do unto others what you would have others do unto you." Is there a significance in the fact that one of them is negative, and the other is affirmative?

TU: In the Confucian sense, to know that what is best for me is not necessarily best for my neighbor is the beginning of wisdom in human communication. I ought to understand myself. This is my project of self-realization. But I cannot understand another person to the extent and in the same degree that I ought to know myself. So that which is best for me may not be the best for him or her. I like spicy food a lot; I don't want to impose that on my children. I know they would not be able to enjoy it. And some kind of path of self-realization is particularly important to me, but I'm not sure whether that is necessarily the best for someone in a totally different cultural context.

So the Confucians, by deliberate effort, try not to be missionaries. In fact, the *Book of Rights* says going out to teach is not in accordance with propriety. When I came to the States, and I took up a teaching position, an older teacher of mine jokingly remarked, "You've already violated a basic Confucian rule." The proper way is to wait at home. When people really want to learn from you, they'll come to you. To go out to teach, already you've compromised one thing—you've opened the possibility of the imposition of something upon an alien structure, which may not be the best for that structure.

MOYERS: So it would have been improper of you to call me and say, "I would like to talk about Confucianism," but totally acceptable for me to call you and say, "Would you talk to me about Confucianism?"

TU: Oh, your calling me would be perfectly all right. But now I think I'm properly Americanized enough—I'd probably call myself as well.

MOYERS: Friends of mine who have lived in China say that, as beautiful as the Confucian idea is aesthetically, it is nonetheless very stifling in practice, because the free spirit of the West does not feel at home in the elaborately prescribed network of kindred ties—ruler and follower, father and son, husband and wife—you just get smothered in this tissue.

TU: Well, you can also say that about the highly ritualized societies of South Korea or Japan, or even Vietnam, because these are also societies under Confucian influence.

MOYERS: Westerners admire the tradition from afar, but when they get there, they feel stifled.

TU: That's right. But I think that ought not to be the case. Even in traditional China, there's been a debate between the Confucian idea of the five relationships, and the Confucian obligation of the three bounds. The Confucian idea of the three bounds is the authority of the ruler over the minister; the father over the son; and the husband over the wife. So in that idea you have all sorts of things feminists are fighting against, and liberal democratic thinkers, and some scholars who think that the primordial tie between father and son will have to be overcome for the ego to be fully developed, not necessarily in the Freudian sense, but in a generic psychoanalytic sense.

But the five relationships, as we understand it, really talk about a mutuality. Here the relationship between father and son is defined in terms of affection—ruler and minister in terms of rightness—husband and wife in terms of division of labor—friendship in terms of trust, and siblings in terms of a sense of sequence. So within the Confucian tradition, you have a major conflict between the five relationships defined in terms of mutuality and support, and the three bounds as a kind of mechanism of ideological control.

MOYERS: But every religion contains the seeds of its own contradiction.

TU: Yes. But I think the Confucian situation is more pronounced in this case, because in many other great religious traditions, there is a spiritual sanctuary which is outside of this world, here and now, so there is a different kind of arena in which some of these ideological conflicts are being played and developed. In the Confucian tradition, they become part of a political culture. It's happened in China, in Korea, in Japan, in Vietnam. So it is politically significant in this connection. What I see within the Confucian tradition is the continuous struggle and conflict between two types of force. We have to be patriotic Chinese: don't criticize the government! We have to be obedient; we work hard; we try to follow the rules, and not to raise any kind of rebellious questions.

On the other hand, it's always been a major tradition in Confucian humanism to understand politics not simply as distribution of power, but to try to moralize politics,

to argue that only the people who are exemplary teachers ought to be politically influential. And that struggle continues. Before the Tiananmen massacre, the students who mobilized themselves against the current regime didn't at first invoke Western ideas of democracy or freedom. They talked about the public accountability of the government; they talked about corruption of the government; they focused their attention on the inability of the government to develop itself as the leader of the land. That's one of the reasons why not only the citizens of Beijing but government officials, too, and members of the security police were moved. The students used a language which is very deeply rooted in Chinese consciousness. They are not representing their own interests. They are really the voice of the people.

MOYERS: The Confucian intellectual is supposed to be the eyes and the ears of the people.

TU: And if the intellectuals, who always constitute a very small minority, manage to articulate the voice of the people for the well-being of the society as a whole, they, in fact, perform an important function not only social, but cosmic. They help the people to be able to voice their concerns. And the government will have to respond to that particular kind of challenge.

MOYERS: The paradox, though, is that the intellectuals who are still espousing this tradition in Confucianism are a minority. The Party runs China, and the Party is mostly peasants and military and workers.

TU: On the other hand, the sinister side of Confucianism, with its emphasis on authoritarian control and obedience, doesn't rely on any base of Western democracy or human rights either. You should exercise your duty, because duty consciousness has always been pronounced in the Confucian culture, whereas rights consciousness, up to this day, has never been fully developed.

MOYERS: What do you mean by "duty consciousness"?

TU: You have to prove that you are a worthy member of the community as a whole to be able to voice your demands for certain kinds of rights and ideas.

MOYERS: You can't just say, "I have the right to say this!"

TU: Right. So when I was in China, my main concern was not whether they managed to understand Confucianism correctly because the negative side of Confucian culture is also obvious in the political system in China. I was concerned about how to develop a narrow bridge between the fruitful interaction of Confucian humanism on the one hand and liberal democratic ideas on the other.

The tragedy in China now is this: the students, overwhelmed by the irresponsibility and insensitivity of the regime that was using all these traditional symbols of patriotism, loyalty, filial piety, and so forth, have become totally westernized. In so doing, unfortunately, they gave some powerful weapons to their adversaries, because even the workers, the peasants, couldn't fully appreciate what the students were striving for. But they *could* hear the inauthentic but still persuasive "politicized Confucian voice" of obedience, duty, commitment to the goal of socialism, and so forth. So unless a fruitful interaction becomes possible between liberal democratic ideas on the one hand and the indigenous resources in Confucian culture as a defining characteristic of the mode of protest of the students, the future of the democratization movement in China is still quite bleak.

MOYERS: So there has to be a fusion. Something of the West, but not so much of the West that it overwhelms the indigenous tradition.

TU: It's not even just the conflict between the West and China; it's really a fusion at many different levels. Look at Eastern Europe, with the power of Christian symbolism on the one hand, and on the other the power of liberal democratic ideas. From the Marxist point of view, they're totally contradictory. "Religion is an opiate of the people" and so forth. The liberal democratic ideas are sort of bourgeois mentality, but they fused in a beautiful way. That's true with the Polish situation, certainly true with the Czechoslovakian. It is a fusion of powerful, indigenous, traditional spirituality on the one hand and a universal demand for freedom, for equality, and for universal love. And if this fusion does not take place, and the students become westernized only in the sense of making iconoclastic attacks on the tradition, and the regime becomes totally manipulative in using their symbols, the vicious circle will continue.

MOYERS: Every major religion, particularly the fundamentalists in the religion, is grappling with how to integrate scientific inquiry, democratic values, feminism, into its traditions. What about Confucians?

> *But within the Confucian symbolic system, there's virtually no sense that women are not full participating members of the society. There's nothing comparable to the idea that only men can be rabbis, and only men can be bishops and cardinals, and so forth.*

TU: The fascinating thing for me is that for years and years, Chinese intellectuals and of course Western intellectuals have concluded that Confucianism is a form of male chauvinism—or at least that it's male-oriented, because it grew out of a male hierarchical system. All the major thinkers in the Confucian tradition turn out to be males, as well. But within the Confucian symbolic system, there's virtually no sense that women are not full participating members of the society. There's nothing comparable to the idea that only men can be rabbis, and only men can be bishops and cardinals, and so forth. So the possibility is great that women Confucian thinkers might emerge in our generation, and the possibility of women Confucians as educators, scholars, leaders, politicians, has already been realized.

And unless the Confucian tradition can creatively transform itself into a humanistic tradition that can embrace feminism as a humanistic movement, it will not be able to survive very well into the twenty-first century—nor will other major religious traditions confronted with the same issue. In order to do that, my own sense is that the notion of the division of labor is still a valuable one. Many people who are concerned about male domination are willing to sacrifice the notion of gender-specific ideas of any kind, requiring that everything be gender neutral. But if we recognize our concrete human condition, every human being is defined in terms of not just ethnicity and language and culture but also gender. This is irreducible.

Even so, it is not necessary to build anything like a false consciousness upon gender. We should recognize it as one of the vehicles for self-realization and self-transformation. I happen to be male. I will never be able to enjoy or endure the experience of child-bearing. But sympathetically, not only do I respect child-bearing, I also cherish it as a common and honored human concern. I have to realize that no major humanistic enterprise is restricted to only half of humanity.

Now this notion of mutual appreciation, based upon a division of labor, I don't think is totally incompatible with the twenty-first-century idea of human compatibility. And I think that one thing we learn from the humanistic movement is that history will have to be not only reinterpreted, but partly rewritten. The power structure that we understand to be enduring, including the family system and so forth, will have to be readdressed, reformulated.

MOYERS: You've been here a long time now. Do you feel at home in America?

TU: I feel at home in a number of senses. First of all, I strongly believe that a spiritual tradition, like a stream, has to change continuously, in response to new conditions, new challenges. When I first came to the States in '62, I told myself I'd be willing to totally change my own conception of the Confucian project, which I had been seasoned into believing as a viable one. I'd even abandon the things that my teacher told me if I learned something from my colleagues at Harvard and other places that was more viable, more persuasive, more in keeping with my experience as a modern human being, in a different environment. So I went through a period of self-questioning, self-doubt, and search, and also gradually more encouragement from my American professors to appreciate what I was able to offer; they gave me a new insight into my own tradition. It was different from the instructions I had received in Taiwan, because there, everything was taken for granted, everything had to be true because it had been tested, and it had been understood through a very long period of time. So the new challenge provided me with an opportunity to reexamine that tradition.

MOYERS: Being Confucian is not easy!

TU: Well, I think being Christian is not easy. Kierkegaard once remarked, "I am not a Christian. I'm only in the process of trying to become one!" I think that's true also with Jews, with Buddhists. They all ask the ultimate question. They are not satisfied with our living as ordinary human beings; simply as economic beings, political beings, and social beings. They want us to be more, and in fact, we want to be more. It is in this sense that religion is extremely powerful, explosive, and demanding.

Joanne Ciulla
ETHICIST

A Senior Fellow at the Wharton School at the University of Pennsylvania, one of the nation's leading business schools, Joanne Ciulla teaches career-minded students to think critically about the role of ethics in management. As a philosopher, she challenges them with the fundamental question: What is the ethical price of the bottom line? Ciulla is writing a book about the meaning of work in our culture.

MOYERS: Peter Drucker, the guru of business management in this country, says that there really is no such thing as business ethics. Ethics, he says, is for everyone, whether we work in a corporation or a factory, as a journalist or a florist. What do *you* think is distinctive about business ethics?

CIULLA: The other thing people usually say about business ethics is "Isn't that a contradiction in terms?" And yes, it is. When we think of ethics, we think of people doing good things or performing good actions because they want to and because those are the right things to do. When we think of business, we think of actions, of strategies, and behaviors that are all geared towards a particular end: making profits. So it is a contradiction.

One of the chief questions in business ethics is whether a business can act ethically. The philosopher Immanuel Kant said that the only good is a good will. Now, can business have good will? For example, suppose a company sets up a program for local schoolchildren that involves donating computers and staff to teach the kids. Is the company doing it because it has a good will, or is it doing it as good public relations? This is a crucial question. The answer is probably that they do it for both reasons.

On the other hand, I'm not saying that ethics in business is different from ethics in the rest of life. What I am saying is that in business, ethics functions in a particular context, and the problems of business make it difficult to understand how to apply the ethical principles we know.

For example, I don't sit around telling my students that you should be honest and fair and just. That would be a fairly silly course. The point is, how are you honest in a variety of business contexts? What does honesty mean in the sales department? Does honesty mean you tell them every single little thing about that product? Does honesty mean that you tell customers that they don't really need all the stuff you're selling them? So business ethics is trying to help people to understand how moral behavior can function in the complex business environment in which we now operate.

MOYERS: Can a corporation really have a good will?

CIULLA: I struggle with this problem. I think there are cases where corporations do have a good will. Those corporations have usually, over the years, developed standard behaviors and practices and procedures and values for dealing with problems. One company that comes to mind is Johnson & Johnson. When someone poisoned bottles of Tylenol and planted them in stores for people to buy, Johnson & Johnson immediately pulled all the bottles from the shelves. Now, this was a very dramatic case, and business people will repeat it to you over and over. The company involved had a strong tradition, a strong set of beliefs, and they maintained them even in this difficult situation where they could have lost a whole bunch of money doing that. So you can say, yes, there was a good will there. You can usually tell if a company acts with a good will because they're taking a huge risk. They're saying it's more important to behave this way than it is to make the money.

MOYERS: But couldn't one also make the counter-argument that Johnson & Johnson had no alternative? That if they had not responded openly, if they had not removed all of the bottles from the shelves, they'd have been out of business?

CIULLA: Yes, one could respond that way. But if you look at the history of problems like this, the usual pattern of response starts with a denial phase. Think about what happened with Ford in the Pinto case, for example. There were serious problems with the Pinto gas tank. It was exploding, people were suing, the alternative solutions were expensive. The company waffled back and forth on how to deal with this problem. They put it off, they denied it and tried to get around it before they finally had to give in.

So Tylenol was interesting because it was a different response, it was a right-way response. They said, "This is important. We care about the safety of people absolutely first," instead of, "Well, it's not really our fault, let's see if we can catch the guy."

MOYERS: In the eighties it was said that rules are for fools, greed is good, he who dies with the most toys wins. Do you think that was exaggerated or is there something new and different at the heart of entrepreneurial capital today?

CIULLA: They were exaggerations to some extent. There was an awful lot of fun in the eighties, too. Many of our students came from Wall Street into business school. They had been in the thick of all the excitement during this time. Working on Wall Street was a great adventure for some students. It was a terrific place to be. Young people were given lots of responsibility, they were making lots of money, and they were working long hours.

The eighties was also a period of deregulation. It was as if the harnesses had been taken off. There was all of this enthusiasm on Wall Street. People were pushing the limits of the law, inventing new financial tools, and seeing how far they could go. So I don't take some of those slogans too seriously. They reflect an attitude that's questionable, but on the other hand, knowing the young people, it also reflects an attitude of fun.

MOYERS: Many still admire Michael Milken. I've talked to students who think he did no wrong. They consider him, in effect, one of the heroes of the eighties.

CIULLA: The eighties did have some peculiar heroes. Milken is an example of someone who was very bright, very inventive, very creative, but he got caught up in the heady times and the environment he found himself in and the things he had created. So once again, he started pushing limits, and I think this happened to a lot of people. It was a kind of intoxication.

MOYERS: But deregulation wasn't supposed to mean the removal of societal sanctions against unethical behavior.

CIULLA: No, and deregulation, in a sense, goes hand-in-hand with the new interest in business ethics. Deregulation meant that instead of regulating by law, people regulate themselves and companies regulate internally.

MOYERS: It's been said that the symbol for our culture and the business culture in particular has become the digital clock. It looks at only the present moment, with no hint of yesterday or tomorrow, of the past or the future. Only the present is what counts. Do you think that's so?

CIULLA: American business is realizing it had better not be so. Here's where I think business schools and business strategists are starting to change. Instead of the fast killing, we need to think about a sustainable competitive advantage, which is something we've been learning from the Japanese. It means you need to understand what's transpired in the past and what the future's going to look like if you want your business to last and grow and develop.

MOYERS: Yes, but the Japanese themselves have been through a round of ruthless business scandals lately. Are you holding them up as an ethical ideal?

CIULLA: No, but there have also been scandals on the Hong Kong stock exchange, the Swedish stock exchange, the French; everywhere we've seen a mirror image of some of the things that have happened on Wall Street.

Part of what's happening around the world is that business practice is changing. We're living in a global economy. But business isn't just the laws and regulations that make it up; it's also a set of unsaid understandings. When you start buying stocks on the Hong Kong stock exchange and you live in New York, you make certain assumptions about what you and the other party are doing. People in Hong Kong may be making different assumptions about what they're doing. For the unsophisticated, it's almost madness to buy stocks on certain foreign exchanges, because locals may have a different set of understandings of what they, as insiders, might do.

MOYERS: Is it becoming a more amoral international culture?

CIULLA: What's going to eventually happen, I think, is that we're going to have to come up with some international sets of norms. A good example is the question of bribery and questionable payments. You may argue that in a particular society bribes are common, everybody uses them, it's understood, fine. Why should we, as Americans, be so edgy about bribes? We have the Foreign Corrupt Practices Act that says we're not allowed to pay bribes. But when you start doing business with lots of different people from lots of different cultures who don't share the same business practices and customs and aren't sensitive to other cultures' norms, does it make sense *not* to pay bribes? Is it an efficient way to do business? And if you do pay bribes, is it ethical? It may be ethical among the people who possess a certain set of understandings, but when people start playing from the outside who don't share those understandings, then the game changes. So the Japanese have had scandals because their business practices and norms of doing business are changing. They are no longer a closed club. A free market demands that everyone have the opportunity to play the game. Here is where we enter into discussions of fair play.

MOYERS: Wasn't it Lockheed that got into trouble for paying a bribe to a Japanese airlines company in order to keep a contract? The company got in trouble here for playing the game the way the Japanese were playing it.

CIULLA: Right. Eventually there's got to be a convergence of rules so that we can all do business with each other. It's not that our standards are higher than anybody else's or better than anyone else's. It's not that we're ethical imperialists. It's rather that at some point we need standards that everybody understands, in order to make this kind of global business possible.

MOYERS: If I were one of your students and came to you and said, "Dr. Ciulla, one day I want to be the president of Lockheed. What's the more ethical course for me to follow? Should I pay the bribe to the Japanese company, or should I not pay it and put five thousand of my workers out of work if I don't get that contract?" Is the obligation to the American ethical norm, or to the American worker?

CIULLA: Well, you see, that case is easy, because we've got a law, and you have to follow the laws, period. If you don't agree with the laws, you must go through legitimate channels to change them. But if you were one of my students, I'd first give you a little lecture on how to set up the problem. You've set it up with only two alternatives. This is a common mistake. There have always got to be more than two alternatives to a question. Students always tell me, "Well, if I see wrongdoing going on in my company, I either tell the boss and get a bad evaluation, or I don't say anything and the harm is done."

It seems to me there are a whole lot of other alternatives in between these two. It's not "I will lose my job or we lose the contract." There are ways of fulfilling ethical norms. There are ways of negotiating how to meet standards. You understand what the Japanese want in this case. They want a payment, a facilitating payment. It's understood as a part of their whole concept of reciprocity, a part of the business relationship. You need to first understand why they want the bribe, what role that bribe plays in their culture. The second thing you might want to do is figure out some way of satisfying those needs without paying a bribe. Are there other ways of building this kind of business relationship up? Are there other people in that decision-making process, which is usually a sort of complicated, consensual process among the Japanese, whom you can use? If people put as much energy into trying to figure out creative solutions to ethical problems as they put in trying to keep their tax bill down, I think the world would be a much better place.

MOYERS: But how do we do that?

CIULLA: You need to entertain different alternatives. I guess the first thing is to be committed to the ethical principle itself and decide it's important. We want our students to be good business people. In teaching ethics we want them to be not only technically good, creative entrepreneurs—people who can run companies and make profits and employ people—but we want them to be morally good people. A really good business person is not just technically good, he or she is also morally good. He doesn't harm people, he's concerned about his employees, he may be concerned about the society he lives in. "Good" in this sense is a broader notion. If you're committed to doing both, to being technically good and morally good as a business person, then you'll be committed to thinking out the ways to work through this problem. There's no reason to let the Japanese be the imperialists in this case. Why do we have to go by their bribery standard?

MOYERS: Because we want to be as strong economically and competitively as they are.

CIULLA: But why does it have to be a bribe to fulfill the needs of that standard?

MOYERS: If I were Japanese and I said to the representative from Lockheed, "You've got to pay this, it's not a bribe, it's the way we do business; it's reciprocity," what would you say to me?

CIULLA: I'd ask what the point was of reciprocity. "Tell me why you need this bribe. What does the bribe mean?" I would want to dig deeper. I would want to really understand what the function of it is.

MOYERS: But the frank answer for the business person is "I make money out of it."

CIULLA: Here we get to the heart of the issue. Bribery has always been considered wrong. From ancient Egypt all the way through, people have never thought bribes were right. I've done some work down in the Caribbean, where there's a great deal of bribery, and many Americans argue that bribery's okay down there. That's not true. You can tell it's not true because it's always done in secret. You never bribe anybody publicly. If everybody in this society believed "Bribery's fine. That's just the way we do business. That's how I get paid," then why can't you just write him a check and give it to him in front of his whole staff? Why can't it be in the newspaper that Lockheed just had this transaction, and they gave Mr. So-and-so 2 million dollars, and now Japan has this contract with Lockheed? Why don't they do that, if it's so right?

If everybody in this society believed "Bribery's fine. That's just the way we do business. That's how I get paid," then why can't you just write him a check and give it to him in front of his whole staff?

I think we also need to look at the impact of bribery on these societies. Are these people going to starve if we don't bribe them? In the past few years there's been an enormous interest in business ethics in South America. The South Americans have been realizing that corruption is strangling them economically, that they cannot make economic progress without getting rid of corruption. You can't have a good competitive market, with thriving small businesses and generous foreign investment, in a country that needs bribes for everything under the sun. I know countries where you can't open a fruit stand without paying somebody a bribe. How do you expect these countries to develop if people can't even start small businesses? So when you get to the real moral issues, and say, well, maybe it's just Americans, we have this funny way of thinking about it, you have to ask whether bribery is good for people in other places. Do people in other cultures really think it's an ethical thing to do? And the answer is usually no.

MOYERS: Everything you're saying raises this question: can ethics be taught to students this late in life, or has the twig already been bent by the time you get them in class?

CIULLA: If we make the assumption that ethics can't be taught to people who are twenty-five, twenty-seven years old, it's saying that people don't continue to learn all through their lives; it's saying that you get ethics and then it stops, that there's no moral development among people, there's no moral learning throughout life. I think those assumptions are wrong.

In teaching ethics, we're really trying to expand people's ability to use moral language in a business context. We all know the meaning of moral terms; we use them all the time. We know justice, fairness, honesty. The question is how you apply moral concepts in different social contexts. Do they expand your understanding of morality? Do you use moral concepts in the same way when you're at home as you do at work? Well, to some extent you do, but to some extent the context will change how you use the terms.

This may make some people nervous, because they can say, "My God, this means you don't have to be honest in business, or that honesty means something different in business." Well, honesty never means the same thing all the time for everybody anyway. We're always interpreting circumstances. We're saying, "Am I being honest here? Am I being fair here?" We don't have a definition that we just plunk down and say, this fits the definition, this doesn't fit it.

MOYERS: So how do you teach people to interpret circumstances?

CIULLA: High school students often assume that you always act dishonestly in business. They assume that you've always got to do the dishonest thing because you get fired if you don't. One day I was talking to a group, and a student gave me an example of an ethical problem he faced. He worked for a sporting goods store. The head of the city Recreation Department would come into this store and buy all sorts of goods that weren't for the Recreation Department. The young boy thought that this was wrong, obviously, because it was on the city budget. So his question was "What do I do about it?" His first assumption was if he said something about it to his boss, he would get fired. Which is a kind of crazy assumption to make, but he was very uncomfortable with the situation so he never said anything about it.

You see, some people just don't know how to act when they get in business. You've got to remember the power relationship in business is not very even. Young employees who come into a corporation aren't covered by a union. They want to get good evaluations, they have career choices to make. But there are things that strike them as odd. They don't know, for example, whether in sales situations or in negotiation situations, there may be different sets of understandings regarding candor and truthfulness. The fact that something is totally dishonest may be understood by both parties, and they both know that everybody bluffs a little bit. But the newcomer doesn't know how much. So part of what someone does when he or she begins work for a company is to try to understand what is considered ethical in that environment.

MOYERS: What do you say to our young student we left back there pondering this question?

CIULLA: First of all, I don't go giving them answers. We discuss these things in great detail, and we look at them from several angles. We ask: "What are your duties in this situation? What kinds of obligations do you have? What are the harms caused? What does your conscience tell you in this?" The main thing we try to avoid is this bimodal suggestion that you either tell and get fired, or you keep your mouth shut. We look at all those assumptions. "Who can you go talk to about this? Let's figure out how you can do something about it."

Usually we decide that something should be done. So let's get clear on it. Let's understand what it is. You've got to get information, ask questions. One thing young people have in their favor is they can ask a lot of questions. Often people assume that in order to do what is right they have to ride in on a white horse with a flag flying, and say, "This guy is unethical, and he's lied, and we should throw him in jail." They don't have to do that. They can go talk to a superior, maybe. We play through the whole scenario of the avenues of redress.

The final question is "How would you feel if you didn't do anything about it? Would you regret it? Would it make you uncomfortable? Would you like that job? Do you want to work at a place where you have to do things like this all the time?" So I don't give people answers.

MOYERS: Don't you sometimes use fairy tales in your classroom? How do they help develop the moral imagination?

CIULLA: I don't actually use fairy tales in class, but I do think that there is an analogy between moral learning in fairy tales and real-life cases. Bruno Bettelheim has written on morality in fairy tales and children. And I got to wondering, "What is moral learning like in a lifetime?" You could say it starts with fairy tales, and it moves on through life and we see things that impress us. There are people who impress us, there are actions that impress us, there are events that impress and inspire us. They teach us lessons and give us models for how to act.

Now Bettelheim points out that a lot of fairy tales convey to children the idea that they can overcome evil if they use their wits properly. There's the story of the genie in the bottle, for instance. A fisherman is out fishing. The first time he casts his line in the water, he gets a dead donkey, and throws it back in the sea. The next time he gets an old wheel that had fallen in the water. The third time he gets a little bottle. He opens the bottle and out comes this great big genie who says, "I'm going to kill you."

The fisherman's really scared, but instead of giving in and saying, "There's nothing I can do, he's going to kill me," he uses his wits. He says, "How did such a big genie like you get into such a little bottle? I can't believe you can do that." "Yes I can," says the genie. "I don't believe it," the fisherman says again. "Well, I'll prove it," says the genie. So the genie gets back into the bottle and the fisherman puts the lid on, and of course he lives happily ever after.

In a lot of fairy tales, people win the kingdom by doing the right thing. They save the princess, they slay the evil dragon. But morality requires encouragement. What's most frightening in our society is cynicism. You know, doing good is only for suckers, and nice guys finish last. That's why a story like the Tylenol story is analogous to a fairy tale. Not only did Johnson & Johnson do the right thing, but they got back their market share, and they did a greater good. So it's the kind of fairy tale businesses like.

MOYERS: As a child I took from fairy tales the lesson that doing the morally right thing is difficult and costly, but that in the end you can win the kingdom back. But I'm not so sure now, at fifty-five, that the world agrees.

CIULLA: As people get older they don't really think they're always going to win. Part of what that story does is encourage you, because you don't always see how morality always pays. But the other thing we learn as we get older is related to the idea of regret. A student told me a story once about that. "I was driving along the road," he said. "I was in a hurry to get to work, I was late. I saw a car accident, but since I was in a hurry, I didn't stop." And he said, "I was tormented all day long. Absolutely tortured. What if those people had died? What if nobody else was going to stop?" I asked him what he learned from that. And he said, "If that ever happens again, I won't pass by. I'll stop." That's part of the way we learn morality—by our mistakes, by the things we regret. We also learn that doing good is not always rewarded. There are lots of reports of whistle blowers who ended up losing their jobs.

MOYERS: And never getting a job again. I can give you chapter and verse.

CIULLA: But ask them if they'd do it again. The other part of morality is the intrinsic good of it, that people feel good about themselves when they take moral action. It doesn't always pay. But in a sense, it does pay. You've got to live with yourself. You can be as tormented with a job as without one. Everyone must choose how he or she wants to live.

MOYERS: It used to be the storytellers, the poets, and the priests who taught morality. They told us about the hero's journey, or what the church expected of honest merchants, or whether we could sell our goods on Sunday. Who's teaching ethics in the large sense today?

CIULLA: Well, that's a good question. I guess we'd have to turn to the media. When I talk to young people, they're getting a lot of their ideas about morality from the media. Our popular culture tells us all sorts of things. We watch soap operas, we watch talk shows and dramas where people shoot each other, et cetera. There are all sorts of messages coming in. And good people aren't usually on the news, so you rarely hear about companies that do really great things, or businessmen who do. But we always hear about the bad things. This helps keep businesses honest, but it also raises the level of cynicism about ethics in business.

MOYERS: What about the business executive? I know you've expressed some discomfort with the likes of T. Boone Pickens and Donald Trump because their wealth and power seem alienated from some broader aim of society. What are we learning from them?

CIULLA: We have this wonderful system of democracy, we have business laws and regulations, and all sorts of safeguards that allow businesses to operate. Any business person should operate in a way that does not destroy those things which make the business possible. Now Pickens is interesting because he provides a moral argument for what he's doing; and that's why he's particularly suspect. He says he's trying to save American business because it's not well managed. So when he takes over companies he's really just doing society a favor by getting rid of bad management. But the question is, should he make that judgment? Let us really understand what's behind it. It looks like a moral argument. It was presented like a moral argument. But is it? Is he really doing this for some greater good? What does it mean to be in business? I think we're going to have to seriously think about that question in the future. This gets back to the long-range view. We cannot have businesses that destroy those elements of our society that make business possible.

MOYERS: But this gets us to another point. Are activities like bribes and contract riggings and cheating at the office really the main ethical concerns today, or is it the whole new structure that came about in the 1980s, the leveraged buyouts, the greed, the takeovers? How much is enough? Are we into a new consideration of ethics for business today?

CIULLA: Part of what's been happening since the beginning of the Reagan era is a shifting concept of public and private responsibility. We have moved into an era where business has taken on greater responsibilities for a variety of things, partly because governments don't have as much money as they used to have, partly because people think businesses can do things better. There are suggestions that private enterprises should run prisons, day care centers, even schools. So business has been put in a role where it has to take on more social responsibilities. This opens up a set of dilemmas. There are certain areas where we don't want business taking control. We don't want business setting the curriculum for schools, for example. They weren't elected by us, they're not representatives of the people. How can we be sure every company has the common good in mind? The interesting question is what this type of private initiative does to our notion of the common good, which we always depended on government to have.

Trust and loyalty are reciprocal relationships; they have two sides. You can't expect someone to be trustful or loyal if you aren't going to be in return.

Inside businesses, concern over ethics is part of a crisis of trust. How can a company have loyal employees when the employees don't know whether tomorrow their company will get taken over? Companies demand an enormous amount of loyalty and commitment from employees, and yet they're not willing and/or able to give the same back to them.

Trust and loyalty are reciprocal relationships; they have two sides. You can't expect someone to be trustful or loyal if you aren't going to be in return. So this has caused an enormous problem inside companies. They're trying to find ways of dealing with this.

Another question is participation, and the great change in how employees think about their role in the workplace. In order to have employees involved in things like quality circles and team efforts, you need to yield some power to them and you need to give them responsibility. From them management needs a certain amount of good will, good judgment, things like that. Then there is also the question of justice. Today we see enormous wage disparities between what people at the top of the company and people at the bottom of the company make. Americans do have, deep down inside, a strong strain of egalitarianism, and we may have reached a point where it's become downright offensive that heads of corporations that can be taken over tomorrow and throw everyone out are being paid enormous sums of money.

MOYERS: The *New York Times* had an article recently anticipating the day when some corporation executives—obviously just a few—might be making a billion dollars a year.

CIULLA: Does that really make sense? What does that say? Are we creating a kind of monarchy or aristocracy in the corporate world?

MOYERS: Do you feel like a subversive here in a business school?

CIULLA: Sometimes I do. I am a subversive in the sense that I don't see business ethics as some kind of Sunday school for business people. I see business ethics as having a much larger role to play in changing business studies and business practice. In my opinion, business ethics really just involves rethinking the way we do business, rethinking issues like equity in companies and fairness in companies, rethinking the kinds of strategies that businesses have had in the past. Just the fact that we've moved to the service business makes ethical questions even more urgent, because we're talking about dealing with people all the time, and most ethical problems have to do with relations between people. The kinds of commitments, the kinds of attitudes people have towards the company in a service business are much more complicated on an emotional level, a psychological level, and an ethical level than the kinds of relationships people have in the old-time companies making widgets.

Business affects so many facets of our life right now. It's affected families enormously. Companies are realizing, for instance, that it's not a great idea, particularly with two-career families, to make employees move every few years. Then there are questions of day-care policies. Can businesses become more sensitive to the needs of families? There have been some rather frightening studies done on the effect of women entering the workplace, on problems like the relationship between that and child obesity and the number of hours spent watching television and the decline of SAT scores. There have been enormous changes going on in our society that all relate in some way to the business world and the way in which employees respond to that world and the way in which that world shapes their personal lives.

MOYERS: Some people say the only social responsibility business has is to make money. Let society then figure out what to do with it, but our job is to make money. That's what we exist to do, that's all we exist to do.

CIULLA: That's the usual straw man that business ethics has to beat up on. Milton Friedman is the most famous proponent of it, and everyone beats up on poor Milton Friedman. While I don't agree with that statement, I think you have to understand the context in which someone like Friedman argues that point. He says that profits are the only responsibility that business has because companies are not elected officials; they're not part of the political system. So they don't have a right to make social policy. The government should take care of social issues.

Now, against that point I would argue that everything has shifted. Perhaps fifty years ago, in the heyday of the welfare state, that was true, because the welfare state took care of things like health care and child care and Social Security. All of those things are in question right now. We can't just get away with saying that the only responsibility of business is to make money, because business can't even do that unless it helps take care of some of these bigger questions first. The real question for the future is how we delineate the appropriate role of business and government in taking responsibility for filling the needs of society.

Ruth Macklin

BIOETHICIST

For more than fifteen years, Ruth Macklin has worked with medical students and professionals to suggest intelligent ways of thinking through the moral obligations they face in their daily work. In her book *Mortal Choices*, she defines the philosophical principles that doctors and patients face when confronted with such issues as prolonging life, controlling pain and suffering, choosing who receives care, and allowing dignity to the dying. Macklin is professor of bioethics at Albert Einstein College of Medicine in New York.

MOYERS: What's a philosopher doing on the staff of a hospital? What do you have to offer that they need?

MACKLIN: Let me start with saying what I *don't* have to offer. I don't have any easy answers. I think if intelligent, concerned physicians, nurses, and other health professionals who care about their patients and have been thinking about these issues have not been able to resolve them, neither I nor any other philosopher can come with a magic wand and provide answers. But there are some ethical principles that underlie the ways of thinking about these issues, and there are also analytic skills that, as a philosopher, I learned in graduate school and applied in my writing.

MOYERS: Skills of thinking?

MACKLIN: Skills of thinking, skills of clarifying issues. For example, if two physicians or others disagree, are they disagreeing about the facts of the matter, or are they disagreeing about values? Now, that may seem like a simple and easy distinction to make, but often it's not. And one of the things that is most enlightening to physicians is to understand that often their values are not in conflict, and they may not be in conflict with their patients' values, but they disagree in their factual beliefs about outcomes, about probabilities, or even about quality of life. My goal is to get them to understand the nature of the conflict, in the hope, perhaps, that the disagreement or dispute will be resolved. Now, that doesn't always work, but it is a way of trying to think clearly and analyze the nature of dilemmas in ethics.

MOYERS: Are doctors beginning to recognize that the best medical outcome is not always the most desirable alternative for the patient?

MACKLIN: Many do recognize that, and in fact, they would have to be blind in today's world not to recognize that. Strangely and interestingly, though, it often doesn't change their feelings of obligation to what they believe is, if not the patient's best medical interest, then their obligation as physicians. If something is truly hopeless, and they know that the modern medical armamentarium does not have the tools to stave off end-stage cancer, or to prevent the patient from deteriorating with chronic illness, then eventually they may have to give up. But if a patient refuses a treatment that the doctors know will be successful in curing that particular illness, even if it doesn't bring the patient back to normal functioning, then many doctors come up with this duty, "We have an obligation to treat what's treatable."

MOYERS: But do they acknowledge it's the *patient's* life?

MACKLIN: They acknowledge that it's the patient's life, but there are a lot of defenses that doctors have built up: patients are sick, they're not always rational, they may have given up hope, they may be depressed, perhaps the oxygen content in their blood has been diminished to the point where they cannot think clearly. So there are many rationalizations that physicians will use. While recognizing that it's the patient's life, they wonder whether the patient is thinking rationally about his or her life.

MOYERS: Do you consider yourself an advocate for the patient, the doctor, the hospital, or society?

MACKLIN: First and foremost, if I have to call myself an advocate of anyone, I like to think of myself as an advocate for truth and justice and the right thing. But I think it's truly the patient I'm the advocate for. The patient's right to self-determination, the patient's right to informed consent, and the patient's right to decide, even if that means deciding against medical treatment. I also think of myself as an advocate of physicians, because physicians should not be adversaries of their patients; they should be allies of the patient. What's somehow getting lost is the doctor-patient relationship. I would like to be an advocate of doctors in conjunction, or in alliance, with patients. When it comes to the hospital, however, I'm afraid I must frankly say that I cannot be an advocate of the hospital, since the hospital's interests are sometimes, and I'm afraid increasingly, at odds with the patient's.

MOYERS: How so?

MACKLIN: Well, hospitals have two main concerns, even though they are, after all, institutions that were established for the purpose of taking care of sick people. Hospitals these days have overriding concerns about liability, about a prosecutor swooping down if a plug is pulled. So even if there is the remotest possibility that someone will arrive from a distant place and bring a lawsuit, hospitals try to guard against it.

Hospitals are also concerned about their costs. I do think that's a legitimate concern; everyone in any endeavor has to be concerned about costs. But when the hospital's concerns about costs begin to have consequences for the care and treatment of patients, perhaps discharging them early, perhaps denying them a treatment that might otherwise be beneficial, then hospitals are not acting in alliance with patients but out of their own interests.

I find that hospitals are concerned about their image. How often have I heard someone say, "Do you want to be the headline in tomorrow's *New York Post*?" So the concerns of the hospital seem often not to be focused on the care and treatment of patients. That's why I will not consider myself an advocate of hospitals.

MOYERS: What's the most difficult dilemma you've seen so far in your career as an ethicist, a philosopher inside the inner sanctum of the hospital?

MACKLIN: It's hard to pick out one case, but a certain kind of case is common and will continue to be common. That's when family members request doctors to withhold or withdraw life supports from a patient who is no longer competent and has either never stated, or not clearly stated, what he or she would want. Therefore the withholding and withdrawing of life supports will most likely result in the death of a patient who has not expressed prior wishes to a physician or to the family in the form of a living will. That's a very difficult range of cases.

MOYERS: Why?

MACKLIN: Well, we have to ask under what circumstances it is permissible to allow a life to end. Life and death are not coequal choices. We're not talking here about flipping a coin. Since the presumption does, and I believe should, lie in favor of preserving life, we have to ask under what circumstances that presumption in favor of preserving life may be altered.

We're not talking here about flipping a coin. Since the presumption does, and I believe should, lie in favor of preserving life, we have to ask under what circumstances that presumption in favor of preserving life may be altered.

There are two different principles for working with this. One is the request by a patient, either at the time that life, in the patient's view, has become intolerable, or through a prior wish, in the form of a living will or the appointment of a family member to make these decisions. This is the principle of autonomy. Certainly in America we believe that people have the right to self-determination in many other spheres and so they ought to have the right to determine the time and the manner of their own dying. So it's the principle of autonomy or self-determination that underlies the right of patients to decide about these things.

MOYERS: Except when they're mentally incompetent.

MACKLIN: That's right, and if they have not made any statement while they were still competent about what they would want done once they're incompetent, then we can't use that criterion anymore. Then we have to use a very different principle, the principle of proportionality. Do the burdens of the patient's illness or medical treatment outweigh the benefits of that life, from the patient's point of view? That's the critical part: from the patient's point of view. Not the burdens to society but the burdens to the patient.

We can ask how anyone can say that about another person. If we're talking about ourselves, we can judge whether the burdens outweigh the benefits, or vice versa. But how can anyone make that judgment for another person? So the difficulty then, in this range of cases, is having to make that judgment, whether the burdens of continued life outweigh the benefits, for someone who's never exercised the principle of autonomy by saying this is what I want, or this is what I don't want.

MOYERS: So you consider consequences—both good and bad.

MACKLIN: Yes. Now when the patient is no longer able to speak, to think about benefits or burdens, the question is what considerations determine what is a benefit and what is a burden. Often, but not always, in these kinds of circumstances, the patients have lost consciousness. They're in a coma or in a persistent vegetative state, something like Karen Ann Quinlan was in.

This is a philosophical problem. How do we conceptualize people who are in that circumstance? Is life a burden to them? Well, if they can't think and they're not aware and they cannot feel pain, does it even make sense to say life is a burden to them? Surely it's not a benefit, but is it a burden? Here is another layer of philosophical analysis. Some people claim that a person has dignity interests. And this is what underlies this notion of death with dignity. A dignity interest in this circumstance would be looking at someone and asking, would that person have wanted to live like this, and does it preserve the dignity of the vital human being that once was?

Others will argue as long as the patient is not at the point of suffering, feeling pain, or feeling lack of dignity, then dignity interests, or other interests from the patient's point of view, don't enter in at all. In that case, some argue we have to look at burdens to the family, burdens to the hospital, burdens to society. I think it's a dangerous path to begin to go down.

MOYERS: Why?

MACKLIN: I don't myself like to use analogies with the Nazis, but we do have to remember that there have been cultures and societies that have viewed some lives as not worth living. They were called "useless eaters" during the Holocaust. They were people who were viewed as a drain on society—mental patients, mentally retarded people, severely demented elderly people. If we start making our ethical decisions based on what is a burden to society, on who is not only unproductive, but who may be a so-called "drain on society," a "useless eater," then I think we're in a worrisome area.

There is another consideration, and that's the family. Patients who are in a coma, or persistent vegetative state, may become a burden on families. It raises the question of whether a family should be granted the right to make decisions, even if the decisions are made in the family's self-interests, not selfish interest, but self-interests, without regard to the continued life of the patient. This is perhaps the most controversial area, since if a patient has delegated decision-making authority to a family, then it's an extension of the principle of autonomy. If a patient has never made such a delegation, or given that wish in advance, then we're asking the family to speak for the patient, when it's very likely that the family will be speaking from its own interest rather than the patient's interest.

I must confess, I'm of two minds. On the one hand—and we always do have these two hands—who better than a family to make a decision that may be consonant with what the patient's values were when the patient was capable of expressing them? Furthermore, we do presume that families care about their loved ones. Only in a minority of cases are families trying to do the patient in. So both the natural identity of interests and the familial feelings and attachments make the family an appropriate decision maker. Where the other hand comes in is that we know family members don't always have each other's best interests at heart, not only in the kind of horror stories where people are actually trying to get rid of them, but also when advanced age, financial burdens, the burdens of actually physically caring for someone at home who may be ill, can begin to be a drain. So families' motives are likely to be mixed. They may not be base or evil, but they may be mixed. My uncertainty lies in whether anything other than the patient's interests should be allowed to govern these decisions.

MOYERS: The paradox is that physicians are not paid for talking to philosophers; they're paid for doing procedures, and I'm wondering if that's not a deterrent to ethical reflection.

MACKLIN: I think it's worse than you have just described it. Physicians aren't paid for talking to patients either. There is no reimbursement for having a conversation with a patient. It's a sad fact of today's practice of medicine. It's surely true that physicians are not paid for talking to philosophers or ethicists, but neither, strictly speaking, are they paid for talking to a neurology consultant, or an oncology consultant, or a radiology consultant. They're paid for doing procedures under a scheme that pays doctors for the higher technology procedures that they perform. It places a premium on doing procedures and tends to minimize what's very important in caring for people, and that is talking to them, their families, and having consultations with medical specialists and perhaps ethicists.

MOYERS: What's frightening is that so often people lose their liberty and their privacy as well as their health. Since all of us are likely to be patients at one time or another, philosophers included, what can we do fundamentally to maintain control over our lives right up to the end?

MACKLIN: We can make certain efforts. Whether those efforts will succeed depends upon all these forces we've been talking about—physicians, hospitals, and so on. I think what any of us should do, and I've done it, is have a living will. In contrast with the normal will that goes into effect once a person has died, the living will is a statement made by a person while having mental capacity about what that person would want by way of medical treatment once the capacity is no longer there. Usually what a person envisages is loss of consciousness, being in a coma, perhaps severely demented, but typically in something like a persistent vegetative state. In a living will, a person, while still having mental capacity, says, "I wouldn't want to be sustained on those life supports indefinitely, I wouldn't want to live with tubes coming out of every orifice, and especially where I can no longer get any pleasure out of life, no longer recognize my loved ones. Mere biological life doesn't matter to me, and I don't want it to be prolonged by any of those means."

MOYERS: Have you signed a living will?

MACKLIN: Yes.

MOYERS: Why?

MACKLIN: Well, I think for the reasons I just gave. The will of what happens to your possessions after you're dead is a statement that's honored in law, and normally we think people's wishes after death should be honored. Why not their wishes before their biological death, but after their psychological death, so to speak? It's a way of extending autonomy to the point where one can no longer speak for oneself.

MOYERS: If you were on an ethics committee for journalists, I would ask you for counsel in responding to the parents who come and say, "Our child, our grandchild, is dying of leukemia, and we need a bone marrow donor, and we can't find one. Please use your air time to promote his need." But suppose there are three others who've written or called to ask the same thing for their children. What would be your response if you were on my ethics committee?

MACKLIN: I would counsel the broadcaster not to be unjust by publicizing the case that comes to him when there are many others out there that will never gain the attention. It's an injustice in the allocation of these resources to allow the patient or parent who gains access to a person who's in a position of national visibility to come to that individual and say, could you make this appeal? There are not only the other three who may have written or requested it, but there are the hundreds of others who don't have access and can't gain access.

MOYERS: But that's troubling, because you're asking me not to be just in the particular opportunity I have to be just. And the question is, if we don't do something because we can't do everything, will we wind up not doing anything?

MACKLIN: I don't think so, and here's why. If you or any other national broadcaster does not publicize the need that one particular child has for a bone marrow transplant or a liver transplant, it's certainly not the case that no child will get it. It may be true that that particular child will not get it, but there are many bone marrow transplants, there are many liver transplants, and there's a system for allocation.

What people who come to a broadcaster are looking for is special privilege. They want their case in the limelight, rather than in the queue or in the lottery. A child who's in need of a bone marrow transplant will be on a list. A child who's in need of a liver transplant will be on a list. There's an organ-sharing network, and there are bone marrow procurement networks that exchange information and that place people on these lists, and that moreover use other criteria in moving people up and down the list. What the people who come to you are seeking to do is bypass the list altogether. So it's not that no one will get these bone marrows, it's just that that particular child won't have a better chance at it. Now, my question is why should the family who gains access to you be given a more-than-fair chance?

MOYERS: The honest but unphilosophical answer is that you look these people in the face, you see them, they're sitting as close as you and I are sitting, and you see the photograph, you know the child.

MACKLIN: Do they deserve it more because of that? This comes into ethics in a strange way. It's the case you know that prompts sympathy and concern. A child across the world who's dying of liver failure is a statistic. The child across the room or across the street is someone you know and can see. I'm not arguing that should never enter one's ethical sensibilities, but it's not an even-handed way, nor a perfectly just way. It's emotionally difficult to deny the person who makes a personal appeal.

MOYERS: But there is not a perfectly just way, not in this world. And in my tradition, in the stories of the miracles in the testament of Christ, he healed the lame he saw, not those he didn't see; the woman who came to him looking for grace didn't preclude others from coming, but he dealt with the one at hand.

MACKLIN: That's an interesting analogy. The most any one individual can do is deal with the case at hand. The most any individual doctor or healer or religious figure can do is deal with the case at hand, because he can't be everywhere at once, and can't be expected to go across town, or across the earth in order to be able to save a life there. But there do exist mechanisms for a more just allocation.

I guess as a broadcaster, you are in a somewhat different position from the physician. Suppose the physician, the transplant surgeon, sat in his office and the people who came to his office and showed him the picture, or brought the child in, were wealthy, and could afford to take the airplane, come there with the child, stay in an expensive hotel and clinic, and bring the child into his office. Would it be fair for him to treat only those who were able to come because of their wealth and who made that personal appeal because his heart went out to them? Again, I don't think so.

MOYERS: I understand that, but if the individual has to abdicate, then who is responsible for so improving the process of distributive justice to ensure that that fairness is involved in the choices that are finally made?

MACKLIN: That's an important question, and it's a policy question, to which I wish I knew the answer. I think we have to fashion a response in our society and make people responsible; that is, have some systematic way of making these judgments. My objection to the individual making the judgment is it's not systematic, it is ad hoc. With all due respect to broadcasters and others, it seems to me there's no expertise in making these allocation decisions.

MOYERS: But we have expertise in news, and this is news. This particular child needs a bone marrow donor. That's news.

MACKLIN: Right. A complete presentation of the news possibly should also add how many other children need bone marrow transplants, where are they located, whether they are more likely to get a bone marrow transplant if their parents are knowledgeable and gain access to a national news broadcaster than they would be if they lived in the inner city. That's news, too. Who gets onto the news and the means of getting onto the news is something that the news perhaps ought to present. So the news is not complete in presenting the need that child has.

Of course, you could take up the whole news every day by listing all the children in the nation. But maybe you should report on how many children there are who need bone marrow transplants. What is the supply of bone marrow and the compatibility with the donations? How might bone marrow donations be improved so there would be a much better supply, enabling more children who need them to get them? That I think should be news in a sense, too.

MOYERS: Let me ask you about another tough issue. There's a lot of talk nowadays about the behavior of women while they're pregnant. Some women are being arrested in the hospital after their newborn babies are found to have drugs in their systems, and women are being warned that they face criminal prosecution if

they drink during pregnancy. Does a woman's autonomy over her body extend to smoking and drinking even though she knows that harm may be done to her unborn child?

> *I believe a woman has a moral obligation—a moral obligation, since I'm talking about ethics—to do what's best to promote the birth of a sound, healthy child. . . . my argument is that not all moral obligations should become legal obligations.*

MACKLIN: The short answer to the question is yes, I do think that a woman's autonomy does extend to her behavior while she's pregnant. But having said that, I want to quickly add that I believe a woman has a moral obligation—a moral obligation, since I'm talking about ethics—to do what's best to promote the birth of a sound, healthy child. So having said that she has autonomy, how does one analyze that in light of the obligation that she has to try to ensure that she gives birth to a child who is sound and healthy?

Succinctly, my argument is that not all moral obligations should become legal obligations. And although I think a woman does have that moral obligation and should be educated, urged, exhorted, even persuaded by physicians, and by the person who will be the father of the child, that moral obligation should not be transformed into a legal obligation that brings the full force of the state and law into her life, allowing the state to incarcerate her during pregnancy, assign criminal penalties after pregnancy, and essentially view her as a fetal container.

MOYERS: But this means, then, that the individual who fails her moral obligation in this sense is essentially without consequence for herself when that child is born poisoned by her addiction, whether it's alcohol or nicotine.

MACKLIN: No woman wants to have a child who's poisoned. So there are indeed consequences—the same consequences that might befall a woman who did *not* engage in behaviors that risked the health or life of her fetus during pregnancy.

MOYERS: But the chronic smoker or the woman who consumes even a normal bit of alcohol is now said to be potentially dangerous.

MACKLIN: Potentially dangerous. Now, here I think the conclusions and society's concern for the fetus are outstripping the medical evidence. What we need to ask about is the probability that a woman who is smoking tobacco, drinking alcohol in moderation, much less in extreme, will have a child who has one of these bad consequences, a birth defect. And what's the frequency of impairments in the birth of those children, and what's the magnitude of the impairment?

It would be folly to think that we can prevent all birth defects by controlling women during pregnancy. Women have many kinds of reproductive rights. For example, if a woman refuses to have amniocentesis—that is prenatal diagnosis—she may give birth to a child with a serious genetic disorder. Furthermore, suppose she has amniocentesis and the child is found to have a birth defect or is discovered to have an anomaly that can be detected in utero. In our society no one is going to insist that she abort that fetus. So on the one hand we have a range of reproductive freedoms for women who are not engaging in these specific behaviors that are thought to risk the health or life of the child. Moreover, genetic disorders are more frequent than the anomalies that have come to light caused by women who smoke and drink and use drugs. So we must look at this against the backdrop of reproductive freedom, and the freedom that women have *not* to have intrauterine diagnoses, the freedom they have to choose *not* to abort even if a fetus is found to have a birth defect, and compare that with the extreme behavior that is now being urged, if not carried out, with women who use drugs and alcohol even without evidence that there is impairment. Something else is going on here.

MOYERS: But we do have some evidence that the babies of crack users are impaired.

MACKLIN: Yes, we do have evidence, and we have evidence that babies of women who drink alcohol to excess are, too. But we don't have evidence about this particular woman's fetus at the time the woman's liberty is taken away. That is, we're using a statistical analysis of a certain probability.

Our society has agreed that people are not going to be sterilized if they have a 50-percent chance of having a child with a hereditary birth defect, the kind that's called autosomal dominant. No one is arguing that these women should be sterilized and prevented from having children, and yet the likelihood that a woman or a couple with two of these chromosomes will lead to one of these birth defects is much higher statistically than the risk of impairment if the mother drinks. So I'm saying that there's not a very good balance in the concern on the one hand in the general arena of genetics, where women are not being enforced to have abortions or sterilizations, or even amniocentesis, and the very different situation with the use of alcohol and drugs, in which it's being urged that women should be detained in hospitals and put in jail based on a statistical probability of an impairment that's lower.

MOYERS: But if one purpose of law is to give collective societal moral force to an ethical imperative—thou shalt not kill—would you be in favor of a law that said a woman whose child was born with impairment as a consequence of drinking or drugs should perform some kind of community service in teaching other women what she has learned from that experience?

MACKLIN: Community service is an attractive idea. It is, however, a punishment. Let me separate the idea of calling these women criminals from the nature of the punishment. You've suggested a somewhat more benign punishment than incarceration, and one that actually may have some good consequences if it succeeds in teaching other women. But we can't deny that this community service is a legally enforced punishment for what the woman did to her infant.

I must go back to the question of the voluntariness of the behavior. If there's anything that we know medically and psychiatrically about the use of crack, it is that it's a highly addictive substance. The question of whether or not the behavior of crack-addicted women is voluntary and that therefore they ought to be blamed punitively and have legal sanctions imposed on them after the birth of a child comes back to the question of whether people should be held morally and legally responsible for their behavior when in fact their behavior was beyond their control. This is not the same as a woman in a restaurant taking a drink, and someone who sees that she's pregnant shakes a finger or comes over and whisks the glass of alcohol out of her hand. I believe that taking a drink of wine during dinner while you're pregnant is a fully voluntary act. It's not at all clear to me, with the horrible tragedy of crack addiction in our cities and in our nation, that the women who are addicted to crack have become so voluntarily, nor that their choice to become pregnant is voluntary. So it's a complicated issue of laying moral and legal blame.

MOYERS: Let's talk about abortion. Many people in the abortion controversy say that if we could only reckon when life begins, when the fetus becomes a person, we would finally be able to solve the abortion dilemma morally. What's your response to that?

MACKLIN: Well, I think I have a more philosophical response than an ethical one, and it's a piece of bad news. I'm afraid that the effort to determine when human life or personhood begins as a way of concluding when or whether abortion is permissible is bound to fail. I had those hopes myself once, and undertook a study of the literature on personhood and humanhood. This was philosophical literature, religious literature, and legal literature, and I really studied it quite thoroughly to see what people said about personhood, and whether that could illuminate the abortion problem.

MOYERS: The premise is that once you know when life begins, or the fetus becomes a person, then that person assumes certain rights, the right to life in this case.

MACKLIN: Yes. You and I and infants and children and anyone who is an individual born alive, this is what we mean by "person." We believe that persons have a right to life. The question is when a fertilized ovum, which is human genetically, becomes a person and therefore acquires rights just like persons who are born. The answers in very thoughtful and lengthy treatises include the following: life begins at conception, by which is usually meant fertilization of the woman's ovum; life begins at implantation of that fertilized ovum into the uterus of a woman; personhood begins at the onset of electroencephalographic activity, that is when brain waves begin—that's an interesting one because that's our definition of death, death occurs when brain waves cease. So some have thought symmetrically, that life begins with the onset of brain waves, which comes fairly early, in something like the twelfth week. A traditional and older criterion was quickening, when a woman feels the movement within her. Viability is one of today's leading candidates for personhood, and that's because the Supreme Court made viability important in 1973, in the *Roe* v. *Wade* decision. That's when the fetus can survive outside the womb, even with the aid of life supports. We don't mean it could survive without ventilation or artificial respiration.

MOYERS: You've just given five different answers to the question.

MACKLIN: There's a sixth one, and that's birth. Since at least these six, and possibly even some other nuances, have entered in, we'd have to decide among these candidates. There has to be a way of deciding among these proposals for a criterion for personhood or human life in order for it to be of any use in trying to answer the abortion question. Some of these writers in the literature—theologians, philosophers, lawyers—spoke to each other on this issue, and began criticizing each other's criteria for personhood.

When I reviewed the literature and saw these arguments, it became apparent to me that the view that the writer or thinker already had on the ethical permissibility of abortion then determined what that individual thinker or writer said about when personhood began. So very thoughtful and articulate Roman Catholic spokesmen said that personhood begins at conception. Some radical feminist thinkers, who not only believe that women should be able to control their own bodies, they should also have control over their infants after birth—said personhood begins a few months after birth. And there were others in the middle. People who are pro-choice tended to make the criterion for personhood a very late one developmentally, typically at birth, and people from religious and other value perspectives made the criterion for personhood the kind that a blastocyst, that is a few cells of life, could meet. Well, if there could be no agreement on what seemed not so much to be a value question but a philosophical, biological, and conceptual question, it became quite clear that that was not going to be a successful way of trying to resolve the abortion debate.

MOYERS: What you found out is that the position they already held about abortion was imported into their answer to the question of when life begins.

MACKLIN: Those who think that abortion is wrong under any circumstances are those who hold that life begins at the moment of conception.

MOYERS: What does this say then about arriving at an ethical resolution for this controversy that is tearing this country into pieces?

MACKLIN: It says, and it may already be evident to people, that there will never be an ethical resolution if what that means is agreement. I believe that agreement will never be forthcoming on the ethics of abortion. However, we must have public policy, and we do have public policy; it's changing all the time. We had public policy before *Roe* v. *Wade*, we had public policy for quite a while after that, and now public policy is shifting. Perhaps it shows that although public policy may in some ways follow ethical analysis, when ethical agreement or consensus is impossible, we must go forward anyway with public policy, and then we're talking about politics, and not ethics.

MOYERS: That's where the battle is now.

MACKLIN: It's also where it will remain. The difference between ethics and politics is that if there's an ethical right answer, or if people believe there's a right answer, that right answer doesn't change from 1973 to 1990. If abortion was not legal before 1973 and was legally available after 1973, it surely does not mean abortion was ethically wrong before 1973 and became ethically right after 1973. Similarly, if *Roe* v. *Wade* is overturned or eroded, as in the recent Webster decision, it does not mean that the ethics of abortion is any different.

This comes from the standpoint of trying to gain agreement in a virtually irresolvable ethical conflict about which some people are quite certain about the rightness or wrongness, and others are highly ambivalent and very troubled. But given the likelihood that people hold a firm view about what is a person, and therefore about when life may be taken or when it may not be, I think public policy will continue to shift as politics moves in different directions. Politics will never settle the ethical question.

MOYERS: Democracy rarely rests its ethical case permanently.

MACKLIN: No, but I think there are some issues that we've seen in our society and in our lifetime and in recent times when ethical viewpoints have changed, and we have gained a consensus. I think particularly of the civil rights movement, where people had sharply different views, not only politically, but ethically, and actually came to change those views. Despite the racism that still exists, the remarkable changes in a very short period of time and the fact that people even pay lip service to ethically appropriate conduct and rejecting racism show that there was moral progress in the area of moving public policy into a more just resolution of what was a terrible problem of racism. I don't see that happening, or the likelihood of that happening, in the abortion controversy.

MOYERS: Because each philosopher's contribution to the controversy depends upon the philosopher's philosophy.

MACKLIN: And upon premises that one's unwilling to change or alter. It's true that almost everything we do depends on our philosophy, but sometimes we alter or change our premises when new evidence comes to light. Sometimes we change our value position if we see that something that we thought had some consequences actually has different consequences. Reasonable people do come to change some of their values and some of their beliefs. It doesn't seem to me that the evidence that's presented in the abortion debate is likely to change the fundamental value premises that any individual, much less group, holds and cherishes.

MOYERS: That leaves it to politics.

MACKLIN: It does. I think there are unfortunate consequences of leaving it to politics. I applaud the political arena for the many things it does in a pluralistic, free, democratic society. But when ethical issues have to be settled purely by politics, the danger is that we may not come to the right answers.

MOYERS: You're really on the frontier here, aren't you? It's all happened in the last ten years. Bioethicists serving in our hospitals.

MACKLIN: About ten years ago, perhaps a few years longer, the field got started, but it's important not only in the hospital and not only for someone who does it as a professional activity. I'm in the hospital, I teach medical students, I write about obligations of the medical profession. But I think it's important for everyone to think about issues in bioethics, to talk clearly, and in fact for patients to raise with their physicians issues surrounding life-and-death choices. Since we know that doctors aren't raising them with patients, maybe we as citizens should be taking the initiative. Any person with a private physician can raise this discussion long before terminal illness strikes, and long before the heat of the moment, when decisions may not be as rationally made and as carefully thought out.

Perhaps if doctors aren't going to take the initiative, patients might. Hospitals have an obligation to institute some patient-education programs, to give some information to patients about how they may choose to exercise their self-determination. A lot of the kinds of problems we've discussed could be headed off in advance by talking to patients prior to the time when they become incapable of making decisions for themselves. Patients, perhaps along with families, could be enlisted in a discussion that can enable them to express their wishes and express them clearly so that people don't have to guess what they might be, and so that hospital personnel might not have to be called in and say to families, "We're not sure this is what your relative wanted, so you may not make this request."

So part of the burden lies with each of us if not in the form of drawing up a written living will, then at least by talking to our families, talking to our physicians, so that when we're in the hospital the physician won't come to the ethics committee and say, "I don't know what this patient wants because the patient never told me."

FACING
THE WORLD

Ernesto J. Cortes, Jr., organizes people—mostly poor people, people on the margin—to bring about change in their communities. The key to good organizing is "a love of politics, in the Greek sense, not in the electoral sense. We have to understand that we are social beings, that our development only takes place to the extent that we engage in public life and public discourse. That there is, in Hannah Arendt's phrase, the joy of public happiness."

Cortes is good at what he does, and the people he works with often learn how to be good activists, too; their efforts have brought better water and better schools to many towns and neighborhoods in Texas. However, there is something of the oxymoron about the idea of "public happiness." Fewer and fewer Americans seem to be connected to the nation's public life.

Michael Sandel worries about this estrangement. As a political philosopher, he sees "a widespread sense that power is located in distant places and that, individually and collectively, we're less in control of the forces that govern our lives." In part, he says, that is a consequence of the reflexive impulse of many mainstream politicians to "banish religion and morality from public life." The better impulse would be "not to flee moral argument in politics, but to engage in it, to make it better, to offer a richer, more pluralistic, more democratic moral vision, drawing in some cases on religious traditions and on religious arguments."

It is not just politics that is gnawing away at our public happiness. Jacob Needleman, a philosopher and professor of religion, has recently turned his attention to money, something more provocative than politics and more intimate than sex. "In our present day and age, to be in the world is to be involved with money. I don't care what you do or who you are, you are going to be involved with money. There are no caves left anymore to retire into," says Needleman. True, but the popularity of Needleman's seminars suggests that we have not reconciled ourselves to the high price money exacts from us. "The question is, how to separate all that is involved with money from this search for yourself. It's insane to turn away from that. It's impossible. But we have to turn toward it without being fooled by it."

Equally inescapable is the reality of the global life. There is a growing recognition that just as Americans make up only part of the human population, so too do humans make up only part of the world population. And there is a growing commitment in many people to foster and honor the health and integrity of our planet. If money is the practical reality we cannot escape, cooperation is its moral equivalent.

Some of this wholeness and interconnection is grounded in religion. Steven Rockefeller, a convert to Buddhism, argues that democracy is as noble an ideal spiritually as it is politically. We cannot find God as "an isolated self," he says. "The mistake made, I think, by many people in the midst of their religious quest is their belief that by just doing meditation or by seeking a God outside the world, they will somehow find wholeness. But we as selves are intimately related to the world of which we are a part. We can only find psychic wholeness when we find a relationship with the larger world."

For some among us, a relationship with the larger world—and the older and younger worlds—is an ancient tradition. Like the other chiefs before him, Chief Oren Lyons of the Onondaga makes his council decisions based on the welfare of the seventh generation to come. Native Americans "have a long perspective. We've been in one place a long time. We've seen the sun come up at the same place many many hundreds, thousands of years," he says. "I'm sitting here as the seventh generation because seven generations ago, those people were looking out for me."

Enter physics, itself a search for wholeness at its smallest common denominator. Physicists looking for fundamental laws of the universe are used to dealing with large questions. But Murray Gell-Mann, who won a Nobel Prize for discovering the quark, the tiniest particle known in nature, spends much of his time now pondering how simplicity produces serendipity. He studies various complicated systems capable of changing or adapting—biological evolution, the global economy, the development of language—in order to understand their similarities and relationships. "It's impossible to get a grasp on the global properties of any complicated nonlinear system by deciding in advance that you're going to look narrowly at this aspect, and that aspect, and that aspect, and then trying to put those aspects together to make a picture of the whole thing," says Gell-Mann. "It just doesn't work! You can find out whether there are some simplified aspects that allow you to get a grasp of the global behavior only by studying the global phenomenon and allowing those aspects to *emerge*. You can't decide them in advance."

Surprise, C. S. Lewis taught us, is the joy of life. It is also, we are beginning to understand, the nature of the universe.

Ernesto J. Cortes, Jr.

ORGANIZER

© 1990 K. C. Bailey

Ernie Cortes empowers. He is a member of the national staff of the Industrial Areas Foundation, a nonprofit organization that helps "ordinary" people organize to make positive changes in their communities. In his home state of Texas, where he heads a statewide coalition of some three hundred church-based IAF member organizations, he teaches citizens to take on issues that matter to them: water and sewer systems, roads, education, worker safety, health care. Named a MacArthur Fellow in 1984, he is currently organizing new projects in Dallas, Phoenix, and Tucson.

MOYERS: What kind of people come to you for training in the art of public life? And what is it they want to know?

CORTES: They care deeply about cities. They care about the city as a place where people come together and enter into relationships, where people's families are raised, and children are mentored, and old people are cared for. They see that cities all over the country are having very great difficulties.

The economy of the city is in great disrepair. The infrastructure is crumbling. There's urban violence, drugs, alcohol, and gangs. None of these things are conducive to families developing and growing and nurturing. There are all kinds of pressures on families in the city—economic pressures, cultural pressures. So they need mediating institutions, intermediate institutions which enable people to negotiate with those pressures and with the corporate people who sometimes stand behind those pressures—the developers, the utility companies, et cetera.

They're also worried about the educational system, which is in very great difficulty in the United States. But most important, they're deeply concerned about the need for meaningful and nurturing relationships, which are so hard to maintain in the isolation and alienation of our cities today.

MOYERS: Some of your critics say that you are actually too conservative. They say you're bringing more people into a system of existing institutions that are ossified and out of date, when you should be changing that system.

CORTES: Well, I've very seldom been privileged to be called too conservative, but I guess in some ways, we are advocating a culturally conservative strategy. It's important for people to be connected to institutions. We have to make a distinction between tradition, which is the living ideas of the dead, and traditionalism, which is the dead ideas of the living. If you say I'm conservative because I think the family's important, I plead guilty. If you say I'm conservative because I think the church is important, I plead guilty. If you say I'm conservative because I think communities are important, I plead guilty. If you say I'm conservative because I think the public schools could be made to work, then I plead guilty. And if you say I'm conservative because I believe America can work, then I plead guilty as well.

MOYERS: I don't see much evidence over the last fifteen years that the poor are a lot better off than they were when you began organizing.

CORTES: There's no question that we've got some serious problems. In San Antonio, my own city, studies have demonstrated that over the last ten years people are getting poorer. We're dealing with some very powerful global economic forces, but we're also dealing with some very powerful and somewhat mean-spirited political forces in this country, and we haven't been able to overcome them yet. But people still have hope. We've been able to do some things that I think are important.

MOYERS: In San Antonio you took some housewives and turned them into experts on zoning, on sewage treatment facilities, on sanitation. What was that all about?

CORTES: First of all, I appreciate the compliment, but I'm not sure it's fair. All I did was point them in the right direction by teaching them how to build the COPS organization—Communities Organized for Public Service. They were very bright, eager, energetic people—housewives, Kelly Air Force Base workers, priests, nuns—just a whole range of people who were really concerned about what was going on. So there was a great deal of commitment and energy and desire to do something: flooding, toxic waste, the city water supply. People wanted to fight the development that was going to degrade that water supply.

But in order to do so they had to learn things. They had to learn about water and how it worked. They had to learn about development strategies and policies. They had to present alternative solutions. Saul Alinsky used to say that the price of a constructive criticism is a creative alternative. You have to not only organize against, but organize for. You have to come up with some alternatives.

MOYERS: What's the key to organizing?

CORTES: A love of politics, in the Greek sense, not in the electoral sense. We have to understand that we are social beings, that our development only takes place to the extent that we engage in public life and public discourse. That there is, in Hannah Arendt's phrase, the joy of public happiness.

MOYERS: But there doesn't seem to be much discourse in politics today.

CORTES: There's not much discourse in the quadrennial electronic plebiscite that we have every four years in this country, but that has very little to do with politics. It has more to do with marketing strategies, marketing segments, direct mailing, polling. That's not what de Tocqueville talked about as America's great strength—the people's love of public discourse and debate, and willingness to deal with local issues from an institutional base, working through these mediating institutions. He was enormously impressed by the potential these institutions offered. Of course he also saw some serious problems, like slavery. People were left out.

One of the things in fact that we're most interested in now is making sure that people who are normally considered the have-nots don't get left out. The IAF wants to organize people who are not part of decision making in communities to be part of the decision-making process. To be involved in politics. For them to see that there is a way in which they can qualitatively improve their lives.

MOYERS: Not just to turn out and vote?

CORTES: Voting is important, but it's the least important aspect of any democratic decision making. It's the affirmation of a decision that was made through a process of discussion and debate. They have voting in totalitarian countries, too.

MOYERS: Gorbachev was just elected president with virtually no opposition.

CORTES: Yes. Augusto Pinochet used to have plebiscites in Chile, which was not a very democratic society under Pinochet. There was no discussion. There was no debate. There was no free press. There was no opportunity for people to engage.

Timothy Garton Ash says that in Central Europe an internal immigration takes place where people withdraw into their own cocoons. It takes place when there's no public space, when there's no opportunity for debate. I see some of that occurring in the United States. Not because of some totalitarian dictator, but because of the role that the media play in politics. People feel alienated and disconnected from it.

We can't rely on people by themselves to be good. They have to participate through institutions. We need institutions and a political culture that hold people accountable and teach them certain values. We're bombarded by all kinds of information, but there's no framework for developing political judgments. The institutions that used to teach people—whether they were political parties, labor unions, churches, voluntary associations—those institutions have been weakened, or they've been rendered incompetent. That's why the IAF seeks to build some sort of institutional framework to enable people to acquire the requisite skills and information so they can make political judgments. In a real sense, organizations like COPS or United Neighborhood Organizations in East Los Angeles are mini-universities for these skills.

MOYERS: What kinds of skills?

CORTES: Our leaders need to understand power. How it operates, who wields it. You have to know not only what a politician says, but who gives him money and how those people influence his decisions. You have to know his record. You have to understand how to negotiate with people. You have to know how to present your issue carefully. You have to understand how to do the research behind a particular issue. Secondly, our leaders have to know how to build what we call public relationships. An organization like Valley Interfaith or COPS is not going to work unless ordinary people can build relationships with other people they don't know very well. The IAF organizers must teach people how to develop sustaining mechanisms for maintaining a collective leadership.

MOYERS: Who has been the world's greatest organizer?

CORTES: Moses and Paul.

MOYERS: Moses was an organizer?

CORTES: Oh, sure. Moses took a divided people, a mixed multitude, people from Sinai and Egypt and all kinds of different traditions, and taught them how to come together under one faith.

MOYERS: It took him forty years to get them out of the wilderness. And then they wanted to go back.

CORTES: But to me the most important part of the story of Moses is the burning bush. Moses was a prince in the House of Egypt, raised to be a leader. I don't know why, but evidently he felt deeply about the way the Hebrew people were treated. In other words, Hebrew is not an ethnic term. It refers to people who are outcast. It refers to people who have no status.

Moses identifies with the Hebrews, the outcasts, who are being pushed around. But even so, the people aren't grateful. They turn against him and hand him over to

Pharaoh. He leaves, but he can't forget. The memory is too great. The pain is too great. The burning bush symbolizes his confrontation with himself. He hears the people. He hears their misery. He hears their agony. And he goes back and he begins to teach them how to organize.

MOYERS: There's that wonderful moment which is a key insight for me into your own work when Moses says, "I can't handle this burden, I just can't do it."

CORTES: Yes. Moses is confronted by the people. They want meat to eat, they're tired of all this manna, and they wish they were back in Egypt, where they had garlic and leeks and cucumbers. Moses in anguish confronts God and says, "Why do you treat me so badly? Where am I going to get meat for all these people? Am I a wet nurse that I've got to carry them on my breast?" And God says to Moses, "Moses, I have taught you how to do it." God tells him to gather together all the leaders of the people—the seventy elders—the people he knew and had tested. "Bring them together," God says, "to take the burden that's on you. Don't be a charismatic leader. Don't think that you're going to solve all their problems. Put it on them. Agitate them. You want meat to eat? Go out and organize—there's some quail over there. Go out and organize hunting parties. Go get it." And Moses still doesn't buy it. He says, "Where am I going to get meat?"

Now, what's great about the story, which most people don't see, is the humor. How do we know about this story? We know about it because Moses is telling the story about himself. But he doesn't tell the story in a way which makes him look good. He tells us all about his anxieties, his fears, his anguish, his desperation. How he wants to quit. How he's depressed, he can't move, he's paralyzed. Moses has a great perspective on himself, a great sense of humor. He's not thin-skinned like some of our best politicians. They can't learn from their mistakes. They can't be critiqued. They always have to look good. They've become tinsel personalities. One of the things we need to teach people is not only to critique, but also to be critiqued.

MOYERS: But the real lesson for Moses was that an organizer ought to get the people to help.

CORTES: The job of an organizer is to agitate. Now, people have the stereotype of what agitation is. But in the sense the IAF teaches it, the agitator raises questions, gets people to look at their choices, to look at their options, to understand that power depends upon consent. The ethics of power really hovers around the question of how you go about obtaining consent. You can obtain consent by force or violence. You can obtain consent by deceit, by lying to people. You can obtain consent by manipulating people, withholding information, rendering them incompetent. But finally you can learn to obtain consent through informed judgment.

There is a tradition in south Texas I call "learned helplessness." People have been taught to be incompetent by all the institutions: family, the church, the school. There was a tradition among the *quinieros*, the workers of the King Ranch. They didn't have to worry about their retirement, they didn't have to worry about their kids' education, they didn't have to worry about anything, because the boss would take care of them. Well, the King Ranch is no longer owned by a family; it's now owned by anonymous corporations. The *quinieros* who are now out of work have no skills, no education, nowhere to go because they've been raised in this almost feudal system where they were taken care of. They were taught to be dependent upon the *patrón*.

MOYERS: They never questioned his authority?

CORTES: Why should they? He always took care of them. If he told them how to vote, what did it matter? In those days, those things weren't important. What was important was the integrity of that relationship between you and the land, and between you and your work, you and your family. I'm oversimplifying it just a bit, but that tradition holds all across south Texas. Part of what these organizations do is to teach people how to exercise responsibility with power.

MOYERS: Give me an example. How do you teach the consequences of actions?

CORTES: One of the most confrontational actions COPS ever organized in San Antonio involved window shopping. My mother and my aunts used to love to browse in the department stores. We didn't have any money so they'd go downtown and window shop, just look at things. The sales clerks would call them "pills" because they never bought anything.

We were having trouble getting the City Council in San Antonio to pay attention to our counterbudget, which included provisions to fight flooding and all kinds of public improvements in the city. So we decided that we had to take it outside the conventional political establishment and get the corporate community involved. I said, why can't we get a whole lot of people to go window shop at Josky's of Texas, the biggest department store of San Antonio? COPS took five hundred folks and we went window shopping. They went in and they looked at furs and sables and so forth. More than five hundred of them went up to the most exclusive department store in town, just trying things on. They didn't hurt anything. They didn't do anything illegal. Window shopping is legal. But they did it at one time and one place.

MOYERS: And the owner got the message?

CORTES: Yes.

MOYERS: What was it Saul Alinsky said? Make the enemy live by his own book of rules. That's what you were doing there?

CORTES: COPS had made this commitment to justice and equality and fair play, and we were trying to get the corporate community, the political community, in San Antonio to be responsive. Sometimes you've got to get people's attention first. You've got to get recognition. And sometimes you've got to deal with the most disenfranchised force to get everybody else to deal with what's not going right in the culture. In religious tradition, the poor have got to evangelize the rich. It's a responsibility of poor people to teach rich people how to be human.

MOYERS: What do you think we are when we are most human?

CORTES: We're rational. We're caring. We are reciprocal. We give and take. We share. Bernard Loomer wrote an essay called "Two Kinds of Power." He says that most of our institutions practice what he calls unilateral power, the power of domination, what Lord Acton would call unaccountable power. Power which is inaccessible and, therefore, unaccountable. We think that people can learn a different kind of power. Power which involves sharing and collaboration. Power which involves people learning how to work together. I'm not trying to preach pie in the sky, but I'm saying that people have got to recognize other people's interests. Sometimes there has to be hard bargaining, hard negotiating. Sometimes arguing, sometimes confrontation. Alinsky used to say that if you had to define democracy in one word, it would be *compromise*. There has to be a deal. A political philosopher said once that in politics, it's not enough just to be right. You also have to be reasonable. You have to give and take. You have to compromise.

MOYERS: It's easy to say that to the poor, though. How do you say that to the rich who have been winning in this country all along?

... the rich have got to understand that they've got a stake in this too, unless they want to live in a Third World country. I'm not sure that America can make it without a decent public school system. I'm not sure America can make it without cities.

CORTES: That's true. But the rich have got to understand that they've got a stake in this too, unless they want to live in a Third World country. I'm not sure that America can make it without a decent public school system. I'm not sure America can make it without cities.

MOYERS: I agree with you. But parts of our culture, parts of San Antonio, are already a Third World country. All the border of Texas-Mexico is a Third World country. You're not talking about something that *could* be, you're talking about something that *is*.

CORTES: That's correct. And that's why I think Texas has a real role to play. We could be a model, or we could be an example of the future that doesn't work.

MOYERS: The Nigeria of America?

CORTES: That's right. That concerns me. I know there are people in the corporate community and the political community who understand that. Ross Perot, for instance, is deeply involved in the education issue. He tells his friends, "I know you don't like black. And I know you don't like brown. But I know you love green."

MOYERS: It comes down to that, doesn't it?

CORTES: Sometimes. One of the things that IAF teaches is that people sometimes do the right thing for the wrong reasons. Some of my friends who are idealists expect people to do the right thing for the right reason. They want people's motives to be pure. But with the world as it is, people operate on the basis of their own interests. We have got to find out what is the interest of people.

MOYERS: What's going to happen in Texas and in California when the people who are now in the minority become, in another fifteen years, the majority?

CORTES: Well, that's a good question. I would ask it of people who think that it's not in their interest to be concerned about those people. Just ask them how their Social Security checks will be paid when the ratio of workers to retired people is two to one, and one of those workers is uneducated, can't read, can't function in a working environment. Now where is that Social Security check going to come from? Where is his pension going to come from?

MOYERS: You're asking us—rich and poor—to think of self-interest as something more than just our own aggrandizement, our own reward.

CORTES: That's correct. Properly understood, self-interest leads people to be their brothers' and sisters' keepers. You recognize you need people. I can't get what I want unless you get what you want. We're in this together.

MOYERS: That's not the way the world seems to have been working.

CORTES: No question about it. But that's why we need to build broad-based organizations. That's why the IAF is recruiting organizers. That's why no matter how hard I work myself out of a job, I'll always have one, because people need these organizations that teach them how their self-interest is connected to other people's interest. How they're not going to get what they want unless other people get what they want. How compromise is not a dirty word. Half a loaf is still bread, you can still eat it. But then there's the compromise of Solomon, which is half a baby, a corpse. The question is, which compromises do you take? Which compromises are appropriate?

MOYERS: What does it mean when you say you want to empower the poor?

CORTES: In a word, I want to teach people. I want to teach people how they can take their private pain, their private hopes, their private aspirations, and translate that into public issues that are going to qualitatively improve their lives and those of their children. But that's going to require work on their part. It's going to require responsibility, because the flip side of power is responsibility. It means they have to be owners of their own destiny. That means everything from raising the money to build an organization so that the organizers work for them and aren't being paid by some outside sources. It means understanding the issues. They have to be their own spokespersons. They have to speak for themselves. They have to understand the arguments, because they have to engage in the discourse with the mayor of San Antonio, or the mayor of Houston, or the bank president. It means they have to be willing to teach others.

MOYERS: How do you do that, though? Because in Texas, as you said, the Hispanics have been taught for so long to conform that it must be very difficult now for them to learn to challenge authority or to believe that authority will deal with them.

CORTES: You take institutions—the family, the church—and you use them as a source of power, of confidence, of authority. If you get people to talk about what's in the interest of their families, what are the threats to their families, what are the threats to the churches and community, then they're willing to look at things like zoning, and they're willing to look at things like the school.

The most important lesson IAF has to teach is the iron rule. The iron rule is never, ever do for people what they can do for themselves. It's the opposite of learned helplessness. The iron rule respects people's dignity. It says, "You have to challenge people." It's the opposite of what Alinsky called "Welfare Colonialism," where you treat people as if they were children. John Stuart Mill wrote an essay on representative government which said that the act of participation teaches people confidence in their own competence. That's central to understanding the iron rule. People have got to have the opportunity to learn. It's what we teach our kids! We enable them to grow and develop through victories. And we teach them how to manage their own lives, their own destinies. We do a horrible thing to them when we take away that responsibility.

MOYERS: The organizer is not more important than the organized.

CORTES: Well, he is and he isn't. She is and she isn't. That's part of the contradiction, if you will, the dialectic involved in this business. It won't happen without you, but it can't be dependent upon you.

MOYERS: Sometimes you don't even lead them into the Promised Land. Moses didn't get there finally. But he organized the people so they did!

CORTES: Yes. And it's important to have a vision of where you're going. It's important to have a vision. Without a vision, people perish. The Scripture tells us. People have to be challenged to develop their own vision and their own values about what's important. Otherwise it's not their thing, it's your thing.

MOYERS: What have you learned—in almost a generation of organizing—about power in America?

CORTES: You don't see enough examples of it, but you see when it can work. You can teach people. You can teach people to be effective. I've learned that.

MOYERS: Have you had it confirmed for you that absolute power is corrupt?

CORTES: Lord Acton was on the money! Unaccountable, inaccessible power is corrupting. Not only corrupt, it's corrupting.

MOYERS: But absolute powerlessness corrupts, too, doesn't it?

CORTES: Yes. If the flip side of power is responsibility, then people who have no power are irresponsible. They become wards of the state. And you see it all the time. The worst example, of course, is a fourteen-year-old girl who's on cocaine who has a child. Children having children. Now to me that's a product of absolute powerlessness. The degradations of people who have no choices; who don't see any options; who are victims.

MOYERS: Do you believe God is just?

CORTES: Yes.

MOYERS: Then why so much suffering? Why so many poor?

CORTES: I don't know! I'm not an expert on all this business.

MOYERS: Are you still a practicing Catholic?

CORTES: Yes. I see a great deal of beauty and joy in my own children. They're wonderful people. My son, my daughters, my wife. I've been gifted with a good relationship; I've been gifted with what the Hebrews would call *"Shalom"*: family, health, friends, meaningful work . . .

MOYERS: In this case, God is just.

CORTES: He's been good to me! I feel that we're responsible, though, for creation. I believe Genesis is the most important book in the Bible sometimes, and that we've been given lordship over creation. We're responsible for what happens, and I think we can make choices. We can make choices whether or not we blow up the planet. We can make choices about whether or not we degrade it. Or we can make choices to leave our future generations a legacy, a heritage.

MOYERS: The future is not something abstract to you.

CORTES: No, my future is in my son. He's my future. My future is in my daughters. My future is in the children they're going to have. A political scientist once wrote that political decisions revolve around a relevant time period. The relevant time period for a politician is two years or four years; for a general it's five years; for a corporate executive, it's every quarter. He said, "But the relevant time period for a grandmother is a generation, because she's concerned about her grandchildren." Well, I'd like to appropriate that time period into our IAF organizations, into our culture, into our psyche, into our political leadership, too.

Michael Sandel

POLITICAL PHILOSOPHER

"Justice," the class that Michael Sandel teaches to undergraduates at Harvard University, has the largest attendance on campus. Leading his students through works by Plato, Aristotle, Locke, and Immanuel Kant, he helps them to understand that they have a stake in ideas about the common good, distributive justice, and democracy. While earning his Ph.D. at Oxford, he began writing his book *Liberalism and the Limits of Justice*. In this and other writings, Sandel is concerned with the civic challenge of our times—self-government.

MOYERS: What do you think are the questions we should be asking as we move now toward the twenty-first century?

SANDEL: The first is whether self-government is possible under modern conditions. And if so, what do we need to do to revitalize it? I don't think the answer to either of those questions is obvious. We know that a certain minimal, not-very-demanding democracy is possible—

MOYERS: One votes for whomever one can identify on the ballot—

SANDEL: Right. We do vote in elections, and that's something. That's of great moral and political importance, especially in contrast with countries around the world that don't enjoy such freedom. But that isn't genuine, full democracy. It's not the kind of democracy that Jefferson, for example, had in mind for this country. Or that even some of the Progressives of the early twentieth century had in mind for this country.

MOYERS: A lot of Americans are congratulating themselves because of the apparent triumph in Eastern Europe of liberal democratic capitalism as an aspiration over communism. Do you think that battle is over?

SANDEL: George Bush, in his inaugural address, said that for the first time in this century we no longer have to debate long into the night about which system of government is best; we know. That seems wrong to me.

No one worth taking seriously is debating very long into the night defending communism. But the real question now is: *what do we know?* What do we have that we're so proud of? Democracy, to be sure, yes. But what counts as democracy? What's the meaning of democracy? Is democracy just a question of counting up people's preferences and managing their self-interests in a way that satisfies them as the consumer society might satisfy their consumer preferences? Or is democracy a more demanding thing, something that makes a claim on the moral character of its citizens and demands of them an exercise of self-government that is more than just pursuing their preferences in the public realm as well as in the market? It seems to me that's a debate that's very much alive, and it's a debate that the Eastern Europeans themselves are going to have to confront very soon.

MOYERS: This isn't something only Harvard professors should be thinking about, is it?

SANDEL: I certainly hope not. The questions are philosophical questions, but the aspirations that they speak to and the political circumstances that give rise to them are the concern of every citizen of this country. To be a citizen in a democracy means being a little bit of a philosopher.

MOYERS: What has happened to our public life? We've seen a trend for years now—declining voter turnout, eroding party loyalties, diminished confidence in government.

SANDEL: There's a widespread sense that power is located in distant places and, individually and collectively, we're less in control of the forces that govern our lives. This is happening despite the fact that individual rights and entitlements have actually expanded in recent years. People have a sense that something has gone wrong with the enterprise of self-government.

MOYERS: You've said that we're facing a world that we can neither summon or command.

SANDEL: Yes. The present generation was weaned on a confidence in America's unrivaled power in the world and a faith in unprecedented growth in the domestic economy. It comes as a source of great frustration that suddenly we no longer seem to be the masters of our collective life in the way that we had come to expect.

MOYERS: That old notion is weakened—that the individual matters, that I can signify, that I'm an autonomous individual in a self-governing political culture.

I had an interesting experience after reading your essay in which you wrote about how de Tocqueville in the nineteenth century marveled at our custom of town meetings. He said, "The town meetings are to liberty what primary schools are to science. They bring it within the people's reach." Just after I finished that article, I picked up the *New York Times* to read the story of a New England town that has stopped holding its town meetings. No one had the time or the deep desire to come. And I thought, "What takes its place?" The institutions that used to inform our public spirit—the local precinct, the party, the church, the neighborhood association, the community—have all been rendered impotent or irrelevant to many people's concerns.

SANDEL: Yes. There are still forms of public life that can command the allegiance and the participation of their members, but they're on the defensive, and they're in danger of being eroded. Politicians in recent years have tried to speak to these frustrations—Jimmy Carter in his way; Ronald Reagan in his. Reagan used largely nostalgic terms, talking about small-town morality and the neighborhood, but he didn't address those genuine concerns with any political programs that could begin to satisfy those aspirations.

MOYERS: Reagan talked about traditional values while espousing a modern free-for-all economy that undermines those same values. As you point out, capital flight and the power of the modern corporation have rendered communities almost helpless before forces that decide their fate from thousands of miles away.

SANDEL: It's not simply that the nation-state is controlling the economic forces which the local community can no longer control. Even the nation-state now is increasingly disempowered in the face of capital mobility and international markets. What was once a problem for local self-governance only is now becoming a challenge to governance even at the level of the nation-state.

MOYERS: Think of the contradiction right now in Eastern Europe. They want the consumer goods this new international economy can generate, but as the coercive rule of the Communist Party diminishes, they are threatened with a breakup into ethnic and religious and linguistic groups that threaten the consensus which they need to compete in this world.

SANDEL: It's true, yes. And the problem of the nations within Europe is now suddenly arising again after forty years of Soviet domination that suppressed that whole question. In a way, encompassing different nationalities within one country—the question of how they can express their autonomy, whether through federal systems or local systems—is going to be a serious question for the Eastern European countries as well as for Western Europe and North America.

MOYERS: What about the United States? Do you see us reweaving ourselves into more viable smaller groups that satisfy the need for some sense of belonging?

SANDEL: There have been gestures in that direction, but for the most part so far, those attempts have been more symptomatic than constructive. The Moral Majority made this point. It spoke to the sense of a certain emptiness in American public life, the sense that our public life is not a place where people can address larger questions of meaning. So fundamentalists tried to fill the public space which had been left empty by the political agenda with a very narrow and intolerant version of morality and religion. The impulse to try to achieve, within public life, some way of expressing larger concerns was authentic and admirable. What was wrong with the Moral Majority was not that it tried to bring morality and religion into the public realm, but that its vision of morality and religion was narrow and cramped.

What was wrong with the Moral Majority was not that it tried to bring morality and religion into the public realm, but that its vision of morality and religion was narrow and cramped.

MOYERS: What's clear after a decade is that we're not getting a new sense of our public life either from the militant moralism of the fundamentalist right or from militant secularism.

SANDEL: I think that's true. The moral of the story is not that we have to banish religion and morality from public life, which was very much the reflexive impulse of many mainstream politicians. The better response would be not to flee moral argument in politics, but to engage in it, to make it better, to offer a richer, more pluralistic, more democratic moral vision, drawing in some cases on religious traditions and on religious arguments. One of the lessons of the Moral Majority is that a public life that's empty of moral meanings or larger meanings is not a place that's safe for pluralism and toleration. To the contrary, it's a place that's all the more vulnerable to narrow moralisms and intolerance.

MOYERS: What do you think is the moral base for pluralism?

SANDEL: There are two philosophic grounds for pluralism. One is it's a fact of our life. We're never going to persuade people to change. We have different conceptions of the good life, so let's just try to accommodate and put up with the diversity that's hopelessly with us.

A better philosophical ground for pluralism is to appreciate the distinctive goods that these different ways of life represent. Not just to put up with them, but actually to try to cultivate them through the educational system, and through the content of our political debate, to appreciate and to draw energy from the distinctive moral visions and religious traditions that comprise American pluralism.

MOYERS: I agree with that, but you're running right into the buzz saw of reality. Let's just take two examples: abortion and homosexuality. If the state says that it's a woman's right to choose an abortion, isn't the state, in effect, saying that for those women who choose it, abortion is a good?

SANDEL: Abortion is a very good example of the problem with the version of liberalism that tries simply to set aside moral and religious controversy. It's important to see what the mainstream Democratic and Republican parties share in the way of philosophical assumptions. For all their differences about how big the role of the federal government should be or how generous or skimpy the welfare state should be, what they share is the idea that government should try to be neutral on moral and religious questions. In a pluralistic society like ours, they say, you can't hope to affirm in politics, or even to entertain in politics, controversial moral and religious conceptions, because that will tear us apart. The debate is largely conducted in the language of rights, on the assumption that to argue in the name of rights avoids taking a stand on controversial moral and religious questions.

MOYERS: In other words, the government will not try to decide that abortion is good or bad morally, but will leave it to the individual to decide.

SANDEL: That's right, but that isn't a compelling way of dealing with the abortion question. Even though our public philosophy aspires to neutrality and tries not to take sides on moral and religious questions, in a case like abortion it's impossible not to. Either abortion will be permitted or it won't, under these or those circumstances; underlying that decision will be some implicit, maybe unacknowledged answer to the question of who is right in the debate over when life begins in the relevant moral or political sense.

MOYERS: That's what I was trying to say. If the state agrees with a woman that it's her decision to terminate a pregnancy, the state is implicitly, it seems to me, admitting that for her, abortion is a moral good. It is sanctioning the view of abortion as a moral good for her.

SANDEL: Not necessarily approving it as a moral good, but at least saying that it's morally permissible. That rejects the position of the Catholic Church, for example, which says it isn't. The way to address that issue is not to pretend to a neutrality that can never be achieved, but to try to draw on the various moral and religious arguments and traditions that confront that question politically.

MOYERS: Are you saying that the state should play a positive role in bringing the different theologians and moral philosophers together to arrive at a definition of abortion that would be acceptable to the body politic?

SANDEL: Yes, ideally. At the level of the Supreme Court, it's disingenuous of judges trying to decide this question to deny that they have to confront the moral and religious questions that arise. And politically, yes, the debate would be informed and enriched and perhaps made more politically manageable if we were to explicitly admit into political discourse the competing moral and religious views, rather than to try to set them side.

MOYERS: Isn't that what the Supreme Court did when it said that abortion is permissible in the first months of pregnancy? It was saying, in effect, that abortion is morally permissible during that period of time, but in the third trimester, it's not morally permissible. So the Supreme Court, as one arm of government, was in fact doing what you have suggested.

SANDEL: They were taking a moral stand in that respect. But they weren't explicitly saying that they were taking a moral stand. They weren't acknowledging that they were making a judgment that was consistent with some moral and religious views and inconsistent with others.

MOYERS: But isn't that the necessary strain of a democratic state: you are not supposed to choose between the Catholic position on abortion and the Congregational position on abortion?

SANDEL: But how could the Supreme Court do otherwise? The question really is how explicit it will be about what it is doing. To what extent should the Supreme Court acknowledge what it can't avoid doing, namely, making decisions about law that presuppose some answer to the moral and religious questions? Let me give you an example that's far removed from the abortion case and that for most people cuts the other way.

Back in 1858, Abraham Lincoln and Stephen Douglas debated the question of whether moral judgment should play a part in political decisions. Douglas's position was a precise parallel to the position of those who today say, "Let's keep moral and religious convictions out of political debate." He said, "Let's not take a stand on the morality of slavery. Let's just leave that to the territories to decide for themselves." Lincoln said, "That's wrong. You can't separate moral questions from political questions. Slavery should be treated as the moral wrong it is and so it should be banned from the territories."

MOYERS: Well, I agree with Lincoln. Do you?

SANDEL: I do agree with him. In fact, in one of his perorations in the final debate with Douglas, he said, "Isn't it false statesmanship to try to make policy based on caring nothing about the very thing that people care the most about?" He drew laughter from the audience. But it was a telling point against Douglas. I think that's right.

MOYERS: And the parallel today?

SANDEL: In the case of abortion, for the most part, people who argue for the woman's right to choose want also to say that they're not making any moral judgment. The state shouldn't make any moral judgment at all. I'm sympathetic to their actual position. But I disagree that you can really defend that position without acknowledging that you are taking a stand in a moral and religious controversy. So, in that respect, Lincoln's position in his debate with Douglas—that morality has to play a part in politics—actually argues for those who would say the abortion question can't be separated from the moral and religious controversy that surrounds it.

Abortion is a morally difficult choice. There are powerful arguments, serious arguments, both ways. What I resist, though, is the thought that runs through liberal political philosophy and also the actual opinions of judges: that in allowing women to choose for themselves, we're rising above moral and religious questions.

MOYERS: Okay, now let's take homosexuality. If the state says that what consenting adults do in private is their business, isn't the state, in effect, requiring that for those who practice homosexuality, it's a good? That, of course, deeply offends those who believe it's a sin. So, in effect, the state is taking a moral stance.

SANDEL: If that were the reason the state gave for saying that what people do in the privacy of their own homes is their business, then that would be taking a moral stand. But in their recent opinion in the case of Michael Hardwick of Georgia, the Supreme Court refused to strike down the antisodomy law. They said it didn't violate privacy rights. The four dissenters on the court said, much as you've said, that it should be up to the individuals to make their own choice. But I think the dissenters' argument is misplaced.

I agree with the result they reached. I agree the law should have been struck down. But the dissenters simply took the position that people should be free to make their own choices in private. The analogy that's often used in these cases is with pornography: if people want to watch pornography in the privacy of their own homes, they should be allowed to do it. But when they use pornography as an analogy for homosexual intimacy, they demean the very practice that they would defend. They demean it by saying homosexuality is not analagous to heterosexual intimacy, which the court has protected, but that the relevant analogy is to a base practice that we put up with so long as it's done in private.

This is a weak case for toleration. It accepts the practice, not by affirming that there may be some human good realized by the practice, but instead by saying it's a base thing that we should put up with because we'll never get agreement about it. It doesn't cultivate appreciation for the diverse ways of life people may pursue. It doesn't cultivate appreciation for the distinctive goods that different ways of life represent. It puts all of those questions aside and says, maybe it's a bad thing, maybe it's a base thing. But let's just put up with it. Because otherwise, we would come apart at the seams.

MOYERS: Are you suggesting that the Supreme Court should try to encourage an appreciation for the good as defined by consenting homosexuals?

SANDEL: Well, I'm suggesting a form of argument for those who would argue before the court.

MOYERS: You're certainly arguing that the state should not be neutral on these issues.

SANDEL: No. I don't think the state can be or should be neutral on moral issues. I think that at its best, public life is a kind of civic education. The relevant education for the questions of toleration and pluralism is an education in the appreciation of distinctive ways of life. The content of the pluralism, not just the fact of it, is something that our public life should address and appreciate.

MOYERS: But as you said, for the state to argue that there is a good in abortion or homosexual intimacy is to take a stand against the teachings of, say, the Catholic Church in this regard. Isn't that another form of majoritarianism, where the majority decides what's good, even though the minority does not accept it morally or religiously or philosophically?

SANDEL: That's a real worry—the tyranny of the majority. One of the reasons that philosophical liberals leave religion and morality out of politics and out of the law is just that worry about the majority imposing its own convictions and prejudices. The answer to that majoritarian threat is to try to appeal to a richer conception of democracy than just adding up votes. At its best, democracy fosters argument and debate and political discourse about the good life, about the common good.

MOYERS: If our public debate changed in response to some of the things you're saying, what would we be hearing differently? How would we be speaking differently?

SANDEL: To some extent, we would be speaking in ways that we naturally, normally speak, just as you and I sit here and debate this. We would be speaking the way, for example, that the Catholic bishops spoke, when they appealed to their own religious traditions but made arguments directed toward the larger public on issues of nuclear deterrence or economic justice or abortion. We would appeal without embarrassment to moral and religious traditions in the hope that they might inform public debate, rather than contaminate it with intolerance.

MOYERS: But ultimately, the state would have to take sides.

SANDEL: Yes. Ultimately, the state does have to take sides. The strength of a federal system is that there are different levels of government and different forms of public life that can decide different questions. At more local levels, we can give more genuine expression to people's collective identities and to their aspiration to work out a common good in public, not just in private.

MOYERS: You said that in recent years liberalism has faltered because of its failure to argue for a vision of the common good. Why has that happened?

If I have a right to something, say if I have a right to free speech, it can't be one thing in New York and another thing in Alabama.

SANDEL: I think partly it's for laudable reasons. After all, liberalism from the New Deal to our time has been combatting some genuine and seemingly intractable ills. One of them is racism. In fighting the civil rights battles, local control was often a code word for racism and prejudice. So liberals, rightly, wanted to argue for rights that would belong to all American citizens. If I have a right to something, say if I have a right to free speech, it can't be one thing in New York and another thing in Alabama.

But when our idea of what counts as a right is enlarged beyond legal and political rights to social and economic rights—to a minimum income, say, or a minimum level of education for my children—we tend to provide them at the largest, most comprehensive level of political association. For us, this has meant the nation rather than the community or the state. That has the effect of draining political importance from those smaller forms of political association. That's one reason that contemporary liberals have not been as alive as they might be to the importance of local communities to self-government.

MOYERS: Is that the real flaw of liberalism? That by attending only to needs at a national level we are neglecting the localism of America?

SANDEL: Well, smaller forms of political association and of community life are necessary if public life is to have a genuinely civic dimension and address the moral character of citizens without imposing values that people may not genuinely share. So it's community for the sake of a civic project that's my concern, and that seems to be missing from the reigning public philosophy.

MOYERS: In part, it's missing because the sources of it have disappeared. We don't live in small towns anymore. The town meeting has been interred. People live in one state and work in another. They don't have time to be volunteer firemen. Or to go to town meetings—if there were town meetings. Are you suggesting that we put something back in the bottle that no longer exists?

SANDEL: No, and that's the difficult thing about it. It may be that geographical location may no longer be available as a primary source of community. So I think the question is: what other forms of genuine political community and public life, less expansive than the nation-state, are available? Some of the answers may come from religious traditions. Others may come from social movements, from protest movements. One of the shining examples of political communities that actually did provide an exercise in civic education is the civil rights movement. It wasn't just a way of achieving certain ends politically. It was also, itself, in the debates, in the arguments, and in the sympathies and public awareness that it generated, an embodiment of the kind of civic life that citizenship in a democracy ideally realizes.

MOYERS: How would we define this republic as a caring and sharing community?

SANDEL: On rare occasions, we can act from a sense of shared purposes as Americans. Historically, those have been times of war or crisis. That explains the attempt, in times of peace, to galvanize a sense of shared purpose in the name of a war on poverty or war on crime. But the shared self-understandings on the national level are hard-won and will only be available at best as glimmers, as brief moments.

So even as we try to be alive to the possibility of a shared national American culture, we shouldn't rest everything on that national commonality. We should also appreciate and cultivate and foster, in our political life, the particular forms of life in communities and convictions and moral and religious traditions that make for the plurality, and to enable our politics to draw strength from those particular forms of identity, as well as from the community we share as Americans.

MOYERS: Are we too noisy, too raucous, too pluralistic? Are there too many of this race and too many of that race, too many tongues and too many different gods, for us to expect that our democratic culture can reflect some shared sense of human enterprise?

SANDEL: I don't think it's a question of different tongues or convictions or gods because numbers aren't the problem. It's a question of the way we address and even appreciate those different tongues and convictions. We must include them and draw strength from them politically within our public life, rather than excluding them, requiring them to rest at the entry way, to remain in private life. A politics that's empty of larger meanings—moral, spiritual meanings, or for that matter, that's empty of any sense of a shared project—is not a democracy that can sustain itself.

MOYERS: Conservatives are going to applaud you. They're going to say you are arguing their case that government has a role to play in the civic virtue of its people and the moral education of its citizens.

SANDEL: What I want to argue is that the progressive tradition, the liberal tradition in American politics should grasp the insight that some conservatives do see, and to use it to reinvigorate the liberal democratic tradition with arguments that attend to the moral character of citizens, rather than ignoring it and setting it to one side.

Jacob Needleman

PHILOSOPHER

Jacob Needleman says he writes for people like himself who want to return to the basic questions: Who am I? Why am I on earth? How can I find meaning in my life? A scholar and seeker, he is professor of philosophy and comparative religion at San Francisco State University. His new book is about money and its power to shape our culture and our souls.

MOYERS: You've spent so much of your life wrestling with the big ideas of religion and philosophy. Why are you now writing about money?

NEEDLEMAN: Because money today has entered into every aspect of human life. Much more than any other previous culture, money is in everything. You have to face the money question no matter what you're doing.

MOYERS: You said recently in one of your seminars that money is more intimate today than sex.

NEEDLEMAN: In earlier generations, there was a lot of ambiguity and hypocrisy about sex. People wouldn't talk about it. Nowadays, after two minutes of conversation with most people you can find out, if you're so inclined, more than you ever wanted to know about sex in their lives. But ask someone how much money he has. Oh no! It is the most secret, most intimate part of many people's lives.

MOYERS: And you say that our culture is drenched in money.

NEEDLEMAN: Absolutely. We want it more than anything else, but the things that we're supposed to buy no longer bring us joy. Home, family, education, travel, art, the pursuit of knowledge. All those aspects of human life for which money was meant to serve as a means are more and more becoming drained of intrinsic meaning, and the only thing left that has any meaning is the means itself. Money becomes more vivid, more intense, than any of the experiences it brings us.

MOYERS: You can see that in art, where vast sums of money are paid, not for the purpose of pleasure, not for what we take from it, but because art is a commodity to be bought and sold.

NEEDLEMAN: It's very hard for us to look at things themselves just for what they are, particularly if something costs 40 million dollars. It's very hard not to be influenced by the 40 million. Or even 4 million. Or even 400. The dollars are the thing. So the art world, really, has been devoured by the money.

MOYERS: Is it fair to say that money has become the chief representative of the life force?

NEEDLEMAN: Yes, I think so. It's what everybody wants,

everywhere. It's the one thing we all have in common. Somebody has observed that World War III is now being fought on the financial battlefield. It's money that's making things move around between Japan and the United States and now Eastern Europe. Hasn't it been remarkable how many things have happened in Eastern Europe without bloodshed? It may have to do with the fact that economics is moving things around.

MOYERS: Is that really new? Hasn't the human pursuit always revolved around the acquisition of wealth and the comfort and privilege and protection wealth can bring?

NEEDLEMAN: Yes. There's always been greed, there's always been avarice. There's always been a problem with people wanting more than they need. That's caused more problems for the human race than almost anything else. But cultures have always wanted other things, too. They've wanted honor. They've wanted power. Love. Respect. Beauty. It's hard to say now, though, that our culture wants anything else as much as it wants money.

If you walk through a museum you see that tremendous energy has been put into creating works of art. What we have put most of our energy into is the financial structure of our culture. We have an incredible financial structure in our country. I don't think any other culture has had quite the highly developed financial structure as America. Someone said that the aim of America has been to make the world safe for money.

Now I think there is a negative side to all this, but we can try to avoid the hypocrisy about money and take it seriously. It's a force. I think people need to take it quite seriously and recognize that it is a force and that it's through this thing called money that things actually happen in life. The art of living is to be engaged in the money game without being devoured by it. And that's what I've been exploring in all my work.

MOYERS: How does the pursuit of money affect our understanding of self?

NEEDLEMAN: Well, that's where the action is now. If we're going to live in the world, we have to live in the world. In our present day and age, to be in the world is to be involved with money. I don't care what you do or who you are, you are going to be involved with money. There are no caves left anymore to retire into. If you want to go to a cave you have to get the real estate agent to find one for you. You have to pay the taxes on it. Now the question is how to separate all that is involved with money from this search for yourself. It's insane to turn away from that. It's impossible. But we have to turn toward it without being fooled by it. In other words, the world of money has this power to fool us, to deceive us into thinking that it's really the most important thing.

MOYERS: You write that our pursuit of money has us living in one sense like animals?

NEEDLEMAN: I was thinking of the Buddhist tradition, in which the animal world is the next level down from the human world. The animal is constantly looking for food, constantly preying on other animals. And we're constantly looking for more money and more money. In order to get that money in certain kinds of economic structures like our capitalistic system, sometimes I have to do it by making someone else lose something. I don't think capitalism has to be like that, but very often my profit depends on someone else's loss.

The medieval laws against usury were based on an attempt to understand what money really meant. Money was a means of organizing the material needs of human life, at the same time recognizing that we are dependent on each other in the human family and that we're meant to serve something much higher. In other words, you didn't go for a loan in medieval times unless you really needed it. So if I loaned you money, it's because you needed it, and I should not profit from your desperation. But now, our whole society's based on loans.

MOYERS: So that's why usury was considered a sin.

NEEDLEMAN: Absolutely. What does it mean that our whole society is based on debt now? Everybody owes everybody, and there's no longer money in the old sense of a coin that was itself of some intrinsic value. What is going on here? This is a big riddle.

MOYERS: What have you learned in your study about the history of money?

NEEDLEMAN: Well, I was brought up to think money is like stones or something, it's just there. But somebody invented it, somewhere in the seventh century B.C. in Greece. It was a big thing. People could carry money with them instead of doing a transaction on the state level. It brought a certain amount of freedom. And democracy was possible. It was an ingenious, brilliant device. A brilliant invention.

The whole idea of the bank was a relatively recent invention. Somebody had the brilliant idea of having a bank to give pieces of paper in exchange for people who deposit their money. Eventually, a man named John Law, in order to get a particular king out of trouble, said, in effect, "You know, King, not everybody is going to come for this money at the same time. We could issue *more* receipts than we have money to cover it." "*Bravo!*" Immediately, with one stroke, the "wealth" was doubled.

Law eventually came to a very bad end, as most monetary innovators do. But it was a very creative discovery he made—that now we can have less money on hand than we have bills out for. Money has become a promise and not an entity in itself. Inflation, in that sense, is what I would call a slowly breaking promise, because the money we have is, in a certain sense of the term, losing value. If money is meant to be an index or an instrument involving human relationships, then money has to do with ethics. It is a way of our exchanging with each other what we need, of implementing the human-to-human relationships. So, if there's such a thing as inflation or that sort of thing, it means something is going wrong in the human relationships.

MOYERS: It certainly has changed human relationships, whether it's good or bad. Coming here I had to stop at the bank and use my card to get a little cash. I saw no human being. I said "Good morning" to no one; no one said "Good morning" to me.

NEEDLEMAN: It's affected everybody; I'm not going to be idealistic about it. For the convenience and the flexibility and instrumentality of the money, we have lost a great deal of the human relationship.

MOYERS: What intrigues me about the notion of money is the fundamental paradox at the heart of it. It is an illusion. It is not that the dollar bill or the ten-dollar bill has value in and of itself. It is based upon an unwritten agreement that we will treat it as valuable.

NEEDLEMAN: Exactly. And if the faith in what's behind the money begins to disappear, then there's financial panic and the civilization crumbles.

MOYERS: Maybe this is part of what's behind this fierce notion that you describe as driving the modern society—this fear that somebody will pull the agreement apart.

Somebody will renege on the promise, and if I don't make sure I have more than I need, however much that might be, I'll be left in a hole when that happens. That's why I drive myself faster and faster to get it.

NEEDLEMAN: I think money has to do with security. We all feel that. But what is real security in this world? That's another question. There is the illusion that if I have a lot of money, I'm going to be secure. But we here in San Francisco recently had a very strong earthquake. And, I would say, for fifteen seconds, 4 million people in this area suddenly realized that all they thought of as security was not secure. When you're in the middle of an earthquake you begin to question, what is it that I really need? What is my real rock, as it were? In my opinion, it's something much more inner. I would bet that 4 million people for the fifteen seconds of that earthquake suddenly questioned all their values as things started to come tumbling down. So money brings security, but only if the civilization you're in is firm. I think you're right, none of us feel it's going to last.

MOYERS: Security is also, though, the sense that there is someone else upon whom I can rely and in whom I can trust. Another person, another group of people. A society that, if I fail or if I'm ill or if I am desperate, will come to my relief. There is a sense of security in family, in neighborhood, in congregation, in our communal effort. When that is impersonal, when only a piece of paper becomes the means of transaction, I'm not sure I can rely on other people when I most need it. What struck me most about the earthquake was that those people learned in that moment of crisis that they could depend on each other.

> *People think it's a great, human, spiritual act to rescue a drowning child. It's not. It's normal human nature. But we've gotten so far from being normal that we think it is a magnificent deed to help someone who's in trouble.*

NEEDLEMAN: Yes. They could. But again, it only lasts for a little while and then, a few days later, a few weeks later, it disappears. Why doesn't that lesson enter more deeply into our lives? It should be absolutely natural! This is one of the weirdest things that's happened to ethics in our world. People think it's a great, human, spiritual act to rescue a drowning child. It's not. It's normal human nature. But we've gotten so far from being normal that we think it is a magnificent deed to help someone who's in trouble. The normal being, the natural man, the real self, is by nature relational and sharing. The old view used to be that we are basically selfish animals, and we join together in a society in order to keep from hitting each other over the head. I don't think that's based on a real view of human nature. Human nature down really deep in the real self is sharing.

MOYERS: Well, look at Jesus' story of the Good Samaritan. The Good Samaritan stopped and picked up the fellow on the side of the road and cared for him. He was sharing himself at that moment with that beleaguered soul. That is at the heart of what we're talking about. He had nothing to give at that moment except himself. He was doing a normal thing.

NEEDLEMAN: Can I tell you a story? I was invited by *Time* magazine to be a participant observer at the launch of Apollo 17. At that time, there were a lot of cynical people complaining about the space program, that it was taking money away from the poor and all that. But I went down. It was a night launch, and there were hundreds and hundreds of reporters all over the lawn, drinking beer and waiting for this tall, thirty-five-story-high white rocket lit by these powerful lamps. We were all sitting around joking and wisecracking and listening to the voice of Walter Cronkite like the voice of God coming over the loudspeaker telling us what was going on.

Then the countdown came, and then the launch. The first thing you see is this extraordinary orange light, which is just at the limit of light that you can bear to look at. It's not too bright. You don't have to turn away. It's beautiful, everything's illuminated with this light. Then comes this slow thing rising up in total silence, because it takes a few seconds for the sound to come across. Then you hear a "WHOOOOOH! HHHHMMMM!" It enters right into you. This extraordinary thing is lifting up. Suddenly, among all these cynical people and the wisecracking people, myself included, you could practically hear their jaws dropping. The sense of wonder fills everyone in the whole place, as this thing goes up, and up and up and up. The first stage ignites this beautiful blue flame. It becomes like a star, but you realize there are human beings on it. And then there's total silence.

Then people just get up quietly, helping each other up. They're kind. They open doors. They look at each other, speaking quietly and interestedly. These were suddenly moral people because wonder, the sense of wonder, the experience of wonder, had made them moral.

By the time we got to the hotel, it was gone. But my point is, in the state of wonder, no one can commit a crime. When you're in touch with something inner, you just are naturally sharing and caring to other people. So to me, the pursuit of understanding ethics without trying to understand this inner self won't go past a certain point. It won't take us where we need to go.

MOYERS: You used the word "moral," not "ethical," for that moment of knowing and sharing. Why?

NEEDLEMAN: Ethics refers to outer actions, what you do. But inwardly, you are moral. That is, you are in touch with something that's truer, more your right nature, your real nature. As a result of being moral, you act in a way that could be judged ethical.

MOYERS: But when you got back to your hotel rooms it was gone?

NEEDLEMAN: It left a trace for a little while. But on the whole, it disappeared under the usual social conventions, and by the time we were ready for bed, we were our usual egoistic selves. But it shows that even in everyday life, we sometimes experience a change of what you might call "state." A state of consciousness, as it were. In that state we are closer to being loving people, caring people.

MOYERS: You have said that human time is conscious time. I think of that as you talk about being conscious of ourselves.

NEEDLEMAN: Well, "conscious time" happens in certain moments of one's life, maybe great crisis or emergency or great joy. It's an unforgettable, vivid moment of being present in oneself. Suddenly time has quite a different sense. Time passes very slowly, sometimes we say it's as though time stood still.

There's a wonderful passage in Dostoyevsky's *The Idiot* when the hero is about to be hanged. He has one minute left before he's hanged and he begins to say to himself, "What an enormous amount of time I have! I have sixty seconds. I'll have ten seconds to think about my family and there's still time left." So at that moment time simply opens up. In that one minute he goes through a lifetime of intense subtle impressions and experiences. That is conscious time. I don't think you need a death sentence in order to have it.

MOYERS: What are we conscious of?

NEEDLEMAN: First of all, we are conscious of our world around us. We're conscious of a sense of our own being, our own self. *My* self, here. In the middle of that, there is something which you would call the sublime; if you like, call it God. But there are many levels to that. Consciousness doesn't have to be of something in the usual sense. It's in itself a valid and reverberating inner experience.

MOYERS: Have you had moments like that?

NEEDLEMAN: Yes, I think everyone has. But our culture hasn't enabled us to value them properly. We take them as extraordinary, and then we say, "But it was just a momentary thing." And we go on. Our culture hasn't enabled us to say to ourselves, "Wait a minute! What is this that I've just experienced? Is it something I need to develop more? Is it really myself? Is all the rest of what I call myself and what people call me and think of me and how I regard myself—is all that secondary?"

MOYERS: Do you believe that in some way we human beings are intended to live in two worlds?

NEEDLEMAN: Absolutely. The one world is the world we live in every day, this world of action and activity and doing. It's usually governed by our everyday thoughts and emotions and so forth. The direction toward the other world appears in these special moments. We have intimations of it in our feelings, sometimes when we come in touch with great art, or literature, or philosophy, or nature. We have a certain feeling, a certain longing that we can't quite put in words. It is like what Plato called "eros." It's a striving. A longing. A wish towards something greater and higher in ourselves.

MOYERS: We have a spiritual nature as well as this nature that depends upon food and drink and sex—

NEEDLEMAN: And social recognition. And money. And all that. This other direction—you can call it spiritual, but spiritual is a word I have trouble with because to many people spiritual means something insubstantial, and this is damned real. This is more real than anything! But it's a longing. I would say it's a love. A love of that which is greater, higher, and more inclusive than my ordinary self. Call it God. Why not? But it's inside, as well as above.

MOYERS: It is the experience of God which comes from being a part of God's creation.

NEEDLEMAN: Yes. And we human beings, as far as I understand it, are meant to be in contact with this higher nature. So we are two. This is our great possibility, and our great sorrow. It's a very difficult spot to be in. The human being is uniquely a being of two natures and our task and difficulty is to find a relationship between them in our lives.

MOYERS: In one of your seminars, you say we are simply not living our lives.

NEEDLEMAN: Yes. We are being lived, by the forces around us and the influences that impinge on us from all of the media and all of the books and educators and all of the other things we hear about and the values that come from outside. But a conscious self, an autonomous individual, intentionally choosing, after pondering and reflecting and consulting with his or her neighbor, consciously choosing what to do and how to live—almost none of us live like that. Part of the illusion of our culture is we think we are free and independent beings, when actually we are being pulled by the forces outside of us. We have no time, no inner space, to search for something higher than that.

MOYERS: You mention time again. I keep hearing in my mind as you speak so many of my friends, and myself included, saying, "I have no time. I'm so busy. I have no time." Do you hear that often?

NEEDLEMAN: Always. This is one of the things that most interests me in the study of money. We're coming to the end of a hundred years or more of devices that were invented in order to save time. What has become of time? Nobody has enough time anymore. We are all completely taken. The way I would put it is that time is slowly disappearing. We are a time-impoverished society. We have lots of material things, but we have no time left. Human time has disappeared, and we're in animal time. Or vegetable time, if you like. Or mineral time. The time of computers. The time of things. Of mechanical devices. Animal time is literally the time of the rat race. It's the New Poverty.

MOYERS: And yet there are still sixty seconds in a minute, sixty minutes in the hour.

NEEDLEMAN: But we don't experience it that way. We don't experience the present moment. Time is real only in the present moment. And we're never in the present moment. We're always worrying about the future, regretting the past, trying to do three or four things at one time. We never have a sense of: "I am here . . . now . . . in this time." And this is reality. It has been said, and perhaps there is some truth in this, that when the clock started striking the quarter hour, that was part of the beginning of capitalism as we know it. Time is money. When you started measuring time in that way, it became a tyrant. A clock is a very good servant, but it becomes master. I'm no longer looking to measure how much time I have to do something I have consciously chosen to do. I am asking my clock if I have time to do something I want to do. And it's saying, "No, you have no time."

MOYERS: Is all this a way of saying that money itself is dirty?

NEEDLEMAN: Not at all.

MOYERS: Money by itself is neutral.

NEEDLEMAN: Yes, like every invention, it's neutral.

MOYERS: You're not urging us to go live in the mountains or in the caves, or turn our backs upon this world.

NEEDLEMAN: Not at all. But to be more consciously involved in understanding the money game that we're in. It's just as wrong to live in beautiful fantasies of being free of money and craving, as it is to be absorbed in and devoured by the rough and tumble of money life.

MOYERS: That's what I like about some of your earlier writings, *The Art of Philosophy* and *Lost Christianity*, where you say that the meaning of life is found on the verge of the two realities, the reality of the spirit, and the reality of this world of getting and spending and being very much involved with the mechanics of society and the way life is lived. That's where meaning comes from. It's not in isolation.

NEEDLEMAN: Exactly. Human meaning comes from being in two worlds simultaneously and it's a very difficult place to be. People often try to find meaning in one world alone. Either the world of outer life, or in the world of some mystical reverie. Neither one's going to bring real meaning. This is what's unique about a human being.

MOYERS: There's a psychiatrist in New York who told his patient, "When you talk about money, it's never money you're talking about."

NEEDLEMAN: That's the secret. It's not just money I'm talking about. It's money as a way of speaking about the human condition. It's what human substance is invested in money. That human substance is something all of the traditions of all time need to speak about.

MOYERS: You also say, "Hell is the state in which we are barred from receiving what we truly need because of the value we give to what we merely want." How does one arrive at understanding what it is we truly need?

NEEDLEMAN: I could give answers which have been given throughout the ages, and everyone would agree with them. Like we need to love and we need to serve. We very much need to serve something other than ourselves. Without that, we'll wither away. We need physical food. We need shelter. We need to pay back nature, reproduce if we can, if we want.

But this is a serious question. It's the kind of question more and more people are asking now. It's that kind of question that, when you really feel it in your guts, begins to give you meaning. Strangely enough, meaning can come from the search for meaning. When I have a real question like that, I have something that directs me. "What do I need?" That kind of a question can really bring meaning to my life because it makes me inquire. It makes me try to understand. And when I do it with another person or two or three people together, when we begin to inquire, we already begin to have a new human relationship, which is what used to be called friendship.

> *Questioning makes one open, makes one sensitive, makes one humble. We don't suffer from our questions, we suffer from our answers. Most of the mischief in the world comes from people with answers, not from people with questions.*

MOYERS: The great philosophers felt that meaning was in the experience of the question and not in the discovery of the answer.

NEEDLEMAN: Questioning makes one open, makes one sensitive, makes one humble. We don't suffer from our questions, we suffer from our answers. Most of the mischief in the world comes from people with answers, not from people with questions.

MOYERS: You're holding seminars on money. Do the people who come there know what they're getting? Or do they think they're going to get advice on the stock market?

NEEDLEMAN: I tell them, "This seminar will not help you make more money. It's not for that. It's to understand yourself in the midst of the world we live in, which is a world of money." And people come in large numbers for that.

MOYERS: What are they looking for?

NEEDLEMAN: I held a seminar a few weeks ago and I asked them what their questions were, and almost all of them had the same question: "How do I engage in making a living and still keep my soul?" They feel that the world of money, the world they are forced to live in, is sucking their soul dry and they cannot keep their self-respect, or their sense of inner worth, and still participate in the money world. They want meaning. People come for meaning.

There's this idea, "Do what you love, the money will follow." I think it's one of the New Age fantasies. Many people say, "No, I have found that when I'm there making my living, making money, I am completely wasted on meaning. My life is meaningless. I'm manufacturing widgets or I'm selling this or I'm writing these things that are totally without any nourishment to my inner life and I come away from that tired and exhausted. I have no time for anything that I consider meaningful. Now, how can I relate to money in a way that doesn't destroy me in some way?" Almost all of the questions are of one variation or another of that. One thing that helps them is to hear great ideas of the ancient traditions, restated in ways they can understand. When these great ideas are really given in the real way, they come in touch with another world. This is the world of ideas. If people come in touch with that they immediately feel a shock of recognition. It opens something, a part of themselves that they haven't been in touch with. And it may not be spiritual realization in any grand sense, but it's the beginning of a contact with a part of themselves that isn't concerned just with making money.

MOYERS: Are you saying people are hungry for philosophy?

NEEDLEMAN: I planned at first to be a doctor, and my parents were so happy. Then when I said, "I'm going to be a philosopher," they were very nice, but they couldn't help being a little disappointed. One day at a party, after I'd gotten my Ph.D., someone introduced me to someone as Dr. Needleman, and my mother immediately said, "Oh, he's not the kind of doctor who does anybody any good."

MOYERS: Well, there you are, that's the prevailing sentiment of society about this. Philosophy bakes no bread. It builds no buildings. It makes no deposits.

NEEDLEMAN: That's right. All it does is open a human being to the most important things in life.

Steven Rockefeller

P R O F E S S O R   O F   R E L I G I O N

The path Steven Rockefeller has taken on his intellectual and spiritual journey would very likely surprise his great-grandfather, the tycoon and philanthropist John D. Rockefeller. A convert to Buddhism, he has been teaching in the Religion Department at Middlebury College in Vermont for almost twenty years. Centering on what he calls "the democratic reconstruction of religion," Rockefeller has steeped himself in the writings of Walt Whitman, Ralph Waldo Emerson, and John Dewey, about whom he is writing a book.

MOYERS: The poet Walt Whitman wrote about America as a "sublime and serious religious democracy." What do you think he meant by that?

ROCKEFELLER: Whitman believed that America had at its core the values of a spiritual democracy in the sense that it had faith in the common people, an Emersonian faith in the capacities of the individual, and a sense of the beauty and wonder of the whole natural world. For Whitman, the objective was to encourage men and women to realize their distinctive capacities at all levels of society. To do this, to create a culture in which people are genuinely set free and are able to realize and express themselves, gives to the democratic life a kind of religious depth and meaning.

MOYERS: Do *you* think America is a religious democracy?

ROCKEFELLER: I don't think it is today. I think a religious democracy is a meaningful ideal we need to strive towards.

The American philosopher John Dewey once said that modern Western civilization stands or falls with the capacity of the individual to be its bearer. Now, I think this is the issue in a nutshell. If we're going to have a free world, we have got to create schools and social organizations that develop in people the intellectual, the emotional, and the spiritual capacities to be independent moral beings. The objective is an autonomous individual who also is willing to develop his or her capacities by using those capacities in the service of the community.

MOYERS: Didn't Dewey also say that the next prophet to command our hearts will be the person who enables us to experience democracy as a religious vitality?

ROCKEFELLER: Yes. He meant that the ultimate religious meaning is to be found in everyday life. Dewey was very concerned that many ordinary people felt their daily lives were really not all that important and lacked any ultimate meaning. That ultimate meaning had to do with relating to a God who was outside the world, and with fulfilling some exalted ethical ideal that had nothing to do with taking care of the cows, or washing dishes, or bringing up children, or being kind and compassionate in one's daily life. What Dewey wanted to do was to give people a sense that "ultimate" meaning can be realized in one's daily life by living as a responsive, caring, compassionate person.

MOYERS: So it's up to each of us to express the religious meaning of democracy in our own lives. Is that what you're saying?

ROCKEFELLER: That is exactly the case. Many people turn to religion to find wholeness, to find inner peace, to find a sense of belonging if you will, with God or the larger universe. But one cannot find this as an isolated self. The mistake made, I think, by many people in the midst of their religious quest is their belief that by just doing meditation or by seeking a God outside the world, they will somehow find wholeness. But we as selves are intimately related to the world of which we are a part. We can only find psychic wholeness when we find a relationship with the larger world.

It makes me think of the story of Viktor Frankl in the concentration camps. Many people have said that the evil of the Holocaust has made impossible any faith in God or any sense of ultimate meaning in life. But Frankl's experience is to the contrary. In the midst of the suffering he was able to find meaning through his relationship with others. One example will illustrate the point.

He was a doctor, and he decided to remain in his camp when the Allied forces were approaching, giving him a chance to escape. He stayed with the sick and the dying at the risk of his own life because he was the only doctor left. After making that decision, he reports, he was filled with the deepest sense of peace that he had ever experienced.

There are many illustrations of this kind of experience throughout human history, whether you look at Euripides' Iphigenia, Socrates, Jesus, or Martin Luther King, all people who in the midst of suffering and evil have been able to find, if you will, meaning and the face of God. This is the deepest answer we can come to in wrestling with the problem of evil. There is no satisfactory explanation for the problem. But what you can say is if you live a certain way and if you carry within you this compassionate, democratic spirit, then you will be upheld.

If men and women come to realize that, and pursue their own religious quest through living as responsive and responsible persons in their everyday life, they can overcome one of the great splits in the modern psyche.

MOYERS: The other side of religious democracy, though, is the danger that theology will produce empire. There's the old idea that Americans are exclusively God's holy and chosen people and that the United States is the kingdom of God.

ROCKEFELLER: Yes, but the values associated with democracy don't belong only to America today. They are shared widely by people in all different parts of the world. Democracy is not just an American imperial export. The Chinese and the Rumanians and the Russians claim democratic values as their own. And I think that we will be seeing new ways of embodying these democratic values and ideas.

Still, America now has an opportunity to export something that can be genuinely helpful to the rest of the world. I mean, we've been criticized for exporting consumerism and destructive forms of industrialism and so forth. Yet America does have a real treasure that goes back to the work of the Founding Fathers and that needs to be rediscovered, retrieved, and shared more widely in the world.

MOYERS: But even if many other nations are embracing democracy now, they also embrace very different religions—Judaism, Buddhism, Hinduism. Do these religions connect somewhere at some crossroad?

ROCKEFELLER: Yes, I do believe that there are commonalities. And I believe that all the great religions teach that the truth ultimately is realized in and through the quality of one's actions in relation to the world. St. Francis, for example, said that he could not really hear the gospel until the day he embraced a leper. He could not hear the gospel until he actually practiced it. Then it came alive.

There's a wonderful story about a Buddhist philosopher named Asanga who had a very complicated problem he couldn't work through. So he decided he would go into meditation and try to contact the great bodhisattva Manjusri, the bodhisattva of wisdom. For many years he sat in a cave and meditated. Several times he thought about giving it up because he couldn't make contact with Manjusri. On one occasion he looked up and saw a little bit of water dripping from the ceiling of the cave, and he realized he'd been sitting there for three years and the water had worn away the stone a bit in that three years. If water could wear away stone, he thought, maybe his concentrated practice would get somewhere, too.

But after nine years, Manjusri still had not manifested himself. Asanga gave up in discouragement and left the cave. Just then, a mangy old dog came by with a terrible wound in its side. Asanga's heart was filled with compassion, and he took the dog in his arms and cleaned the wound and bound up the dog's side. There were maggots in the wound, and out of compassion for the maggots Asanga cut off a piece of his own flesh and placed the maggots on it. As he finished caring for the dog, he noticed a great radiance all about him and he looked up and there was Manjusri standing right next to him.

At first he was annoyed, and he said to Manjusri, "Where have you been? Why did you not come through all these years of meditation?" And Manjusri said, "I've been here all the time." He said, "Look at your robe. You can see the lint of my robe on your robe. I've been sitting right next to you." Asanga said, "Why couldn't I see you?" And Manjusri said, "The one act of compassion that you undertook for this dog did more to awaken you to see me than all the nine years of sitting in the cave."

MOYERS: But then I think about this dichotomy: about how the great religions have indeed inspired faith and wisdom and tradition and compassion, but at the same time, they've been the source of corruption and war and belligerence and prejudice. They've been so exclusive and so vengeful at times that trying to imagine a spiritual democracy where the great religions dwell in peace and ethical flowering strikes against the face of our history.

ROCKEFELLER: This is why I would argue that what is needed today in the world is the democratic reconstruction of the world religions. The greatest single moral failing of many religious traditions is their inability to teach their followers to respect people of a different tradition the same way they respect the people of their own tradition. Some people have tied this to the theistic concept of God. Because if God is a being upon whom your salvation is dependent, and God's will is expressed in a certain set of laws and doctrines, then those people who do not adhere to those laws and doctrines are your enemies. They might lure you away from the source of your salvation. You relate to those other people in and through your relationship to a God who is outside the world.

Now, if you give up that monarchical, patriarchal concept of God, and think of your relationship with God in and through your relationship to all kinds of people, then this problem begins to dissolve. So there has to be an embracing of the democratic principle of respect for every individual regardless of race, religion, ethnic origin, nationality, and so forth. At the same time, I think, there has to be a surrender on the part of many religious traditions of their discrimination against women. This is also part of what I would call the democratic reconstruction of the religions.

MOYERS: You're talking about something that goes beyond just simply tolerating one's differences.

ROCKEFELLER: Yes, I am. I'm talking about enabling or teaching people within the framework of these traditions to positively respect others in spite of their differences. I remember a teaching of a rabbi along these lines. "A strong man," he said, "is someone who can control himself. A rich man is someone who is satisfied with what he has. And a wise man is someone who learns from everyone." Now, the democratic spirit in the religions has to have something of that. That is, a Christian can learn from the Jews and the Buddhists, and vice versa. There has to be an openness to others, without surrendering the uniqueness of one's own tradition.

MOYERS: Can that happen? Can we promote this spiritual democracy of respect for the other, the recognition of our commonality, while each religion honors that particular revelation that gives it its own force, tradition, power, and subsistence?

ROCKEFELLER: I think this is possible. You can find at least a seed of the democratic idea in all the traditions. All of them have a capacity to move towards this kind of democratic ethical attitude. The task is to develop those ideas in each of these distinctive traditions that will lead people to a common center where there is a shared set of democratic moral values. All of these religions originally were intimately related to a particular society at a particular place in time on this planet.

MOYERS: Beirut, Belfast.

ROCKEFELLER: But the world society that is emerging is obviously bigger than these communities with which these religions originally identified themselves. So people who are part of these religions are caught in a bind. They now are part of a world community but their religion is tied to a more narrow community. The only way to reconcile this tension between membership in a global community and their being tied to a local religious tradition is for there to be a democratic evolution of these different religious traditions.

MOYERS: This is a very exciting time for religious inquiry. In Eastern Europe we see an outburst of religious sentiment behind the toppling of the Communist empire. Feminists are bringing insights to the notion and image of God. A swift running current from Buddhism and other world religions is arriving in this country. There's something very exciting going on.

ROCKEFELLER: There clearly is. When I think about the struggles in Eastern Europe I cannot help but think about Dostoyevsky's parable in *The Brothers Karamazov* about the Grand Inquisitor and his encounter with the figure of Christ. The Grand Inquisitor has a very negative view of human nature and, therefore, supports an authoritarian form of government. He believes that human beings are basically like a bunch of unruly schoolboys who, given some freedom, will make a terrible mess out of things and then, realizing they can't control themselves, will return and submit themselves again to authority. The Christ figure in this story, on the other hand, believes firmly that the meaning of human existence is linked with the realization of freedom, and that freedom is perfected in faith. This is true even though the realization of freedom involves tremendous risks, and often it's abused. It is ultimately humanity's destiny to wrestle with freedom and try to find its way to faith.

Even though Dostoyevsky was powerfully drawn to Christ, he predicted that the future of history was with the Grand Inquisitor. He thought people really couldn't deal with freedom, that democracy would ultimately fail and totalitarianism would be the future of the world. Now the democratic vision is very different. It is a vision that has faith in the common person, like Dostoevsky's Christ does. It recognizes that there's great risk in freedom but it is worth the risk. Indeed the whole meaning of modern history is tied up with this search for freedom and its perfection and realization.

So in Eastern Europe today there is again a great experiment going on as to whether Eastern Europe can deal with freedom, and surmount the ethnic rivalries, the religious conflicts, and the nationalism that is liable to make this experiment in democracy impossible.

MOYERS: On a related subject: what did you mean when you wrote that we have to extend the ethics of democracy to nature?

ROCKEFELLER: I want to argue that our sense of democratic community today has to be expanded so that it embraces and includes the whole biosphere. We are now faced with an environmental crisis that is bringing us to the realization that nature also has rights. Animals have rights. Species have rights. Plants and flowers and even rocks in a certain sense perhaps have rights. We need to sort all this out; I don't think that these issues have been fully explored. But I am convinced that only when our notions of moral democracy are integrated with a sense of environmental ethics and a sense of the intrinsic value that exists in the natural world, quite apart from what its utility is for the human being, will we find the kind of integration and wholeness as people and the kind of health and well-being as a society that we're searching for.

MOYERS: But we have such a hard time extending the idea of rights to other human beings, to people who are different from us, who don't speak the same language, or agree with us politically, or worship the same God. It seems almost an impossibility if not an absurdity to try to extend it to the rest of the living world. To the animals and the plants and the other forms of life.

> *I think that one of the great challenges to religion today is to become more articulate about the relationship between the human and the nonhuman world.*

ROCKEFELLER: Well, I think that two issues are involved here: one is the very survival of human society in a biosphere that has been seriously damaged and that presents us with enormous problems. If we don't change the way we are relating to this whole world, the consequences for human life are going to be disastrous. From a selfish human point of view, if we don't change our way of relating to the natural world, we may not survive. But there is a deeper spiritual issue here, which has to do with this sense of community with the whole world of nature. I think that one of the great challenges to religion today is to become more articulate about the relationship between the human and the nonhuman world.

MOYERS: It's hard to see that religious values can withstand the economic imperatives of the modern world.

ROCKEFELLER: The only thing that will change this is for the wise businessman to recognize that the capital that he depends upon involves natural capital, which is not usually part of the balance sheet. When air, earth, and water are being polluted and when the burning of fossil fuels is creating serious damage to the ozone level and raising the temperature of the planet, his possibilities of doing business are going to be jeopardized. For that reason, if for no other, many of these industrialists are going to have to reevaluate their calculations.

A new term being used these days is "eco-economics." In the eco-economics approach you try to integrate environmental concerns with economic decision-making. The UN report on the environment called "Our Common Future," which has been translated now into seventeen different languages, is a basic document in the world discussion of sustainable development. One of their major recommendations is this integration of economic decision-making with sound environmental policy. This is going to cause a major restructuring of the way we do business and the way governments go about developing policies. But I think there is a growing recognition among world leaders as well as business people that this must happen.

MOYERS: It's going to require a major change in how many Christians think about the world, because their tradition is one of being told they are to have dominion over, to conquer and master. That's not what you're talking about.

ROCKEFELLER: However, if you look in the ancient Hebrew scriptures, along with those passages about dominion you find, for example, in Deuteronomy and other parts of the Torah, a very clear teaching that the promised land is a gift of God and that the gift is conditional upon its being cared for properly. Human beings have a responsibility that goes with the land. It is not just there for them to use wantonly.

MOYERS: You have undergone an unusual spiritual journey. You were reared by your parents in the Christian tradition, and now you are a Buddhist. How has that journey shaped your thinking about our relationships with the world?

ROCKEFELLER: I was raised in a Baptist and Protestant tradition, and early on in my life I developed a deep religious interest. I took lots of courses at college in religion but I didn't think that it was appropriate for me to major in it. Then I went into the Army, and politics, and business, but I finally decided that I'd better just stop and give my full attention to religion, because if I didn't, at the end of my life I would regret it deeply.

So I went to theological seminary. Initially I tried to find answers basically through intellectual analysis. But I found increasingly that religion is not something that can be acquired through the head.

MOYERS: The intellect was not enough for you? There was still something missing?

ROCKEFELLER: In Union Seminary in those days people discouraged one from pursuing mysticism. They said, "Well, this is an interesting subject, but not worthy of a term paper." But I felt an impulse in that direction. It was a side of my nature that wanted to find expression. It wasn't until some years after I graduated from Union Seminary that I found what I was looking for in a book by Philip Kapleau called *The Three Pillars of Zen*. He gave instruction in meditation. And so I turned to the Zen tradition.

MOYERS: Why? What was different about it?

ROCKEFELLER: In the 1960s, when my own quest was at full swing, there still was not a great deal of interest in the contemplative life. Since then, of course, there has been an explosion of interest in contemplative prayer, and many of these rich contemplative traditions that are part of the Christian heritage have been recovered and retrieved. But in those days it was difficult to find. I was also troubled by the dualism between God and the world that is involved in Christian theism—the separation of God and the world, God and myself. I felt there a sense of remoteness and isolation, if you will. So I turned to Zen and through Zen and meditation I found a direct personal realization of spiritual truth. The core of Zen is an intense spiritual quest to see into the truth of yourself and the truth of reality.

MOYERS: And how does one do that?

ROCKEFELLER: The basic Zen practice is sitting meditation, which involves concentrating the mind. It also may include working on "koans," or spiritual puzzles that cannot be resolved by the intellect alone. They are intended to jam the intellect and to engage your whole personality so you come to encounter the truth on that deeper level.

Let me give you a short poem of a great Zen teacher—Dogen. He's the Thomas Aquinas, if you will, of the Japanese Zen tradition, a thirteenth-century master, almost a contemporary of St. Francis of Assisi. Dogen has some lines that run like this: "To study the Buddha way is to study the self. To study the self is to forget the self. To forget the self is to be enlightened by the ten thousand things. To be enlightened by the ten thousand things is to free your body and mind and those of others."

What did Dogen mean by that? He meant something not unsimilar to what St. Francis meant when he said the brother sun and sister moon and animals and earth, air, fire, and water all reveal the glory of God. If you are awake to this divine presence in the world, then God is all about you. And there is no separation of yourself from God. St. Francis was very concerned about trying to break down that dualism of God and the individual. Dogen again is saying that if your way of relating to others, including animals and rocks and stones and rivers and mountains and trees, is genuine and open, then the truth of life is manifest all around you.

It is not a truth that can be stated in words. It has to be directly experienced and lived. The important thing is that when one experiences it, there arises deep in the heart the fundamental core of religious faith, which is the great Yes to life in spite of everything that would lead us to say no. It is the affirmation of life which gives one a sense of belonging to the world—a sense of inner peace and a sense of courage.

MOYERS: This was quite a quest for a Rockefeller from a conspicuous American family, a Protestant family and a powerful one. You went into what to many Americans would appear to be an exotic religion, certainly exotic in terms of the American tradition. It's a tradition that seems to many people not of this world. Is that a stereotype—that the Buddhist is not of this world?

ROCKEFELLER: It is a common criticism of Buddhism—that it does not have a social ethic comparable to that of Christianity, that it has been otherworldly in its orientation with a heavy emphasis on monastic withdrawal. But one of the things that has always appealed to me about Zen is that it uses concrete imagery to express saving truth or the divine. A wonderful little Zen poem that I encountered several months ago runs something like this: "Gone my fine old hopes. Dry my dreaming. But still iris blue each spring." In that poem somehow the iris is able to communicate something about the meaningfulness of existence and the value inherent in it that comes through in spite of the fact that all the poet's hopes and all his dreams have crumbled and gone.

I am reminded again of Viktor Frankl. He provides this account of an exchange with a dying woman in a concentration camp. Through a small window she could see the branch of a chestnut tree on which there were two blossoms. "This tree here is the only friend I have in my loneliness," she said. "I often talk to this tree and it replies." Somewhat puzzled Viktor Frankl asked: "What does the tree say to you?" She answered: "It said to me, 'I am here—I am here—I am life, eternal life.'" Now there is an experience of a Westerner that is comparable to the experience recorded in the Japanese poem about iris blue. These experiences occurred in two different parts of the world, but in both cases the divine made itself present through concrete everyday reality. They were experiences of what some mystics call the Eternal Now. So there is that dimension in Buddhism.

But you've asked about Buddhism and its being otherworldly. There's one kind of otherworldliness which is very misleading because it takes one's attention away from this world and turns the attention to another world, causing believers to neglect their everyday relations. The Marxist critique of religion is rather valid in criticizing that.

MOYERS: No justice now, justice later.

ROCKEFELLER: Exactly. But there is a certain kind of otherworldliness that Jesus expressed when he said, "Be in the world but not of it." Now what does it mean to be in the world but not of it? To be not of it is to give up those illusions, those rationalizations, those prejudices, those attachments, which distort our relationship to the world. The objective is to be an individual at one with the world. To be a person who is free from illusions and prejudices that prevent us from encountering the world as it really is. That kind of otherworldliness has a certain constructive function. One sometimes has to withdraw in order to enter more fully into the world.

Oren Lyons

ONONDAGA CHIEF

For hundreds of years, the Haudenosaunee people have been talking about democracy, community, and reverence for nature—and Chief Oren Lyons of the Onondaga is helping to continue that conversation. As faith keeper of the Turtle Clan, he preserves and transmits the memories and traditions of his people. And as director of the Native American Studies Program at the State University of New York at Buffalo, he shares with others the ancient wisdom.

MOYERS: Why did you come back here to live on the reservation? You gave up a successful career as a commercial artist in New York City.

LYONS: Well, in 1967 I was condoled as one of the faith keepers.

MOYERS: Condoled?

LYONS: Yes, condolence is a process of raising leadership among our people. It's what we call the great event. You see, if you're raising a leader it means that the previous leader is not there. So you're condoling the loss of the previous leader. It's a long ceremony. It's fifteen separate wampums that are spoken maybe twenty minutes apiece.

MOYERS: A wampum is a—

LYONS: Wampum is a seashell. And these are strung in different ways, and they have different meanings according to the strings. So when the condolence begins, it's quite a process.

The condolence is always a renewal. And there's a peace to that, an underlying process of peace which talks to the person who suffered. It says: You've lost your leader, we know how you feel. We have to clear your throat so that you can speak and we'll have to clear your eyes so that you can see and we have to clear your ears so that you can hear again. And now we know that you can't see color, that everything looks the same because you're feeling so bad. There's no night and there's no day for you because of how you feel. But we have this great condolence for you. We have this great feeling for you. And so all the wampums go one by one across the way and then the speaker on the other side of the house stands up and returns the wampums again with the same speech. But in the meantime, there's been a closing of a curtain between the two. It's like between death and life. And then there's great song, the song which unites, sung only by the chiefs. It is a great, powerful song, with ancient power, and when you hear it, it sends shivers through you.

Then it's sung by both houses and then the curtain is opened, and the condolence comes back to the new and so you can let go of the past and you come back to the new. When the sun is just setting, they bring forth the candidate for the new position. That's when you see who's coming forward. All the people are there. They have a right of veto.

Now he's brought in front of the two great houses. Both sides of the house will pass on him. If they agree, then they turn to the people and they say: Does anyone here know a reason why this man should not be our leader? Now you must stand and speak. If you know a reason and you do not speak, then you are never to speak again. And so it all goes back to the people. That's democracy. That's power. It goes back to the roots of democracy.

MOYERS: Among the Six Nations?

LYONS: Yes. A long time ago when we first began the process of our governance, the Peacemaker—we call him the Great Peacemaker—came among us. He brought peace among the Mohawk and the Oneida, the Onondaga, the Cayuga, and the Seneca. We don't know how long ago. Maybe a thousand years ago, maybe two.

MOYERS: Maybe more . . .

LYONS: Maybe more—it doesn't matter. This is the story. The Peacemaker was a spiritual being. He was a messenger. He brought a message, the Great Peace. It was our second message. We were brought a first message which was long prior to that. The message of How to Live. The Way of Life. And everybody learned that message. And then somehow people forgot it, and there was warfare.

MOYERS: That's an old story, too.

LYONS: Yes. This is a human story about human beings. And so then the Peacemaker came with the second message: the Great Peace, the Great Law. Same word for both. And he changed the minds of all of these men who at that time were leaders by strength and by force. And he stepped in and changed the whole process to deliberation and consensus. It took a long time.

MOYERS: You were a stubborn people?

LYONS: Very stubborn. In particular the leader at that time, the Todadaho, was fierce. He was a man with snakes in his hair, who was twisted and deformed and feared—a cannibal. He was so powerful that people feared him. He just stayed in the woods. Hard to reach. And so people were given help, spiritual help, in the form of a song from a bird.

This song is what they learned and what they came to him with. And they said that if he agreed to join this Great Law, this Great Peace, that the Onondaga would be the fire keepers. Haudenosaunee would be the name of the federation, which the French call Iroquois and the English call the Six Nations.

The names of the fifty original men from those nations became offices. And when one passed on, then the ceremony was performed, the condolence of replacement. It was the peaceful replacement of authority, exactly the opposite of aristocracy. As you know, being an heir to the throne in Europe in those days was a very dangerous position. There was a lot of murder and intrigue in the courts. But here, in this country, among our native peoples, it was different. What the Peacemaker established in our laws was that each of those leaders was leader of a family, a clan. Clans were given designations—of Wolf or Turtle, of Snipe or Deer or Eel, or Bear, or Beaver, or Hawk, or Heron. There would be in each of these clans five leaders. There would be a clan mother, whose purpose was to choose the chief.

MOYERS: Why the mother? Why did that role go to the woman?

LYONS: Because in the Peacemaker's first encounter as he landed on the eastern shores of what is now called Lake Ontario, he stopped overnight at a lodge of a woman. And this woman took him in and said that this was a place where people could rest and refresh themselves and could eat. A neutral place, even though it stood on a warpath. Everybody who came there recognized that this was a neutral place.

MOYERS: So they'd leave their weapons outside.

LYONS: Yes. And they'd pass that time together. Now when he told her of his mission and what he was about, she said it was wonderful. The Peacemaker and the woman worked together. They were in the lead of the men who were approaching the Todadaho with the song. And as they approached him he transformed and agreed to this Great Peace.

MOYERS: This creature in the woods with wild hair and twisted body, he responded—

LYONS: He responded. He agreed. He changed. And now there was a law. There was a lesson there for everyone. And that lesson was, no matter how bad a person is, he could change to be the very best.

MOYERS: He could be born again.

LYONS: I hesitate to use that word because it has such a different connotation.

MOYERS: But really, it was a spiritual conversion . . .

LYONS: Yes. It was a spiritual conversion. And because the woman was the first to recognize this, the Peacemaker said society will follow the women's side, and become a matrilineal society.

MOYERS: Because the woman would recognize the importance of peace.

LYONS: Because she was the first to recognize the Peacemaker.

MOYERS: Like Mary in the Christian tradition.

LYONS: Right. Again, you see, a very powerful metaphor of equality.

MOYERS: So the woman would chose the leadership.

LYONS: Yes.

MOYERS: Who chose you?

LYONS: Well, my clan mother at that time. She was a Turtle. Although I am a Wolf, I was borrowed into the Turtle Clan at that time by a wonderful woman who raised many generations of children. She carried at one time here, at the Onondaga Nation, four clanships in her hand, because of the inability to find a clan mother for those clans. So she carried all that extra work. And she asked me whether I would consider becoming one of the representatives of the Turtle Clan in council. And I said, "Well, I don't know." You see, your first reaction is that you don't want to do that because the chiefs are always busy; they're always working. They're never home; they're always in meetings. And it seemed to be quite a load. The only words she ever said to me were "Think of what you can do for your people. Take your time, and if you have questions, come and ask me." So I thought about it. I did have questions, and I did ask her. And she explained everything. So finally I said, "Well, I'll try." She said, "That's good; that's all I want to hear."

MOYERS: And you became faith keeper. The faith you're keeping is the memory of these stories, of the traditions.

LYONS: Yes, and you sit in the council of chiefs. And you sit in as one of the chiefs.

MOYERS: Representing the Onondaga.

LYONS: You're representing first the clan. You're representing the Turtle Clan in the council. And when the councils of the Six Nations meet you sit as a representative of the nation, the Onondaga in my case. And then when you sit in the large circle, you are representing the total of the Six Nations. So you sit in three positions: the clan, the nation, and the grand council of Six Nations.

MOYERS: When you returned to be a chief, was it a hard choice to bring your kids back to the reservation?

LYONS: No. One reason I came back was that I didn't want the kids being brought up in the atmosphere that's out there. We're talking 1959 to 1970. You could watch the deterioration of New York City even then. Even though now people talk about 1960 in New York as the good old days.

MOYERS: Where do they belong now that they are grown, here on the reservation or out in the other world?

LYONS: Everybody belongs here. All Onondagas belong here. Whether they live elsewhere or not. It's the same as if you had a U.S. citizenship and were living in Paris. You know, you always go back to America, right? It's the same. So if you're an Onondaga and you're living in Boston, which some are, and if you're living in New York, which some are, your home is here.

MOYERS: Did your children watch television when they were growing up?

LYONS: Oh yes. This is a television-oriented society. We're surrounded. You know, we have this little square here of land—six square miles—and every day you're impacted by television.

MOYERS: Doesn't television seduce them away from intuitive thinking?

LYONS: Oh yes, no doubt. There's an attrition. Every generation has faced an attrition. But on the other hand there's also a distillation of these ideas, of these thoughts. The leadership and the chiefs and the clan mothers and the messages that we have are extraordinarily important in these times. I mentioned the second message, which was the Great Peace. Now, we had a third message. The third message came around 1799. This was directly after the Revolutionary War. You're looking at the turmoil that was in Indian country, particularly the Six Nation country during that time. We had a third message from Ganeyodio, whom people call Handsome Lake. Handsome Lake was taken on a journey, for four days. And during that time he was shown the future, what was going to happen. And he was given instructions on how to deal with the white man, instructions by the four protectors, from the spiritual side of our life. They told him what was coming. And this summer that story will be told again here in our longhouse, as it's told every year in every longhouse across the Six Nations.

MOYERS: What did the protectors say to Handsome Lake?

LYONS: The central message is that there's going to be a deterioration and a falling away of life as we know it. Well, I have to be quite careful about how I do this because we're on national television. I don't have the authority or the right to begin discussing things at large without the consent of the nation or the group. I'm not free to do that. But it's clear enough and people have known enough, for instance, about water. The protectors talk about water. Handsome Lake was shown things in vignettes. They asked him: "What do you see?" He said, "I see a river." And they said, "Pick up the water to drink." He reached his hands in to pick the water up and he said, "I can't. It's filthy."

They said, "What you say is correct, and at some time the water's going to be that way."

MOYERS: Are you suggesting that the story anticipates the environmental degradation that we now see?

LYONS: Yes. And at one time he was shown some corn. A man was working in the garden. At one point the man reached down and pulled up the plant to see what was on the roots. And there was nothing on the roots. Handsome Lake was asked, "What do you see?" And he answered, "There's nothing there." And the four protectors said, "What you say is correct, and at some time that is going to happen."

MOYERS: What do you make of that?

LYONS: Well, as he was being told about these things that were coming, he asked, "What is the hope?" And the answer was that it's up to each generation to see that it doesn't happen in that generation.

MOYERS: So the vision he received was that destruction, environmental destruction, could come in each generation. But each generation is charged not to let it happen.

LYONS: Yes, actually the hope lies in the intensity of the life of that generation.

MOYERS: The publication that you edit, *Daybreak*, is dedicated to the seventh generation unborn.

I'm sitting here as the seventh generation because seven generations ago, those people were looking out for me. Seven generations from now someone will be here, I know.

LYONS: That is the instruction given to the chief. When we are given these instructions, we are told that when we sit in council for the welfare of the people, we counsel for the welfare of that seventh generation to come. It should be foremost in our minds. Not even our generation, not even ourselves, but those that are unborn. So that when their time comes here, they may enjoy the same things that we're enjoying now. I'm sitting here as the seventh generation because seven generations ago, those people were looking out for me. Seven generations from now someone will be here, I know.

MOYERS: You have a moral obligation.

LYONS: Well, I believe that all discussion between human beings is about morality. We have both good and bad in us and we must strike a balance at all times. The balance is what's important. Your conduct should reflect a balance. For us, this is what the great tree of peace is, the spiritual center.

MOYERS: When the Peacemaker came, he planted a tree of peace.

LYONS: The Great Peace, the Great Law, is a spiritual law. He said, "When you become afraid or when you become weak or when you are not able to carry on, it's the spiritual law that will stiffen your spine." He said, "That's where your strength is. So you must make your laws in accordance with those spiritual laws. And then you will survive." He called that council the Council of the Good Minds. So that's what he set up, and he asked the nations to come forward and cast away their weapons of war. He said, "We now do away with the warriors. And we do away with the war chiefs. And in their place we plant the Council of the Good Minds who will now counsel for the welfare of the people." He said, "I shall not leave you defenseless."

And that's why this peace is so foremost in our minds. He said the three principles will be peace, equity, and justice—and the power of the good minds. And when your people think that way and everyone has the same position, then being of one mind is the greatest power there is. We witnessed it just recently, when we saw three hundred thousand people move into the streets of East Germany and say, "We want freedom." That's one mind. Those people were saying one thing. One mind. When it moves like that, it's a great power.

MOYERS: But the history of your people since the Peacemaker came a millennium or so ago has, like all people's, been one of enmity, conflict, and competition. These are great teachings. It's a wise and wonderful philosophy you espouse, but look what the gun, the church, the dollar, and the bottle did to your story. You got run over.

LYONS: We did and we didn't. We're still here. We're not through. The story's not over. You're still talking to a chief. And you're sitting in the Onondaga Nation. The tree is still here. The roots are still ours. And if anything I see the roots growing.

MOYERS: What's the evidence?

LYONS: Well, I watch, especially in the Eastern bloc of Europe, how these people are clamoring for freedom and for democracy and how they're looking toward the Americas for democracy, and how the Chinese were using the symbol of the Statue of Liberty. And they were saying that it's great that it's coming from America. But America got it from the Indians. America got the ideas of democracy and freedom and peace here, among the Six Nations. When Columbus landed and later on when the Pilgrims landed, freedom was rampant in America. All the nations here were free. The native people, I mean. Everybody was equal. There was a great society here, if you want to call it that. All people understood about freedom. They were masters of freedom.

MOYERS: But they were not without conflict, enmity, and war. Those are not just attributes of the white race.

LYONS: But what kind of a war is it when the bravest of them all carries no weapon and touches his men in combat? What kind of war is that? That's not really a war, is it? I mean, it's some sort of a very lethal game at times perhaps but . . .

MOYERS: Indians died.

LYONS: Of course they died. Of course they did. And sometimes there were great conflicts. But Indians had a lot of time for the ideas of councils and the ideas of talking. We've been here a long time, you know, thousands of years. You're talking about twelve thousand years. We were people who sat under a tree for a long time talking about things. About society. About law. About rules. Lots of rules here. None of it written down. Everybody understands the rules, though.

MOYERS: I read that when the first Europeans arrived, the council of chiefs was already established here.

LYONS: Oh yes. We had a process of peacemaking and peacekeeping. And confederations, there were many confederations. The Six Nations wasn't the only one. There were confederations in the South of what is now the United States. There were great confederations in the West. And the Sioux were a great confederation of seven nations.

MOYERS: Do you subscribe to the opinion of some researchers that some of the people we call the Founding Fathers were affected directly by what Indians were doing and thinking?

LYONS: Oh yes. They were affected very directly. The Wampanoags met the Pilgrims. There was a great leader by the name of Massasoit. And Massasoit saw to it that there was peace between the two. When Massasoit died, one of his sons was killed. And his other son Metacom, whom they called King Philip, died in a swamp, hunted down in the swamp by the English and by what you call renegade Mohicans.

MOYERS: The quislings of their day.

LYONS: Yeah, for whatever reason. They were very powerful. You know, James Fenimore Cooper wrote about the "last of the Mohicans." Well, you can go out to Wisconsin and find Mohicans there. Not the last at all. But the Mohicans were powerful among the Haudenosaunee.

MOYERS: The . . .

LYONS: The Haudenosaunee. It's the proper name for our people. It means the people of the longhouse. And sometimes they use the metaphor of the longhouse to mean from one ocean to another.

MOYERS: The whole continent itself.

LYONS: Or it's the length of our nation, the longhouse, and all these fires in the longhouse, put together, were family. Indigenous people talk family all the time. The basis of our politics is family. And one of our young people—I think it was John Mohawk—said that spirituality was the highest form of politics.

MOYERS: What do you take that to mean?

LYONS: Well, I go back to the center tree of peace, that spiritual center. That is the highest form. That's what everything has to come around. Because it's what we call the great law, the common law, the natural law. The law says if you poison your water, you'll die. The law says if you poison the air, you'll suffer. The law says if you degrade where you live, you'll suffer. The law says all of this. And if you don't learn that, then you will suffer. There's no discussion with this law.

MOYERS: There's no mercy in nature. You can't get down on your knees and beg forgiveness.

LYONS: There's no mercy in nature. And there's very much something that people should understand, that you suffer in direct ratio to your transgressions against the natural world. The natural world will prevail. You know, human beings are still a biological experiment as far as the world's concerned. We've only been here a short time. In the time of the earth and the time of the world, the human being is here a short time. You see, when you're dealing in the time of an oak, or the time of one of the great sequoias, you can take a chainsaw and in ten minutes kill a tree that's four hundred years old, and there's no way that you can make that tree grow back. You'll have to wait another four hundred years for another. So the technology has overtaken the common sense of human beings and the understanding of time. And just as the time of the ant is very very short, the time of the mountain is very very long. If you don't have a good understanding of what this time is, then you can get yourself and your people and your generation into a lot of trouble. And I think that's where we are right now.

MOYERS: You're talking about environmental trouble.

LYONS: Yes, indeed. I'm talking about making payment now. For as long as I can remember and longer in the memory of our people, we've had celebrations for the thundering voices, our grandfathers, the rainmakers, the people who bring the rain and the fresh water that refreshes the springs and the lakes.

MOYERS: You refer to the rain as grandfather? Nature is personified as a member of your family, not as something to be dominated.

LYONS: Yes. Indeed. We are literally a part of nature. This was a statement of Audrey Shenandoah, one of the clan mothers from here who spoke at the global forum in Moscow last February.

MOYERS: In both Jewish and Christian scripture nature was something to be dominated. God said go and have mastery over what I've created.

LYONS: Well, we weren't taught that. Our leaders, our spiritual guides, never said that to us. They said we must respect the earth. When our young people are married in the longhouse, the ceremony begins with the words "When the creator made the earth . . ." to give them a context of why they're here and why they're being married and what their purpose is—you know, to bring forth a family, to protect the family, to work in the community. It's all instruction.

MOYERS: To share in that ongoing story, to write their own chapters.

LYONS: Yes, yes. I mean, we can say that it looks like things are lost. But I've seen the spirit and I've seen the fight of the young people. I love those young people. And I think they've got enough within them to do it. Certainly they're a lot more active now than we were when I was a young man.

MOYERS: Our problems are also more complex.

LYONS: Yes. When suddenly the rain that we celebrate and the rain that we pray for and the rain that we give thanks for begins to kill, we ask why is that? What happens when your grandfathers begin to turn on you? And your great brother, the elder brother, the sun—when suddenly people begin to suffer from cancer from the sun, the sun worshippers, all those people who've been out on the beaches are beginning to experience the loss of the ozone, and it's become quite dangerous to be in the sun for very long. What are people going to do when these lifegiving forces that you've depended on, that you've prayed to, that you give thanksgiving to, suddenly turn on you? What happens?

MOYERS: In this regard, exactly what do indigenous people, Indians, have to offer the rest of us?

LYONS: Well, first of all we have a long perspective. We've been in one place a long time. We've seen the sun come up at the same place many many hundreds, thousands of years. And so we have a familiarity with the earth itself, the elements. We know about them. And we know what it is to enjoy them. The ceremonies, which are as ancient as we are, carry forward this respect. Our children are not sat down and taught about what's good and what's wrong. They see their grandfathers or they see their fathers or their grandmothers going to ceremonies. And they say, "So that must be the right thing to do. The old people do it. Everybody does it. That's good." So they do it. And so they learn in the process. "The thanksgiving, what is it for?" "Well, this one is for the maple, the chief of the trees. We're giving a thanksgiving for the maple." "Good. Let's respect the tree. We must respect all the trees." So respect is learned through ceremony as a process. It's an old one. Thanksgiving comes as a natural way of being. It's part of life. It's not something that you do occasionally. It's something that you do all the time. And that's how the process has been passed down. So we have these wellsprings of knowledge, about places that only aboriginal people would know. Because we've lived there. We have intimate knowledge of what's there. And when people are destroyed and languages are destroyed, you destroy that knowledge along with it. Indigenous people may have the long-term thinking required for proper context.

MOYERS: Context being . . .

LYONS: Life as it functions in the cycles and the great cycles of life, our cycle of being born and going back to the earth again; as the tree, there's a sapling and it grows to full being and then falls. As it goes back to the earth again, as the spring comes and the summer and the fall and the winter. And it comes again. The cycle is endless; it's endless as long as you protect the cycle. As long as you participate in the cycle, as long as you honor it and respect it. Then it will continue. But it doesn't have to.

MOYERS: You said a moment ago that the tree of peace is still here, in Onondaga.

LYONS: Spiritually, yes. It was a spiritual tree to begin with. You know, again, people are so literal. It's hard at times to have a discussion with people who think in linear terms, because they say, "We've come to see the tree." And you tell them, "It's a great tree. It reaches to the heavens. You can't see it. We can see it. It's there. And it's very real." As we were told, sometimes the most real things you can't see.

MOYERS: You've said on other occasions that there has to be a spiritual change if we are going to face these environmental issues. What kind of spiritual change?

LYONS: We don't preach here in this, our country. You know, we don't proselytize. As a matter of fact, we try to protect what we have from intrusion. And yet at a meeting that was held in Hopi back in 1969 when we sat there with many Indian leaders from around the country, spiritual leaders, they talked about these young people who were sitting on our doorsteps every day when we got up. They had come from all over the country, and they had come to learn something about us. And we said this is a very strange phenomenon, you know, that our white brothers' children are now coming to our doorstep and wanting to be part of us. What do we do with this?

So one of the Hopi elders said, "Well, we have a prophecy about that. It said that there would be a time that they're going to come and ask a direction. Maybe this is what's happening." So it came under discussion by the elders, and it was agreed upon that perhaps this may be true. And if it is, then we should be more responsive to the questions. We should maybe try to help to see what we can do, to pass on whatever we can, however we can. So it was agreed upon at that time that we would work more directly then. How much can be imparted is hard to say. But the "isms" of this world—communism, capitalism, all of these "isms"—are really quite bereft of a spiritual side.

MOYERS: But the reality of human nature keeps intruding on your stories and philosophy.

LYONS: Well, what Indians are about, first of all, is community. They're about community. They're about mutual support. They're about sharing. They're about understanding what's common—common land, common air, common water. Common—and for all.

MOYERS: But Indians are divided and separated on the reservations. Many of your people who come into the larger world perish—psychologically, emotionally, spiritually.

LYONS: And on the reservations as well. But this is an intrusion again, by our white brother. He has made these reservations. You know, we've gone from a great power to a small power, and Chief Seattle said, as the waves come one behind the other, so nations come, and as a wave disappears, so nations disappear. So perhaps, he said, this is what will happen to us. But you know, human beings are very powerful creatures.

MOYERS: Well, the species is a stubborn resister.

LYONS: We're spiritual beings. Each one is a spiritual being with great power. And every once in a while you have a manifestation of this. For instance, Adolf Hitler was a manifestation of one kind of power an individual can wield. And on the other hand, you have Gandhi as another kind of power. Each of us is capable of, has within us, this great spiritual power. So around the earth, you have all these spiritual beings and they have options.

MOYERS: You and I can go this way or that way.

LYONS: Every day's a discussion, isn't it? There's nothing for sure. Every day as you get up, there's going to come a point where somebody is going to tempt you or try to influence you. This is what happens every day, so every day you have to make small and big choices all the time.

MOYERS: What sustains you?

LYONS: My belief in the people, my belief in the ceremonies, my belief in the earth, and I'm really kind of optimistic.

MOYERS: Václav Havel said recently that hope is a state of the spirit, a state of the soul.

LYONS: Yes, I think I deal in reality. I deal very much in reality. In order for us to have survived up to this point, we have to deal in reality.

MOYERS: Indigenous people have lived for centuries close to nature, in harmony with this world, and yet you've been overwhelmed by the material progress of the industrial society. Have you really survived or is it just the stories that survive?

> *As long as there's one to sing and one to dance, one to speak and one to listen, life will go on.*

LYONS: No, I don't think so. I think that the spirit is quite there. And then I think the spirit's manifested outside as we look about here. It's all here. We're told about the longhouse, about the ceremonies. The power of the ceremonies and the thanksgiving that we were instructed to do. As long as there's one to sing and one to dance, one to speak and one to listen, life will go on. So it's the instruction. Sing what? Dance what? Speak what? Listen to what? So it's the instruction. As long as the instructions are being carried out, even if it's down to the last four people, life will go on.

MOYERS: What is your mission? You strike me as a man on a mission.

LYONS: Well, I think we have a common mission, you and I. From the time that I walked the streets of New York and tried to get directions uptown and I couldn't get directions uptown, to the time now when people will come and pick me up at the airport and take me uptown, there's been a change which is quite profound, actually, in a short time.

MOYERS: What kind of change?

LYONS: Well, people are interested in the spiritual side of things. I believe that there's a real groundswell of people wanting to understand that there's more to life than what the media moguls on Wall Street and on Madison Avenue put forward. That there are other values—the old values—the ancient values—the constant values—and they are the ones that have to prevail and will prevail. And I think what we're feeling now is people beginning to respond and they're saying, "The leaders are trying to catch up to the people these days. The people are moving so fast—and the leaders are behind them."

MOYERS: My wife and I saw a bumper sticker the other day that said, "If the people will lead, the leaders will follow."

LYONS: Well, that's what is happening. The Six Nations have been lucky to have leaders of principle who do their best, quite simple people but quite profound in their belief, who are steadfast in the face of everything.

MOYERS: We watched the children playing lacrosse yesterday. An old native game—does it teach them something?

LYONS: Oh yes. It's about the continuity of community. Everybody's involved. Children are involved. Parents are involved. Our greatest fans are the women.

MOYERS: You were a star goalie back in the fifties. Wasn't it just a game to you then? Just play?

LYONS: No. You could have called me a ringer because I'd been playing lacrosse for so long by the time that I got to the university that I had a great deal of experience. Because our people do it from these little fellows on up. And my grandfather was a lacrosse player. My father was well known as a goalkeeper. Some of the great leaders were players. Tecumseh was a great lacrosse player.

MOYERS: Is there a connection between being a goalkeeper on the lacrosse team and being the keeper of the tribe? Are both a metaphor?

LYONS: Well, that's an interesting thought. Of course, there's the intensity of the game. And the spiritual aspect again. Yes, it is. In its origin, it's called the creator's game. Lacrosse is the creator's game. And he loves to have the contest in its vitality. You're supposed to play it as hard as you can. But don't cheat, you know. You do things fair. It's a spiritual game. We are at one on the same field. You know, I was lucky enough to play a few games with my father. And I've been lucky enough to play a few games with my son. We've shared the field, and the transference comes with that and I know my son Rex's kids are already out there in the field. Rex will be one of our main shooters when we go to Australia this summer, for the international games.

MOYERS: So it's a sharing—in a way, it's another kind of condolence. I mean, you pass on the leadership of the game.

LYONS: Yes, in that coming to the condolence ceremony is a process of governance. It's like the generational accountability we talked about. The other thing, though, is that we shouldn't take ourselves so seriously.

MOYERS: Even a chief?

LYONS: Especially a chief, I guess. You're just a human being, really. And you happen to take on a responsibility that anybody else could have taken on if he wanted to do it and took the commitment to do it. And you begin to see the serious side of things quite a bit but, nevertheless, there's life to be lived. I told you the instruction was to give thanks. There was a second instruction that I didn't mention. That was to enjoy life. We're instructed to enjoy life.

Murray Gell-Mann

PHYSICIST

© 1990 Charles-Henri Sanson

Theoretical physicist Murray Gell-Mann received the 1969 Nobel Prize in Physics for his discovery of quarks, the elementary particles of matter. But his interests extend to a wide range of subjects: archaeology and anthropology, language and linguistics, natural history and conservation, population growth and arms control. His recent research, centering on complex adaptive systems, integrates these areas of study. Gell-Mann, a member of the faculty of the California Institute of Technology since 1955, is a founder of the Santa Fe Institute, devoted to the interdisciplinary study of complex systems.

MOYERS: When did you realize that science was your calling?

GELL-MANN: It depends on what you mean by "science." I learned such a lot from my older brother about many different things. About nature, about history, about many branches of knowledge. Bird-watching was an early enthusiasm. I remember once when I was about ten or eleven, we went on a quest to see as many kinds of birds as possible in one day.

MOYERS: Where was that?

GELL-MANN: Here in New York City where I grew up. We saw a hundred and three different kinds of birds, and that was without the benefit of a car. We were too poor to have a car; we used the subway, the Staten Island Ferry, and buses. We started very early in the morning and came back after dark. We used to think of New York as a hemlock forest that had been logged too heavily.

MOYERS: It used to be a hemlock forest, didn't it? Right where we are now, not far from Central Park!

GELL-MANN: When I was a child, a little bit of that hemlock forest was still left, just north of the Bronx Zoo. We used to go there a good deal. It's probably still left! I haven't been there in many years, but I assume those hemlock trees are still standing.

We went to art museums, too, and I was fascinated by archaeology. But we didn't really think of what we were doing in terms of separate branches of science or the arts or humanities. I have never really emphasized distinctions among different subjects. The unity of human culture is what really impresses me, with science being an important part of that culture.

MOYERS: But you're flying in the face of the prevailing intellectual tendency of our time toward increasing specialization.

GELL-MANN: Specialization is important, too. It's necessary that people study particular fields deeply, simply because our knowledge has become so detailed in those fields. But that shouldn't lead to the exclusion of a concern with the unity of human culture. I see them both as very important. It's impossible to carry out today's activities without delving very deeply into particular subjects, because there's so much to know about an individual subject today. At the same time, I think it's very important to keep emphasizing the unity of human culture, and for some people at least to be concerned with transcendent, overarching principles that cover many different kinds of subjects.

At the Santa Fe Institute, we try to do that. Our principal mission is to study issues that transcend specialized subjects, while utilizing the skills of people who are responsibly familiar with the facts of various different specialties. To look for principles, laws, that cover many of them at once, in particular in the study of complex adaptive systems.

MOYERS: What are complex adaptive systems?

GELL-MANN: Those are systems that can evolve or learn or adapt. They would include biological evolution as a whole; that is, the evolution of biological organisms and ecological systems on the earth, as well as the chemical evolution that preceded the first life, what's called prebiotic chemical evolution. They would also include many things that arose as a result of biological evolution—for example, individual learning and thinking (in human beings and other animals) and human cultural evolution, including such things as the evolution of languages, and the global economy as an evolving complex system. All of these have a great many things in common, because learning, adaptation, and evolution are all very similar phenomena.

MOYERS: Are there practical implications of looking at these systems?

GELL-MANN: Oh yes. We can understand every one of these subjects better by seeing the relation that all of them have to one another. It's very important that people, while pursuing specialization, also concern themselves with taking a crude look at the very large issues and the interrelation among many aspects of a large issue.

MOYERS: What do you mean by "a crude look"?

GELL-MANN: Well, it's impossible to get a grasp on the global properties of any complicated nonlinear system by deciding in advance that you're going to look narrowly at this aspect, and that aspect, and that aspect, and then trying to put those aspects together to make a picture of the whole thing. It just doesn't work! You can find out whether there are some simplified aspects that allow you to get a grasp of the global behavior only by studying the global phenomenon and allowing those aspects to *emerge*. You can't decide them in advance. But what a specialist does, typically, is to look at some narrow aspect of a very complicated situation, and then other specialists look at other narrow aspects, and so on, and then whoever it is who's supposed to make a decision, for example, has to synthesize all these narrow views somehow and try to understand how the whole thing is working. It's no good!

MOYERS: Were you performing as a specialist when you discovered the quark?

GELL-MANN: Oh yes, very much so.

MOYERS: Because you were looking for the fundamental building blocks of matter. First scientists had told us that the fundamental particles are molecules and crystals. And then they told us molecules were made of atoms, and then they told us atoms were made of nuclei with electrons around them, and then they said the nuclei were made of neutrons and protons, and then you came along and won the Nobel Prize for discovering that "No, neutrons and protons are not the smallest; they are made out of quarks."

GELL-MANN: That's right; quarks are the fundamental constituents of neutrons and protons. They are as elementary as the electrons that are found around the nuclei.

Actually the Swedish committee that very kindly awarded me the prize didn't mention the quarks in the award. I guess they were worried that those wouldn't turn out to be correct!

MOYERS: And the committee said?

GELL-MANN: They mentioned earlier work that I had done, which the notion of quarks summarized and synthesized very nicely, but they didn't go so far as actually to recognize the quark in the award.

MOYERS: Did you name the quark?

GELL-MANN: Oh yes, I chose the name.

MOYERS: Does a scientist get that privilege? If you discover something new in the universe, you can name it?

GELL-MANN: I guess that's right.

MOYERS: Why "quark"?

GELL-MANN: Well, I could easily have invented some pompous name, derived very carefully from some apparently appropriate root. But names like that often turn out to have been derived from something *in*appropriate as you understand more about the phenomenon. With a meaningless name like "quark," that could never happen. I had the sound first; I didn't know how I would spell it. And then while I was paging through James Joyce's *Finnegans Wake*, I came upon the line, "Three quarks for Muster Mark."

MOYERS: Before you found a name, you knew a sound.

GELL-MANN: A sound, yes; it might have been spelled K-W-O-R-K, or something like that.

MOYERS: But how did you know the sound? Did you just make it up?

GELL-MANN: It just seemed like the right sound. It seemed a natural name for the fundamental constituent of nuclear particles. Whether it was natural or not, it is now the name.

MOYERS: And your new book is going to be called *The Quark and the Jaguar*?

GELL-MANN: I have thought of calling it that, yes, and I may do so. A friend of mine, Arthur Sze, a wonderful Chinese-American poet who lives in Santa Fe and is married to a Hopi weaver, has a poem in his book *River, River* that starts out: "A Galápagos turtle has nothing to do with the world of the neutrino." Actually, he's used poetic license to turn the tortoise "Galápago" into a turtle. Later on he says, "No!" and changes the tone: "The world of the quark has *everything* to do with the jaguar circling in the night." I think that's a very good line.

MOYERS: You believe that, don't you? The fundamental particle of the universe has to do with everything, including a jaguar's movement in the dark.

GELL-MANN: And the relation between the two is just what fascinates me. The relation between the fundamental, simple laws that underlie the operation of the universe, and the enormous complexity of the actual universe as it's observed. The relation between those two is what I think about most of the time these days.

MOYERS: Do I understand you to say that if we found the fundamental law of the universe, and if we found the initial condition of the universe, we would be able to explain all human behavior?

GELL-MANN: That's just the point. We would *not*, and for very fundamental reasons. In fundamental physics, we believe that there exists a simple law of the elementary particles, the fundamental building blocks of the universe, and their interactions. Indeed that may already have been written down by my colleague John Schwarz and his friends in the form of "superstring theory." It's the first viable candidate there has ever been for a unified quantum field theory of all the elementary particles and all the forces of nature.

MOYERS: I'll take your word for it!

GELL-MANN: It may even be right. It may not, but what's astonishing is that there is a candidate that might be right. Similarly, my friend Jim Hartle, a former student of mine twenty-something years ago and now a professor at the University of California/Santa Barbara, and Steve Hawking, who has made himself wealthy and famous with his best-selling book *A Brief History of Time*, proposed some years ago a candidate theory for the initial condition of the universe at the beginning of its expansion.

Now, whether those two principles have been correctly written down in the form of superstring theory and the Hartle/Hawking condition doesn't matter so much as the fact that when those two principles *are* written down correctly, they will be the fundamental principles of the universe. In fact, they may be related to each other. Jim and Steve have a proposal according to which the same formula that gives the fundamental equation for the elementary particles and their forces will also give the initial condition of the universe. So the two laws may actually be just one.

Now, given that law, your question is the most natural one. Would we then know how everything works? And the answer is no. There are actually some complicated reasons for that, but the simplest reason is that the world is quantum-mechanical.

MOYERS: Which means?

GELL-MANN: It means the fundamental law does *not* tell you exactly the history of the universe, but only gives *probabilities* for a gigantic number of alternative histories of the universe, and we can learn the particular details of the history that we experience only by looking around us. Therefore, the idea that the fundamental law can tell us what the complexity of the universe is like just isn't true.

MOYERS: But what will we know, then, if we do know these two laws?

GELL-MANN: Oh, we'll know a lot! We'll know a huge number of correlations, a huge number of relationships among different things that are going on in the universe in the form of scientific principles.

MOYERS: But how would you know you've got the correct fundamental law? There's no way to confirm it.

GELL-MANN: That's another good question. Let me answer that one, too. Suppose that we take the superstring theory as a candidate for the fundamental law of the elementary particles and their interactions, and suppose we take the Hartle/Hawking proposal as the candidate for the initial condition of the universe at the beginning of the expansion. Together, these constitute the fundamental equation for the universe. How can we check that it's true? Well, obviously, we can never *prove* it's true. But what one can do is to try, with better and better calculations, to extract more and more accurate predictions from the theory. At the same time, with more and more careful measurements in the laboratory and the observatory—using the great accelerators and underground labs to study the elementary particles and using the great telescopes to study the cosmos—increasing the accuracy and the scope of the observations (as well as the care with which predictions are extracted by calculation from the theory) one can keep comparing theory and observation better and better. If that comparison keeps going well for a very long time, eventually, of course, humanity will declare we can't afford any further calculations or any further observations, and the theory is right!

You can never finally prove it, but in the meantime, it could be disproved. If careful calculation and careful observation lead to a discrepancy, and that discrepancy persists with further calculation and further observation, then one will have to modify the theory.

MOYERS: It's all mathematical formula, isn't it?

GELL-MANN: Yes. That formula has to be revised if it turns out to be wrong, if there turns out to be a serious discrepancy between calculation and observation. But the proof that it's absolutely right can never be forthcoming. All you can have is a long period of coexistence of observation and theory without any contradiction appearing. As the consequences of theory are extracted more and more carefully, and the observations are done better and better, and no contradiction emerges after a long time, people would decide that it must be right.

© 1990 Charles-Henri Sanson

MOYERS: In layman's terms, aren't you talking about what happened 10 to 15 billion years ago?

GELL-MANN: In the initial condition of the universe, yes.

MOYERS: And all one can do to address that is to apply a beautiful theory. Einstein was said to reject ugly theories; he only wanted beautiful theories.

GELL-MANN: Yes, and it's a very deep question as to why our sense of beauty and elegance should be such a useful tool in discriminating a good theory from a bad one. It's true, but the reason why it's true has caused many scientists to scratch their heads over the years.

MOYERS: But can you put into layman's terms what a beautiful theory is, as opposed to an ugly theory?

GELL-MANN: Well, roughly speaking, a beautiful theory in basic physics can be written down very simply in terms of what appear to be fundamental mathematical quantities. Now why we consider those familiar mathematical quantities to be fundamental is, of course, the mystery. Take Einstein's theory of gravitation, which he liked to call "general relativity." He wrote down that theory utilizing very fundamental quantities referring to the curvature of space and time, and in terms of those, it's very beautiful. My father was an amateur of math, physics, and astronomy. He wasn't very well versed in them, but he used to try to read books on those subjects and try to understand what was going on. He would look at Einstein's equation for the theory of gravitation in empty space, for example, which reads, roughly speaking: $R_{\mu\nu} = 0$, and he would say, "Gosh, that's a simple equation! The only thing is, what is 'R sub mu nu'?"

MOYERS: Your father and I share a lot in common!

GELL-MANN: And, of course, he tried to understand what $R_{\mu\nu}$ stood for. It stands for something very simple and fundamental about the curvature of space/time. But the issue is, why should that work? Well, I can tell you my explanation. My personal view of why simple, beautiful theories work in fundamental physics is that "simple and beautiful" means that we have the mathematics available already. That we have already heard of $R_{\mu\nu}$ in some other context and can therefore write down "$R_{\mu\nu} = 0$." In other words, at an earlier time in history when we were formulating the laws of nature more crudely, we ran across the same kinds of mathematical quantities that we now have to use for a more sophisticated attempt to understand the laws of nature. Now, why should that be? The reason is, I believe, a tendency of the laws of nature to be self-similar to a considerable extent, to resemble themselves at different scales. So that the earlier attempts to understand nature at a scale of larger distance, lower energy, and so on, would yield some of the same kind of mathematics that later proved useful for smaller distances and higher energies.

MOYERS: What happens when we think we've got it right?

GELL-MANN: The fact is, knowing the fundamental formula by no means predicts everything about the universe, because we live in a universe with an enormous amount of uncertainty. A quantum-mechanical law, such as these laws are, can only give probabilities for different alternative histories of the universe. And all the things that are not predicted are nevertheless very important for determining the outcome. The particular events of the history of the universe are codetermined by the fundamental law and a whole series of intrinsically unpredictable accidents.

MOYERS: What do you mean "intrinsically"? I know there are accidents, but do you mean they are built into the nature of the universe?

GELL-MANN: They're built into the nature of the uncertainties of quantum mechanics. You cannot ever predict those. They're just random. They're just accidents. For example, take the existence of our galaxy. Now the existence of a statistical ensemble of different kinds of galaxies is probably predictable, but the existence of this particular galaxy with its particular structure follows, among other things, from some set of accidents that could never be predicted from the laws. The development of our particular star, the sun, similarly depends on accidents, fluctuations, that are intrinsically unpredictable. The emergence of the particular planets of our solar system, likewise. The details of the development of life on the earth, likewise. The evolution of particular forms of life, likewise, depends on these utterly unpredictable accidents. Within a given species, such as ours, the emergence of particular individuals depends on intrinsically unpredictable accidents.

> *So it's the combination of the fundamental law plus this host of completely unpredictable accidents that determines the actual history of the univese as we see it.*

MOYERS: For example, if your parents had coupled two days before or two days later, you would not be the same person sitting there.

GELL-MANN: Or some random cosmic ray could have changed my genetic composition, and so on and so forth; and the same is true of you. So it's the combination of the fundamental law plus this host of completely unpredictable accidents that determines the actual history of the universe as we see it.

MOYERS: So what's the practical consequence of the rest of the story?

GELL-MANN: The practical consequence is that there are simplicity and complexity in the universe. There are simple underlying laws, but very complex results, and among the complex systems in the universe are systems like us that can process information.

MOYERS: Human beings.

GELL-MANN: Not just human beings; other animals as well. And there's no doubt life in many places in the universe, on planets of other stars, and there may be complex adaptive systems that don't closely resemble life, but are also processing information. Complex adaptive systems include computers that have been programmed to evolve new strategies, say for playing games. It's part of the work of the Santa Fe Institute to try to understand what the general laws could be that govern such complex adaptive systems throughout the universe.

MOYERS: What good will this do us?

GELL-MANN: If we understand those principles, it may help us to understand the different systems better by looking at what they have in common.

MOYERS: Could you learn anything about human violence from this? We don't really know how human violence arose.

GELL-MANN: That's right. Let's look at that as an example. The thing that's characteristic of complex adaptive systems—whether we call them evolutionary systems or learning systems or adaptive systems—is that they take their information about the world and don't simply record it in what a computer person would call a look-up table. It's recorded instead in highly compressed models or schemata. Take biological evolution, for example. Virtually all the lessons of biological evolution for a particular organism are expressed in the DNA, in the genetic material.

MOYERS: Sort of a biological "chip."

GELL-MANN: Yes, a little chip, exactly. Now, that doesn't determine the adult organism, does it? What happens is that this schema or model that the DNA represents develops in the presence of environmental situations to produce the actual organism. There's always a further input from the environment in the unfolding of this highly compressed schema to produce an actual situation in the world, like the development of an adult organism. In the case of human societies, what are these chips? They are things like traditions, institutions, myths, and so forth, and in particular circumstances for the society, these combine with the external circumstances to produce some sort of result.

Now how does the adaptation or the learning or the evolution take place? It takes place through a kind of feedback loop. When the schema, together with the external events, produces a situation in the real world, that situation then feeds back and affects in some way the viability of the schema. For example, in biological evolution, the ability of the adult organism to have offspring influences whether that DNA will continue to exist or will die out. In the case of a society, whether the reaction of the society to external circumstances, as codetermined by those circumstances and the traditions and myths and institutions and so on of the society, will lead to a favorable outcome for the society helps to influence whether those particular institutions, myths, traditions, and so on will survive.

MOYERS: You've helped me to see why there is so much emphasis these days on religion and the environment. People say that what one believes theologically about the earth—whether it's our purpose to dominate it or to live in harmony with it— really affects how we respond to such things as the greenhouse effect. We're coded that way with our beliefs, our mythologies.

GELL-MANN: Yes. This can occur in various ways. Some of our coding is biological; some of it is cultural, behavior learned over a long, long time by the society; some of it is individual and has to do with thoughts that develop in the individual human being in a cultural context. One has to distinguish among those different levels. What happens with these schemata is that, as in biological evolution, as in cultural evolution, and so forth, the schema may not be very adaptive. An idea can survive in a human being for a very long time, even though the idea is wrong. A behavior pattern can survive for a long time, even though it's neurotic. So, in other words, a schema has to be robust, has to be persistent, but it also has to be liable to change. Now, sometimes that's not very efficient. For example, early in life, many of us form "person schemata," ways of interacting with other people which are based to some extent on our earlier experience.

MOYERS: Some people are competitive, some cooperative—

GELL-MANN: We may have an experience with a parent or a nurse or a sibling which later on influences our behavior with other people. Now that pattern of behavior may be quite maladaptive. It may also be persistent. That's when we have what we might call a neurosis. It's notoriously difficult to cure. In the same way, a society can have developed patterns of behavior which are rather persistent and they may not be sufficiently changeable. For example, we human beings seem to have a tendency to divide up into groups that dislike one another.

MOYERS: Ethnic groups, religious groups—

GELL-MANN: It could be anything. I call it "generalized tribalism." It can be based on language, on religion, on the shape of the ear, on all sorts of different things. You even notice it in trivial matters, like whether you have an office on the third floor, or you are one of those nasty people who have an office on the second floor. Now we don't know to what extent that tendency may be built in genetically or culturally. People argue about it a lot. Not being an expert on that sort of thing, I won't try to give an opinion on that. But whichever the combination is, it is no longer very adaptive. It is claimed that perhaps it was adaptive when we were bands of hunter-gatherers a long time ago. But now that we live in a world of very destructive weapons, I think most people will agree this is no longer such an adaptive trait as it once was. But we've found it hard to change.

As you pointed out, another such trait is our tendency to trash the environment. At one time, our aggressiveness toward the environment may have been adaptive. It presumably is no longer adaptive now that we're reaching the finite limits of what the earth can take, and we need to find ways to alter our schemata, our programs.

MOYERS: Is there a connection between tracing the delicate balance of elementary particles in physics and appreciating the delicate balance of this ecosystem?

GELL-MANN: Well, certainly in the context of understanding simplicity and complexity there is a connection. And I'm very pleased after all these years of thinking about those things separately, to be able to think about them in a more unified way. But what's even more important in our age is to integrate an awareness of the delicate balance in ecological systems and the delicate balance in our economic system.

MOYERS: You've just helped me to understand a question that's plagued me for some time. The physician and writer Lewis Thomas wrote recently that if he could ask the world of medical science to settle one thing for him, it would be to tell him what happened in the mind of a honeybee. Is a honeybee's mind a machine or does the honeybee know it is thinking about what it is doing? And I thought, "What would be the one thing I'd like to have settled for myself?" And it is this: Why is it I can't change my ways? Now you're suggesting there are a lot of reasons why I as an individual and we as a species don't easily change our habits.

GELL-MANN: The same kind of thing comes up in another study that interests me: creative thinking and how we get our creative ideas. We are constrained in our choice of schemata. It's as if we had what in mathematics are called basins of attraction. As if our thoughts keep running back to particular points of attraction. It's very hard to get them to go over a barrier into another basin where the thoughts would tend to run to some other end.

MOYERS: Well, how do you do that?

GELL-MANN: The way it usually happens was summarized a long, long time ago, for example by the great scientist Helmholtz. I discovered it myself in my own work and in that of colleagues and in talking with artists and all sorts of other creative people. We had almost identical experiences. It's actually very well known. There are stages of thinking. First comes saturation. You fill yourself full of the contradiction between the problem you are working on and the existing ideas that are somehow not good enough, or the existing methods that are somehow not good enough to deal with the problem. After you've confronted for a long time this contradiction between what's available and what's needed, apparently further conscious thought is no good anymore. And at that point some sort of mental process out of awareness seems to take over, involving what the psychoanalysts would call the preconscious, and starts to process this material. That's

And then one day while cooking or shaving or cycling or by a slip of the tongue, or even while sleeping and dreaming according to certain people, you suddenly have an idea.

called incubation. And then one day while cooking or shaving or cycling or by a slip of the tongue, or even while sleeping and dreaming according to certain people, you suddenly have an idea. That's illumination. Maybe the idea is right. There's a final, fourth stage, seeing if it's a good idea: verification.

MOYERS: Did it ever happen to you?

GELL-MANN: Oh yes, very much so. I discovered the notion in physics called "strangeness" by a slip of the tongue. I was giving a lecture in Princeton on why a certain idea I had tried didn't work. And while describing that wrong idea and trying to say why it didn't work, instead of saying "five halves, two and a half," I said "one." It was a mistake, a slip of the tongue. But I realized that if the quantity in question was one instead of two and a half, the idea would work.

MOYERS: You realized that while you were standing in the seminar. You knew instantly?

GELL-MANN: I knew instantly. The reason why the idea didn't work collapsed if the quantity was one instead of two and a half.

MOYERS: But you had been thinking about it a long time, obviously. Saturation. You let it lie there. Incubation. It grows. And then suddenly, illumination.

GELL-MANN: And verification was instant.

MOYERS: Do you think that scientists and poets differ in their methods of creative thinking?

GELL-MANN: I don't believe there's much difference. We had a seminar in Aspen about twenty years ago at which a biologist spoke on his work in theoretical biology, and I spoke on work in theoretical physics, and a poet talked about a case in which he had a problem that he needed to get over and finally figured out how to do it. Two painters were there, and they talked about their work. And the stories all sounded very, very similar. They all had these features of saturation, incubation, illumination.

MOYERS: Can creative thinking be learned or is it a gift?

GELL-MANN: That's very interesting. I would put it a little bit differently. Are there ways of speeding up the process of creative thinking so that one doesn't have to wait for mental processes out of awareness to cook the saturated material for an indefinite period of time? Is it possible to stimulate our ability to think of the right idea? To use the other analogy, can we knock ourselves out of our old basins of attraction into some other basins of attraction where better ideas may lie? And it's possible that we can, that creative thinking can be taught and learned to some extent.

MOYERS: Do you have an unsettled account like Lewis Thomas's? Is there something in your mind you'd like to have science settle for you?

GELL-MANN: There's one question scientists are mostly scared to discuss. What is the nature of self-awareness? Dare we utter the C-word—consciousness? What is the nature of consciousness? What kind of threshold of complexity is there for consciousness? What does consciousness mean? Well, you're not thought to be very scientific if you use words like that. Even the word "mind," the M-word, is one that can get a scientist into trouble.

MOYERS: We certainly have the notion that there is such a thing as consciousness; why not try to understand more precisely what we mean by it? What it corresponds to scientifically, and what is the threshold of complexity necessary to reach it.

GELL-MANN: Whatever it is, it's presumably widespread in the universe. I refuse to believe there's anything special about the complexity of life on this planet or of human beings.

MOYERS: Nothing special?

GELL-MANN: No. It seems terribly unlikely. There must be complex adaptive systems all over the universe.

MOYERS: You mean we're not alone in the universe.

GELL-MANN: It seems extremely unlikely that we are, because, at least according to present theory, there's nothing very special about the solar system. There must be somewhat similar systems in many, many different places in our galaxy and in other galaxies. And as far as we know, the development of life is nothing particularly special either, given the appropriate chemical and climatic circumstances. The cartoon character Pogo said it all very well. Pogo, speaking to another one of the creatures in the Okefenokee Swamp, said, more or less, "Just think! There may be many planets in many systems out there that have life, intelligent life, and there may be many creatures out there that are more intelligent than we are. On the other hand, it may be that we are the most intelligent creatures in the universe. Either way, it's a mighty sobering thought."

LOOKING AHEAD

Remember when 1980 was the future? We are closer now to the new millennium than to the day Ronald Reagan was elected. But while the future has a way of creeping up on us, it never quite manages to catch us. Ambrose Bierce defined "future" as "that period of time in which our affairs prosper, our friends are true and our happiness is assured." No wonder it's never now.

Some of the people I've interviewed think that if we continue to live as if there's no tomorrow, we may indeed make prophets of ourselves. That looming and definitive date 2000 is adding both anxiety and punch to our prognostications of what our future will hold.

Thinking ahead can be fun, nonetheless. Robert Lucky of AT&T Bell Labs, who is paid to think about the future, envisions the day we'll have micro-robots that perform surgery from the inside, and huge computer networks connecting every one of us to all the knowledge in the world. But, says Lucky, the computer will never replace the human being. It can't think, its speech is vacuous, its art is soulless—and it doesn't even smell.

The future also invites dreams of grand reform. Louis Kelso believes every American has the right to be a capitalist. He says there is only one cause of poverty in the modern world: "failure to own an adequate holding of capital." So Kelso has been advocating an Employee Stock Ownership Plan to end that poverty by redistributing capital more equitably.

Keeping our future hospitable to visionaries, inventors, reformers, and dreamers will require taking some very practical steps. Education, for instance. Mike Rose teaches people on the margin—underprivileged children, older students, dropouts back from Vietnam. They may be the last believers in the classic American dream that education saves. This, despite the reality that our educational system does not really know what to do with their unfulfilled dreams. "The presence of such a huge number of people in America who are so marginal runs counter to the best story that this country tells itself about itself," says Rose. "Unless we do something, the falseness of that story will slap us very hard in the face." This, he believes, is the crisis of the democratic promise.

Education is at the heart of the environmental crisis, too. Earth Day 1990 drew people from around the world who were concerned for the future. But between Earth Day 1970 and Earth Day 1990, says Lester Brown of the Worldwatch Institute, the planet lost ground. "We've reached a point where more and more of us have to become environmental activists," Brown maintains. "If more of us do not become politically active, we're not going to make it."

Most of all, says one famous scientist, we have to learn to think like nature—consciousness of the future precedes the future. How can we rebuild the future? How can we make it what we would like it to be? "Are we being good ancestors?" he asks. "Are we contributing to shaping the human beings of the future by what we do now?"

Compelling words from Dr. Jonas Salk, the man who discovered a polio vaccine, thus saving the future for millions of children.

Can we live up to that promise?

How could we *not*?

Robert Lucky

ENGINEER

As executive director of research at AT&T Bell Laboratories, Robert Lucky leads a team of scientists and engineers who are inventing the future. He spends his days thinking about people and machines and the different ways of knowing things. Some of these thoughts he put into his book *Silicon Dreams*. From advanced computer networks to a robot named Sam who understands human speech, Lucky and his colleagues are exploring how technology will touch our lives in the year 2000 and beyond.

MOYERS: When you think about the future, do you think of a vast canvas out there still to be filled, or do you think only about specific things you're working on at the moment?

LUCKY: No, I think of a vast canvas, but I'm a "techie," I'm a technologist, and I'm looking at possibilities. I have got a palette of paints to paint on that canvas. But I don't control the motion of the brush on that canvas. Technology throws certain kinds of things out there, capabilities, you know, computers and what they can do for us and communications possibilities. But the people decide what they want and what they don't want.

MOYERS: But there are no councils of citizens sitting around saying, "Let's ask Bell Labs to do this or to make that."

LUCKY: No, that's the wonderful thing about it. See, I don't even know we're doing these things until I read it in *Time* magazine. I think that journalists are creating the future. They tell us what we are doing. And we don't even know these trends are emerging until the media tell us about them. In communications, for example, we tried to market a picturephone in 1971.

MOYERS: The video phone . . .

LUCKY: Yes, I could see you while I talked to you. And nobody wanted it. That's an idea that people always think of for the future of communications—you're going to see the person you talk to. But we actually had that in 1971 and people didn't want it.

MOYERS: Why do you think they resisted it?

LUCKY: Well, I had one myself for two years in my office. I think I had the last one in the world actually. There wasn't anybody left to call. You don't want to be the only one in the world with a picturephone. But I thought that it used too much of me up. It took too much out of me.

When you talk on a regular telephone, it doesn't involve all of you. You know, you doodle. Now I type quietly at a keyboard while I talk to people, and they don't know it. And you can use only part of your mind for the conversation. But when you have a picturephone you have to stare at that person. I find it intrusive, like you're sitting home on a Saturday afternoon and the doorbell rings. You feel that someone has come in to where you live.

MOYERS: I wouldn't have wanted to comb my hair before I answered the phone.

LUCKY: In fact, we had one switch on the picturephone, it was a privacy switch; you turned that switch and the other person couldn't see you. But in the two years I had one no one ever threw that switch because there was a social compulsion against it. If you threw the switch you had something to hide. So you couldn't do that.

MOYERS: But who threw out the idea of a video phone? Was it technology having the capacity or did someone say, "Maybe the customer will want this, maybe people will like this, so we will create it for them?" In other words, do you think about what people want or what's possible?

LUCKY: Both. But I'm coming from the technology side. I think a lot about what's possible. And then I think, "Are they going to want this?" Usually I think about, "Am I going to want this?" first—

MOYERS: The engineer becomes the customer.

LUCKY: I fell in the trap many times of saying, "I don't want this but it ought to be good for people," and I always find that's wrong, you know. If I don't want it, no one else is going to want it either.

MOYERS: Do you think the day will come before this decade is out when, as the predictions were made in the late seventies, we will be working primarily at home?

LUCKY: No chance. That's something I think I've learned about people. We're social beings, and I really don't believe that telecommuting is going to be a big factor. There's this dream that you can choose to live wherever you want to because it won't matter as far as your work is concerned. You can work from wherever. If we all want to live in Hawaii or Tahiti or whatever, we can do that because it won't matter. Place won't exist anymore. Place won't be important, or what has been called the passing of remoteness. No longer will any place be remote.

Now maybe technologically we could do that. But people don't like to be like that. If I have only an electronic presence I'm not really there. I think the workplace is a social place and you have to get physically immersed in the social place to be effective. You have to be people-networked. It's just not an electronic network. It's really people-networking that counts.

MOYERS: Geography may not be important but society is.

LUCKY: And I'll give you one little story that underlines the point. I was talking with a Minister of Commerce in England about this—Lord somebody or other—and he said, "Teleconferencing will never work." And all of a sudden, he reached out, and he embraced me. And he said, "I need to smell the person I'm dealing with." And I was just frozen. You know what I mean? I thought, "My deodorant has failed!"

And when these things happen, you can't think of a single thing to say. My mind was a blank. And I never thought of a reply. But I finally understand what he meant. He meant smell as a metaphor for something that was human, that wasn't conveyed by the electronics. See, I'm an engineer, and if he tells me he wants smell, I just say, "Hey, he wants smell, give him smell." We go design a smell board, you know, to put in the computer. But that wasn't what he meant at all. He really captured something there. He was saying, "Hey, there's something about a human being that isn't conveyed by a picture of his or her speech. There's something else there."

MOYERS: Well, you said once that people still share information primarily by talking, just the way you and I are doing it.

LUCKY: Talking is the best way of exchanging information because I think we really learn to do it well. If you go back to the early advertisements for the telephone, they were trying to convince people to use this new device. I mean, it seems natural today—who wouldn't want to use a telephone? But back in the late 1800s people were afraid of it, and they didn't know how to use the thing. So the advertisements carried instructions on how your voice is going to be carried and you shouldn't be afraid of this thing, talk right into it clearly and distinctly, and it's going to work!

I think that some people in the older generation never really learned to use this very well, but now, of course, business people—all of us really—have learned how to use the telephone effectively. Maybe in the future we can also learn how to use visual images at a distance better, like the picturephone. We're learning with fax, and we're introducing other media like electronic mail that have a completely different nuance.

MOYERS: What kind of nuance?

LUCKY: Electronic mail, of course, is where I can talk into my computer and send a message to your computer. And it's developed an entirely different social feel from the other mail. Like I would never send you, Bill Moyers, a letter because I'd be too abashed to do that, because you're a famous person and I'm not.

MOYERS: I'm an intimate stranger, that's what television makes us.

LUCKY: Right. But electronically, if I knew you had a computer and it could accept messages, I would not feel the same compulsion about not sending you a message. This cuts across the normal social hierarchies—in a corporate organization, for example, where an employee can't talk directly to the president. You don't call the president of your corporation if you're a lowly employee. But you can send this person electronic mail because it depersonalizes; there's no letterhead, you see? There's nothing that carries a status in the electronic mail. It's an anonymous kind of a medium. None of these trappings of office are present in electronic mail. So you can get to the famous people, to the high people, you can cut across organizational lines.

MOYERS: I looked at Sam, the talking robot here at the Bell Labs, and I thought: "Is there a Sam the robot in my future?"

LUCKY: Certainly there's a computer in your future that's going to befriend you. At least I hope he'll befriend you. I hope you'll think it's a friend. I don't know that there's going to be a robot that walks around and does things. You know one of the most wanted inventions would be a household robot, to take care of your house for you.

But those things are really hard to invent. Because these are tasks that really just involve human judgment, and they seem simple to us because we do them all the time. One example would be a robot carrying a broom around, and it walks through the door. It doesn't know that it has to turn the broom vertical to get through the door. You know that because it's obvious, but think of all the reasoning that the robot has to know to do that.

MOYERS: So there are things you'll never be able to command?

LUCKY: I think there are. There's just an accumulation of these little things. For example, people think computers are so intelligent, yet they're so stupid in plain old human ways. We can build computer programs that play chess at a master's level now. We just had a tournament and the computer lost to the champion. But it can beat just about everybody else. To us, this is the highest form of intelligence—the computer that can play chess. But no computer can walk into a room and find the chessboard. You see? Just a simple human thing.

MOYERS: Then why is there so much experimentation with robots? Why do robots occupy such a place in the imagination, not only of scientists and inventors and engineers but of ordinary folks?

LUCKY: It's anthropomorphic—manlike. You know, the idea of something that looks like us and moves like us sort of grabs us. You don't like to think of a computer like a toaster, sitting there looking uninteresting. In fact, when the lights were taken off computers I thought to myself they should blink or do something to show they're alive. But technologically, robots are really pretty far out. They only do little simple mechanical tasks by rote.

MOYERS: What about the robot cockroaches that I heard were running around here?

LUCKY: Well, we did start out some work on what we call silicon micromechanics, making very small mechanical things the way we make very small electric circuits. That is, when we make computer chips, we make them from design masks, and then we project that mask onto a little wafer of silicon of a very small size. And we etch out the silicon to produce microscopic circuits. So someone said, "Well, why can't we make mechanical things that way, very small mechanical things?" And we did some of that but not anymore.

MOYERS: What would be the value of that?

LUCKY: Well, the real dream—and this is only a dream, I have to say—you build a little robot that could do microscopic things for you. Our first thought was that it would crawl around inside these microscopic circuits and fix them, but actually there's only one little thing that's worth crawling around in and fixing, and that's the human body. That's worth a lot to fix. So the dream for some century is that you have a little pill that is a microsurgeon. You swallow it and the thing runs around inside your body fixing things up.

Now that's appealing. It's a lot better than the surgeon cutting a hole in you and sticking his hand in there and doing things. So you would have this little microsurgeon inside your body working away. And then you have the real surgeon working on something that looks like a steam shovel, he's operating the little guy inside your body. I picture that you're lying there on the operating table and you can see the doctors out there watching the computers as those things are inside fixing you up. And then I see their expressions start to darken, and then they're all concerned. And the thing has run amok inside your body!

MOYERS: I'm not even going to smile at that. I used to think that not everything that could be imagined could be done, but I'm about to decide that everything that can be imagined can eventually be done.

LUCKY: Eventually. I mean, this is going to take a long time, and I wouldn't want people to get the idea that we're actually building anything like this microsurgeon. You know, the only thing we did was to build little gears and little mechanical assemblies to show that it could be done. So perhaps in the next decade you'll have not only big robots, but little robots. Because that's one of the things that we humans aspire to do. To be someplace we're not. And usually I think of that in terms of communications. To be somewhere we're not. In the case of the microrobots it takes our presence places we can't go, like inside the human body. Or into far space. Into fires and nuclear reactors and places we could not go we can send our surrogate. So in this case it's a physical surrogate, a robot, but we think these days about virtual surrogates—computer programs. For example, a phrase which has been used with respect to information is a knowbot.

MOYERS: That's a new one to me.

LUCKY: Well, a knowbot is an information robot. And it's not a real thing with arms, but it's a computer program. Say you need some information. You're doing an interview with someone and you need to get some background information for it. Right now you probably have a research assistant who goes out and does spade work. So that maybe you turn this over to your knowbot and you say, "I need some information." And the knowbot goes out onto the computer networks and it rummages around and it looks for this information and it puts it together, and finally it reports back to you. And says, "Here's what I found out." You know, "Is that what you want?"

MOYERS: I could just hear Andie and Judy and Becca—my colleagues—all quaking for their jobs.

LUCKY: No, they don't have to worry. They don't have to worry at all. Some of this is far out in the future, but I think that getting specific information is not hard. You could have knowbots that go out and get a specific fact for you.

MOYERS: Where do they go?

LUCKY: Oh, they go out into virtual space. Out into the computer networks.

MOYERS: Virtual space.

LUCKY: Virtual space. Right. Outside of these walls the wires run into the walls out here and there's an electronic space out there where the information is floating around. It's in the computer banks of the world. And it's forming sort of a distributed intelligence. All the libraries of the world, all the databanks of the world—they're all getting connected electronically.

I'd like to think of it as sort of an electronic commons out there. This is my dream, anyway. In old New England you had town commons, where you went when you wanted to find something. You could exchange information with people and talk to them. But now the towns have grown in size and the world's a busy complicated place and there's no simple little town commons. But now there's this virtual space out there, an electronic space where you can go and engage people all over the world. It's an electronic meeting place. We can go out and barter information on those networks. They exist today.

In fact, I'm really a devotee of what we call electronic bulletin boards. That's very much like a fence where people can pin up notes. Imagine you live in a small town and you want some little bit of information. You don't know who to ask. So you put up a note on the fence where everyone's passing by and people see it and someone knows the answer and they write the answer to you and then you find it there. The fence is a meeting place. Now we have that electronically.

I'll give you a simple example. Somebody wanted to buy a humidifier for his house. But he said, "Isn't it going to rust my heating ducts?" Now this is the typical kind of information that you need in everyday life. You can't get this in an encyclopedia. You can't get this in a library. There's no place you can get this. You have to get it from other people. But who do you ask? So you send a message out there into virtual space: "Hey, does anybody know about heating ducts and humidifiers?" You just punch in this message.

MOYERS: There's no address on it?

LUCKY: No, no address. It goes into the consumer network. And people sitting throughout the world at universities and in companies like mine, or sitting in their basements at home, on their computers read the news on the Consumer Net, and they see this message about humidifiers. Actually, this particular question drew dozens of responses. Some from plumbers who knew about this, or claimed to know about it. Some from scientists who knew about the theory of corrosion, and some from just plain homeowners who had one experience or the other. And at the end of the day this person had scores of responses from the wisdom of the people out there on this particular subject. It's a way of going into virtual space to get information.

MOYERS: A whole new way of sharing.

LUCKY: A whole new way of sharing human information. And this isn't some mystical database out there. These are real people putting in real messages. Real human information.

MOYERS: You're talking about another category of haves and have-nots. The world's going to be divided into those of you browsing through this virtual space and the rest of us living in a world we only see.

LUCKY: I don't worry about that. Because I feel that more and more people are learning to deal with computers. I don't think you have to go to the computer; I think the computer's going to come to you. I think that's happened a lot already.

When I went to graduate school I met my first computer. And it basically didn't want to talk to me. It was really hard to use. And the people who owned it didn't want me to touch it. This is our computer, you know, keep your grubby hands off our computer! They said, "If you want to use our computer you've got to submit a pile of punchcards." So it was very impersonal. I had to submit punchcards like I was an outcast. And they deigned to look at my punchcards.

But eventually we got time-sharing computers—computers where I could deal interactively with a computer via some terminal. And then we got the personal computer. You could own this thing in your home. And I built a computer in my home, even before there were Apples or machines like that. The idea of having a computer in your home is so alluring and obsessive to me. Owning this kind of power.

Now we're working very hard, and making very good progress, in computerized speech. So the computer is going to learn to deal with you eventually. It's an awfully hard task. It's going to take us decades and decades because we humans are so complex. But the computer already knows how to speak pretty well. It can read a book to you, for example.

MOYERS: You can program the text into the computer and the computer interprets the data to speak—without your having spoken the words into the computer?

LUCKY: Right, exactly. You can take a book and put it in the computer, the computer looks at the book, scans it, and electronically finds out what the letters are and then eventually pronounces the words to you.

MOYERS: What a boon that will be for the blind.

LUCKY: Yes. There are machines like that now. But they don't work perfectly. Because it's not just a question of learning the pronunciation of an individual word, or looking a word up in the dictionary and finding out how to pronounce it. It's the cadence from word to word. The rhythm of speech. And that's very hard. It's a very human thing to know how to modulate your tone. Basically you've got to know what you're talking about. And the reason the computer doesn't sound right is it doesn't know what it's talking about. These are just words to it.

MOYERS: It's had no emotional experience with the words.

LUCKY: That's right.

MOYERS: So when it says "love" it has no sense of the pain or the joy.

LUCKY: Could you imagine a computer reading Shakespeare to you? It would sound dreadful. It doesn't know how to emote its words.

MOYERS: We're going through this silly stage now where cars speak up and tell you to buckle your seatbelts and where magazines talk about their products and greeting cards sing to you and security alarms shout "Burglar! Burglar!" But they're all in these inhuman voices.

LUCKY: Yes.

MOYERS: And I feel jolted.

LUCKY: Somebody told me once that he didn't want to listen to anything that didn't want to listen to him. And I feel that way too. There's an emptiness behind this computerized speech. There's no intellect behind it. You can sense it in the emptiness of the words, that there's no intelligence behind it.

But I'd have to ask you— Do you really want the computer to sound human? I'm not sure I do. Suppose the computer can be programmed to be seductive or persuasive. I'm not sure I want that. I think I really want to know that it's a computer. Yes, let it sound stupid, as long as I can understand it. Information is one thing. I want to understand it. But I'm not sure I think that I want this thing to mimic being a person.

> *Do you really want the computer to sound human? I'm not sure I do. Suppose the computer can be programmed to be seductive or persuasive.*

MOYERS: Do you think we human beings are thinking differently because of the computer?

LUCKY: I really don't know. The computer is an ordered world. It appeals to me as a scientist, an engineer, because everything has a rule and an order. In order to explain things to the computer we have to translate things into rules. And organize things. Take the question of understanding language. I keep saying, "The computer doesn't know this, or doesn't know that," but in truth it's *we* who don't know it. The reason the computer can't understand our language is that we don't understand our language. We can't understand it well enough to explain it to the computer.

Every little child can go out in the schoolyard and learn the English language. But we still don't understand the rules well enough to teach them to the computer. Now suppose we think like this computer that says, "I've got to understand English." For that to happen, we've got to make a whole table of the rules of English. However many rules there are, the computer doesn't care. It could be a million rules. The computer says, "All right, just give them to me. I'll learn them all." But it has to know the rules. And we don't yet know these rules well enough to program it so that the computer can "learn" them.

MOYERS: Well, look at what Shakespeare did without "knowing," in the technical sense, the rules of English.

LUCKY: That's the difference between humanity and the computer. A friend of mine once wrote that in the future, computers were going to produce all of the art and music of the world. But they wouldn't know when something was good and when it was bad. They would just spew it all out. There would have to be a human critic who would take these pictures and this music and decide—this is good; that's bad. That's the role of the critic. In the end, the critic would become known as the artist. The computers can do art now. They write music. But they don't know whether it's any good or not.

MOYERS: You play the piano.

LUCKY: Yes.

MOYERS: Is it good music, the computer music?

LUCKY: I feel funny about that. Because when I hear computer-composed music I sense an emptiness in it. There's no emotion behind this. You know, when you hear Mahler or Chopin you think about the troubles of their lives. The anguish. The emotions that are coming out in their music.

MOYERS: They evoke in me a similar response.

LUCKY: And then when I hear this computer music I think "What does this computer know about life?" It hasn't experienced love and death and the sensations that make human anguish and human joy what they are. Who is it to tell me about such experience? To try to convey that experience to me?

The catch is, that's when I know it's computer music in the first place. You see, if I don't know it's computer music and I start thinking "Oh, the anguish of the music . . ."

MOYERS: Then we've crossed into another world. What do you think is the most human about humans?

. . . the more you study computers, the more you realize how beautiful it is to be human.

LUCKY: Well, the most human thing about humans, I think, is language, art. Those are the two things. Art is only an expression of language anyway. We don't know where language came from. But there it is, and we all have it. And the more you study computers, the more you realize how beautiful it is to be human. How we can look and see things and recognize objects and how we can express our thoughts in language. I doubt that if they took away my language, I could even think.

So there's a world of difference between us and the computer. Sometimes I think of myself as a walking VCR, because all my life I've been recording images inside my head. And I can replay them whenever I want to. I can remember when I walked on the beach in Tahiti, and I can bring that back in my mind and replay it. A computer doesn't know pictures at all. A few pictures use up its memory. It knows no language of pictures. It doesn't know about a beach in Tahiti. It doesn't know a beach from anything else.

MOYERS: What more do we need technology to do?

LUCKY: There's a lot we can do with the technology we already have today to improve our life in the future. In the last decade we've rewired America with optical fiber. The first optical fiber went out in 1980–81. And we've built a whole new telecommunications system. Now it sits there buried under the ground, these little hair-thin strands of glass. And they offer us an overwhelming new amount of communication. We could send a whole *Encyclopaedia Brittanica* on optical fiber in a half a second.

MOYERS: You did this without thinking of whether society really needed it. The old satellite system seemed to be working all right for me.

LUCKY: But we used it up. The sky is filled with these satellites now. All the parking slots are gone. We've always used up every bit of communication that technology has offered us in the past. Now the optical fiber can carry a tremendous amount of new television, if we want it to. What we'd like to do is bring that fiber into your home. It's as if we've built a superhighway across the country, but so far, we don't have any on and off ramps.

MOYERS: No off and on ramps?

LUCKY: Well, there are, at the major interchanges at cities. But it doesn't come to your home. To get to it from your home, it's like going through a drinking straw. There's this giant pipe out there, but you've only got a little straw. So what we'd like to do is put this superhighway into your home in the next decade. And it can bring you a thousand television channels, all the communication you might need for the next decade.

MOYERS: It's not just a cliché then, the information age?

© 1990 K. C. Bailey

LUCKY: I hope not. No, it isn't a cliché. And my only hesitancy comes from my realization that it's not enough just to exchange information. We also have to make things.

MOYERS: Which we're not doing very much of. What do you think is the significance of that? That we Americans are not making things anymore?

LUCKY: It gets to the heart of the economy. I think one of the most pressing problems for us in America is to find a way to derive economic benefit from intellectual work. Because we're very good at intellectual work, but we're bad at getting a return for it.

MOYERS: The Japanese do that better. The Germans do that.

LUCKY: Well, the Japanese are dealing in material goods. And there's a tried-and-true system for deriving material benefit from that. One of the presidents of one of the large Japanese corporations told me, "The reason that you're failing in America is that you've moved into the information age, while we're still in the industrial revolution."

MOYERS: We have to nurture information, harvest it, shape it, program it, package it, and merchandise it.

LUCKY: Yes. We can do all those things. But we have to learn to get money for it. And that's one of the tasks. Look at the problems of software. The problem about information is that it's too easy to copy. It's leaky. Information is made out of nothing. And once you've made it, you can't destroy it. My image of the factories I worked in when I grew up was of a railroad track coming in with raw material. And the railroad ran out the other side of the factory and took out the finished goods. That was the world to me. In came the raw materials, out went the finished products. But with information, for the "factories" of today, nothing goes in, and only information comes out. It's a virtual thing, and we have to find a way to sell that.

MOYERS: Right now we create the information, and other societies sell it back to us in the form of hard goods.

LUCKY: Exactly right.

MOYERS: That's behind the trade imbalance as much as anything. Doesn't part of that answer require redirecting some of the research? Research is now backed by billions of dollars. Much of it comes from the government, aimed for military purposes. And much of it is now bankrolled by corporations whose main interest is the next quarter. We don't have patient capital in this country. Do you think that's one of the reasons we're having such a difficult time competing?

LUCKY: Absolutely, yes. Research is a long-term investment. And it requires patient capital. There's no question about that. It requires someone to look past the next quarterly return. We think of research as being in the five-to-ten-year interval. You're not going to see a return on this until you're downstream five to ten years. And what American business leader can persevere in investments like that?

I used to blame the people on Wall Street. I thought they were greedy and were endangering my livelihood by their short-term greediness. But as you grow up a little, you realize that it's not just them, it's all of us. It's our American system that demands this. So we have to change our basic habits as a nation in order to get this patient capital.

MOYERS: There's something else, too. We are an adversarial society. And so many of the other societies that we're competing with are cooperative societies.

LUCKY: Yes. Japan has a system where the various corporations in Japan cooperate on research projects. And then when it comes to fruition, they each take their own directions. But they have a government consortium that puts companies together to do basic kinds of research. And we're looking at that as a model of behavior that perhaps we should emulate more in this country. We set up Sematech, which is a consortium here in America of electronics companies to build basic electronic circuits. We're experimenting. We don't naturally cooperate nearly as well as the Japanese do. Maybe their island culture of togetherness, forced togetherness, makes them cooperate better than we do. But all we know how to do is compete. Our laws are structured that way. Antitrust laws. Thou shalt compete.

MOYERS: The anthropologists will tell you that over time, cooperation has paid off more often than competition. But it's not a lesson we seem to have applied successfully in this country yet.

LUCKY: No, I don't think that's in our nature as Americans. We've learned to compete. That's where we're coming from.

MOYERS: You manage hundreds of engineers and inventors, very creative people. What drives them? What makes them tick?

LUCKY: Fame. Fame. You want to be the first to do something. You want to create something. You want to innovate something. And you want the world to know about it. I often think of Edison inventing the light bulb. That's what I want to do. I want to drive over the bridge coming out of New York there and look down on that sea of lights that is New Jersey and say, "Hey, I did that!" I mean, just to have invented the light bulb. Could you imagine?

Louis Kelso

CAPITALIST

Louis Kelso is a crusader for a more democratic form of capitalism. Early in his career, he developed the Employee Stock Ownership Plan (ESOP), which is based on the idea that every employee—not just corporate officers—should be an owner of stock, paid for out of the company's earnings. Endorsed by Congress in the 1970s, ESOPs have been put into effect by companies across America. Ten million people belonged to ESOPs by the end of the 1980s, but the results have been mixed. Continuing to champion the worker-owner, Kelso heads a firm that advises companies on creating ESOPs for their employees.

MOYERS: There's a widespread perception in the country that something is fundamentally wrong with our economic structure. Our debt has tripled in the last ten years. There are thirty-two million people living in poverty. Twelve million of those earn less than five thousand dollars a year. It's harder and harder for even two spouses in the same family to do for their children what one spouse did twenty-five years ago. Working couples have a hard time buying a home. More and more people, by your own statistical studies, are falling out of the middle class. Something is wrong here.

KELSO: Well, the purpose of the Industrial Revolution was to free people from toil and poverty. But that hasn't worked for a large part of the population. They're working harder and longer under less homelike conditions than they ever did before. The poor live in a very lousy fashion. The Department of Housing and Urban Development estimated there are 25 million people in the United States who would love to have homes and want to buy them who will never be able to buy them in their lifetimes under present conditions.

MOYERS: Is this why you say that in the United States today, we have a political democracy within an economic plutocracy? That's strong language. "Plutocracy" is not a word we normally hear in our political discourse. But you have said that the concentration of wealth in the United States today is as great as Marx and Engels found in Europe when they wrote the *Communist Manifesto*.

KELSO: It's even worse. They said most of the wealth was concentrated in the hands of the wealthiest ten percent. I'd say that now all the nonresidential capital is in the top five percent. Ninety-nine percent of all the capital assets in the United States have been bought out of the income of capital.

MOYERS: During the 1980s, we saw capitalism in its heyday. The free marketeers had their decade with Ronald Reagan and the mergers, the leveraged buyouts, all of that. Wasn't the result of it to further concentrate the ownership of capital?

KELSO: There's no question about it. They concentrated the

heck out of it. Look at the Forbes 400. That's a study by *Forbes* magazine that identifies the four hundred largest family holdings of wealth in the country. You used to be able to get into that club with $100 million or so; now it's almost $500 million. And it'll be a billion sooner or later if we keep on the way we are.

The interesting thing about that is that the minute your income exceeds what you will spend on consumption for yourself and your dependents, you're no good to the economy anymore. You only use the excess for one purpose and it's a bad purpose. You accumulate more excess. The thing is out of control.

MOYERS: You've said that one of our problems is the rich don't spend enough.

KELSO: They can't spend enough. And they only spend it for the wrong thing. Accumulating more excess. Capital is too fabulous a thing to be owned by the few. We're violating that all over the place. The earning power of a large part of the population is inadequate, and even with all the redistribution and the damage that that does—and it does tremendous damage—we can't get everybody under the redistribution rug.

Obviously we haven't mastered the art of redistribution. That is, we're saddling the highly productive with the cost of the underproductive and the nonproductive. We've had to grant more and more pay for the same work input or even diminished work input. The result is, we price ourselves out of the international competition. Countries like Japan, where wages historically have been controlled by tradition and fear, have been able to easily undersell us.

MOYERS: If you were advising the new governments in Eastern Europe, would you advise them to follow our model or Japan's?

KELSO: Neither. I would say, "You are dead right in seeking democracy, but for heaven's sake, don't pretend that you only have to democratize political power. You have to democratize social power, too, and a major part—more than half—of the total power of a society is economic. You have to democratize both. You have to adopt a national economic policy that recognizes that capital is a main source of productive input and that acquiring and owning it is a human right." The right to life implies a right to earn a good living. When 90 percent of the goods and services are produced by capital workers—people who own capital—as it is in an industrial society like ours, you can't earn a good income without owning capital. You need to have both. Therefore, you need to have a reasonable opportunity to acquire it.

MOYERS: And by capital you mean—

KELSO: Land, structures, machines, capital intangibles, processes, tools, all of which are normally represented in our economy by common stock, since most assets are held in corporations and most production is carried on in corporate form.

MOYERS: You have written that what we need in this country is 200 million capitalists. What's the definition of capitalist in this instance?

KELSO: A family that earns a significant part of its income through the ownership of capital. As I say, that's normally land, structures, machines, processes, capital intangibles. Capital is a major source of economic power. We need to imitate nature's pattern in the distribution of that: One person, one capital power. It's a constitutional right. The right to life doesn't mean a thing without the right to earn a good income.

MOYERS: Where do you find that in the Constitution? Is there a constitutional right to be a capitalist?

The Roman arena was technically a level playing field. But on one side were the lions with all the weapons, and on the other the Christians with all the blood. That's not a level playing field. That's a slaughter. And so is putting people into the economy without equipping them with capital, while equipping a tiny handful of people with hundreds and thousands of times more than they can use.

KELSO: I find it in the fine print and in the development of the law. You don't have to jump very far philosophically to realize that the right to life means the right to earn a good income to support life, as good an income as the system could provide if it were properly used. The idea that the level playing field is a field on which every individual is treated as economically equal is absolutely insane. The Roman arena was technically a level playing field. But on one side were the lions with all the weapons, and on the other the Christians with all the blood. That's not a level playing field. That's a slaughter. And so is putting people into the economy without equipping them with capital, while equipping a tiny handful of people with hundreds and thousands of times more than they can use.

MOYERS: But you're defying the very nature of capitalism itself when you make this argument. Capitalism is essentially competitive and essentially ruthless.

KELSO: No. The claim to capital ownership is one of the expressions of the law of private property. Now, the law of private property is part of the common law. We acquired our common law from Great Britain. Great Britain refined it for seven or eight hundred years. And the roots of it go right back into Roman law. So we're talking about human concepts that are a couple of thousand years old.

Now, the relationship between an individual and his capital is subject to three limitations. Private property does not vest an owner with the right to use his property to injure a fellow man. It does not vest him with the right to injure the property of a fellow man. And it doesn't vest him with the right to injure the public welfare. The moment you recognize that capital is man's invention to combat toil and poverty and that every person needs to have it, those three principles of limitation which come out of ancient common law of private property become operative. Every once in a while you'll find some wise guy, usually a billionaire, who says, "It doesn't make any difference who owns the capital." He is speaking from a very safe position, you can see. The truth is exactly the opposite. Owning capital is the difference between being poor and being not poor. There is only one cause of poverty in the modern world: failure to own an adequate holding of capital.

MOYERS: You propose that employees of a company should be able to obtain access to credit and use the profits from the company to pay back that credit.

KELSO: Right. All employees should have the right legitimately to acquire stock in their company and pay for it out of the company's own income.

MOYERS: Pay for it out of the profits of the company? Not out of wages or salaries?

KELSO: That's right. That would be Adam Smith's private property free market economics, modified to recognize that owning capital is the way to engage in production and earn income.

MOYERS: But even this idea of yours, the Employee Stock Ownership Plan, has been corrupted—

KELSO: No question about it.

MOYERS: Eastern Airlines gives 25 percent of its stock to workers, but not much democracy. They had to sit around helpless when Eastern Airlines was sold. Dan

River Company down in Virginia gives 25 percent of the stock to the employees. They feel good about it. Bang, it all goes badly and the workers now feel they've been had by a management that is out to protect its own interest and preserve its own privileges at the expense of the workers.

KELSO: Anything can be misused. But the right of everyone to buy, in the same way that the rich have bought their capital—out of its own income—that is a human right.

MOYERS: When you came forward with that idea in the fifties and sixties, and when Congress finally acted in the seventies, I thought we were really going to see a new form of capitalism in this country. But one team of management after another has subverted that idea to protect its own interests. They share the stock, but they don't share democracy. They don't share participation.

KELSO: That's because we simply haven't gone far enough to make it clear what the principles are and to adopt them as policy. People act on their knowledge. People act on their impression of things. Our national economic policy is to solve all income problems through jobs. We don't even recognize that a basic American human right, a constitutional right, is the right to acquire and own capital.

MOYERS: But you're challenging the theoretical basis of capitalism, that privilege always protects its own privilege.

KELSO: It does. But the purpose of the state is to lay down a sound policy. To make it possible for people to live well and peaceably and prosperously and competitively. The United States is going downhill in the world competitive society. The evidence of it is all over the place. Unfortunately, the double-entry bookkeeping logic on which a market economy is built doesn't require that the consumers be in the same economy with the producers.

MOYERS: What would it take to bring us all into the same economy? You're talking about changing American economic policy from full employment to—

KELSO: Full employment and capital ownership. Efficient, effective capital ownership as early as possible in your life.

MOYERS: But how?

KELSO: We need one leader. One leader who says this present economic policy is insane. We have an economic policy that was very appropriate in the Stone Age, but we've passed that now. We haven't yet upgraded the assumptions underlying free market economics that were made by Adam Smith.

MOYERS: But the tendency of society is not in that direction. Look at the 1980s; look at the wild euphoric romp that the free marketeers had on Wall Street.

KELSO: It wasn't free marketeers exactly. It was a greed romp. It was an absolute greed rage. But we had a leader who didn't recognize it, and who thought it was good.

MOYERS: Isn't that the nature of this capitalist system?

KELSO: I don't think so. I think it is the misused nature. The *real* nature hasn't been aroused. I don't think that anyone can defend his position in seeking to own more than about $25 or $30 million, at most, when he can't use it, won't use it, can't take it with him. And when his ego is imposing enormous harm on his fellow man.

MOYERS: You are arguing against the dominant tendency in American capitalist development. Here you are saying that with the right leader we could make America truly a capitalist society, and you're up against the way we've been doing things for the last twenty-five years.

The New Deal made a great discovery, one great discovery, and that was that in a modern industrial world, only government can be responsible for the prosperity of an economy.

KELSO: Yes, but we've been getting deeper and deeper in trouble. We have reached the limits of redistribution. We've been running this society on redistribution since the New Deal. The New Deal made a great discovery, one great discovery, and that was that in a modern industrial world, only government can be responsible for the prosperity of an economy. It's only government that can set the policy. Only government can police the policy to make sure it's followed. I think that's an absolutely valid principle, and we have followed that even more than our laws would suggest. But then it made a second great decision. Looking at that first decision as the highway out of the wilderness, we put the economy down on that highway faced one hundred and eighty degrees in the wrong direction.

MOYERS: Towards what?

KELSO: We launched a war on the *effects* of poverty. The effects, not the cause. There is but one cause of poverty in the modern world: failure to own an adequate holding of capital. That's all.

MOYERS: Isn't there more to it than that? There's the old saying in Texas, where I come from, "Play the cards fair, Reuben, I know what I dealt you." Isn't that what the wealthy and privileged do? The concentrations of wealth concentrate more wealth which concentrates their power. They deal themselves a good hand.

KELSO: But they're leaving out 95 percent of the American public. I say that in a

democracy, with odds of ninety-five to five, you should be able to win. The good should be able to win. The sensible should be able to win.

MOYERS: Would you be undermining capitalism?

KELSO: Quite the reverse. You'd be establishing it. You'd be putting it on a sound, powerful footing. A footing where it can really spread all the way around the world.

MOYERS: You wrote a long letter to Mikhail Gorbachev. What did you say?

KELSO: I said to him that to think that democracy depends merely on democratization of political power is to miss the big ball. It requires the democratization of economic power. And that requires the democratization of capital ownership.

MOYERS: You are arguing beyond Marxism. Beyond Adam Smith. Beyond liberal and conservative. Beyond Republican and Democrat. Which opens you to the charge from these people: "He's a crank. He wants to take our system and radically change it."

KELSO: Nothing would be taken away. Nothing would be given. Everything would be bought and sold. Those are people who live on the buying and selling. When I invented the ESOP, I started a whole new industry. There are thousands of people engaged in setting up ESOPs, in financing ESOPs, in buying and selling ESOPs. A society that's prosperous all the way down to the shoe soles is a good place to work and a good place to make a living.

MOYERS: Do you consider yourself a capitalist? A socialist?

KELSO: I don't know what I am. You just said that I don't fit any of the definitions. I think I'm the capitalist of tomorrow.

MOYERS: You've been at this now for forty years. You were a voice in the wilderness for a long time. Finally, by coincidence, you met Senator Russell Long and he listened to your idea about employee stock ownership. And while that became legislation, I think the jury's still out on it.

KELSO: ESOPs are now protected by the law of one of Aesop's fables.

MOYERS: The other Aesop?

KELSO: Yes. This is the story of the man and the tiger. You can give meat to a tiger but you can't take it away from him. For two hundred years, two centuries, people have been coming to America in search of the American dream, to acquire capital holding that'll stand them in good stead. The Homestead Act, which offered free land out West to any settler who would work it for five years, was, in a sense, the first governmental tool recognizing that capital ownership is essential. But we were still an agrarian economy when Lincoln pushed it through. It'd been debated for about twelve years.

MOYERS: It made landowners of lots of ordinary people.

KELSO: It made landowners of people who couldn't earn a good income without that capital. It was paid for by sweat equity, but it was paid for. It was bought with very dear labor. But the logic of the Homestead Act was never followed through into the industrial society. It should have been but it wasn't.

MOYERS: In part, the resistance comes because the capitalist is a tiger. Once he gets it, he doesn't let go.

KELSO: But he's not the only tiger in the jungle. And the hungry tigers are going to beat the greedy tiger every time, especially when they outnumber them ninety-five to five. All they have to do is get the issues straightened out.

Mike Rose

TEACHER

Born to immigrant parents in a poor neighborhood in Los Angeles, Mike Rose was not expected to make it in school. He did—and went on to become a teacher, working with people on the edges of society: inner-city children, Vietnam veterans, adults trying to overcome a lifetime of disadvantage. Now, as associate director of the writing program at UCLA, he continues to teach underprepared students how to enter and succeed in the academic world. In his book *Lives on the Boundary*, he writes about his students, many of them poor, all of them labeled failures—as he once was.

MOYERS: You've been teaching . . .

ROSE: Twenty years.

MOYERS: And you can still write that teaching is a romance?

ROSE: Yes, it *is* a romance. It's a romance, the terms of which are language, mathematical formulas, facts, dates, theories, opinions. It's easy to lose faith in that. Education has often functioned as a gatekeeper. With so much of what goes on in education—testing, assessment, grade levels—the intent is to evaluate people and keep them out or let them in. The way I view education is really very different from that. It's an invitation. It is an attempt to bring people into a kind of conversation, into a set of ideas, into ways of thinking, talking, writing, and reading that are new to them. If you see education as an attempt to bring people in, then you automatically see it as a relationship. And if the relationship works right, it is a kind of romance.

MOYERS: Just before we began this conversation, you said you just didn't think you had the right to be heard discussing education. Why did you say that? After all, you've been teaching for twenty years. That's experience.

ROSE: I know. Isn't it foolish? You know, for the two days before we were to get together, I played out every awful scenario you could imagine, from throwing up on my shoes to passing out in my chair to embarrassing you or embarrassing myself. I realized finally that it was all based on the long-standing feeling that develops in a lot of us who grow up in the working class and then find ourselves in arenas that are very different from our origins. I continue to live with that sort of nagging doubt that I have the right to speak to a public about many of these issues.

MOYERS: Because you're from the working class?

ROSE: Well, it's not that neat and clean. I wish I could say it that articulately to myself because then I could prove it to be nonsense, right? I like the phrase from that wonderful book by Richard Sennett and Jonathan Cobb—*The Hidden Injuries of Class*. It's a kind of lingering doubt that's hard for me to voice, but it's there. I think that doubt stays with a number of us who move up through the class system and end up in a profession that is highly status-laden.

MOYERS: What does that say about the mystique of education in this country? That somehow, even after twenty years of teaching street kids, slum kids, illiterate adults, people who can't get out of the neighborhoods, the lost people of our society, that you don't take yourself quite seriously as a competent authority?

ROSE: Interesting, isn't it? The raw power of education, particularly higher education, is so strong, I think, that it can act to deny our most immediate and true experience. That's the sort of power that education has in the minds of many of the folks who come from where I come from. I see it all the time with the people I teach.

MOYERS: What do you see?

ROSE: It manifests itself in lots of ways. People who are sullen and silent, or people who make lots of noise, or joke around a lot, or become the class clown. People who get stoned. People who are absent a lot. All of these are ways that they're defending against that very feeling that we're talking about. The feeling of not belonging. Of being inadequate.

MOYERS: Your parents were immigrants from Italy who came here looking for opportunity?

ROSE: Yes. Both of my parents came from dirt-poor peasant backgrounds. They arrived at Ellis Island in the 1910s and '20s, as literally millions of other Italian and Central European immigrants did at that time. It's the classic immigrant story. Coming to America for a better life, only to find a very hard life.

MOYERS: So you were poor.

ROSE: We were pretty poor. We lived in South Central Los Angeles. We were able to rent a house. We had some furniture, although I can remember the furniture being repossessed and we had to get used furniture. My parents managed to scrape their money together to send me to a parochial school, because they had it in their minds that such a school would guarantee me a better education. It's a tremendous testament to them that they pulled money out of God knows where to do that sort of thing for me. They bought me a telescope once when they realized I was fascinated with astronomy.

MOYERS: They got you on the right track.

ROSE: They sure did. Now, the elementary school that I went to was okay. You know, it was so-so. I didn't excel particularly. I was a decidedly average student. I look back at my old report cards and there were all these C's speckled throughout them.

When I went to high school, an interesting thing happened. My entrance tests were confused with somebody else's, and I was placed in the vocational track, which is, with few exceptions, a euphemism for the bottom level. I stayed there for a couple of years, and drifted more and more to the level of a really mediocre and quite unprepared student.

What's interesting to me about that experience is not that an unusual thing happened, but that it shows how arbitrary placement in "fast track" and "slow track" can be. It also shows how students placed in the slow track live down to the expectations of their classrooms. And finally, it suggests to me that for parents who are not socialized into that whole way of thinking about education, it's very easy not to realize that something is amiss.

> *. . . students placed in the slow track live down to the expectations of their classrooms.*

MOYERS: And to fight back.

ROSE: And to fight back. I mean, my father got through the second grade in Italy. What would he know about tracking, different curricula, all that? My mother was an exhausted waitress. Where would they get the confidence to go and even question a school about these things? That's why I get a little short-tempered with the blue-ribbon reports telling us that parents are not doing enough and need to be more involved in the schools. That may be true, but we also have to have some compassion for people who are terrified by the schools and don't know how to even begin to interact with them.

MOYERS: You got on a dead-end track, but your parents didn't know it was dead-end because authority had told them that was the way it would be.

ROSE: That's right. I was the first one in my family to go to high school. So what did I or they know? But a funny thing happened. I finally found a course that interested me, and I kind of caught on. It was biology. And the fellow who was teaching the course noticed that this Voc. Ed. kid was racking up 98s and 99s on these biology tests, and he went and looked at the records and found the mistake.

So in my junior year I suddenly found myself sitting in college preparatory courses, for which I was utterly unprepared. Then in my senior year I had a teacher who was a latter-day beatnik, a bohemian sort of guy who had come out to California because he wanted to teach school. He ended up in my school just by some wonderful twist of fate, and he caught me. I was so taken by a man who had such presence and gained his presence through the use of his mind. I had grown up with the presence and the power of brawn. This was the first person I ever met who could captivate people with language. And I wanted to be like him. It was simply because of that. I'm convinced of this—it was because I admired his potency and his presence that I wanted to be like him. So I started working hard. As I started to write essays and work with books and got some reward for it, I took to it. I liked it. And that's where it started for me.

MOYERS: So you became—a teacher.

ROSE: My first teaching experience was many years ago in an old War on Poverty program called the "Teacher Corps." I worked for a couple of years with kindergarteners through sixth graders in a pretty depressed school. Then I worked for about five or six years with returning Vietnam vets, many of whom had never made it through high school. They had seen a lot of terrible action, and now they wanted to reenter society. It was a kind of preparatory program. The vets called it academic boot camp. It got them ready to enter into some forms of higher education. From there I moved on to a whole series of other teaching jobs, working with people in low-level law enforcement jobs, parole aides and things like that, with CETA workers, with community college students. I even did a poetry appreciation class by telephone hookup with old folks who were shut in. So I've worked in all these different settings.

MOYERS: With people on the margin.

ROSE: People on a variety of margins. And all different sorts of folks, from little kids who had the misfortune of being born behind the economic eightball, to old folks who were closeted away in rest homes in fairly poor areas of town.

MOYERS: What did all these people teach you? You had to learn from them.

ROSE: Did I ever learn from them! I learned that virtually any person who has been written off—virtually any child or adult who has that thick folder full of failure—has an ability and a potential that we simply don't see.

MOYERS: An ability that doesn't show up on the tests.

ROSE: It certainly doesn't show up in the work they do in the classroom because the classroom is such a mysterious place to them. Or they have already, at a young age, turned off because of the hurt and the disappointment and the incompetence that they felt at an even earlier juncture in school.

What I found again and again was that they had all this ability: to tell stories and write them, to talk to each other about the reading they did and create interesting kinds of connections between the readings. They had an ability to get very excited about language use in a way you could have never predicted from what the so-called objective test scores in their cumulative folders indicated. Some powerful stuff emerged in those bits of writing they did. Some were powerful because they were so wistful; there was so much longing for a life other than what they had. I remember one migrant worker's son who himself worked in the fields during the summers. He wrote about a place with trees and snow that was quiet and cool. And that was very powerful in its way. But another kind of powerful writing drew on some of the horror that these kids lived with. People getting shot. Brothers in prison.

MOYERS: Writing has something to do with the impulse to survive, doesn't it? If you can put it on paper you somehow have a foothold.

ROSE: You see your experience validated in a medium that has always seemed very foreign to you. Even for kids in the fourth and fifth grade, writing had become something distant, even frightening. I was able to get them to see that with writing they could render some of the things that they saw, some of the things that were important for them to talk about. They could also play. They could play with writing.

MOYERS: Was this true also of the adults you taught? The men who came to you back from Vietnam looking for a way to change their lives?

ROSE: Yes, it certainly was. These were guys who did not have a good time of it in high school. To tell the truth, many of them were probably hell on wheels in high school. It was a terrible place for them. After the experience of Vietnam, though, what they saw with blinding clarity was that they needed to get up and out of that pool of men who could be called on so readily to go into the horror of a meaningless jungle war.

MOYERS: Those who shoot and get shot at. That's where we took most of our fodder in the Vietnam War.

ROSE: That's right. These guys knew what cannon fodder was. And they no longer wanted to be fodder.

MOYERS: We use a lot of clichés about people like this. That they've abandoned the word, they've ceased to care about ideas. Simple reading is beyond them.

ROSE: Yes. Pick up the newspaper. Look at the crisis reports. Hear the cloistered academicians giving their opinion about our eventual cultural demise. And those are the kinds of phrases you hear about these folks. But what was striking was that virtually to a man these vets were curious. They wanted to know how to do things with language. They knew damn well that to be able to do things with language was going to enable them to improve their lives. They held on to that American dream about education improving one's lot. I mean, by the time I was teaching them I was already beginning to get cynical about the reality of that dream. But for them it was real and vital.

MOYERS: In your book *Lives on the Boundary*, you quote a woman named Ruby, who wrote, "I myself I thank God for the dream to come back to school and to be able to seek the dream I want, because I know this time I will try and make my dream come true." And she said to you, "I ain't givin' up the ship this time, though, Lord, I might drown with it."

ROSE: Pretty powerful, isn't it?

MOYERS: People like that have not given up on education. They still have faith in that old dream that education equalizes.

ROSE: Yes. It's astounding how tightly folks like Ruby have held to that American dream. She hoped that education was going to give her the ability to do things with her life that she wasn't able to do before. I was also taken by that statement, "I ain't givin' up the ship this time, though I might drown with it." In that comic line there is both the expression of tremendous optimism and real despair.

MOYERS: So they do know, your students, that this is a very tenuous dream and that America has in many respects been moving away from its dream of social equality.

ROSE: Yes. They're not stupid people. You just cannot write these folks off—as we have so often done—as being in some way incompetent, incapable, damaged, deficient. It's that they never had the right kinds of opportunities. The right chances.

MOYERS: Is that what you mean when you say that poor performance in education is more often a social failure than an intellectual failure?

ROSE: So often we assume that miserable test scores or a failed performance of some kind—you know, the stunted piece of writing that we always see in our national magazines as evidence of our cultural demise, the low reading scores, the dropout and truancy rates—we assume all this is hard evidence of the intellectual failure of our population. We less frequently ask what kind of a society is so organized that so many people fail in school.

MOYERS: What does misery do to learning? What impact does poverty have?

ROSE: I think it's valuable that some of our social theorists and policymakers have admitted the degree to which poverty can constrain a life. But the problematic side of that analysis is that often they also start to talk about the "culture of poverty" and the deficiences in intellectual growth. What that easily leads to is a kind of deficit notion that everybody in the working class is somehow stunted linguistically and cognitively.

MOYERS: There is a continuing tendency in our society to look upon the poor as somehow different. Different in terms of soul or mind, in resources of spirit and intellect.

ROSE: It goes way back. You know, when you read reports from nineteenth-century educators about teaching the urban poor, there the whole discussion is cast again and again in moral and spiritual terms. To be poor suggests a flaw in character or spirit. In America we have this tendency to equate being poor with being innately damaged.

MOYERS: What about a kid like Melvyn? The student who told you, "Teacher, English is not my thing"?

ROSE: This was in a "remedial writing" class in an Ohio college that I was visiting. They were doing all the awful things that we do in so many of our high school and college classrooms under the name of remediation in English. They were going through one of those endless, tiresome workbooks, circling "who" or "whom" and the correct spelling of "their" and "there." Some were doing it, some weren't; some were doing their nails, some were looking out the window for the whole fifty minutes. When I caught up with this guy after class and asked him about English, he said, "No, you know, English is just not my thing."

But I noticed he was listening to some rap music on the radio. The lyrics were particularly interesting in their cadence and rhyme, so I asked him about the song. He said, "Oh yeah, I really like this." What was interesting was that he liked the music and liked the words for the very reasons that someone who was "very literate" would be drawn to language. He liked rap because it could do things. It enabled you to express an opinion. It built you up. And also, he said, "It helps you get women."

MOYERS: Another way to get women is "How do I love thee? Let me count the ways . . ."

ROSE: That seemed to work, too, didn't it?

MOYERS: So rap is just another form of language.

ROSE: That's right. When Melvyn was in his classroom, he was being subjected to the most deadening sort of language use, and he, of course, felt either bored with it or inadequate to do it. But ten minutes later, out in his real life, he was surrounded by language. He was surrounded by words and appreciated the various things that they can enable him to do in the world.

MOYERS: But the language of rap is not the language of the marketplace, or the workplace, not the language he will need to function economically if he is going to gain some means of support and some place in the larger world. So you're not saying we have to go the way of rap and forget Shakespeare and Marlowe and Hemingway and Faulkner or the ordinary language we're using here.

ROSE: I think one powerful educational principle that we need to keep in mind is that you meet people where they are. Now if rap is the kind of language use that's the most scintillating and exciting to a guy like Melvyn, that makes the most sense to him, that's embedded in his immediate experience, let's start there. Because if you can start there, if you can get him interested in that, maybe getting him to write the lyrics out, think about the lyrics, play around with the lyrics themselves in print, then you can move into less familiar domains.

MOYERS: Do you ever see your students surprised by the joy of discovering that, hey, after all, I can talk with this fellow Shakespeare, and he can talk with me?

ROSE: Oh, you do. Of course you do. But again, literature like Shakespeare has to be presented in the right way. You have to lead up to it. You have to do a lot to demystify it. Remember back to your own first encounter with the language of Shakespeare. If it was anything like mine, it was distant and strange. I couldn't really understand it. I got angry at it. I couldn't work my way through it. Well, that's the sort of experience that so many of these folks have had.

MOYERS: So they begin to feel incompetent and unworthy and mad.

ROSE: And as soon as that happens, then they put it away. I had one student, an older woman, who was a pretty tough customer. She had had a rough childhood, and a rough early adulthood. She came back to school and was doing well. Now she was trying to advance herself, and one of the things she had to do was take an introductory humanities course that included *Macbeth*.

I knew that I had to get her through this somehow. She fought me all the way on it, for all the reasons that I could understand, because I had felt that way myself fifteen years before. She said, "This stuff is so hard to read. It's so distant. What's it got to do with us?" I spent a lot of time with her. I would drag her through scene after scene and act them out with her, and make her speak the words. When she finally got through this—and it was a battle—she said, "You know, Mike, people always hold this stuff over you. They make you feel stupid with their fancy talk. But now, I've read it. I've been Shakespeare. I can say, 'I, Olga, have read it.' I won't tell you I like it, because I don't know if I do, or I don't. But I like knowing what it's about."

That was powerful to me, because that is not the sort of thing you read in the humanist tracts on the great books. It's not that Olga became a "better human being." It's not that she gained a kind of "discriminating vision" that allowed her to better distinguish between good and evil. It is not that her linguistic capacity was enriched by the encounter with the great word. What she got from her reading of *Macbeth* was a sense that she was not powerless, and she was not dumb. She understood something that had become a symbol of everything that limited her before. And she felt good about the kind of power she had.

MOYERS: It seems to me that one of the first purposes of education is to open our eyes to our own worth, to our own capacity to change our lives and to understand the lives of others.

ROSE: Yes, it is. And if we really want our educational system to achieve that, then we have to truly think of rigorous ways to bring people into that encounter who traditionally have not been brought into it. We must begin where folks are, but we must also remain true to the commitment to continually move them outwards, into other worlds, other means of expression—and to get better with those means of expression and facilities that they bring with them. To truly nurture that kind of growth, it seems to me, is a very rigorous and demanding pursuit.

I'm calling for an educational philosophy that is more compassionate and more of an invitation than the ones we've often had. But that at the same time is not soft-hearted, not patronizing, and finally, doesn't abdicate the responsibility of the teacher.

MOYERS: Beyond the humanistic values of knowing, seeing, and perceiving, survival is at the heart of it.

ROSE: If you hold to that belief, then you also have to hold to the belief that the social order has to respond, and make jobs and opportunities available. What disturbs me sometimes about policy is that education gets castigated on the one hand as a sort of bogeyman, the root cause of all our dilemmas; but then, on the other hand, the economic sphere does not respond in a synchronous and appropriate way to open itself up and make more opportunities available, so that the pursuit of knowledge will lead to something in the world.

MOYERS: But what about the argument that I don't care if my plumber can read *Macbeth*; I want my plumber to know how the pipes fit together. Or I want the clerk to operate that word processor swiftly and accurately; whether he or she can read *Macbeth* is another thing.

ROSE: Yes. I think it's a legitimate thing to say. But the best programs that train people to do the plumbing right, and to make the word processor work, are ones that build off of the belief that the development of a kind of critical literacy, and the ability to troubleshoot problems and articulate them, are the true job skills. Those skills are what's going to make the plumber the best plumber, and the computer operator the best operator. Now, *Macbeth* may not be an essential part of that curriculum, but certainly the stuff of language—learning, reading and writing, critical thinking, expressing oneself, articulating an idea, troubleshooting—those are important literacy skills. And those are woven into the best kinds of job training programs I've seen.

MOYERS: And those are rigorous.

ROSE: Those are rigorous.

MOYERS: There is no easy way to reading and writing, no easy way to survival in our society today, is there?

ROSE: No, there isn't. We have to be very levelheaded. What we're talking about is the ability to gain a kind of facility with language that's going to help people gain some power in their lives and maybe make a little more money, maybe be able to defend themselves a little bit better, and not feel so excluded from the world of reading and writing. But we also have to remind ourselves that human interest and curiosity are tremendously diverse. There are twenty different reasons that bring people to a writing and reading classroom. Often, those are reasons of economics, gaining a facility that will enable them to do things in the world. However, if you can create conditions in the classroom so that people can play with words, and discover an interest in them, well, some people will respond to that, too. And that's fantastic.

MOYERS: Do you think there will be a place in the economy for all of these people whose potential you would like to tap, whom you would like to turn on to the joys and power of reading, writing, and communicating?

ROSE: I don't see that we have any choice but to figure out how to invite more people from the poor and disenfranchised groups into our economy. First of all, we need to do it for very pragmatic reasons. We hear all the time that the kind of work that people are going to have to do is shifting and changing, and that more problem-solving skills are needed. That's the pragmatic way to look at it.

I think we're headed for troubled times in this society, unless we do something to help more people enter into the educational system in a more productive and powerful way.

But I also think that the presence of such a huge number of people in America who are so marginal runs counter to the best story that this country tells itself about itself. The existence of a vast underclass does not speak of equality; it does not speak of a country that is an open society, with an open educational system. And I think unless we do something, the falseness of that story will slap us very hard in the face. I think we're headed for troubled times in this society, unless we do something to help more people enter into the educational system in a more productive and powerful way.

MOYERS: You just used that word again—invite.

ROSE: Yes, I did, didn't I?

MOYERS: Education is invitation.

ROSE: It is to me.

Lester Brown

ENVIRONMENTALIST

Early on, Lester Brown sounded a trumpet for the planet. One of the founders of the environmental movement, he tackled head-on the problems of pollution and toxic waste, deforestation and a decreasing global food output by founding the Worldwatch Institute. Brown and his colleagues have suggested solutions for a wide variety of environmental problems, and have published over ninety papers on topics ranging from nuclear power to deforestation to world health. He was named a MacArthur Fellow in 1986 and awarded the United Nations' environment prize in 1989.

MOYERS: The environmental movement has been an astonishing propaganda success. But what has it actually achieved? By your own measure, between the first Earth Day in 1970 and the most recent Earth Day in 1990, the world's population increased by over 1.5 billion people. The earth lost 500 million acres of trees, 480 billion tons of top soil. Carbon dioxide in the air increased by 9 percent. Thousands of plant and animal species have disappeared. What do you really have to show for the last twenty years?

BROWN: If we look at the condition of the planet, every major indicator shows deterioration since 1970. No question about that. The gap continues to widen between what we need to do and what we are doing to reverse the degradation of the planet. What we have to hope is that the environmental movement, which is now a worldwide movement, will become strong enough, and enough people will become involved with the issues, that we can begin to take some of the steps necessary to reverse the damage.

MOYERS: Why haven't the environmental leaders been able to persuade the politicians to do more, given the almost indisputable character of so much of the evidence that has been marshaled?

BROWN: For one thing, enough people have to understand an issue in order to bring about changes in policies. We change our perceptions and our behavior in response to new information and new experiences. And much of what is happening goes on so fast that we literally have trouble absorbing and understanding the consequences of our actions. For example, you mentioned that since 1970, the world has added a billion and a half people—to be precise, 1.6 billion people. That's more people than we added during the twenty centuries preceding this one. It's very difficult to picture that.

MOYERS: Yes, because I don't look out and see all those people. I still see just the same number of people who are in my circle of daily habit, and in my neighborhood, or in my community. I don't see that exponential growth.

BROWN: And you don't see so many of the consequences either. As one who's been very much involved in international agriculture over the years, I've traveled a lot in Third World countries. And what I see is not only the population growth, the villages with two or three times as many people in them today as thirty years ago. I also see the deforestation, the soil erosion, the desertification.

MOYERS: You can actually see the loss of those 500 million acres of trees.

BROWN: You can see a lot of it.

MOYERS: Five hundred million acres, that's equivalent to the United States east of the Mississippi.

BROWN: It's a lot of trees. It's a big area of forest. And we're continuing to lose forest now each year. The consequence is increased flooding, soil erosion, and land degradation. I think it was the French philosopher Chateaubriand who said that the forest precedes civilization—the deserts follow. And in a sense, that's true.

What we do at the Worldwatch Institute, in our annual state of the world report, is in effect to give the world a physical examination each year. We check its vital signs. And each year, the forests are getting smaller, the deserts are getting larger, the topsoil layer is getting thinner on much of the world's cropland. The ozone layer in the stratosphere that protects us from ultraviolet radiation is being depleted. The number of plant and animal species is diminishing. The level of greenhouse gases in the atmosphere is rising.

MOYERS: In fact, as you concluded in this most recent report, "We are losing the battle to save the planet."

BROWN: We are. But I think Earth Day '90 provides at least some basis for being hopeful that enough of us will become concerned about what's happening to the planet that we can begin to turn some of these trends around. One of the big differences between Earth Day 1970 and Earth Day 1990 was that twenty years ago Earth Day drew mostly Americans concerned about air and water pollution. Earth Day 1990 drew people all over the world concerned about the future of the planet. It's a much more fundamental set of concerns that people have today.

MOYERS: Yes, but there's still a limited appeal. *The National Review*, the conservative journal published by Bill Buckley, recently ran an article arguing that the environmental movement remains altogether too elitist. It took certain satisfaction, I think, in polls that show that middle-class and working-class Americans are either indifferent to or ignorant of these environmental concerns.

BROWN: Indeed a lot of people do not understand the consequences of environmental degradation. The issue has often been presented as a choice between the economy and the environment, so it's not surprising that the people interviewed for this poll saw it this way. But that's almost a trivialization of the issue. The real issue is, can we protect the environmental support systems on which the global economy depends? If we cannot, then we're obviously in trouble. We're already beginning to see real trouble in parts of Africa, for example, where the forests are gone and the soils are gone. Ethiopia is probably a cutting-edge example of what happens. At the beginning of this century, half of Ethiopia was covered by forest. Today, it's less than 4 percent. And as the trees have gone, the soils have gone. In parts of northern Ethiopia now there's simply not enough topsoil left to support even subsistence-level agriculture, much less a market-oriented surplus-producing agriculture.

MOYERS: Those facts are indisputable. But there is conflict in some of the scientific advice. Just recently, the magazine *Science* came out with a report by two reputable scientists saying that they had studied the satellites gathering information about the warming of the earth, and there is no long-term warming trend evident in the earth's atmosphere. So a lot of people who have not yet joined the environmental movement look at that and say, "Well, I don't know what to get alarmed about if I can't believe a scientist."

BROWN: Right. What this article said was they now have satellite data—the most accurate data we have on global average temperatures—established for the 1980s. We have ten years of data. But what they said was that ten years does not show a long-term trend. And that is certainly true. You can't determine a long-term trend based on ten years. The scientists were trying to be cautious in presenting the data, so that people wouldn't read too much into it. As a result, the headlines almost without exception said, "SCIENTISTS SAY GLOBAL WARMING TREND NOT IN EVIDENCE," or something to that effect. That's not what the scientists intended to say.

Six of the ten warmest years of the last century occurred during the 1980s. And that suggests—it does not prove scientifically, but it suggests—that the warming is underway. If one were to take a poll of the world's meteorologists, my guess is that the vast majority would say it is likely that the warming has begun. But there's no way of scientifically proving that, because weather always changes and fluctuates over time. Nothing that has happened over the last decade, for example, exceeds what has happened at some time during the past century.

MOYERS: Where would you bet your bottom dollar if you were president and had to choose between conflicting pieces of evidence?

> *Those who don't want to do anything can seize upon enough uncertainty to avoid doing anything. That's what we're seeing with a lot of political leaders. I think we're clearly seeing that in the White House.*

BROWN: I don't think the evidence is so conflicting for those who are prepared to be objective. Those who don't want to do anything can seize upon enough uncertainty to avoid doing anything. That's what we're seeing with a lot of political leaders. I think we're clearly seeing that in the White House.

MOYERS: I suggest that politicians are unwilling to act because despite the publicity around Earth Day, the constituency isn't mobilized. A lot of people still say, "Look, I like the way of life that creates the problems that Lester Brown and other environmentalists deplore. I like my cars, I like my clothes, I like throwaway containers. I like this way of life."

BROWN: I think most of us have those inclinations. Certainly I don't like to change. If I have established a certain behavioral pattern, it takes some effort to get me to change. But behavior will change dramatically when people begin to see that the lifestyles they now enjoy are not sustainable.

MOYERS: How can you say that with such certainty?

BROWN: Well, look at the food sector of the world economy, the most vulnerable part. As we look at the various forms of environmental degradation, every one of them affects the food prospect negatively. And we're already beginning to see a slowdown in world food production. The world's farmers are losing about 24 billion tons of topsoil a year from the cropland. That's about the amount of topsoil on Australia's wheatland. So each year, the world's farmers are now trying to feed 88 million more people with 24 billion fewer tons of topsoil than they had the year before. You don't have to be an agronomist to understand that those two trends cannot both continue indefinitely. I cite that as an example.

Or I could use air pollution. The Department of Agriculture and the Environmental Protection Agency together have done a study of the effects of air pollution on U.S. agriculture. Their conclusion is that in this country, our annual harvest has now been reduced at least 5 percent across the board by air pollution—and perhaps as much as 10 percent. Now, if our harvest is being affected that much by air pollution, what about Western Europe, where the concentration of automobiles and population is far greater? What about the coal-burning economies of Eastern Europe and China? How is *their* crop output being affected by air pollution?

MOYERS: But how do you reach the masses of people if the environmental movement remains in this country, as it is, essentially lily white, composed mainly of people who are socially secure? I mean, we're living in a nonwhite world. The Indians in Brazil say they don't appreciate white Europeans and white Americans coming down and appointing themselves guardians of their land. They want an economy that's going to produce a way of life for their children not unlike what Europeans and Americans have had. How do you reach those people? How do you reach the coal miners in West Virginia, who are disaffected by the recent Clean Air Act that's going to put their sons out of jobs—sons who would normally have expected to take on the life of the coal miner and carry it forward into the next generation? How are you going to reach those people?

BROWN: A lot of people are being reached by environmental conditions that are deteriorating already. For example, in Louisiana there's a so-called cancer corridor, named "Odor Alley" because you can just smell the odor for miles around. A lot of low-income communities are really up in arms protesting this, because they see the health effects on their children and themselves. It's not too different from Eastern Europe where they're now beginning to realize that they've got serious, serious environmental problems—so much air pollution and water pollution that it's actually reducing life expectancy in many of the cities in East Germany, Czechoslovakia, and Poland. Male life expectancy in both Poland and the Soviet Union has fallen in recent years, apparently partly because of environmental pollution and workplace exposure to hazardous chemicals. So a lot of people are being affected in one way or another.

But what I think is likely to be the Pearl Harbor in the battle to save the planet, the event that will really rally people, will be the next year in which we have severe heat and drought in the United States. In the summer of 1988, when we had a very hot, dry summer, our grain production actually fell below consumption for the first time in our history. Now the drought didn't create a crisis then, because we had enormous reserves to draw upon. We produced 196 million tons of grain, and we're consuming 206 million tons. So we took 10 million tons out of reserves.

But we're committed to export about 100 million tons, because there are more than a hundred countries around the world that get at least part of their grain supplies from us. We satisfied those commitments by exporting our reserve. As a result, world grain reserves are way down now, at one of the lowest levels since the years immediately following World War II. Now, if we have another summer soon like 1988, then there won't be any reserves to draw upon, and world grain prices could double or triple almost overnight. When that happens, then we'll begin to see that the combination of soil erosion and climate change and air pollution is beginning to affect the ability of the world to produce enough food to feed 5.3 billion people. At that point, I think we'll begin to realize that we have to make some course corrections.

MOYERS: Perhaps it will take the equivalent of a Pearl Harbor. The Americans, in particular, didn't respond to the terrible reality of slavery in time to prevent a civil war. We didn't respond to the threats of the totalitarian powers of Germany or Japan until we were attacked at Pearl Harbor. What if it takes some grave ecological strike before we wake up?

BROWN: My concern is that we will not move fast enough to reverse the trends that will eventually lead to this sort of catastrophe. If I had to guess now, I would guess that we're not more than a few years from a world food emergency, where food prices would increase to the degree that they would lead to political instability in many countries in the world, industrial as well as developing. It could create a situation, for example, where American consumers would be competing with Japanese consumers for our grain. Or consider what could happen to the international banking structure if Third World countries, faced with soaring world grain prices, use all their foreign exchange to import food to avoid starvation and maintain political stability. They'd literally forget debt payments. At that point, the stability of the international banking system would become a major issue for the world.

If we were to have another hot, dry summer this year or next year, then we could see a situation where by fall, governments in the industrial countries would be meeting to discuss whether or not to tap the only remaining food reserve in the world, the grain fed to livestock, in order to avoid starvation in Third World countries. The question then would be, how would you do it? Would you impose a meat tax, like the gasoline tax we keep talking about? Or would we impose rationing of livestock products, like the rationing we had in World War II of sugar and rubber and gasoline and other scarce commodities? We could be only one year away from a situation in which these issues would have to be considered.

MOYERS: That kind of doomsday talk does frighten some people.

BROWN: I'm not sure it's doomsday talk. I think it's a realistic scenario, based on a very detailed analysis of what's happening in the world.

MOYERS: But here's what you're up against. For a long time now societies have gauged their successes by materialism. Self-worth is often determined by one's possession of goods, just as national greatness is determined by the gross national product. You're really challenging the materialistic life that we have developed in the West. Are you opposed to materialism?

BROWN: I'm not challenging it. Nature is challenging it.

MOYERS: But what if the survival of the human species is not intrinsically a part of the laws of nature? What if God or nature assigned to our interest no greater claim than that given the dinosaurs? The assumption is human beings must survive. Why?

BROWN: I think we're somewhat enamored with ourselves. I mean, evolutionary biologists say that the fate of all species is extinction. That's been the history of the last few million years.

MOYERS: Thousands have disappeared.

BROWN: Most species that ever existed are no longer here, and there's no reason to assume it won't happen to us. We like to think that because of our intelligence and our uniqueness we can survive. Most of us have an innate desire to maintain ourselves as a species, to maintain civilization. But it seems to me, as one who spends most of his waking time trying to analyze what's happening in the world, that the trends of the last few decades cannot continue without jeopardizing our future.

MOYERS: Then other questions arise. If a throwaway culture leads inevitably to pollution and resource depletion, how are we going to satisfy our material needs? If not fossil fuel, what? And if forests are no longer to be cleared to grow food, how are we going to eat?

BROWN: Let's take fossil fuels. We are now burning in the world enormous quantities of fossil fuels. It's fossil fuels that drive the world economy for the most part.

MOYERS: Four fifths of the energy in the United States comes from fossil fuels.

BROWN: Right. Worldwide, fossil fuels completely dominate—that's coal and oil and natural gas. What we're now faced with, if we want to stabilize the climate, is phasing out fossil fuels. To most people, that's a rather shocking sort of thing. The first thing they say is, "Oh, my God, there goes my car."

MOYERS: And my job, if I work in the petroleum industry or the automobile or petrochemical industry.

BROWN: Not necessarily if you work in the automobile industry, because we may have other sources to power automobiles. But we need to be more energy efficient than we are now. For example, we now have light bulbs that can replace the traditional incandescent bulbs and reduce electricity use by three fourths. There's no reason why the entire world can't make that shift within the next few years if we get serious about it. Look at automobiles. The U.S. fleet now averages about twenty miles per gallon. New cars sold this year will average, by law, twenty-seven miles per gallon. There are cars in the showroom that get more than fifty miles per gallon. There are prototypes that have been developed, not yet on the market, that are in the seventy-to ninety-mile-per-gallon range. I think we have to begin moving quickly toward the more energy-efficient cars. The second thing we have to do is to improve public transportation. Public transportation, particularly in this country, is not very well developed.

MOYERS: That's because Americans like to go it on their own.

BROWN: That's right. If the costs of continuing to drive automobiles become great enough, people will reconsider. The automobile culture has probably evolved further in Southern California than in any part of the world. Yet it is in Southern California where the future of the automobile is being reexamined. They're actually investing heavily in rail systems now in Los Angeles, San Diego, and other major communities. They're talking about mandatory car pooling. They're talking about alternative sources of fuel to run automobiles. There is an environmental protection initiative on the ballot for the election coming up in California this fall that would require a 20 percent reduction in fossil fuel use by the end of this decade, and another 20 percent by the year 2010. If that is passed, and it has a decent chance of passing, then California will be leading the world in phasing out fossil fuels. They are also developing wind power in California. It's extraordinarily impressive to see miles of wind turbines turning in the wind and generating electricity—as much as three or four nuclear power plants. Enormous outputs, supplying a substantial part of San Francisco's electricity. That's just one example.

MOYERS: Well, windmills used to sustain cattle in this country.

BROWN: And they still pump much of the water on the Great Plains for cattle. Another source of energy—and this may be the most promising of all right now—is the solar-thermal power plants being built in California. One was completed in December in the Mojave Desert. These plants use mirrors to concentrate sunlight on a vessel that contains a liquid, and they generate temperatures of seven hundred degrees. This heat is then used to produce steam and drive steam generators. The newest solar-thermal plant is producing electricity at eight cents per kilowatt hour, versus twelve cents for new nuclear power, and six cents for coal.

MOYERS: Everything you're talking about requires a global consensus—global treaties, global management, global organizations—that impinges on national sovereignty. Do you think powerful politicians, backed by powerful groups, are going to tolerate it?

BROWN: It's not going to be easy, because it's going to require a lot of change in behavior in a very short period of time. And a lot of things will occur at the national level. But many others must be done in concert with other countries. Very few of the things that need to be done can actually be done by a country acting alone. If we phase out CFC's in this country tomorrow—the chloro-fluorocarbons that are depleting the stratospheric ozone layer that protects us from harmful ultraviolet radiation—and the rest of the world continues to produce them, then it makes no difference. We share the global atmosphere with the entire world.

MOYERS: That assumes global treaties, global organizations.

BROWN: We have to work together. In some cases, we're going to see the use of incentives and disincentives. For example, it looks as though environmental taxation is going to become an important component of tax policy in countries throughout the world. We could put a tax on pollution. We could put a tax on the use of fossil fuels, a so-called carbon tax, to reduce carbon dioxide emissions. As we reshape our tax policy, we could actually decrease the amount of income tax we pay and get more revenues from taxing activities that are harmful to the environment. In fact, if we put a tax on fossil fuels that reflects the costs of air pollution and acid rain and climate change, wind and sun technologies will take off because they're clean technologies.

Other things could be accomplished by simple legislation. For example, my guess is that we are not more than a few years away in this country from mandatory recycling programs. It may become illegal to throw away material—whether it be glass or paper or aluminum—simply because of the environmental costs of doing so. We may find ourselves in another decade or two where most of the materials we use will be recycled material rather than virgin material, such as virgin wood cut for paper pulp. If we can do that, if we can make that shift quickly, then we will greatly reduce the amount of energy we use. It's so much more efficient to recycle than to dig iron ore out of the ground and process it. And the amount of air and water pollution would be greatly reduced in the process.

MOYERS: Running through so much of what you say is the assumption that we will have to function as a collective society, acting through legislation to impose mandatory controls. What about the conservative argument that if we extended property rights to certain resources, we would achieve the same result much more efficiently? The argument is that we keep polluting the stratosphere because no one has any proprietary claim on it, and therefore, no need to protect it. If we gave individuals responsibility for it, and property rights in it, we'd come closer to achieving a voluntary sustainable economy.

BROWN: There are some real limits on what you can achieve with that. Those limits are most obvious where we share common resources, like oceanic fisheries, the earth's climatic system, the ozone layer, biological diversity. We have to take inventory as an international community and begin to figure out how to work together at the international level. Individual property rights will not solve the problems of the global commons. There's no way that any individual can be responsible for the earth's climatic system. We all have to be responsible for that together.

MOYERS: What does it say to you that in the Communist bloc, where the state was dominant and wealth was not permitted, pollution has been worse than in the capitalist countries?

BROWN: The socialist planners are somewhat naive in their judgment of human nature. The assumption was that people who were socially motivated when they were building factories and managing them would be concerned about pollution. But we in the capitalist world have not made that assumption. We know that there's a certain amount of greed in any population. And so we've tried to build in safeguards to check the greed. We have controls on pollution, for example. What they're beginning to realize in Eastern Europe is that people are not yet quite as perfect as they assumed.

But there's a more fundamental lesson, I think, from Eastern Europe. We've seen a transformation that none of us could have imagined a year ago. Suddenly it became clear to almost everyone in those societies that the economic system was not working—that it was an inherently unworkable system. And when they realized that, it really set things in motion. There was an inherent contradiction in that system, and they recognized it and responded to it. The parallel at the global level is that there is an inherent contradiction between the economic trends we read about in the daily press and the environmental trends. The economic system, of which we are a part, is sowing the seeds of its own demise. And as that inherent contradiction becomes more apparent, I think we're likely to see some basic changes in the economic system itself.

We tend to look at what happened in Eastern Europe as an isolated event, but in fact it was the beginning of a wave of social change that could engulf the entire world within the next few years. I think we're seeing it in South Africa. I think we're seeing it within the environmental movement and among serious thinkers in countries throughout the world. People are beginning to realize the inherent contradiction between the economic system we now have, and the trends of environmental degradation that it is leading to. As that contradiction becomes more apparent, I think we may see social changes and economic changes on a scale that we've not seen during our lifetimes.

MOYERS: What the collapse of communism said to me is that you can only sustain a society so long through coercion, and that human beings will resist. They must be persuaded and inspired or it won't happen at all. And what the environmental movement has yet to do is to persuade enough people that by voluntary change, we can still maintain a way of life to protect our freedom and provide our children with the decencies of life.

BROWN: We have not done it yet. And my guess is that we are going to see the level of concern about the future of the planet rise, not only in response to events like Earth Day and the intense media coverage of the issues leading up to Earth Day, but also in response to the daily news headlines reporting what's happening to the world's environment. It is now difficult to pick up a major newspaper anywhere in the world on any given day that doesn't have one or two or three stories on some environmental issue.

MOYERS: In the meantime, what can we each do to contribute to this change that leads to the actual, as opposed to the perceived, rescue of the environment?

BROWN: Some years ago, we would have been tempted to say, recycle your newspapers and install a low-flow shower head in your bathroom and so forth. Those things are still important. But I think now we've reached a point where more and more of us have to become environmental activists, or politically active environmentalists, supporting candidates who have demonstrated a concern for the future of the planet. Becoming involved in elections at all levels, from the city council to the White House.

MOYERS: You're saying the only solution is political?

BROWN: Yes.

MOYERS: That means more government action.

BROWN: Without question. We have to become politically active in pushing our governments at various levels to begin to phase out fossil fuels and move toward alternatives. At the local level, that may involve becoming active in pushing for a community recycling program. It may mean working to improve public transportation, and to create a bicycle friendly transport system, one in which the automobile and the bicycle are on an equal footing.

If more of us do not become politically active, we're not going to make it. . . . We're faced with the need for an enormous amount of change in a very short period of time.

If more of us do not become politically active, we're not going to make it. There's too much inertia in the system, too many vested interests. We're faced with the need for an enormous amount of change in a very short period of time. The only historically similar mobilization that I can think of is what occurred during the early forties as we mobilized for war. We're talking about change on that scale, and with that sense of urgency. The threat now is not some alien power in Europe or Japan, but the degradation of the planet. We have reached a point where the principal threats to our security are no longer ideological differences or military aggression. It's degradation of the planet that is now threatening not only our future, but that of our children and our grandchildren.

Jonas Salk

MEDICAL RESEARCHER

Jonas Salk was a young doctor when in the spring of 1955 he announced his discovery of a vaccine that could prevent polio. He was hailed as a modern miracle worker. Recognition for his pioneering research, including the Presidential Medal of Freedom, has continued through the years. Today, at the Salk Institute for Biomedical Studies in La Jolla, California, he leads scientists from the world over in studies of cancer, heredity, the brain, the immune system, and AIDS. Now, as then, Jonas Salk is in search of the next medical miracle.

MOYERS: You have used an intriguing term to describe what you have done with your life. You say you spent your life reading the scriptures of nature. Is there some immortal lesson in those scriptures of nature?

SALK: Well, I believe so. When I discovered there was more to learning than the books we were exposed to, and then when I became interested in bringing science into medicine, I recognized that there was a logic to the magic. Life is magic; the way nature works seems to be quite magical. Look at something as remarkable as the immune system and immunological memory. You vaccinate individuals and they remember that experience. At some later time if they are exposed to the real enemy, they say, "I've seen you before." They respond appropriately and quickly. So I started to try to understand how that system works. I began to tease out the logic of the magic that I was so impressed by.

MOYERS: How old were you when you came upon the polio vaccine?

SALK: I was thirty-nine.

MOYERS: Has your life been anticlimactic since that great breakthrough?

SALK: I've kept on going. I still have the same purpose that I had then, which was to see what I could do to heal, to counter the negative. I was born in 1914. In 1916 came the worst polio epidemic up until that time. I remember when I was about four years of age seeing lots of crippled children.

Then there was the war and I remember seeing our troops coming back on Armistice Day in 1918. I recall even as a very small child being perplexed by seeing wounded soldiers in the parade. Then I became aware of anti-Semitism in the world and the difficulties that occurred during the Depression. These affected me so much that when eventually I decided to study medicine, I could not separate it from these larger questions. The painful paradoxes of life seemed to be so unnecessary. So I think that we have an instinct, an impulse to improve our world. And I think that's quite universal.

MOYERS: I read the other day that by the year 2000, there will be some 20 million people in the world carrying the AIDS virus. Is that a comparable challenge to what you faced with polio fifty years ago?

SALK: Well, it's an even more difficult challenge from a scientific and technical point of view. Nevertheless, it is a similar challenge and I have no doubt that we will rise to that challenge. I think we are on the way. We ask the question, "What effect would we like to produce as far as AIDS is concerned?" We have a pretty good idea about preventing the infection in those who have not yet become infected and controlling the disease in those already infected. By projecting ourselves toward such objectives, we will find a way.

MOYERS: The good news would be a vaccine that could protect us and immunize us against the AIDS virus. Are we going to have that good news in your time and mine?

. . . solutions come through evolution. They come through asking the right question, because the answer preexists.

SALK: That time will come. I cannot imagine that we will not be able to think the way the virus does and figure out how to outsmart the virus. My hope and expectation—I should say my expectation—is that we will solve the problem. It is just a matter of time and it is just a matter of strategy.

Now, why do I say this? It is because I think solutions come through evolution. They come through asking the right question, because the answer preexists. It is the question that we have to define and discover.

MOYERS: You mean when you asked the question about how to defeat polio the answer was already there?

SALK: Yes. In a way, if you think of Michelangelo's statue of David, it was in the stone but it had to be unveiled and revealed. You don't invent the answer, you reveal the answer.

MOYERS: From nature.

SALK: From nature.

MOYERS: But is it conceivable that some other form of life—the AIDS virus, a cancer cell—might have a defense mechanism that protects its own survival over ours?

SALK: In fact, that's precisely how these organisms work. They oppose the defense mechanism that we otherwise erect against them. One of the ways in which the AIDS virus works is to impair the immune system. Not only that, I think that it even induces the immune system to form an antibody that protects the virus.

MOYERS: It's fighting for survival, too.

SALK: Indeed. And it is this struggle for survival that leads me to wonder whether or not the problem will be solved by a resolution in which the objective will be to live and let live so that the virus may remain in the body but not cause disease.

MOYERS: So that's why you suggested a strategy of research that would immunize the victim *after* he or she has been infected.

SALK: Yes. To see if we can't possibly find a phase or a stage in the process of infection before impairment has gone too far. Maybe we can erect or strengthen the defense mechanics before that happens.

MOYERS: Why is it so difficult to explore a vaccine for AIDS?

SALK: Because AIDS takes so long to develop. It was very easy to develop an influenza vaccine. Immunize in October and by January you knew, in the midst of an epidemic, whether you had a result. In the case of polio, a field trial was done just before the summer months when the outbreak occurred. By the end of the summer, you knew what the results were. In the case of AIDS, it's an entirely different story. It's more like trying to find a way to treat or control cancer.

MOYERS: Because the cancer cell is fighting for its survival very effectively in this ongoing struggle of nature.

SALK: And also because of the long interval of time from its appearance to the time when you can see clinical evidence of effectiveness.

MOYERS: When I was out here last year to visit the Salk Institute, you said, "Bill, we have to learn to think like nature." What did you mean by that?

SALK: We are aware that some species that have come before us have disappeared from the face of the earth. We would like to use our intelligence and our creative capacity to prolong our own presence on the face of the earth as long as possible. So we must develop the kinds of tactics and strategies among ourselves to ensure that this can occur, to ensure that we will not destroy ourselves or the planet or make it uninhabitable, and to allow the fullness of individual potential to flower. That's awfully ideal. The question now is how can we translate this, how can we make this happen?

MOYERS: Well, flying in the face of that idealism is what you and others in the world of biology have told us about human beings. Somewhere I remember you saying that the so-called lower forms of life have a certain solidarity that prevents them from preying on each other as ferociously as we humans prey on each other. Is it true that human beings and rats are the most ferocious of the species?

SALK: Well, they certainly seem to be. That is one of the things that distinguishes the human species from other species. When I talk about trying to understand nature, I mean thinking like nature and relating to each other so as to avoid the necessity for war. There will always be disagreements, but there must be more civilized ways of resolving our differences. If we compare ourselves to what humankind was like a thousand years ago or even fifty years ago, we have come a long way.

My hope lies in seeing the emergence of a new generation of young people who were born into a new context with new opportunities and new circumstances. They, in my judgment, are going to act appropriately to improve the conditions of their lives and the lives of others.

MOYERS: Here we are in the last decade of the twentieth century. What's the dynamic that you see at work in the human condition right now?

SALK: I think this is the culmination for not only the last twenty centuries, but millions and billions of years.

MOYERS: Are you saying that we humans were inherently the purpose at work in this whole process?

SALK: If you need to use the word "purpose." I prefer to say that we are the consequence or the result of whatever intelligence exists in the cosmos. The way I like to look at it is that the human mind is the culmination of the organization of complexity to such an extent that whatever was created is now capable of being expressed through human creativity. Were we to have the wisdom, we could shape the future. I like to speak of it as rebuilding the future.

MOYERS: Rebuilding what has not even happened?

SALK: Exactly. So that the future can be what we would imagine it to be ideally. We are at a point in the scheme of things when this should be possible. We are going through a qualitative change, not merely a quantitative change in numbers of people on the face of the earth.

MOYERS: Five billion plus now.

SALK: And in a hundred years it will be ten billion plus. Then it will be maintained. But the quality of human life generally will be as different in the year 2100 compared to now as it was between 1900 and now.

MOYERS: What was the dynamic?

SALK: In the past most of the contributions had to do with reducing the negative. Reducing disease and death. We are now suffering from our success in that regard if you think of it in terms of the population explosion. People live longer, healthier lives. That has added to our burden, but it is the consequence of the success with which we have addressed the problem of improving the human condition.

MOYERS: If reducing the negatives was the dominant force of the past, what is it going to be in the future?

SALK: Enhancing the positive. Improving the quality of human life, the human mind, the conditions under which humans come upon the face of the earth and are given the opportunity to develop.

MOYERS: What do you mean by quality of life?

SALK: Think of it in terms of the children who come upon the face of the earth in different parts of the world. It is clear that in some parts of the world there are more advantages than in others. This comes about not only through nutrition, not only through care, but through education and through the people's opportunity to express themselves. To become positive contributors to the future becomes their purpose in life.

What we are talking about now are the values that we espouse and the values that we instill in the generations of the future. I like to think that we are in a very unique position now, and I ask the question, are we being good ancestors? Are we contributing to shaping the human beings of the future by what we do now? And are we doing what we should to provide for them the optimal opportunities for carrying those values into the future?

MOYERS: What is the answer to the question?

SALK: Yes and no. We are becoming more and more conscious of this. It is this evolution of consciousness, the raising of consciousness and awareness of what the human potential is all about.

MOYERS: Someone just back from Central Europe said that the single most powerful phenomenon of the twentieth century has been this explosion of human consciousness. That is what the people in Central Europe and Russia and the students in China are trying to express. They want their identity on the world stage. Even the smallest creature wants its identity.

SALK: Yes. It's as if we are in a stage of adolescence in human development as a species. We are going through this transition, the same kind of an identity crisis, you might say, that adolescents experience.

Lincoln said, "You can fool some of the people some of the time, but not all of the people all of the time"; you can suppress some of the people some of the time, but not all of the people all of the time. We are seeing how this is breaking out all over. We are observing it now. I sometimes like to refer to the caterpillar becoming a butterfly. We are breaking out of the caterpillar stage into this next stage. It is a form of metamorphosis that is occurring. It is as if the human mind and the human self are maturing to the point where they can no longer be restrained, nor should they be restrained. We have to become oriented to looking upon the future as one that will be governed less by external restraint and more by self-restraint. These are ideas that you might say are quite ancient, but they are essential now. It has become not an ideal but a necessity.

MOYERS: Why a necessity?

SALK: Perhaps because we have so much knowledge. In the past when we had very little knowledge, we had enough wisdom with which to deal with that knowledge. Now, we have so much more knowledge, but do we have the wisdom with which to deal with the power that we have?

MOYERS: What do you mean by wisdom?

SALK: Well, it's awfully difficult to define. It is something that you know when you see it. You can recognize it, you can experience it. Certainly you can recognize individuals who seem to have that quality. I have defined wisdom as the capacity to make retrospective judgments prospectively. The capacity to make judgments that when looked back upon will seem to have been wise. That's just a way of putting oneself into a position of understanding that there is a short-term and a long-term way of seeing the world.

MOYERS: And wisdom involves making decisions in the long run, even at the sacrifices of some short-term gains, or rewards. I like that definition of wisdom.

SALK: You see? And it is more encompassing. It requires a longer and broader perspective. You might think of wisdom as common sense.

MOYERS: In what sense? Pun intended.

SALK: In the sense that people at large if given the options—and I am talking not about limited options but broad enough options—can see what the consequences are and gravitate to making the right decisions. Now, another way of saying this is that I see the process of evolution as error-making and error-correcting. We have to be ever so much better at error-correcting than error-making.

MOYERS: We are quite good at error-making, it seems to me.

SALK: Indeed. And what we have to do now is see how to correct our errors as soon as they occur, or perhaps find a way to correct them before they occur. Let's see if we cannot sign the peace treaty before the war rather than after it. We know that a peace treaty is going to be signed. We know that peace will have to be made. Is there some way for us to avoid that destructiveness? Can we become organized as a species so as to bring about peace for humanity as a whole?

Our principal problem now is not the microbes but the macrobes. *We* are the major cause of disease. If you think of the number of deaths on the face of the earth today, the amount of pathology, you can see how much of that is man-made. Now we may have to shift our attention from our concern with the microbial cause of disease, as Louis Pasteur spoke of it a hundred years ago, to what I am trying to say is the macrobial cause of disease.

Just take the drug problem, for example. There are people who exploit others, who want children to become addicted to drugs so that they will have a market for them. Now, that is a problem that I think can be dealt with rationally if we understand that we have vectors of drugs. Just like mosquitoes transmit malarial parasites, so we have to recognize that there are some people among us who are pathogenic, who are the cause of our malady.

MOYERS: Enemies of society.

SALK: Indeed. And look at the dictators in recent decades.

MOYERS: They have been falling on hard times.

SALK: They are now becoming an endangered species. I fully anticipate that they will not survive.

MOYERS: You use the term evolution quite often. What is evolution to you?

SALK: It's a process by which we came into being. We human beings came through this long trajectory from the beginning of time, through the evolution of matter, through the evolution of life, and now through the evolution of the human mind. And that is all part of a continuum. What is so remarkable is our consciousness of all that. We are conscious of evolution through the evolution of our consciousness and I believe we can engage in that process consciously and intentionally.

MOYERS: The fish cannot analyze, as far as we know, the water that surrounds the fish, but we are able to analyze the environment of which we are a part.

SALK: And which we can improve or destroy.

MOYERS: When you use the word evolution, do you mean God?

© Michael Oletta

If I were to define God, I would say God is evolution.

SALK: If I were to define God, I would say God is evolution. Evolution to me is what God is to others. It's a force that exists, that propels us, that impels us, that causes me to do what I do. It causes you to do what you do. We are sitting here now hoping to communicate some ideas that might be useful and helpful to others, for what purpose? Where have these ideas come from? Go to libraries and see the enormous number of volumes that have been written. There is some force that is inexorable.

Think what would happen if we were to realize the power of that force, and what we might be able to do with it if we were to try to discipline it, to engage it for a purpose. I think now in terms of the next millennium and the millennium beyond. It is remarkable—we are sitting here now at the beginning of the last decade of the last millennium just before the next millennium. When you think in those terms it is a bit awesome to see how much has happened until now and the power we have gained through human ingenuity.

MOYERS: I sometimes wonder if you are not unduly affected by the geography of where you work and think. This is such a beautiful part of the world, looking out on the Pacific Ocean toward the setting sun. I wonder if the geography of this place doesn't inspire more optimism in you than the rest of us have.

SALK: Well, it may well be. It may be that that is why I gravitated here. That is why I looked for an idyllic spot in which to work and to bring together others with similar ideas and ideals and to create a center where we could imagine what the future could be like. The future has been moving westward. The earth is now all going to become one. The cultures of the East and the West are going to have to merge. The center is no longer going to be the Atlantic. The Pacific is going to become another center. That is all part of the maturing process.

I suppose that you do need people who are not only idealistic, but who are realistic idealists. We have attained many of the ideals of the past, but there are new ideals to reach and to imagine. I think that this is what the new generation is all about. I think if we were to look at this as a dynamic process and see what the future might be, we are going to be experiencing more good news than bad news. That would be quite a change, wouldn't it?

LOOKING BACK

"Very few things happen at the right time," Mark Twain cracked, "and the rest do not happen at all: the conscientious historian will correct these defects."

It is all too easy for a conscientious society or nation or people to correct its defects, too—quietly to forget the unpleasant, embarrassing, brutal, and stupid deeds of its past. Yet only by openly acknowledging and airing the true behavior of our predecessors can we correct it. The present tense cannot be spoken fluently unless we first speak honestly about the past.

Two men whose talents I admire insisted on witnessing to the truth in times of epic stupidity and banality, when whole peoples were numbed by lies. They spoke at cost, to embody for us the priceless value of freedom.

William L. Shirer has been a journalist longer than I've been alive. In 1925 he left his native Iowa to see the world, only to see it almost die. As a reporter in Europe, he learned how totalitarianism could crush the human spirit. He came face-to-face with some of history's most evil men, and wondered at their denseness; he met some of the bravest, the rebels who protested and fought back—and sometimes disappeared. The enormity of the evil was, he says, a "stumbling block" to his imagination. "I ask myself, if there's a Christian God, how could he permit Christians to slaughter 10 or 15 million people? If there is a Jewish God, how could he permit Christians to slaughter 7 million Jews? And it's a question which bothers me, and I can't answer."

My fellow Texan John Henry Faulk was a humorist. He was also so ardent a believer in the First Amendment that he staked everything on its principles when they were most beleaguered. During the McCarthy period, Faulk, host of a popular radio show, was disgusted by the strong-arm tactics of the avowed anti-Communist group called Aware, Incorporated. Their strategy of blacklisting entertainers deemed by them to be "un-American" "had nothing to do with communism—anti or otherwise. It had to do with shutting off the lifeblood of this republic, the open and robust and free dialogue that our Founding Fathers had anticipated when they made the First Amendment an absolute mandate."

So when Aware blacklisted him, too, Faulk fought back. He turned to the most American activity he knew: he stood on the Constitution. Risking his career, he refused to consider himself a hero. "When you understand the First Amendment," said Faulk, "it doesn't take a hero to say, 'Well, to me it means what it says.'"

Maybe it doesn't. But John Henry was a hero. No maybe about it.

William L. Shirer

JOURNALIST

In sixty-five years as a journalist, William L. Shirer has been an eyewitness to the history of our times. He started as a reporter in Europe in the 1920s, went to India to cover Mahatma Gandhi, and then joined the pioneers of radio broadcasting. He reported for CBS from Berlin on the rise of Hitler, and watched the surrender of France to Germany from the front lines. His bestselling books, among them *Berlin Diary*, *The Rise and Fall of the Third Reich*, and a trilogy of memoirs, have given readers a front-seat view of major events. Now, at age eighty-six, Shirer is at work on a new book about Tolstoy.

MOYERS: If you were living in Europe today, would you fear a strong and reunited Germany?

SHIRER: I'm sure I would. If I were a Frenchman or a member of any of the nations that were victims of the Nazi Germans, I would feel it, yes. The question is whether the Germans have changed since the end of the war. I've come to the conclusion that we really don't know. I'm a little bit skeptical perhaps because of my experience in Nazi Germany. But we don't know. Once they're reunited, they will be very powerful economically and potentially very powerful militarily.

MOYERS: You wrote once about the fatality of the German character. What did you mean, fatality?

SHIRER: Historians tell us that you cannot indict a race, or a nation, or a people. And perhaps that's true. But in our time, the Germans, it seems to me, have had this fatal urge to expand, to conquer, to glorify militarism. I'm not sure that's dead. I don't think these great historical movements die very quickly. We can all hope they have died. But I don't think the countries in Europe want to take that chance. That's why they're asking for some kind of guarantees.

MOYERS: When you consider how many people have suffered at the hands of the Germans, you can understand why there's no quick inclination to trust them.

SHIRER: I think in this country, we don't realize that. We've never been invaded. But when you go to the Soviet Union, for example, you're struck by what Nazi Germany did to that country—the 20 million dead, the destruction of their cities and towns. No conquering country probably behaves very well. We know that. But I think if you ask a Frenchman about the occupation, he would say it was pretty tough. I think something like twenty-nine thousand French civilians were shot as hostages, for example. So our European friends remember those things. And I'm very much concerned that neither we Americans nor our government seems to realize that. Maybe we don't have much of a sense of history.

MOYERS: Just recently we've been hearing about sporadic outbursts of anti-Semitism in East Germany. How strongly do you think those pro-Nazi sentiments are rooted in that soil?

SHIRER: I had hoped that anti-Semitism was dead in Germany. It didn't start with Hitler. It's been there a long time. But when I went back in 1985, during the ill-fated visit of President Reagan to the Bitburg cemetery, one thing that did surprise me and depress me was a feeling of anti-Semitism that was far from dead. I was disturbed by the language the papers and radio and television used to denounce critics, particularly American Jews, for complaining that the President of the United States was coming to the cemetery, where something like forty-nine SS troops were buried. Now I don't want to say that there's a great outbreak of anti-Semitism in Germany, such as we saw during Hitler's time. But it's far from dead.

MOYERS: What did you think when President Reagan looked at those graves and said that those Gestapo troops were the victims of the Nazis just as the Jews were?

SHIRER: Well, it was a horror. And it was a violation of history. The German soldier did not feel for a moment that he was being done in by Hitler. I followed the German army through Poland. Those German soldiers loved it. I met possibly one soldier, an Austrian, one night, who felt he had been done in by Hitler. To equate the Jews who were done to death in the extermination camps with 4 or 5 million German soldiers was a terrible abortion of history.

MOYERS: We forget how eagerly so many of the Germans greeted Hitler. In your book *The Nightmare Years: 1930 to 1940*, you have pictures of Hitler arriving in a number of German cities. Here's one caption: "Wildly enthusiastic crowds greet Hitler." That is an enthusiasm reserved for the most charismatic.

The hysterical applause of these Germans, as if they were looking at a messiah, I must say not only surprised me but deeply shocked me.

SHIRER: I lived through that. One of the first shocks I think I got when I went off to cover Germany permanently, in 1934, the year after Hitler took over, was the enthusiasm of the crowds. The hysterical applause of these Germans, as if they were looking at a messiah, I must say not only surprised me but deeply shocked me.

What was important and terrible for an outside observer was that the vast majority of people supported Hitler with incredible enthusiasm. Now, why was that? Well, for one thing, he was giving them what they wanted. We forget that. He was giving them full employment. He was improving the economics of the place by borrowing a lot of money that he never paid back. He was building up an army, navy, and air force. The Germans liked that. There's a certain militarism, at least in our time, in their blood. He was telling them: we're going to get back the territories we lost. We're going to take Austria, we're going to take Czechoslovakia, and so forth. Those were things the Germans liked.

I remember going up to Hamburg to try and find out why German workers were supporting Hitler. I said, "Don't you miss the freedoms you had of free trade unions and free elections?" And they said, "Well, I'll tell you, there's one freedom that we don't miss, and that's the freedom to starve." There was no real German resistance. The masses of the workers, of the petite bourgeoisie and so forth, never revolted. There was never the kind of meetings we've seen in Eastern Europe in recent months, where crowds got out into the streets and protested. The Germans didn't seem to care about their freedoms being taken away. Maybe this is true of a lot of countries. It might even be true of us sometime. They didn't seem to care about loss of freedom, as long as they had some prosperity.

MOYERS: All these years later, do you still ask yourself the question, why? How could a Christian nation that produced Goethe and Beethoven and Bach and Immanuel Kant and all those great scientists perpetrate such evil?

SHIRER: It's a question I posed when I got to Germany, and one I've been asking myself ever since. They went to church every Sunday. They had this great culture, a part of Western civilization. How could they slaughter 6 million Jews in the extermination camps? How could they let over half of the 6 million Russian prisoners of war die by not giving them shelter or food—in other words, killing them? But I cannot answer your question, and I wish somebody could. It's a stumbling block to my whole imagination.

MOYERS: You came face-to-face with many of Hitler's top men—the men who were responsible for carrying out the evil he ordered. You describe them in your books

© Tony Dugal

as dim-witted, somewhat stupid, dull, tedious. But these were men who were about to take over the world.

SHIRER: It's amazing. Ribbentrop, who was the Foreign Minister, was one of the stupidest men who ever lived, and Hitler thought he was another Bismarck. Himmler, who built up the SS, always looked to me like a chicken farmer. But behind those glasses of his, and his mild manner, was a terrible killer. Goebbels, the propaganda minister, was a cynical guy.

I remember that Hugh Trevor-Roper, the British historian who wrote that wonderful book *The Last Days of Hitler*, thought Goebbels was probably a very intelligent, clever guy. And maybe he was intelligent about the Germans. He knew his own people. But he was abysmally ignorant of the world beyond the German borders. He had no conception of British character. You see, I'm still maintaining that nations, or people, have characters, and the British had a bulldog character, which I much admire. Goebbels didn't understand the French, either. The Russians were beyond him. The Americans he thought were run by Jews and blacks.

Goering, the aviation minister, was a swashbuckling guy, but ignorant. He couldn't have made it anywhere else but in the Nazi Party.

MOYERS: Do you remember Alfred Rosenberg? Hitler, in effect, appointed him philosopher of the party.

SHIRER: He was the official philosopher of the party. And he was one of the most dim-witted guys I've ever known. He was just outrageously stupid.

MOYERS: But how do you explain it? They took over this country, they perpetrated these horrors, genocide, millions upon millions of deaths; and they were below-average men.

SHIRER: We've got some below-average men in our country, sometimes, too, at the top. But these were particularly so. I think that the conservatives who helped manipulate Hitler into power thought they could control him. But Hitler was a very able guy; you have to admit it. He had a mass following, which they did not have. He also had a ruthlessness, which they did not expect. So within a few months, all the opposition, including the conservatives, was finished. Their parties were dissolved, and this gang of ruffians came up.

MOYERS: When you looked at these men, were you aware that they were capable of such evil?

SHIRER: To be honest, I don't think I was in '34. I certainly didn't think there would be genocide, and what happened after the war started. You had a bit of a taste of it, the weekend that they eliminated the leadership of the SA, during which they also shot a few personal enemies of Hitler and Goering and Goebbels, including a general, the head of the Catholic social movement. We don't know exactly how many they killed, but they killed at least seven or eight hundred in cold blood. So you had a taste of the ruthlessness. But I have to be honest about that. I could not imagine what would come in when the war started.

MOYERS: Do you think they thought that what they were doing was evil? Or does the totalitarian mind obliterate the distinction between good and evil, right and wrong?

SHIRER: It obliterates it, certainly. There's nothing in all the documents I read that indicates they considered what they were doing as evil. I mean, throwing these people into the gas chambers and so forth, we did not predict that. I knew nothing about that for a time, because I left Germany at the end of 1940. They did not adopt "the final solution" until 1940. Terrible term in itself—"the final solution"—awful. Makes my stomach go.

MOYERS: When you first heard about it, when you first were told that a whole people were being systematically obliterated, did you believe it?

SHIRER: I couldn't believe it. No. And that information came very slowly. I certainly missed the story myself. I remember first hearing it in London in 1943, two years after it really started, or at least a good year. I heard it from people in the British Foreign Office.

I remember one weekend I spent down with Anthony Eden, who was then Foreign Secretary. He said there was no truth in it. They were getting these reports, but there was no truth in them. When I came back to America, I checked it with Harry Hopkins, President Roosevelt's aide. He told me that Roosevelt had heard these things, but he did not believe them. During all that time, the Jews were trying to get the word out. It's a very bad record for the British Foreign Office and the American State Department.

I have a bad record, too. I did not get the story, really, until the war-crimes trials at Nuremberg. I sat there one day when they had these terrible pictures, and we heard the testimony of a guy named Hoess, who had been the commander at Auschwitz. He was almost proud of it. I went home that night, and I couldn't eat dinner. I think that would be true of my colleagues too. I was in a daze for three or four days, I think. One's imagination could not grasp it. But we should have learned about it in '44.

MOYERS: Somehow there is a reluctance on the part of an optimistic people like the Americans to acknowledge the real presence of evil and its solid state of being.

SHIRER: I think so. The theologian Reinhold Niebuhr said that a people without a sense of tragedy have difficulty meeting the evils of the day. I think that's true. I don't think we as a people have it. We have our problems and our troubles and our sorrows, but no real sense of life as a tragedy.

MOYERS: Our own forebears committed their own crimes against humanity: the Indians, the slaves.

SHIRER: Yes. I suppose we're all hypocrites, including myself.

MOYERS: You've certainly lived through a century of hate and evil.

SHIRER: Well, at certain times, it seemed to me that that was the only thing the human race was doing. It was committing so much evil, such destruction of life, of people, of the planet, and so forth. But I'm not always in a despondent mood.

MOYERS: No, you've tried to provide an antidote to it, a record. But one of these days the last living witness of what happened in Germany, what happened in this century, will be dead. What do we do about the memory? Do you think enough people will read books like yours?

SHIRER: I don't think so. When I hear George Bush's press conferences about the unification of Germany, I think the memory of the part that I lived through, Nazi Germany, is already dead. As you know, Reagan put out this idiotic idea of history that only Hitler, one man, was responsible for the evil, and that the poor German people, including the soldiers, were innocent victims. History gets distorted all the time. I guess we all do it, and that will go on. It's too bad.

MOYERS: You are convinced that it was a whole people who followed this man and gave their loyalty to him gladly, if not gleefully.

SHIRER: I think so. Chancellor Adenauer, for example, came over here and tried to put through the idea that Nazism was something supported only by a few criminals. But when I was in Germany in '85, President von Weizsäcker made a speech on May 8, the anniversary of VE Day, because there had been so much terrible talk during the Bitburg episode. He said, in effect, "Let's stop kidding ourselves. The whole German people were involved in Auschwitz, and we must recognize that." And Chancellor Helmut Kohl had been up at one of the concentration camps and had made almost the same kind of a speech. He said, "We've got to recognize that those who don't understand the past cannot understand the present." My feeling is, until the German people face the evils of Nazism, their future's going to be clouded. Until we remember it, at least, we're going to make a lot of mistakes. I don't want to be vindictive about it, and I keep hoping for the best, but we have to be honest.

MOYERS: What does the totalitarian mind do to the human being? That's the question that continues to obsess me, all the way through Stalin, and Hitler, and Idi Amin, and Ceausescu. There's some powerful idea at the heart of the totalitarian mentality that seems to drain the mind of its own thoughts and replace them with some fantasy.

SHIRER: Totalitarianism, in Germany or the Soviet Union or anyplace—Rumania certainly—destroys the human spirit. One of the sad things to me about the Russians, whom I like very much—I'm married to a woman who grew up in Moscow—is what it has done to the spirit of the Russian people. After seventy years of crushing their spirits and crushing their aspirations for some kind of freedom, you wonder today what they can do to ever get out of that situation. They've been so formed by this now, and so crushed by it, that you wonder what they can do. You can talk about democracy in Russia, but it's going to be very difficult.

MOYERS: But I do think character changes. Certainly circumstances change, and so much of the drive for freedom in Eastern Europe today, including East Germany, is coming from the churches, whose members sixty years ago often supported Hitler and the Nazis. That's been a remarkable transformation.

SHIRER: It is, I think. Of course, under Hitler, the churches were under pressure to conform. But even though institutions may conform to save themselves, there's always a band of individuals who have a lot of guts and character, and maybe are a little bit mad. That happened in the Catholic and Protestant churches.

I knew one young Lutheran clergyman who had been feeding me information about the persecution of the church. We tried so hard to be secret—we met in toilets, in the railroad station, in the zoo, and so forth. But they nabbed him. It was one of the worst moments of my life.

I was not the only foreign correspondent who knew him. Some of my colleagues did, too. For days, we went around wondering whether any of us made a false step that exposed this man. When he was condemned to death, I just wanted to pull out of the country. Later, his sentence was changed to life imprisonment, and I hope he got out somehow. I never could find him after the war.

MOYERS: One question that seems to me, even in these euphoric days of Europe, to be pertinent is: can it happen again?

SHIRER: Nobody can predict whether they'll do it again. I just think we have to be careful to see that they don't. I don't mean to say that I know an easy solution to the German problem. I don't. But thinking it over, the last few days, it seems to me that if we can enmesh this new united powerful Germany into some sort of a European security confederation, that's the only thing which will really give us security. If you make that coalition, which would have to encompass West and East, strong enough that if the Germans did try to break out of it, the others would be strong enough to restrain her, then you might solve the problem.

I remember, just before the war started, there was a wonderful French editor who used the pen name Pertinax. He said that if we could only convince the Germans that they were no longer strong enough to defeat Western Europe, and the Slavic world in the east, and the Americans, they wouldn't go off to war. But the Germans never believed that, you see. They never believed that we would come in, up until the last moment. Hitler had the most idiotic idea of America you can think of. He didn't even know that our great economic power would give us military strength eventually.

MOYERS: But he didn't misjudge the French. He knew, when he went into the Rhineland in '36, that France was not going to retaliate. The records now show that if the French had stood up to Hitler when his armies marched across into the Rhineland, his army would have collapsed.

SHIRER: They could have crushed him in a moment, I think. But there's a great deal of revisionist history going on now. I saw a piece by a professor recently up in one of the Boston universities. He'd written that the French could not have defeated the Germans in 1936. To me, it's absolutely absurd. They had a great army. The Germans had very little by that time. The German military people knew that they couldn't take on the French. It was a bluff on Hitler's part.

I had been in and out of France during that time, and the two or three years that led up to the war were awfully depressing. You can understand a Frenchman being against the war. They had these terrible losses in the first war. But a country has to fight for its defense. I had a very depressing afternoon once with the French journalist and philosopher Raymond Aron. I went up to his apartment overlooking the Seine River. We looked down there along a highway on one bank of the Seine, and the cars were going by, and there were people in the streets. He looked down and said, "You know, I am beginning to think we were right not to fight when the Germans invaded in 1940. All those happy people down there would not be alive today." I indicated to him, as politely as I could, that I was absolutely appalled. As diplomatically as I could, I suggested that a great country has to defend itself and that France was lucky. It was saved by the British, the Americans, and the Russians. But that's a dilemma, of course.

MOYERS: Was Hitler inevitable?

SHIRER: No. Hitler was not inevitable. If the Germans had worked the Weimar Republic honestly, we never would have had a Hitler.

MOYERS: What do you mean, if they'd worked it honestly?

SHIRER: Do you realize that the Constitution of the Weimar Republic after World War I was probably the most liberal in the world? When I was a youngster working in Paris, I used to get an assignment in Germany occasionally. I sort of grew up at the Sorbonne University in Paris, but I found that as a young American, not long out of college, I was more akin with the Germans then. They were interested in the arts, they were interested in peace, they were interested in social matters. A lot of them were socialists, some were Communists, some were middle of the road, and so forth. All very idealist. And I would come back thinking, "Gee, they're the most wonderful youngsters in Europe."

One of the most disillusioning experiences of my life was when I went back to work in Germany only seven or eight years later and looked up some of those people. Most of them were bigwigs in the Nazi Party, or in the German Foreign Office, where by that time, you had to be a Nazi. It made you think. How the deuce could it have happened? I was full of myself at that time, I guess. I would say, "Come on, we're old acquaintances. How can you believe in all this nonsense?" They said, "Listen, we have a career to make, just like you have in America. And these people are the future. They've taken over the country."

But worse than that, they began to believe in it. That was the worst thing. If they had just gone along, like so many Russians do, you know, in the last few years, knowing that the place was tumbling down, but figuring they just had to eat and so forth. But you didn't get much of that cynicism.

Compare Nazism and Italian fascism. The Italians are a very intelligent people. They have that Latin intelligence that I like. The Italian people were much too intelligent, sophisticated, and decent to go for Italian fascism. Mussolini's fascism was a thing at the top. It never got the mass of the people, as it did in Germany. There was a great difference there.

MOYERS: So you do believe there is something called character—the character of a people.

SHIRER: Oh, absolutely. But of the inevitableness of history, I'm not so sure. I grew up in the Presbyterian church, which believes in the doctrine of preordination. I had a bellyfull of it as a youngster, listening to it all, every Sunday at Sunday school.

MOYERS: How old are you now?

SHIRER: I am eighty-six.

MOYERS: And you're setting out now to write another book, this one about Tolstoy. Why?

SHIRER: Well, I'm interested in his last days. One night, about four o'clock on a cold autumn night, suddenly, something cracks in him. He sees his wife going through his diaries. And it does something to him. As soon as she's gone to bed, he steals out, to leave his wife of forty-eight years, and sets out for he knew not where. He hasn't the faintest idea where he was going. And ten days later, he is dead.

Why had this happened to this great, great man? Tolstoy was not only a great novelist and writer, but he was sort of a Christlike figure in his embrace of the ideas of nonviolent resistance to evil. Gandhi got his idea from Tolstoy. I've often talked to Gandhi about that. Gandhi called his commune Tolstoy Farm.

But why had Tolstoy done this? Why had this happened to so great a man? I read the biographies, and none of them were quite satisfactory. I don't know whether I have the answers. I've just given it a lot of thought. But it's a story of a man running away from himself, despite this uncommon wisdom that he had and all he learned from experience.

> *I ask myself, if there's a Christian God, how could he permit Christians to slaughter 10 or 15 million people? If there is a Jewish God, how could he permit Christians to slaughter 7 million Jews?*

MOYERS: Do you share any affinity with the idea that God died in this century at Auschwitz and Buchenwald and in those trenches of Flanders?

SHIRER: I ask myself, if there's a Christian God, how could he permit Christians to slaughter 10 or 15 million people? If there is a Jewish God, how could he permit Christians to slaughter 7 million Jews? And it's a question which bothers me, and I can't answer. It bothers me terribly. I know religion is a great solace, but it's something that's denied me at the present moment.

MOYERS: Are you still looking?

SHIRER: Absolutely.

MOYERS: Is Tolstoy any help?

SHIRER: Yes, he is, because Tolstoy saw one of the great dangers to religion. It's a danger to all religions, and it's a very great danger in our country, particularly in some of the places that follow fundamentalist religions. Tolstoy was excommunicated by the Church. He began to see the organism of the Church as a poison to the Christian faith. He wrote some wonderful books on Christianity about that. He had this change of life when he was about fifty years old, in 1879. And his writings, of course, won the enmity of the Church, and they excommunicated him. When he was buried, they wouldn't permit an Orthodox priest to take part in the funeral, though some did.

But he has been helpful to me, in a sense, because he went to Christianity. He learned Greek so he could understand the exact words of the New Testament. He found a great deal of solace. He used to repeat "The Sermon on the Mount." He knew it by heart. He was a rather crotchety old man, too. Some of his ideas you can't follow. He actually hoped to form a new form of Christianity. That was beyond him and probably beyond any man. But I think ideas do bear fruit, both good and bad ideas. Nazi Germany went through just one bad idea after another. But there are still good ideas. I don't think Gandhi, for instance, would have evolved as he did if he hadn't read Tolstoy.

MOYERS: You say, "I count the days with Gandhi the most fruitful of my life. No other experiences so shook me out of the rut of banal existence and opened my ordinary mind and spirit." That's very powerful.

SHIRER: I thought then, and I still think, that he probably was the greatest man of our time. He was a great political leader, and he was a great spiritual leader. Despite all the baggage that I brought along from Western civilization, I learned from him that there was another world, a completely different world. A world where force did not always prevail, where nonviolence, if properly directed, could overcome bayonets, and that sort of thing. Above all, he talked a great deal about love, spiritual love.

He used to lecture me by saying, "Love is God." He would say, "That's the only God that I really recognize. Love equals God." Well, that was difficult for me to get. But I got from him a different kind of religion. I could never go back, after two years in India, to my Presbyterian church as a worshipper. He taught me something that's been wonderful in my life, what he called comparative religion. He was a devout Hindu. But the Hindu religion is very tolerant, much more tolerant than any of our religions or Islam. And he said, "I take the best of all religions."

MOYERS: You've experienced both Gandhi and Hitler. You saw both of them close up.

SHIRER: You might say that they were two geniuses. Many people don't like to hear that about Hitler. Hitler was a genius; but an evil genius. Gandhi was a saintly genius. He had his faults and his quirks, but he was one of the few men in the world who practiced what they preached. How many of our leaders do that today?

John Henry Faulk

HUMORIST

John Henry Faulk was a homespun humorist in the tradition of Mark Twain and Will Rogers and a troublemaker in the tradition of Thomas Jefferson and James Madison. They believed in individual liberty and so did John Henry. In the 1950s he staked his livelihood to challenge in court the right-wing blacklisters who were bullying and intimidating the entertainment industry. He lost his job—but he won a victory for the common sense of plain Americans and the uncommon power of American ideals.

MOYERS: I was at William and Mary College recently about two weeks after you gave a speech there, and I was intrigued by all the publicity that was still following in your wake. The students hadn't known who John Henry Faulk was; they hadn't been born when you were suffering your ordeal back in the fifties. Yet when you finished speaking, they gave you a standing ovation.

FAULK: Well, Momma had aimed me towards the Methodist ministry, but by the time I got born she realized she shot a blank. But apparently I still have an evangelical streak in me, because I used it there in that speech. I got to talking about the First Amendment; I got to talking about the McCarthy period, and the trivialization of our most meaningful national experience, the election of our federal officers from the President on down. And I got so carried away I started saving souls. I really did; I got kind of a state of joy at it.

MOYERS: Did these kids at this traditional college know what you were talking about?

FAULK: I do a great many college speeches for that very reason. I am determined that they shall know what the McCarthy period was all about. It had nothing to do with communism—anti or otherwise. It had to do with shutting off the lifeblood of this republic, the open and robust and free dialogue that our Founding Fathers had anticipated when they made the First Amendment an absolute mandate. See, treason is the only crime in the Constitution. Treason shall consist only—and that adverb is very important—of waging war against the United States or giving aid and support to the enemy. Well now, in the McCarthy period, we were told that the Democrats—or anyone who dissented—were treasonous. It was an anti-dissent thing, exploited for political purposes.

MOYERS: To silence the opposition.

FAULK: We were told that there was an international Communist conspiracy afoot, and it had its bony hand right on the White House door, and Roosevelt and that crowd of cronies he had there were nothing but a bunch of old Communists. I had an aunt who said, "Johnny, it just scares me to death when I think they're right there in Washington, D.C., fixing to take over this government at any day." And I said, "Aunt Edith, there's not a Communist officer in the entire United States Government. One's never been elected. People in this country would never put a Communist in charge of anything." But Aunt Edith said, "You just don't know, you just don't know, Johnny."

MOYERS: You tell a story about the time you were twelve years old—

FAULK: Ah well, I use that to illustrate something. Boots Cooper and I used to pretend we were law-and-order men. I was a Texas Ranger and he was a United States marshal. We were both twelve years old and we rode the frontier between Momma's back door and her henhouse. One day Momma told us there was a chicken snake in one of the hen's nests out there, and she asked us mighty lawmen to go and execute it. We laid aside our stick horses, got a hoe, and went in. The hens were in a state of acute agitation. We had to stand on tiptoe to look in the top nests, and about the third top nest we looked in, a chicken snake looked out. I don't know, Bill, whether you've ever viewed a chicken snake from a distance of six inches from the end of your nose—

MOYERS: Not that close—

FAULK: The damn thing looks like a boa constrictor from that distance, although it's about the size of your finger. All of our frontier courage drained out our heels— actually, it trickled down our overall legs—and Boots and I made a new door through the henhouse wall.

Momma came out and said, "Well, you've lulled me into a false sense of security. I thought I was safe from all hurt and harm and here you've let a chicken snake run you out of the henhouse, and a little chicken snake at that. Don't you know chicken snakes are harmless? They can't hurt you." Boots said, "Yes, Mrs. Faulk, I know that," and he's rubbing his forehead and behind at the same time, "but they can scare you so bad it'll cause you to hurt yourself."

MOYERS: And that's what happened during the McCarthy period.

FAULK: See, the men who erected the protections for the individual Americans back there two hundred years ago believed that we would be capable of governing ourselves if they made freedom of speech an absolute mandate. Anything of lesser force wouldn't survive the kind of crisis they knew would come. They were men of great wisdom and vision, literate men.

So in the First Amendment they said, "Congress shall make no law." Well, that's not complicated, is it? You read that to a fifth-grade schoolboy and he'll say that means Congress can make no law. That's what it says, but the Supreme Court has scared everybody so that they have never been willing to see that's what it meant. The great four rights of the people—conscience, speech, press, and right to assemble— are included in the First Amendment because this great notion will guarantee and protect the right of people to voice those opinions we loathe and despise—protect them with the same force it does those we cherish and live by. Now when you catch on to what James Madison and the others were really driving at there, then you see the real genius of this society that we live in.

MOYERS: Which is?

FAULK: A guaranteed right to be wrong. That is the greatest right the American people have inherited. This is what was passed on to us. And this is what some people trivialized when they said children should be required to pledge allegiance to the flag. That kind of argument belongs to those who so little trust the democratic processes, the wisdom of the people, that they feel a man must be forced to demonstrate his patriotism by saluting a flag. Fortunately, the Supreme Court has said you can't do that.

MOYERS: Why are you so passionate about the First Amendment in particular? You brought those students at William and Mary to their feet talking about this.

FAULK: It puts every American citizen of every color, every walk of life, on precisely the same footing, just as your right to vote puts you on the same footing with the heads of the party, the richest men, all the Rockefeller boys. It doesn't make any distinction. It doesn't say, "Congress shall make laws only for this group or for that group." Congress can make no laws respecting the establishment of religion or prohibiting a free exercise. That includes everybody. It is an absolute.

The First Amendment made us a beacon of freedom to the rest of the world. We were the only people in the world who had anything like that going for us. We are the ones who created and committed to paper the proposition that "we hold these truths to be self-evident, that all men are created equal, that they are endowed by their Creator with certain unalienable rights, that among these are life, liberty, and the pursuit of happiness." And here's the important part: "That to secure these rights, governments are instituted among men, deriving their just powers from the consent of the governed." God, it was like a blowtorch in history. It flared up the whole world. It lit the whole world up. It had never been said before that people had a natural right to rule themselves. It meant Boots Cooper and I could get up and stand right next to the governor of Texas. Lord have mercy.

So I try to communicate this to the students I talk to. I say, "Just understand this, and you are armed against any of the slings and arrows of outrageous fortune that might befall you. You are strong." That's the reason people called me a hero for fighting the lawsuit I fought. But I wasn't a hero at all. When you understand the First Amendment, it doesn't take a hero to say, "Well, to me it means what it says." It doesn't say, "Except when Senator McCarthy thinks otherwise."

MOYERS: You're very eloquent and passionate about the First Amendment, but the fact of the matter is that the First Amendment didn't protect you in the 1950s.

FAULK: Oh yes, it did.

MOYERS: You lost your job, your weekly show on CBS.

FAULK: What the hell is a job? Look, we had Mr. J. Edgar Hoover and the FBI spying on American citizens. That's more like a totalitarian country than a self-governing, democratic republic. We had the House Un-American Activities Committee hauling schoolteachers and librarians and ministers of the gospel in. That all added up to an absolute horror to me, and I welcomed a chance to attack this group called Aware, Incorporated, who worked hand in glove with the FBI and the House Un-American Activities Committee.

MOYERS: What was Aware, Incorporated?

FAULK: They were a private group who completely dominated the radio and television industry. They published a list of names of persons, producers, directors, writers, and performers, who had in the past done something that Aware decided indicated less than loyalty to the United States of America. Then they inquired what their employers were going to do. Were they going to support the international Communist conspiracy that had its cold hand on the throat of the American republic or were they going to get rid of this trash?

MOYERS: And of course, the networks knew that when word got out that they were sponsoring a suspected Communist sympathizer the advertisers would disappear, the public would disappear. How did Aware get to you?

FAULK: I belonged to a union called AFTRA, the American Federation of Television and Radio Artists, and a union called SAG, the Screen Actors Guild. Everybody in network radio and television had to belong to AFTRA and everybody doing any film work at all had to belong to SAG. The SAG was headed up by a gentleman named Ronald Reagan, who was informing to the FBI, and anything you got to the FBI seemed to get to Aware right away. Oh yes, it was a nest of rattlesnakes really. Persons named by Aware became blacklisted and became unemployed. They never confronted their accusers, because they didn't know who their accusers were. They were simply washed out of the scene, and you would find them working in delicatessens and shoe stores and what not. The variety-show host Garry Moore said once, "A blacklisted person was like somebody who was blindfolded in a dark closet, with six guys hitting him with clubs. He never knew where the licks were coming from, which direction they were coming from. He was just there; the victim of 'em." And that best describes a blacklist. See, you never knew. At a dinner party, for instance, you never knew whether you were being offensive or being a hero to them.

And Aware made money out of this, you see. The head of Aware, Vincent Hartnett, made a lot of money; he charged the networks and the advertising agencies so much per head to clear names, and your name had to be cleared by Aware before you could legitimately work in a show. So I organized a group of guys who were sitting around bellyaching about the injustice of blacklisting. In the fall of 1955, we ran for office in our local AFTRA union, and swept in. Charlie Collingwood, bless his old sweet heart, became president and I became a vice president and Orson Bean became a vice president. Garry Moore became a vice president, and we were going to save the world.

Of course it made headlines; they literally said "ANTI-BLACKLIST SLATE WINS." So Aware then put out a bulletin on us which said, "This middle-of-the-road slate alleges that it's not Communist. Perhaps it isn't in the Communist movement, but let's look at some of the leadership. For instance, John Henry Faulk, who organized it—" and then they went to town on me. They alleged six different things that I had done.

MOYERS: Were the accusations true?

FAULK: Two of them were true; I'd done them. I had appeared at a dinner at the Astor Hotel in 1946 with a known Communist and never repudiated that appearance. It was an anniversary dinner for the UN Security Council, and the "known Communist" was Andrei Gromyko, the Soviet ambassador to the UN. They also said I had entertained somewhere in 1948 for Henry Wallace, the third-party candidate. Neither one was illegal, and the other four things were totally false—had not even a scintilla of truth in them. But Aware had gotten so reckless by this time, they didn't care whether it was true or false. Nobody ever called their hand on it, so I decided this was a golden opportunity.

CBS got my business manager to say to me, "Look, go home and write an affidavit saying that you were misled, and thanking Aware for calling this to your attention. Say that you are violently anti-Communist. You can't stand them. And you would stomp one if you could see him. And that you are a loyal, fine American, that you served in the American Red Cross overseas in the Middle East and that you served in the United States Army and that you are so patriotic that it just gives you a headache when you get to reflecting on it. Make it very patriotic, but apologize and say that you did get into a couple of these, those that are true. Say that you didn't realize that they were Communist-inspired. It was a very serious misjudgment." See, this is the way you get off Aware's list. Apologize to Aware, volunteer to go to the House Un-American Activities Committee and spill your insides on all your friends on how you got involved in this, and tell the FBI all of this stuff. They were all garbage collectors,

I called them—Aware and the FBI were. They collected garbage and dumped it on your head when they got a chance.

MOYERS: So you're sitting there in your apartment in New York. You've got CBS's offer that if you'll just say, "*Mea culpa,* I didn't mean it; I was just an innocent dupe," Aware would take you off the list.

FAULK: But I also had to say this in a polite way. I got to thinking, and Lord have mercy, it was like wading through my own vomit. I couldn't do something like that. Good God, I couldn't do that to myself, you know.

And I regarded it as an opportunity to fight back. I didn't underestimate their villainy, but I said, "This is an opportunity to haul these people into the courts of justice that the people of the United States maintain for resolving just such disputes as I'm involved in. Where I can confront my accusers and where they are bound by the laws of evidence and by the rules of evidence. I'll know who it is who's saying these things and the lawyer can cross-examine them. And of course they'll have the same right to do that to me.

> *The people maintain our court system and independent judiciary, and I have no doubt whatever that we will triumph.*

"I have no fear whatever that I won't triumph; I know I will triumph because I know who I am and I know who this country is. I know the basic law of this country. I believe that I can destroy them. I believe that when the American people see what these birds are up to, they will take care of them themselves. They maintain the court system; I don't maintain it. The people maintain our court system and independent judiciary, and I have no doubt whatever that we will triumph."

MOYERS: They accused you of harboring Communist sympathies. Had you had any sympathies for the Communist position in this country? Had you been a Communist? Had you joined a Communist organization? Had you had anything to do with the Communists?

FAULK: No, and they knew that. They knew that I'd had to sign an oath, all officers in unions had to sign an oath. "I'm not now and never have been a Communist." Now you understand that I never considered Communists a threat to the United States. But they had no more appeal to me than Roman Catholics. Still the Communists and the Roman Catholics have the same freedom. I believe in Roman Catholics enjoying all the freedoms of any other American citizen. I believe a Communist is entitled to enjoy all the freedoms, register to vote, and so forth. But I haven't noticed any great headway the Communists have made.

MOYERS: But you didn't make any big issue out of it? You didn't go around speaking at rallies for the Communists or anything like that?

FAULK: No, of course not.

MOYERS: In fact, if I remember correctly, John Henry, you were also out making speeches to FBI groups, the Daughters of the American Revolution, Harvard, and Yale, those other subversive institutions. And your subject was the American heritage.

FAULK: Yes. Because I had been a folklorist, and the more I discovered about who we really were, the more uncomfortable I became about the number of people who don't understand the genius of America. The Founding Fathers made the First Amendment an absolute. They said a man's got as much right to be a Communist as anything else. We won't make that decision. We will never let the state make that decision. The people in their wisdom can make that decision. If they don't want to vote for the Communists or the vegetarians or the prohibitionist party, they don't have to. Don't want to vote for Democrats, don't vote for Democrats. Vote for whoever you want to. Listen to all sides—and then you pick. That's what makes this republic great.

MOYERS: And what happened next?

FAULK: I went down and got Louis Nizer to file a lawsuit. He took it on. He understood it would be a very big suit. And he said, "Are you ready to go through a real ordeal? You can be knocked out of work. And you won't work again. But we're going to do our best. We'll take hand in hand and you and I together will put down this terrible plague of blacklisting in Hollywood and New York."

Then Mr. Nizer said he was going to take this at a minimal retainer, and he named the sum. Well, that was about seven thousand more dollars than I had. I was a very improvident person. I hadn't saved money well at all. The next day I had lunch with my colleague at CBS, Ed Murrow, and he was just tickled to death. He thought this was going to be the greatest trial of all time. Mr. Carl Sandburg had called Ed and said, "You tell John that whatever's the matter with America, he ain't." Ed thought that was the best statement he'd heard.

I said to Ed, "Well, you know, I've got to hustle. You have to help me get somebody to hustle up another seven thousand bucks. I hate to go and tell Nizer that he's got a total pauper on his hands." And bless goodness, Ed Murrow said, "You tell Mr. Nizer the other seven thousand will be in his office within the next week or so from me." When I said, "Oh no, Ed, I can't let you do that," he said, "I'm not doing this for you. Johnny, if you needed twenty-five dollars, and I happened to have it, I would maybe lend it to you, although I don't make it a practice to lend money easily. But I'm investing in America, not in you."

MOYERS: You filed the suit against Aware in 1956. What did CBS do?

FAULK: Well, a year later they fired me; said my ratings had fallen. And Nizer said, "Well, they got to you. Aware's lawyer Roy Cohn got to you through CBS. They've hit you." And I said, "No, Mr. Nizer, I trust CBS. I really believe that they've given me the straight dope, because they are the kind of guys who would. They hate Aware as much as I do." Mr. Nizer laughed a cynical laugh. But it turned out he was right.

MOYERS: They had gotten to CBS. You found that out.

FAULK: It was strange as hell, Bill, when I got fired. It's a very strange feeling to be blacklisted. You weren't supposed to be seen with people on the blacklist. The restaurant Toots Shor's was kind of my headquarters over there on Fifty-first Street. I knew everybody who came in. Toots had a table for me and all. But people started leaving, getting up and having to rush out when I came in. It's a strange feeling because you know why they're doing it. Or you're walking down Madison Avenue and you see old so-and-so coming along there, and you see him all of a sudden look over toward Cardinal Spellman's house and start walking across Madison Avenue there at Fiftieth to avoid you.

MOYERS: Friends, too? Colleagues?

FAULK: Many friends were outraged and stood steadfast with me. Walter Cronkite stood steadfast with me. Ed Murrow, of course. Charles Collingwood stood steadfast with me.

MOYERS: The lawsuit dragged on for years and nobody would hire you. How did you survive financially?

FAULK: Borrowed money and cut back sharply. There were people who were very kind. I started this little advertising agency. Many friends were very kind. Myrna Loy was very helpful to me. Mrs. Roosevelt was very helpful to me. She was indignant over what was being done to me.

MOYERS: Do you remember the day you heard the verdict?

FAULK: That's kind of like asking Mr. Bush, do you remember when they inaugurated you President? I mean I sure do remember that. It was in June of '62, and the case had lasted three months. It was beautifully constructed, and it had become exceedingly clear that Aware was nothing more than a barefooted bunch of kids with cans, shaking them to make people believe ghosts were going to attack the Mount Zion Baptist Church. They were fear peddlers, and under the cross-examination of Mr. Nizer that came through pretty clearly to the jury.

So, Nizer got carried away in his summation and asked for two million dollars in damages for me. Well, we hadn't sued but for a million. So we went to have dinner while the jury was out to consider the verdict. And I said, "Lou, you poured it on. Hell, you had me. I'd have voted for me, too. But two million dollars? Lou, they're liable to think I am actually doing it for money." He said, "No."

Then there came a runner from the court to say the jury was returning to the courtroom. We went tearing back up into the courtroom and sat down, and the jury filed in and the judge said, "Have you reached a decision?" The jury said, "No. We have a question we want to ask. Can we give more than two million?" Honest to goodness, and old sweet Louis Nizer, he sat there like somebody'd caught him between his eyes with a ball peen hammer. He'd made a lot of mistakes in his legal career, but asking for too little never had been one of them. And the jury went out and thirty minutes later came back with a three-and-a-half-million-dollar judgment in my favor.

MOYERS: How much of that three and a half million dollars did you finally get?

FAULK: Well, the Appeals Court cut it down to a half million, saying it was an obscene sum of money. It was a record-setting verdict at the time. But we never even got that. The defendant was Mr. Johnson of Syracuse, New York, the head of a bunch of supermarkets, who was the backer of Aware. And he died the night that the jury went out to make its decision.

MOYERS: Six years of your life and you get a few thousand dollars back. You borrowed money all the time.

FAULK: Well, I owed every penny of it. It wiped me out. By the time I got through paying those debts off, I didn't have fifteen cents. But I was out of debt and as Nizer said, "You've now been made whole." We were both under the illusion that the networks would rush out, grab me up in their arms, and carry me around triumphantly down Madison Avenue.

MOYERS: But nobody offered you a job?

FAULK: No. As a matter of fact, they didn't even like to discuss it. See, I had done the unpardonable. I had challenged the establishment.

MOYERS: The irony is CBS, which fired you for standing up to Aware, ten years later made a movie out of the book you wrote about your experience and made themselves a lot of money.

FAULK: Isn't that an ironic thing, though? A reporter called me and said, "Look here, CBS is doing this big show on 'Fear on Trial.' Does this represent a change of heart toward you on the part of CBS?" And for once I ad-libbed brilliantly. I said, "Of course not. CBS has never had a heart, nor has it ever claimed to have a heart. It has a Board of Directors and it has a corporate policy. Corporations don't have hearts. They have policies. Twenty years ago, it was their policy to blacklist anybody who was mentioned unfavorably by Aware. Today, now that things have broken loose some, it's their policy not to blacklist; as a matter of fact, to do a movie and make a lot of money out of telling how they did it once."

MOYERS: Could all this happen in America again?

FAULK: Yes. That's what offended me so grievously about the use of innuendo and the arguments about "I'm a better patriot than you are" in the 1988 presidential race. As though these are genuine issues.

MOYERS: When the trial was over, Louis Nizer wrote in his own book of you, "One lone man with virtually no resources had dragged the defendants into the court, and, although outrageously outnumbered, had withstood starvation and disgrace and summoned enough strength to battle them into submission." Where did you get that strength?

FAULK: Well, of course I appreciate very much Mr. Nizer saying that and I appreciate very much your quoting it as though it were a group of facts. I would like to say, "Well, I'm just such a strong spirit." It came, I would say, from Daddy, from Momma, good Methodist souls. It came from a wonderful exposure I've had to some beautiful, beautiful Americans, in the tradition of Mr. Jefferson and Mr. Madison and Mr. Mason.

But I don't know whether it's strength or not, Bill. You see, Momma had an absolute hard-and-fast rule: "No self-pity," she said. "It's more deadly than whooping cough. No self-pity." And I remembered that time and again during my fight when I caught myself going into a fit of self-pity, "Well, look, those other guys all got their jobs, and one of them is living in that mansion now up there in Connecticut" . . . and then I'd say, "Oh, come off that nonsense. None of them's got your friends and the benefits and the blessings that have befallen you." Which is true.

MOYERS: It meant something to you, growing up in Texas. What did it mean?

FAULK: The real Texas, Bill, is the Texas you grew up in, too. The Texas that has given us substance is not this Wild West of Tom Mix and Hoot Gibson. They used to be Western movie actors that I'd sit watching in Skinny's Theater every Saturday afternoon. But the point is there never was that Texas.

Look, my people came here in 1827. Jesse Tanninghill left Tennessee because he wasn't making it there, and he heard the Mexicans would give him free land over here. And most of the people here were tradespeople. There wasn't a wealthy family out here. There were ordinary working folks. I never saw a pair of cowboy boots on any human being in my life except in the movies of Tom Mix. But you have to understand. Every time the Rotary Club or the Masons would go up East, they'd buy cowboy clothes to wear. And I get up to New York, and that's the first thing CBS wants me to do, have a picture made in cowboy clothes. I couldn't sit down in the pants and couldn't stand up in the boots. But I was from Texas. I was supposed to do it.

The real Texas was founded by people who came here to find a way of life and to build a community and they lived on a very communal basis. It was cooperation. Most cooperative society in the world. That's the way they survived the rigors of a frontier life where you couldn't call a doctor if your child was snake-bit or broke his arm or you were having a child. You called a midwife if you could find a neighbor. It was people cooperating together. If a house burned down, all the neighbors got together. If a woman's husband died and they had a corn crop in the fields, the community got together and helped her get her crop in. It was a cooperative society; it was a beautiful society. That's where the real music of Texas is; that's where the real drama of Texas is, you see.

MOYERS: What's life been like for you since you came home? You've never had a big job in radio or television again.

FAULK: Well, Momma had a cousin who was a state senator and he loved to say, "When my people came to Texas, we found paradise on earth and so we've stayed here in paradise ever since." But Daddy would always ridicule that by saying, "They got here and never could raise enough money to get out of the state on." Well, that's the way I feel about Texas, although I'm very fond of this state and I'm very fond of the people. Even the ones I disagree with very emphatically. They have many fine qualities. I've got kinfolks who are Klu Klux Klanners. I've got all shapes and sizes of the political spectrum. So I have an affection for this state. But I feel repelled by the attitude, "We're the biggest and the best." My uncle Amos said, "Johnny, you know if there's one thing for sure, God made Texas the center of the universe," and I said, "How do you know that?" "Well, he wouldn't have went to the trouble of putting it there if he hadn't intended it to be the center, Johnny." Well, this kind of braggadocio really bores me about Texas.

MOYERS: We don't brag that much anymore after these years of economic recession.

FAULK: That's right. And bless Mr. Bush's heart, he's a sweet man, with all his points of light and everything. But his wanting to make himself a Texan absolutely defies my understanding. I'd think he'd want to say, "Well, I wasn't born there. I went down."

MOYERS: He doesn't strike you as a Texan?

FAULK: He strikes me as a human and a well-meaning human. Now I don't want him to go around bragging that John Faulk supports me. I don't want him using that in his propaganda, though I don't think there's any danger of that. I think that he has many positive qualities, but I don't think that striking oil out in Odessa, Texas, or Midland, or wherever it was, is one of them.

MOYERS: You're seventy-six now?

FAULK: Yes. And I figure, God, I've been blessed. This has been such a full life that I'm not sitting around wringing my hands, saying, "Oh, my Lord, why did it happen to me?" I've been very fortunate. Have the best wife and the best bunch of friends in the world. A sweet and loving family.

MOYERS: So many people say they just don't understand why there's no bitterness in you.

FAULK: Because, Bill, you're sitting and looking at one of the most fortunate people in the world. I had some rough times. I'm not trying to say, "Oh, it wasn't anything." Yes, it was damn rough. It was damn rough when I had to go and borrow money from people to survive, but over all, you see, I won the love and respect and the ardent support of people whose respect I really wanted.

MOYERS: People you cared about?

FAULK: Yes. I'm a free man. I don't have to "crook the pregnant hinges of the knee where thrift may follow fawning." I don't have to any longer hide my opinions. I can look my neighbor in the eye, and say, "This is my opinion on so and so." On racism, for instance, I happen to consider it one of the great threats to our society. Unless we address ourselves to correcting it, we are in real difficulty, because you see a good part of the earth's population now is not pink-cheeked Anglo-Saxons like me. They are people from Asia, from Africa, who are going to inherit the earth. When Jesus said, "The meek shall inherit the earth," he hit the nail on the head.

MOYERS: So after all of this, what have you learned about life?

FAULK: It's the most glorious experience in the world. Now you understand that I have, in a way, been a privileged person. "Well," you say, "you don't sound very privileged to me." I've been a privileged person in a white, Protestant-dominated society. I've been a member of that society. I've been a member of the people who control the show, as it were. And in the process, reckoning with that, I've had to face

> *Whatever we have achieved as far as intellect and spiritual growth are concerned, we still can't conceive of infinity. This is all part of me and I am part of every human life on this globe.*

the fact that basically, I was a member of the species called *Homo sapiens* and that as such I was kin to every single one of them.

Recently when I found out I had cancer, I had to come to grips with something I'd left out of my life for a long time. That's when I got in the habit of going out early in the morning before daylight and looking up into the heavens and becoming part of that. I said, "My God, I'm part of that; I'm part of eternity. This is me." And then I realized it makes no difference when you pass on to Glory, or when you die, if you feel that you are a part of this, all of this. Whatever we have achieved as far as intellect and spiritual growth are concerned, we still can't conceive of infinity. This is all part of me and I am part of every human life on this globe.

John Henry Faulk died on April 9, 1990, in Austin, Texas.

LOOKING WITHIN

Running through so many of the conversations I conducted in 1990, often as a strong undercurrent, was the theme of unfulfilled relationships—one's relationship to one's self and to others. There is within and between us unmapped country that we are often deterred from exploring because of some "No Trespassing" sign erected there by fear or pain we cannot acknowledge or understand.

Robert Bly is exploring this country more audaciously than anyone I know. That a poet should plunge where others tiptoe is hardly a surprise. It takes more than imagination to make a poet, it takes indignation. "To pipe a simple song for thinking hearts" is no mechanical art; poets "learn in suffering what they teach in song." The poet's credential is earned through grief. This is especially so with Bly. Absurd and cruel experience has weathered his life as it has his face.

On the subject of men he is especially provocative. He contends that the models so many of us were given in high school—of John Wayne or Audie Murphy or the Lone Ranger—are inadequate to the task of helping men be both human and male. "Around thirty-five, men begin to realize that the images they were given of what a man is don't work. They don't work in their jobs, they don't work in a relationship, they don't work in the marriage; they don't work!" But when those childhood myths die, what can take their place? Are there new images and stories that can help men? How do we address the "primary experience of the American man now": the experience of being inadequate?

More frequently men are gathering to talk about all these issues: how we think and feel about ourselves, our fathers, our sons, and our roles in society. The conversation that follows took place at one such event in Austin, Texas. What summons men to such gatherings, in my experience, is not a desire to separate again from women or to move back to that destructive, aggressive, and dominating masculine personality of more chauvinistic days. To the contrary. The men with whom I have talked are drawn to these conferences by a sense of loss—the loss of familiar myths and road maps. But they are also drawn by hope. There is something optimistic about the very willingness of men to learn from one another through sharing their confusion over the problems of life.

Robert Bly

POET

Poet Robert Bly has become a familiar mentor at men's gatherings. A prolific writer, editor, and translator, Bly gives frequent lectures and readings and conducts men's workshops around the country. He won a National Book Award for *The Light Around the Body.*

MOYERS: Why "A Gathering of Men"? It's rare, isn't it, to have a workshop for men only?

BLY: Maybe twenty years ago it would have been rare, but men in various parts of the country have begun to gather. It isn't a reaction to the women's movement. I think the grief that leads to the men's movement began, maybe a hundred and forty years ago, when the Industrial Revolution began. It sent the father out of the house to work.

MOYERS: What impact did that have?

BLY: Well, we receive something from our father by standing close to him . . .

MOYERS: Physically?

BLY: Yes. When we stand, physically, close to our father, something happens that can't be described in material terms. It gives the son a certain confidence, an awareness, a knowledge of what it is to be male. In ancient times you were always with your father. He taught you how to do things, he taught you how to farm, he taught you whatever it was he did. You learned from him.

MOYERS: A kind of food.

BLY: Food, yes, food from your father's body. When the father went out of the house in the Industrial Revolution, that food ended. Today, the average American father spends ten minutes a day with a son, and half that time is spent in, "Clean up your room!" That's a favorite phrase of mine, I know it well.

The Industrial Revolution didn't harm the mother and daughter relationship as much as it did the father and son. Mother and daughter have stood close to each other, and still stand close to each other. Daughters receive some kind of knowledge from their mothers of what it is to be a woman. They receive knowledge of the female mode of feeling. The mother gets it from her grandmother, who got it from her grandmother, who got it from her grandmother; it goes all the way down. But, now, I don't know, maybe that'll change too as mothers are going out to work.

After the Industrial Revolution, the male did not receive any knowledge from his father: knowledge of what the male mode of feeling is. And then, too, the old male initiators who used to work with younger men are not working anymore.

MOYERS: Who were those "old male initiators"?

BLY: Well, in traditional cultures, you aren't initiated by your father. You're initiated by older males; they might be friends of your father, or they could be uncles or grandfathers. They're the ones who used to initiate. But since they've disappeared, it falls on the father to do. But the father can't do it either, because he's at the office. You see the picture?

MOYERS: Yes. In some traditional cultures, a night arrives when a group of men show up at a boy's house. They take him away from home and don't bring him back for several days. When he comes back, he has ashes on his face . . . he's been initiated.

BLY: In New Guinea, they still do it today; the men come in with spears to get the boys. The boys know nothing about the men's world, they live with their mothers completely. Now, all over New Guinea, women and men accept one thing: "A boy can't be made into a man without the active intervention of the older men." They accept that; both men and women participate in this drama.

So, the men come to take the boys away, and the boys are crying, "Save me, Mama, Save me!" Now, the men have built a house across the water for the boys' initiation hut. They're taking the boys to the hut, but three or four women get spears and head them off at the bridge. The boys are crying, "Save me, Mama! These horrible men are taking me away!" There's a battle between the mothers and the old men who are stealing the boys. There's lots of yelling and clashing of spears, but it's all show; nobody is hurt. Finally the women are driven back. The men take the boys to the initiation hut. The women go back to the village, have coffee, and say, "How'd I do? How'd I look?"

So that's wonderful. The women are not doing the initiating; they're participating, but they don't do it, the men do it. Then, as you said, the boys stay with the men for a time, for a year, maybe. The initiators will explain that something has to die to be born, and what will have to die is the boy. This isn't happening to the men in our culture.

MOYERS: If we don't have the old initiations, what does happen with younger men?

BLY: As for my father, he didn't teach me much about the male mode of feeling, but he taught me something. But many men have no father at all, or the father left when they were two, or the father doesn't say anything, or the father doesn't talk well about feelings. It seems to be natural in the American male, not talking about feelings.

So then, how does the boy learn the male mode of feeling? He doesn't. It's a problem, and in the sixties, it came to a crisis, during the Vietnam War. The young men hadn't been helped by their fathers, and they were really betrayed by the older men during Vietnam. So, women would offer to initiate the young men: initiate them in wonderful things like respect for the earth, respect for life, respect for feeling, and so on. That wasn't wrong at all, it's just that no one has helped them with the male mode of feeling.

MOYERS: What's the chief difference, as you see it, between male feeling and female feeling?

BLY: A strong part of the women's mode of feeling has to do with pain: moving towards pain, and helping to remove it. And there's also the pain of being devalued. I mean, women's values have been rejected in this culture for over two thousand years, and women feel a strong pain in this devaluation. Men don't feel devalued quite that much. With men it's more an area of grief, as opposed to pain.

MOYERS: You keep using the word "grief."

BLY: Yes, you see, I began as a poet, writing poetry. Poetry deals with feeling, but . . . Until I had really tried to go into some of the grief around my father, I didn't really have access to feeling.

MOYERS: Tell me about that.

BLY: Well, you know, as men we're taught not to feel pain and grief. I remember when one of my boys was about nine years old, he was hit in a basketball game—hit by the ball—and I saw him turn around and bend down and get control of his pain and his grief before he stood up again. That same boy had been so wonderful in being open to wounds and crying and so on when he was very small. But the culture says to him, "You cannot give way to that. Turn around, and when you turn back, you must have a face without pain or grief in it." Right?

I received that too. My father was an alcoholic, and in an alcoholic family, someone is hired to be cheerful. That's one of the jobs. Another person is hired to be a trickster, another is appointed to be . . . well, anyway, *I* was hired to be cheerful. So, when anyone asked me about the family, I'd lie in a cheerful way, "Oh, it's wonderful, yes, indeed, we have sheep, you know, and we have chickens, and everything's wonderful."

If you can deny something so fundamental as the deep grief in the whole family, you can deny anything. So then how can you write poetry if you're involved in that much denial? So the word denial was very helpful to me.

MOYERS: Did you resent your father?

BLY: No, I think what happened was that, being appointed to be the cheerful one in the family, I tended to follow a movement upward. More and more achievement, more and better education, and so on. That's what you do. And so, by upward movement you try to redeem the family's name. You feel there's a shame there somewhere in the name. So you try to get excellence associated with the family name.

I got to be about forty-six or so before I realized how unsteady I was, how my own poems didn't have . . . well, I didn't even mention my father in my poems until I was forty-six. Not once. Now my older poems are good, but there's something, well, missing. And I began to realize that in the ancient times, the movement for the man was downward, a descent into grief. Before you're really a man that descent has to take place. In the fairy tales it's referred to as the time of ashes, the time of descent.

So I wrote a poem, and it's the first poem—I must have been forty-six or forty-seven—I'd written in which there was some sort of grief. It's called "Snowbanks North of the House." Snow comes down from Alaska, and then it suddenly stops, a few feet from a barn or a house. You get a snowdrift.

Those great sweeps of snow that stop suddenly six feet
from the house . . .
Thoughts that go so far.
The boy gets out of high school and reads no more books;
the son stops calling home.
The mother puts down her rolling pin, and makes no more bread.
And the wife looks at her husband one night at a party and loves him no
    more.
The energy leaves the wine, and the minister falls leaving the church.
It will not come closer—
the one inside moves back, and the hands touch nothing, and are safe.

The father grieves for his son, [This is Lincoln] *and will not leave the room*
where the coffin stands,
He turns away from his wife, and she sleeps alone.

And the sea lifts and falls all night; the moon goes on through the
unattached heavens, alone.
The toe of the shoe pivots
in the dust . . .
And the man in the black coat turns, and goes back down the hill.
No one knows why he came, or why he turned away, and did not climb the
hill.

MOYERS: What did that do for you?

BLY: Well, it was the first time my words were not heading towards ascension, that New Age thing. They weren't going for higher consciousness. These words led me to a movement down, where you break off the arc, you move down, you go down towards your own darkness. It had to do with the possibility that my life was not going to be a series of triumphs, that what was asked of me was not to ascend, but to descend. That meant I had to start paying attention to my father.

MOYERS: Here . . . in your mind?

BLY: No, here . . . in the heart.

MOYERS: But he was inside you. You didn't have him out there.

BLY: No, I mean going to the house where he lived. My mother and father were living on a farm a mile from where I was. I'd go over and see them. My father had lost part of one lung and he'd be lying in the bed, next to the living room. I'd go and sit and talk with my mother for an hour. If I remembered it, I'd say good-bye to my father before I left.

Now, my father's lying there in the next room. How do you think he feels about my talking with my mother for an hour? What can he do? He thinks, "Well, that's nice, they have a good relationship." But how about him? I realized I had been in a conspiracy with my mother to push my father out since I was two or three years old. And I decided, about the time I wrote that poem, I decided it was time for that to end. I didn't want to be in this conspiracy anymore.

So I would go in and sit down with my father. My mother would wait for me to come into the living room. And I didn't. I'd sit down next to him, in the other room. He's not a great conversationalist, but we'd talk a little bit. Eventually my mother would have to come in and sit down on the bed. And then we all knew some change had taken place.

MOYERS: It seems to me that you and your mother hadn't pushed your father out. Your father removed himself, like so many fathers do, either through alcoholism or through work or through obsession with the world, through ambition.

BLY: It's possible . . . let me give you something. It's the first poem I wrote that was connected with my father. In fact, it's the first one in which I used the word father. It isn't *my* father; it's a poem called "Finding the Father."

My friend, this body offers to carry us for nothing—as the ocean carries logs.
So on some days the body wails with its great energy; it smashes up the
boulders, lifting small crabs that flow around the sides.

Someone knocks on the door. We do not have time to dress. He wants us to go with him through the blowing and rainy streets, to the dark house. We will go there, the body says, and there find the father whom we have never met, who wandered out in a snowstorm the night we were born, and who then lost his memory, and has lived since longing for his child, whom he saw only once . . . while he worked as a shoemaker, as a cattle herder in Australia, as a restaurant cook who painted at night.

When you light the lamp you will see him. He sits there behind the door . . . the eyebrows so heavy, the forehead so light . . . lonely in his whole body, waiting for you.

MOYERS: Did you find your father?

BLY: To some extent, I did. He died only a few months ago, but one of the things that happened is this. I was in Moose Lake, about five hours away from where my mother and father lived in an old folks' home in Madison, Minnesota. I got a call saying my father was in the hospital with pneumonia. So I drove down to see him, and some change had taken place in me. When I walked into the room, he was alone there. And for the first time, I picked up a book, the book I write in, and I wrote a poem in his presence.

I'd written so many poems in the presence of trees, of the sea, so many poems in the presence of women, never a single line in the presence of my father. So this is the poem I wrote. It's called "My Father at 85."

His large ears hear
everything.
A hermit wakes
and sleeps
in a hut underneath
his gaunt cheeks.
His eyes, blue,
alert, dis-
appointed and suspicious
complain
I do not bring him
The same sort of jokes
the nurses do.
He is a small bird
waiting to be fed,
mostly beak,
an eagle or a vulture
or the Pharaoh's servant
just before death.
My arm on the bedrail
rests there,
relaxed, with new love.
All I know of the Troubadours
I bring
to this bed.
I do not want
or need

to be shamed
by him
any longer.
The general of shame
has discharged him
and left him in this small provincial
Egyptian town.
If I do not wish
to shame him, then
why not
love him?
His long hands,
large, veined, capable,
can still retain
hold of what he wanted.
But is that what he desired?
Some powerful
river of desire
goes on flowing
through him.
He never phrased
What he desired,
and I am
his son.

MOYERS: You say, "He never phrased"—

BLY: He never put into language what he desired. In the United States, we put into language what we want. We want another television set, we want a VCR, we want a refrigerator, we want a good 3.2 beer. We want to have a cowboy hat and have some girl come along and touch it. That's what we want. But we never talk about what we desire. What you desire is something you're never going to get. Desire gives a little fragrance—

MOYERS: Wait, what do you mean by that? We're going to desire something that we're not going to get?

BLY: Look, someone says, "I want to be a great poet, as great a poet as Shakespeare." That's great, but it's not going to happen; still, it's sweet, the desiring. In the thirteenth and fourteenth centuries, they knew about desire, the Provençal poets and the Sufi poets. They desired God, they desired to have God as a lover. You know that Rumi poem?

I want to kiss you.
[Answer:] The price of kissing is your life.
Now my loving is running towards my life, shouting
What a bargain! Let's take it!*

That's a poem of desire, isn't it? It's not a poem of wanting. If our parents could have phrased what they desired, our lives would have been different.

MOYERS: Why do fathers have such a hard time talking to sons about desire, about what they really seek?

*Excerpt from a Rumi poem in *Open Secret*, translated by Coleman Banks (Putney, Vt.: Threshold Books, 1984).

BLY: I don't think the mothers phrase what they desire either.

MOYERS: Yes, but . . .

BLY: Grown-ups don't phrase what they desire.

MOYERS: Why? Do they know? Do we know?

BLY: I think they brood about it a lot. My father spent many hours . . . I saw him lying in bed . . . he was brooding about something. I think he was brooding on what he'd desired. You see, he had to go back to the farm because his own father had a heart attack. Still, he read a tremendous amount. One of his favorite people was the Prince of Wales. He read everything on the Prince of Wales. Now, the Prince of Wales abdicated his throne, and I think my father felt he'd abdicated from what he desired, in order to raise his family, and so on. I think so. That must be one of the connections. He couldn't talk about what he desired. I wanted to have a king as a father, but he was a prince, an elegant Prince of Wales who abdicated. There must have been a disappointment there, he must have felt ashamed. He was so proud. But, maybe to him, keeping all that inside was *his* way to father, *his* way to protect his sons from something.

Everyone comes into the world with a certain way he wants to be fathered. And every father comes into the world with a certain way he wants to father. What if they don't mix? What then?

That's something to think about. How did your father want to father; how did you want to be fathered? Rather than complain about it all the time, we should ask our father how he wanted to father. He might say, "Well, the problem is I wanted a violinist son," or, "I wanted an athlete son, I really did." And then you tell him how you wanted to be fathered; "I wanted this, and I wanted that, and . . ." It takes a lot of work to go down to what you wanted, to see what you still want.

And if you're with a woman, it'd be good to say to her: "Look, this is the way I wanted to be fathered, and I want you to write this down, because sometime I'm going to ask you to do it for me. And you'd better not do it. Don't do it. Write this down, will you?" And when you ask for that, the woman will be able to say, "Wait a minute! That's one of the ways you wanted to be fathered. I'm not your father." Oh wow! And make sure to ask your girlfriend how she wanted to be fathered too. You'll be asked to move into that, to help with that, and try to get that clear. But you'll have to say, over and over again, "I'm not your father, and I wish I were, but I'm not, and I can't give you that."

MOYERS: Why do you think there's so much confusion today over what men are?

BLY: What models were we given in high school? John Wayne? All those models, they don't last past the age of thirty-two or so. Around thirty-five, men begin to realize that the images they were given of what a man is don't work. They don't work in their jobs, they don't work in a relationship, they don't work in the marriage; they don't work!

MOYERS: So what happens when these high school images fade?

BLY: Well, I think there's a deep sense of failure, a sense that you're inadequate. The absence of the father standing next to the son, giving cellular significance—I don't know what you call it, cellular confidence, what we talked of earlier—when that's gone, you judge yourself a great deal more. It seems you're failing in your relationship. What was it that Maggie Scarf said? The typical relationship in the United States involves the woman chasing the man to try to get him to talk more, and the man fleeing? But she doesn't chase him fast enough to really catch him, and he doesn't run away fast enough to really get away. That's the game that's played.

In a way, the man can't turn and face the woman, because without a clear sense of what it is to be a man, he can't stand and say, "Wait a minute, I know what I want in a relationship. It isn't exactly what you want, but let me tell you what it is." And he may fail. Since the woman knows what she wants in a relationship, the man again feels inadequate. I'd say the primary experience of the American man now is the experience of being inadequate. In work, you can't achieve what you want. You feel inadequate as a man because you don't have any close male friends, and you don't know why. You feel inadequate as a husband because your wife is always saying you don't talk about your feelings enough. And you don't know what your feelings are.

But, you know, men are not *hiding* their feelings from women. Men look down inside and they don't see anything in there. There's a feeling of numbness that, for men, comes early in life.

> . . . men are not hiding their feelings from women. Men look down inside and they don't see anything in there. There's a feeling of numbness that, for men, comes early in life.

MOYERS: Do you remember when you first began to get in contact with your feelings, as a man?

BLY: It was because I'd decided in college that I was going to write poetry the rest of my life. It was a very rash decision for a Lutheran. One has to find one's feelings to write poetry. Anyway, my first book was called *Silence in the Snowy Fields*. My feelings are not exactly speaking in that book. I knew there was a kind of envelope around my body which was in touch with wind and air and pine trees. I wrote my poems by sitting down under a tree for two hours. This envelope around the body puts us in touch with the bark and the branches and the birds and the weeds. It's almost as if the tree said something in those poems. As if I heard that, more than my own feelings.

My first book was published when I was thirty-six. Still, I wasn't in touch with many of my feelings. I think I was about forty-six when I wrote "Snowbanks North of the House," and there's some feeling of grief in that poem. That's why I say grief is the door to feeling. Being out in nature is not the door to feeling. Excitement, I thought, was the door to feeling. It isn't. That's why rock music doesn't always work in helping people open to feeling. Excitement is not it.

With men, there's some quality of grief. But men don't know what they're grieving about. It's as if the grief is impersonal with men. It's always present. You don't know if it's about the absence of the father, or if it's about all of the animals we were in touch with the millions of years we were hunters, and all the animals that died. It may be a grief that's in nature itself. You remember the Latin term *lacrimae rerum*, the "tears of things"? Men have lived for centuries out there, and they feel that terrific grief of nature and the out-of-doors and pine trees. There are certain little groves in England; if you walk in there, you'll burst into tears, because there's grief in nature.

MOYERS: I grieve, but I don't write poems. What do I do about it?

BLY: I don't know that you have to *do* something with it. It's a choice, at any second. You know, in a conversation there are little things, things you can turn, up or down. Someone says, "I lost my brother five years ago." Well, you could say, "We all lose our brothers." Or you could touch his hand, or you could go into the part of you that's lost a brother. You can follow the grief downward in this way, or you can go upward in the American way. You can always tell an American on the streets of Europe, because he's smiling.

So grief is really important for us. It must be important, we avoid it at every turn. I mean, we've had four presidents in a row who promised us we wouldn't have to go into the grief about the Vietnam War. If Lincoln had been alive, you know he'd have gone into that grief. He would have gotten everybody . . . five years after the Vietnam War, he would have said, "We've killed so many people, and these veterans are here, we've destroyed them. Aah, let's all weep. Aaah, Aah, AAAH." That's what Lincoln would have done. He'd have encouraged America to grieve over the losses in Vietnam. We still haven't grieved over that. Only the veterans are grieving, and that's not right.

MOYERS: How does a whole people grieve?

BLY: Well, we don't do it by hiring people like Reagan. You know, Reagan's father was an alcoholic. When I look at Reagan, I know he hasn't gone through the grief of that. So he's in denial. When you're in denial over your own father, you can deny the budget deficit easily; that's not a problem. He spent the whole presidency in denial, and the result is we've got the homeless sleeping on vents; we've got— what —a $3 trillion deficit. That's what it's like when you decide not to take that turn down; you decide not to go and face your father and do that work.

It's a very serious thing, because in some way we knew all that when we hired Reagan. If we're so co-dependent as a nation that we'll hire this man who didn't go through the "adult children of alcoholics work," or whatever . . . well, it doesn't speak well for our future.

MOYERS: This is territory I'm not very competent to enter, but America never really has come to terms with the shadow of its past.

BLY: That's right.

MOYERS: The Indians, the blacks.

BLY: We didn't mourn over the death of the Indians. I guess we did moderately well in mourning the Civil War, with Whitman and Lincoln. But after that, it's been a process of not-mourning. Alexander Mitscherlich has written a book called *The Inability to Mourn* about the Germans after the Second World War. We're in the same situation. We have an inability to mourn. How can we have strong men or women if we can't go into grief at all?

MOYERS: I see. But there's more to being a man than knowing how to grieve—

BLY: Yes, you also need to develop the warrior. That means you're not always obeying the demands of the body. Robert Moore of Chicago, who is doing wonderful work on the warrior and the king, said, "All of you who are in graduate school, if you don't have the warrior, you're going to be in trouble, because you have to do a lot of unpleasant things in graduate school." And he said, "I'm writing a book; if I don't have the warrior, I'm not going to finish the book."

MOYERS: The warrior enables us to—?

BLY: When the body says, "Let's quit and get some ice cream," the warrior says, "No, no, no." I mean, your body's okay when you're getting a massage, right? The warrior says, "For now, we're going to do the task, and we're going to continue."

Joe Campbell had a great warrior. In his twenties he read nine hours every day. That's the warrior that enabled him to do that. So, the warrior in men is not always the one that's out there killing people. That's not it. It's the one who is able to pursue a task until it's finished. And the warrior usually has a cause transcendent to himself.

MOYERS: Transcendent to himself? Which means, "I'll do it even if I can't explain it to other people"?

BLY: Yes, "I'm not doing it for my own good. I'm not doing it for selfish reasons. I'm doing this for a cause I believe in." The traditional way it's said is that the warrior works for the king, and the king is the one that's connected to the sun, and to the spirit and to God.

When the warrior has no king then he gets in trouble, like Ollie North. The Japanese tell a story about a little pond. Now, the king of the pond disappeared somehow. So all the animals of the pond hired the heron to be the king. The heron ate up everyone in the pond—because he was a warrior; he wasn't a king. The warrior will eat up everyone in the pond if he doesn't have a transcendent cause.

Americans are very weak in the warrior now, American men. Japanese men were strong in the warrior during the Second World War, and they somehow transferred that into their briefcases and into their VCRs. We don't have warriors to stand up against them, even in the business world.

Robert Moore said, "The only warriors we have in the United States are the negative versions of it, the shadow versions, who are the drug lords." They're the ones. We need warriors in the city who are able to stand against the drug lords. But instead of that, we have only negative warriors.

MOYERS: When you use the word "warrior," most people are going to say, "Oh, he means the slayer, the killer."

BLY: No, that's not it. In general terms, the warrior isn't sent out to harm or damage others. The warrior is a defender of boundaries.

When you live in a dysfunctional family, people in the family invade your boundaries all the time. They will open the door, they'll shout. The mood of the dominant parent is the strongest in the house, one's own mood counts for nothing. You understand what I'm talking about?

MOYERS: Right, okay.

BLY: When you're three and four years old, you have no boundaries in relation to grown-ups. They simply do what they want. And sexual abuse means other people just open the door and walk in and ruin your psychic house. There's no way you can keep them out.

Here's one way I see this. When we're three and four years old, the doorknob's on the outside of the door. Now, I have to understand I'm not three or four years old now, I'm a grown person. If I want to have the doorknob on the inside of the door, it's my job to move it there. If I don't wish to be shamed, I have to do something about it. . . . The hardest thing is to realize you're not four years old. The adult man and the adult woman need to have a warrior, so they can hold their own boundaries.

The line from that poem I just gave you: "I do not want or need to be shamed by him any longer." Well, that means there's been some movement to get the doorknob on the inside of my door. That's called a warrior. Each of us desperately needs our warrior. A warrior is not someone who goes off and kills. That's the negative warrior, the one without a king.

Some women have a very fierce warrior in them, you know, a very fierce warrior. And I would say that the women, in the last twenty years, have a much greater sense of their own boundaries than the men do.

Men have suffered a great deal in losing the wild man, which is a certain form of spontaneity connected with the wilderness itself. And men have suffered a great deal since the Second World War, in losing the warrior. It's very strange how this works. We gave up the king; we founded our country by getting rid of the king. And you know, the king is weak in American men; how can it be otherwise?

MOYERS: The king being . . . ?

BLY: The king, the part of the human being that knows what he wants to do, for the rest of his life, or for the rest of this year, or the rest of this month.

MOYERS: The king can decide that for himself. That's the whole image—

BLY: This is the *inner* king, the one who's in our soul. The king can decide without being contaminated by the prejudices of other people. "Follow your bliss," is what Joe Campbell said. That means that the king decides. You don't join IBM and then do what your boss wants you to do. If you do what IBM tells you, it means you're giving in to the outer king. That can kill your own king.

MOYERS: But that's the way the world works.

BLY: Yeah, it's the way it works. That's the way it destroys inner kings in all of the men and in most of the women. So the king, then, is that part of you that can decide. And I mean it's very private, too, because there are various kinds of kings.

When I'm with a group of two hundred people, my king is fairly strong. I'll decide what I want to happen that day. When I'm with three or four people, my king is moderately strong, but they can still drag me off to a movie I don't want to go to. But when I'm with one person, my king is rather weak. I think that's because of all those crossings of boundaries and so on when I was a child. For example, say I go into a store with my wife, and there's two sweaters: one green and the other blue. I can't decide which one I want, and I ask her, "What do you think?" She says, "Oh, the blue one is beautiful." Immediately the green fades into some hideous color. You understand me?

MOYERS: I do, but I'm troubled by the analogy. We can't go back to being an aboriginal society. We can't become a traditional society again.

BLY: I agree with you. These tribal initiations—as in New Guinea—produce a man, but a rather brittle one. They have to do it in three years because they need to defend their tribe from enemies. We do it slowly; initiation with us could take forty years, but when it happens well, we develop a resilient man, like Martin Luther King. So I'm not saying all of the primitive initiation stuff is desirable. What I'm saying is that we can't go on any longer entirely ignoring initiation. We have to work toward conscious manhood. Each generation, men are more and more separated from the grandfathers, and from the kings, and from the inner warriors. They're weaker, in some way, every generation.

One of the things said is, if you're not conscious about your initiation, it may happen to you unconsciously and negatively. Because it will happen—whether you know it or not.

MOYERS: Aren't we initiated as men by the sergeant in the army, by the corporate executive we take our first jobs from, by the professor at the university?

BLY: To some extent. But the sergeant is not the equal of the old male initiators, because he's not interested in your soul.

MOYERS: In your soul?

BLY: Yes, in your soul. The sergeant is interested in your not dying, or he's interested in your physical health, or he's interested in your obedience. But the old male initiators we're talking about—King Arthur would be one—are interested in the soul of the young man. That's what the young men are missing. They're missing older men who are interested in their souls.

MOYERS: You mention King Arthur. He was a mentor to the knights, but what did he do?

BLY: Here's one way to think about male initiation. The first stage is bonding with the mother and separation from the mother. Now, we bond with the mother pretty well in this country, but we don't do the separation well at all. There's no ritual for it.

The second stage is bonding with the father and separation from the father. We don't do the bonding with the father well. What did Geoffrey Gorer say in *The Americans*? "In order to become an American, it's necessary, first of all, to reject your father." You don't even attack him, as Freud said, you just regard him as ridiculous. Like in all those movies we're seeing, and the filmstrips, and the situation comedies; the fathers are completely ridiculous. You know those?

MOYERS: Sure.

BLY: This is all over television. The father is a fool and the woman is a wonderful person and knows everything. The father, the man, is in bad shape. The woman says, "You should use Comtrex." And he says, "What's Comtrex?" She tells him what it is. You mean the man doesn't know what Comtrex is? The young males writing these comedies are rejecting their fathers all over again in order to become real Americans.

Okay. So the second thing is bonding with the father and separation from the father. In a culture in which you reject the father automatically, as in America, oftentimes you don't become bonded with your father until you're forty or forty-five. That's what I told you in my story.

MOYERS: Well, how do you bond with a father who's absent all the time, who goes off to the office, ten, fifteen, thirty miles away?

BLY: Sometimes you have to wait until he's sixty-five and he's home. It's not easy. One man about forty-five or fifty years old told me a story. He calls up his father and his father says, "Hi, here's your mother." The man says, "Hey, wait a minute. I want to talk to you. I want to take you down to New Mexico. We'll go down there for five days and fish or something." The father says, "No, I don't want to go." But the man says, "Yes, you're going to go. I'm going to pay for it and we're going to go." Well, that's a bonding that sometimes takes place with the father there. The son has to do it. Sometimes the son has to make the motion.

MOYERS: That's the stage of bonding.

BLY: Bonding with the father. After that you still have to do the separation. Then the third stage is called the appearance of the male mother.

MOYERS: Male mother?

BLY: That's a man who does nurturing in a similar way as a woman, only he's not a woman. King Arthur acted that way for those young men.

MOYERS: What does he do?

BLY: Cuts his arm and gives them the blood. He nourishes them and nourishes their souls. So this is like—Pablo Casals was a wonderful male mother.

MOYERS: Yes.

BLY: Many great jazz musicians have had a great male mother. 'Round Midnight was about that. The first scene of 'Round Midnight, he walks into a hotel room in Paris, and you don't know what's going on. And the black musician stands there a long time. And finally someone says, "Is this where he died?" And he says, "Well, I guess so, but these rooms all look so much alike." That was the room where his male mother, his mentor, his male mentor, had died.

MOYERS: When you're talking about a mentor, you're using—

BLY: We're talking about a metaphor. Male mother, mentor, I'm using them as a metaphor. King Arthur was a mentor to those young men. When the male mother, when the mentor, comes along, he helps the young male separate from his mother and from his father. He's not the boy's father. He's acting as both as a mother and a father, but in a different sense. That's the third stage.

MOYERS: Wordsworth has this wonderful poem in which he talks about the old man who sat under the tree.

BLY: You found that too?!

MOYERS: Yes, the old man sits under the tree, and Wordsworth says, "He picked me out from all the rosy boys and I became a comrade for life."

BLY: I couldn't believe that passage when I read it! Wordsworth was in grammar school, and an old man there at the edge of town would talk with him every day. Wordsworth, at the end, says, "I think he had the greatest mind in England." Do you remember that? Because he had given that boy so much. So that's a perfect example. That's how you produce a Wordsworth!

MOYERS: Where do we get our mentors today?

BLY: You have to look for them. Your father came to you, you didn't have to look for your father, but you have to look for your mentor. If you want a mentor, you have to go look for him. That usually means he's in your field, but not always. If you're an architect, you go and look for a male mentor there.

You know, I once met Szent-Györgyi, the one who discovered vitamin C and got a Nobel Prize. He was living alone in Woods Hole, and he told me various things. He said, "When I got out of graduate school, I knew exactly whom I wanted to work with. I would have walked a hundred and fifty miles to work with this man. And I did, I worked with him, I loved him." Then he said, "I've been here thirty years. Not a single American man has ever come and wanted to work with me." I said, "Well, maybe they're not interested in ideas." He said, "They're *not* interested in ideas! You know what they're interested in? Retirement plans!" He was a wonderful old man. He was wanting to be a mentor, a male mother, to young American scientists, but they didn't know the tradition and they didn't go to him.

MOYERS: In traditional cultures, when these older men played this role for young men, what were the older men—the male mothers—doing for the boys?

BLY: One thing he does is bless the young men. And it's so strange, that men need blessing from older men. Robert Moore said, "If you're a young man, and you're not being admired by an older man, you're being hurt." I like that a great deal.

Many women bless young men, but the man still needs a blessing from an older man. I heard Robert Moore say to a group of men, "How many of you have admired a younger man in the last two weeks, and told him so?" Silence. "How many of you were admired by older men when you were young?" Silence. Then he said that sentence, "If you are a young man and you're not being admired by an older man, you're being hurt."

MOYERS: You talk about the old men giving the young men "Zeus energy." What do you mean, "Zeus energy"?

BLY: Well, the way the king is described in Greek mythology is through the image of Zeus. Zeus energy is authority that the male takes for the sake of the community. The American Indians in upstate New York, for example, had a strong chieftainship. The chief was chosen by women, and once the chief was chosen, he had to agree to give up all property. He had nothing that was his. And the authority that he had was for the sake of the community.

We don't have Zeus energy in corporations. With Exxon, you do things for money, for advancement, for power, for security. You're not doing anything for the sake of the community. They take their authority for the sake of the corporation, not for the sake of the community. In the corporation everybody is doing things for himself.

MOYERS: Where did you get your Zeus energy?

BLY: I don't know if I have any Zeus energy. It could be I just have a big mouth, you know. That's always a possibility.

MOYERS: No. I happen to know there are a lot of young writers and artists and students who look to you as a mentor.

BLY: Men didn't trust me until I was maybe forty-five or fifty. I don't know what that was, but I noticed it. And they were right not to trust me.

MOYERS: Why?

If I don't have a connection with my father, where's my grounding? If I don't have a connection with grief, where's my grounding?

BLY: If I don't have a connection with my father, where's my grounding? If I don't have a connection with grief, where's my grounding? So somewhere along the line, because of various disasters in my life, I must have gotten in touch with some sort of grief. Since then I've done a lot of work to try to maintain my connection with my father and deepen that.

MOYERS: How can a forty-six-year-old man bond with his father after those long years of estrangement?

BLY: I don't have a good answer for that. But, well, here's a poem about my experience. Here's a poem about my attempt to thank him for the fathering he gave, even if it wasn't what I wanted.

> *There must have been*
> *a fire, that nearly*
> *blew out, or a large*
> *soul inadequately*
> *feathered, who became*
> *cold and angered.*
> *Some four-year-old boy*
> *in you, chilled by*
> *your mother, misprized*
> *by your father, said,*
> *"I will defy. I will win*
> *anyway, I will*
> *show them."*
> *When Alice's well-off sister*
> *Offered to take your two*
> *boys during the Depression,*
> *you said it again.*
> *Now you speak the defiant*
> *words to death.*
> *This four-year-old*
> *old man in you does*
> *as he likes: he likes*
> *to stay alive.*
> *Through him you*
> *get revenge,*
> *persist, endure,*
> *overlive, overwhelm,*
> *get on top.*
> *You gave me*
> *this, and I do*
> *not refuse it.*
> *It is*
> *in me.*

So I realized, then, that my father gave me this, "I will defy, I will win anyway." It's not the gift I wanted, but it was a gift. My other father was Yeats. He was my male mother. He wasn't alive, but your mentor doesn't have to be alive. Does that make sense?

MOYERS: What does a male mother do that the father doesn't do?

BLY: The father cannot really do initiation with his son because there's too much tension. They're both interested in the same woman, and that's a problem. When men recognize their fathers can't do it, and that the initiators are gone . . . there's no one to welcome the young men into the male world. Young men are angry about that.

When you're looking at a gang, you're seeing young males who have no older men to welcome them into the male world. They're trying desperately to do it themselves. They're trying to teach each other what courage is, how much pain you should endure, what a cause is. They're trying to do it, but it doesn't work, because young males cannot initiate each other. But they're angry at the absence of the older males who are not doing that.

When this group of old male initiators disappears, everything falls on the father. The father's supposed to do everything. When young men realize their father could not have done that, they begin to think of the things their father did try to do. Oftentimes they're touched, they weep when they think of the possibilities.

MOYERS: So when the older men—

BLY: Fathers are supposed to keep us alive to the age of seventeen, make sure we don't get eaten by ants, or packs of wild dogs. Fathers were never intended to initiate sons.

MOYERS: But what happens when the father is gone? In America today, so often it's just a single mother who is left to do it all, the initiation, and . . .

BLY: That's right, and women try very hard. They try very hard with this, but it's hopeless. A woman can bring the boy from being a fetus to being a boy, but she can't move him from being a boy to being a man. Only other men can do that. When I said that in a seminar once, some of the women got angry. But one woman said, "I think he's right, because when my boy was in high school, I know he needed something harder than I could give him. If I did that, I'd lose my own femininity." Women can't really guide a boy all the way to being a man. That's a job for men to do. If a woman is in that situation, she should recognize it.

She should try to find some older man she trusts, and ask him to hold the boy in his heart. It isn't necessary to find a man who will take the boy to the zoo every other day. Many boys don't know a single older man who encourages them, or holds them in their heart. To the men who come to my seminars, I say, "This next year, what I'd like you to do is to go out and find a young man who doesn't have a father in the house. I'd like you to hold that boy in your heart. Write him once a month, take him somewhere once a month, anything, make sure he knows he has a heart-link with the male world."

That's a responsibility men have got to take. They've got to take more responsibility for the younger men: encouraging the younger men, admiring the younger men, and holding the younger men in their hearts.

MOYERS: How do we get in touch with the male mother that's in us? How do I find in myself the male mother that serves another young man?

BLY: First of all, one would consciously reject the idea that all men are in competition. In business, that's a primary assumption. So there are very few genuine male mothers in business. There have been exceptions, of course.

We've got to realize . . . I never realized that younger men needed something I had to give . . .

MOYERS: Except a job.

BLY: Yeah, that kind of thing. But I didn't realize young men are hungry and thirsty for a simple connection to an older man that doesn't involve shaming. What are the older men saying? "Clean up your room!" Right? "You did this wrong. You have to stay after school! You're a fool; you're stupid!" And then they go to women for comfort.

But what if they could go to older men for comfort? Then women wouldn't be so burdened with all these aspirins and stuff. I think it'd be a great relief to women, if men could go to other men for comfort. I have to realize that, by being an older man, I have some substance that's helpful to younger men, and then I also have to realize that I can perform something for them without intending to, by being consciously aware that they need to step from the father, to an older man, to God.

And I'm not a guru, because I need my freedom myself. A young man says to me, "Will you be my father?" There's something touching about that, and I say, "Yeah, I'll do it if it doesn't cost me anything." That's a joke, but I have sons of my own too.

MOYERS: Yes.

BLY: So we have to agree that older men have an important duty. It's an important thing, like supporting your family, loving your wife, or protecting the earth. You can be open to younger men, recognize they can use a blessing from you.

One way it's done in Russia is with the toast. Raising the glass and toasting. It's so fantastic, those Russian toasts. They all toast the younger men. Now, the idea is that they have to see that younger man clearly. No lying, no mere flattery. They have to see the young men, and praise them, praise them for what they carry, for who they are.

MOYERS: Praise?

BLY: Yes, praise. Blessing is a form of praise. Remember what Robert Moore said? "How many young men have you admired in the last two weeks, and told them so?"

MOYERS: Some people say the men's movement is a throwback, a regression to the segregation of the past, to the time when men had their own private clubs and could talk about things without worrying about anybody catching on to their secrets. Is this a throwback?

BLY: No, I don't think so. Women will say certain things when men are not present. They'll talk about certain things, or talk in a certain way, when men are not present. The sexes can shame each other so easily! A similar thing is true for men. For men getting near their grief, it's important it be done in the presence of men. So it isn't an attempt to exclude women in that sense at all.

MOYERS: Do you think that men have a harder time with relationships than women?

BLY: Men can't mix words with feelings as well as women. This has been known for a long time. But sometimes the fury of the male happens because the woman is able to go ahead of him, finishes his sentences for him, goes on ahead. And he cannot do it. The mix isn't there. It takes him a long time to learn how to do that, forty or fifty years. The woman can often do it at fourteen. Some of the rage of men has to do with that. So it's important for men to be together to express their feelings at their own pace, which is slower than women's pace. At their own pace, and then eventually they come down into grief and they come down into some other place.

The amount of feeling on the fourth day of a men's group is unbelievable, fantastic to someone who hasn't been there before. They will show more feelings and amaze themselves with the depth of their feelings. Many times they wouldn't have been able to show that to a woman. Later, they might be able to do so.

MOYERS: So, tell me, what does all this have to do with poetry?

BLY: Well, you know, there are two kinds of men's groups. In one kind of men's group you use psychological jargon. That's okay, but those men's groups usually end up complaining about their wives for three months, and then the whole thing stops. The other kind of men's group uses mythology and fairy stories. The fairy stories were in this territory long before us, and when you go into the male area through the fairy story, you find that many men have had this suffering long before you.

So, I've found mythology to be wonderful in teaching, in trying to teach. To use story and myth . . .

MOYERS: Fairy tales in particular?

BLY: Yes. Fairy tale and myth are similar, but the name of the god is not mentioned in a fairy story. So therefore, fairy stories are a social form, they can be told with jokes, or in any way. But they still contain all the energy and genius.

Now, as for poetry, Gary Snyder said a wonderful thing. "The function of the poet is to find out what part of the mythology is useful in his lifetime." Milton did that. He made the wrong choice, in my opinion, but that's what he did. The connection of the poet with mythology is centuries old. The poet is not connected only to the lyric poem, or the poem of feeling; he filters the available mythology.

People have praised me for what I've done with the men; it's nothing but finding a couple of fairy stories that are useful. That's all it amounts to.

Bill Moyers would like to thank the following people for their work on the television series:

EXECUTIVE PRODUCER
Judith Davidson Moyers

PRODUCTION EXECUTIVES
Judy Doctoroff O'Neill
Arthur White

PRODUCERS
Leslie Clark
Judy Epstein
Betsy McCarthy
Gail Pellett
Andie Tucher

COORDINATING PRODUCER
Judy Epstein

EDITORIAL ASSOCIATE
Andie Tucher

RESEARCHERS
Greg Dillon
Jennifer Mirsky
Kelly Venardos

EDITORS
Michael Collins
Scott P. Doniger

CAMERA
Mark Allan
Stewart Barbee
Eric Camiel
Mike Giovingo
Ricky Lee Harrell
Steve Harris
Richard Hutchings
Levie Isaacks
Marc Kroll
Sam Lopez
Jinny Martin
Blake McHugh
Joel Shapiro

SERIES RESEARCH
Rebecca Berman

PRODUCTION ASSISTANT
Brynne Clarke Ferguson

BUSINESS AFFAIRS
Diana Warner

PUBLICITY
Christine Dietlin

EXECUTIVE ASSISTANTS
Lee Taylor
Rebecca Jo Wharton

STAFF SECRETARIES
Lynnette Caldwell
Naomi Golf

PUBLIC LIAISON
Doris Lang Thomas

INTERNS
Sarah Alpert
Caroline Claudepierre
Karen Levy

VIDEO
Dale Cihi
Daniel Epstein
Bernard Russo
Keith Winner

AUDIO
Thomas R. Bobrich
Mike Cogan
Mark Dichter
Jeff Edrich
Bob Fazio
Al Feuerbach
Galen Handy
Algis Kaupas
Otto Kennedy
Richard Max
Don Miller
Will Wynne

AUDIO REMIX
Barbara Flyntz-Bradley
Grant Maxwell

UTILITY
Rick Albright
Al Byrne
Mark Flint
Stew Gilman
Tom Guarcello
Guy Jaconelli
John Swetye

MAKEUP
Judith Widener Baker
Annie Bean
Eleanor Bogart
Judy Charles
Linda Donvito
Norah Hernandez
Kim Kegler
Michele O'Callaghan
Linda Peterson

ASSISTANT EDITOR
Joseph Annechiarico
Mayra Bustamante
Ultan Byrne
Steven Max Droge
Linda Long
Billy McCarthy
Colleen Quinn
Bob Soond
Andrew Turits

THEME MUSIC COMPOSED BY
Michael Bacon

"A World of Ideas with Bill Moyers" was a production of Public Affairs Television, Inc. The series was made possible by grants from the John D. and Catherine T. MacArthur Foundation and from the General Motors Corporation.

Special thanks to the Florence and John Schumann Foundation.

BILL MOYERS is an acclaimed television journalist, widely respected for his work at PBS and CBS News. His conversations with teacher and mythologist Joseph Campbell were the basis for the bestselling book *The Power of Myth*.

ANDIE TUCHER is Editorial Associate at Public Affairs Television. She has been a writer, associate producer, and producer for various PAT productions and is a coauthor, with Bill Moyers, of *Report from Philadelphia: The Constitutional Convention of 1787*.